CRISIS:
IN THE WORLD ECONOMY

CRISIS:

IN

THE WORLD ECONOMY

Andre Gunder Frank

Holmes & Meier Publishers

NEW YORK • LONDON

First published in the United States of America 1980 by
Holmes & Meier Publishers, Inc.
30 Irving Place
New York, N.Y. 10003

Library of Congress Cataloging in Publication Data

Frank, Andre Gunder, 1929–
  Crisis: In the world economy.

  Bibligraphy: p.
  Includes index.
  1. Economic history–1945–   2. International
economic relations.   3. Economic policy.   I. Title.
HC59.F732 1980   330.9'047   80-14540

ISBN 0-8419-0583-5
ISBN 0-8419-0596-7 (pbk.)

Contents

Preface

This book and its companion volume, *Crisis: In the Third World,* examine the development of the new economic and political crisis in the world. According to my dictionary, a crisis is a decisive turning point, which is filled with danger and anxiety because the issue from the crisis may be life or death for a diseased person, social system, or historical process. The outcome need not necessarily be death, and could be new life, if in our case the economic, social, and political body is able to adapt and to undergo a regenerative transformation during its time of crisis.

Crisis: In the World Economy reviews and in part previews the new capitalist crisis of overaccumulation of capital and some of its economic, social, and political repercussions in the industrial capitalist West or "first" part of the world, in the "socialist" countries of the East in the "second" part of the world, and in the capitalist underdeveloped countries of the Third World in the South, which are sometimes also called "developing" or a bit more accurately "less developed countries" (LDCs). *Crisis: In the Third World* (hereafter abbreviated as TW) examines in greater detail the repercussions in that part of the world only.

This book presents an overview of the whole world economy and its parts, an analysis of the new capitalist world economic and political crisis in the West since 1967, the integration of the socialist countries in the capitalist international division of labor, and the Third World's demand for a "new international economic order" (NIEO). This more general and introductory volume may be read separately. The more detailed analysis of the repercussions of—or more accurately of the participation in—the world capitalist economic crisis of the Third World appears in TW, which may also be read as a study in itself, if the place of the Third World in the global context and the motor force of the industrial center and its economic crisis are kept in mind. That is, both books are part of a single study of the world, or at least world capitalist, system and its present economic and political crisis as a whole; but each book, the present one dealing generally with all three parts of the world and the other devoted more specifically to the Third World, may be read without the other. Although the problems that are dealt with are very serious, it has been my intention in both books, but especially in this one, to use an analysis and to write in a language that any interested reader can understand.

This first of the two books on the world economic and political crisis examines the development of the effects of, and the responses to, this crisis in the industrial capitalist countries of the West, including "Western" Japan, in the "socialist" countries of the East, and in the Third World capitalist underdeveloped countries of the South. The book begins (chapter 1) with a review of the expansive boom years of the two decades following World War II. Chapter 2 traces the cyclical ups and downs of the development of the new crisis of capital accumulation in the industrial capitalist West since 1967. Chapter 3 reviews and in part tries to preview the corresponding political economic responses of capital, labor, and the state in recent and coming years. This chapter lays particular emphasis on the policies of economic austerity and the deliberate creation of unemployment by social democratic governments as well as on the growth of political repression and the apparently accelerating political and ideological shift to the right nearly everywhere in the West. In the presentation of this development in chapters 2 and 3, I have chosen to alternate successively between the recording of a particular historical event, such as the recession of 1970, and the analysis of a particular major problem, such as unemployment. Each such problem is discussed in connection with the period during which the situation first became problematic, even though it may already have existed or may have become more serious later, as unemployment did during and still after the recession of 1973–1975. After analyzing such a problem, I go on to record what happened during the next historical period of the development of the crisis, before turning again to the analysis of another problem of the crisis that is particularly associated with the later period, and so on successively. Chapter 4 examines the accelerating integration of the socialist economies of the Soviet Union, Eastern Europe, China, Korea, and Vietnam in the capitalist international division of labor in part as a response to the crisis of the capitalist system, which affects these economies and societies as well. The fifth chapter examines the demands by spokesmen for the Third World for a new international economic order and considers the not very favorable prospects for the realization of NIEO. A sixth and concluding chapter reviews and previews the entire development of the crisis in the West, East, and South. Thus, this book offers a review of some of the important economic, social, and political developments that the new world crisis is generating in all three parts of the world.

Limitations of time (for my writing) and space (in this already too long book), as well as perhaps in my own theoretical and practical capacity to analyze the world, or at least world capitalist, process of capital accumulation in its new period of crisis, also obliged me to treat the crisis in the West almost as though it were somehow separable from the historical process in the larger economic system as a whole. Moreover, I opted to omit any attempt at profound theoretical analysis of the crisis of capital accumulation (or to leave that for some possible later book). Instead, I decided to devote these, for the purposes short, 200 pages of chapters 2 and 3 to a review of the economic and political development of the crisis since 1967.

The chapters of this book and its companion volume were written and updated at different times. The introductory chapter 1 and chapter 4 on the socialist economies were written in 1976–1977. Since the first chapter is more historical, it has received only minor revision and updating since then. Chapter 4, however, is very topical; and there are numerous and constant important developments in the socialist countries and their relations with the rest of the world. I have thought it best to leave the main body of the analysis in this chapter as originally written, if only as a record of how things looked at that time. However, I added updating addenda in May 1978 (identified as such in the text), and I again updated both the text and the addenda in December 1979. Chapter 5 on Third World demands for NIEO was written in mid-1978 and revised in late 1979 to take account of more recent developments. The core of the book, chapters 2 and 3 on the sometimes nearly day-to-day economic and political development of the crisis in the West, were written in mid-1978, but were substantially revised and updated to the end of 1979. The concluding chapter was written in August–September 1979, but I have taken advantage of subsequent minor revisions to take account of developments that appeared in early 1980.

The companion volume, *Crisis: In the Third World* (TW), examines the effects on and responses to the same world economic crisis in the Third World. That volume distinguishes between the principal kinds of Third World economies and the different modifications of their participation in the world economy under the impact of the crisis. These are principally the intermediate development in the seven major semiperipheral economies of Brazil, Mexico, Argentina, India, Iran, Israel, and South Africa (which are examined individually in TW, chapter 1); the economies in which agricultural export, especially through agribusiness, is important (TW, chapter 2); and the economies promoting other exports of manufactures, oil, and minerals, as well as the expendable regions, which have hardly anything to export at all (TW, chapter 3). The analysis then turns to some features and processes that are more or less common to all of these Third World countries despite their differences. These are the increase in their foreign debt (TW, chapter 4) and its burden, which is paid through the greater exploitation of the local population; the increasing superexploitation of many members of the labor force in the Third World (TW, chapter 5); the political economic repression, which is extensively documented in chapter 6, that is necessary to sustain this exploitation and superexploitation; the transformation of the state (TW, chapter 7) as one of the principal instruments of the adaption of the Third World and its population to its new roles in the world, as well as the militarization of society and other emerging forms of institutionalization; and finally the growing arms economy and military conflict in the Third World (TW, chapter 8). In short, this book examines some of the economic transformation that the Third World is undergoing today under the impact of the world economic crisis; and the volume also tries to document through what political instruments and to suggest at what social costs this economic transformation is taking place.

Both books are the outgrowth of my work on the history—including the present as history, to borrow the felicitous phrase of Paul Sweezy (1953)—of capital accumulation on a world scale (as Samir Amin [1970] calls it) and of dependent accumulation in the so-called Third World. Already in 1965 I wrote in the preface to my *Capitalism and Underdevelopment in Latin America* that there is "the need . . . for the development of a theory and analysis adequate to encompass the structure and development of the capitalist system on an integrated world scale and to explain its contradictory development which generates at once economic development and underdevelopment" (Frank 1967: xv). My own attempt to contribute to this theory and analysis did not begin until 1970 in Chile, when I started to write the book now published as *World Accumulation 1492–1789* (Frank 1978a). The coup in Chile and other considerations interrupted this historical account of world accumulation at the beginning of the industrial revolution. At the same time, my conviction grew that the capitalist world had entered another major crisis of capital accumulation. I had expressed this opinion publicly in 1972 (see Frank 1977c, chapter 1). This conviction also persuaded me that the analysis of current events is now increasingly urgent. I therefore decided to embark on a study of the two centuries since the industrial revolution in order to write a second volume to complement the one mentioned above by beginning at the end, that is, today, and working backward. This work on "today" began in 1973, and it has continued on the contemporary and just-past events ever since. However, I became so engaged in, and absorbed by, the contemporary crisis, that most of the historical work came to be relegated to some time in the future, although I did brush up on part of the historical study of the underdeveloped countries within the world economy until the present, which was published under the title *Dependent Accumulation and Underdevelopment* (Frank 1978b).

Thus, my intention to analyze two centuries of world capital accumulation, became, under the increasing influence of the new world economic and political crisis, a study spanning some two decades past, present, and future of that crisis itself. However, although I tried to analyze the crisis in the world, or at least in the world capitalist, process of capital accumulation as a whole *in theory*, in practice my study seemed increasingly to dwell on the industrial West, the socialist East, and the underdeveloped South each taken individually, albeit in relation to each other. In the case of the "socialist" countries, I did not try to study the internal structures of their societies as much as their economic relations with the West and the South and the political implications of these relations, particularly for the Third World. My study of the effects of the world economic crisis on the South and the corresponding modifications of the economic participation and political response of the Third World became so extensive (though by no means complete) that it is being published separately as *Crisis: In the Third World*. To a significant extent, this separate treatment of the Third World thus violates in practice the fundamental theoretical guideline of this study, which is to analyze the world economic or at least capitalist system as a whole. Of course, the recent developments in the Third World and its parts are herein analyzed as part of a historical process in the world as a whole; but often these developments are presented separately as though they were analyzable in and of themselves. This procedure constitutes an important practical and theoretical limitation, which I believe it is my duty to stress.

Since the parts of the world system are presented separately in each of these books, it is perhaps appropriate to stress here how much of what goes on in each part of the world should be regarded as the various parts of a single process. The overaccumulation crisis of world capitalism manifests itself for capital through a decline in the rate of profit. Like the previous crises through which capitalism passed in the past two centuries, this one can only be resolved through far-reaching and basic modifications in the international capitalist division of labor. For capital this exigency presents itself as the need to reduce costs of production in order to raise profits again. Therefore, capital tries to administer several remedial economic measures simultaneously to the world economic body. Some of these are the austerity policies, rationalization of production processes, and reorganization of work processes in the industrialized West. Others involve the accelerated incorporation of the East through increased trade, but even more significantly by producing in the socialist countries with technically qualified but cheap labor for the capitalist world market. Other economic measures include the "runaway" transfer of some manufacturing industries to the Third World and the increased superexploitation of many parts of the labor force in the South, which are directly and indirectly engaged in the production of manufactures and primary goods as well as services for the world market of capital. All these are complementary and mutually reinforcing measures to confront the same crisis of capital. The corresponding political policies of increasingly conservative social democratic governments and authoritarian tendencies in the West, of uneasy détente and negotiated collaboration between the West and the East, and of military and other authoritarian states and more acute armed conflict in the Third World are the necessary political instruments and manifestations of the aforementioned economic crisis responses by capital and its states. The social, political, and ideological response of labor and other sectors of society to this challenge by capital to restructure capitalism will determine whether, how, and to what extent capitalism will overcome its present crisis and go on to another later period of expansion.

If labor and the population at large are not willing to accept and bear the costs of the new capitalist order that capital is trying to impose on the world, and if these people successfully rebel against this order, then this crisis of capitalism would be its undoing and a really new noncapitalist order would emerge from the crisis. The reading of reality in the pages that follow suggests that, though the measure of social conflict within and between some states is likely to increase, the prospects of such a change are not very large for the foreseeable future. (They are perhaps the best in the "socialist" countries of Eastern Europe, which are least examined in this book.) For this reason also, without fundamental political change within the participating countries, the "new" international economic order that some Third World spokesmen demand among nation states is at best likely to turn out to be the same old order in some new emperor's clothes. Their design and measure, however, may well be the result of strategic and military disputes between the East and West that unfortunately remain unexamined in this book except partially insofar as they are carried over into the South.

Some readers may think that the superexploitation and repression in the Third World during the present crisis contradicts the thesis of the "development and underdevelopment" (Frank 1966, 1969), according to which underdeveloped satellite economies fare less badly during a crisis in the center. But on the one hand that thesis was not meant to suggest that every part of the periphery develops more during a crisis in the center, and some semiperipheries are shown (in TW, chapter 1) to experience a new development—or underdevelopment—today. On the other hand, chapters 5 and TW chapter 8 suggest that other parts of the periphery may still come to fare less badly during the present crisis, if this economic crisis or its political and military manifestations get so serious as to lead to a substantial breakdown of the international division of labor.

The scope, method, and sources of this study may seem to some readers like an unholy mixture of a superficially worldwide sweep with very selective local detail, of scientific (at least pretendedly so) objectivity with (certainly intentional) political engagement, and of standard official statistics with a wide variety of stray newspaper clippings. In part these combinations may be explained, if perhaps not justified, by my work substantially as a "loner" in physical isolation from a library that could offer permanent access to standard reference and research materials and maybe in intellectual isolation from the pressing or fashionable concerns of some institutions and currents of thought. I have sometimes tried to break through this isolation through occasional quick flights to talk with, and collect documentary material from, people at the UN Economic Commission for Europe (UNECE) and UNCTAD in Geneva, the OECD in Paris, the EEC Common Market Commission in Brussels and other institutions (whose abbreviations, like all others used here, are listed under Abbreviations at the end of the book), and to engage in longer political discussions with friends and comrades around the world from Bombay to Belgrade, Lisbon to London, Mexico to Montreal, and Tokyo to Tananarive, as well as the many who passed through Frankfurt and stopped to visit.

In part my scope, method, and sources are, however, also the deliberate (and I hope justified) attempt of a single concerned person to confront some, though certainly not all, of the pressing issues of the day with objective scientific *and* common-sense regard guided by conscious political concern. The examination in historical perspective of these contemporary events and processes, some of which are evident to the naked eye and others less so, is meant to be expository—and sometimes denunciatory—but not prescriptive.

I am trying to "tell it as it is" and not as we might or might not like it to be. I am not trying to say—at least not in these pages—what we should, or would have to, do to change things so as to make them the way we want them to be. Of course, I am also partial; but my—or our—partiality should not blind us, as it unfortunately and often even deliberately does, to reality as it is.

For this reason also I have relied very heavily on the daily press for my sources of information (the list of abbreviations cited identifies over one hundred periodical publications and their respective abbreviations. Some of them I have cited only a few times in the text and others hundreds of times, like the *International Herald Tribune,* which is abbreviated IHT and is published in Paris by the *New York Times* and the *Washington Post*). This does not mean that I regard the press as entirely truthful or infallible. On the contrary, more often than not it has a political and ideological ax to grind; and I have tried to put that ax to good use. Thus, I have sought to rely on spokesmen of business, like *Fortune* (FOR), *Business Week* (BW), *The Financial Times* (FT), *The Economist* (ECO), and *Business International* (BI) or its various regional newsletters (BA, BE, BLA) and other sources, such as official government documents or declarations, as sources that are relatively "unimpeachable" spokesmen or reflections of business and government action or opinion. For instance, the extensive documentation of political repression for economic reasons, recorded in TW chapter 6 for some thirty countries all around the Third World, is almost entirely provided—and deliberately selected—from the business, "bourgeois," and local press as well as from official government documents or declarations, such as that which begins, "Now, therefore, I, Ferdinand E. Marcos, President of the Philippines . . . decree. . . ." On the other hand, though I have had much less access to documentation from the socialist countries themselves, the analysis of their willing and anxious participation in the capitalist international division of labor is based on the evidence supplied by responsible official and other sources and is accompanied by at least a selection of quotations to that effect by their most authorized spokesmen, such as Leonid Brezhnev and Hua Guofeng and others.

Similarly, the analysis—and, if you will, denunciation—in chapter 3 of the deliberate deflationary policy of austerity and unemployment in one Western country after another is not only documented by, but verily distilled from, the reports and declarations of the most authorized officials and political representatives and spokesmen of these Western governments, such as the Organisation for Economic Cooperation and Development (OECD), President Carter and his Cabinet members and Prime Ministers Callaghan and Thatcher of Britain, Schmidt of West Germany, and Barre of France, as well as news coverage and editorial opinion about their policies by the *New York Times* (NYT), the London *Financial Times* (FT), and many other organs of the press. When I have needed statistical series over a longer timespan, I have taken them from United Nations, OECD, U.S. government, and other similar official sources insofar as they were available to me (without direct access to a library); or sometimes, if necessary, and especially for data on the most recent times, I have again relied on the press for reports or summaries of such information provided by these agencies and others such as the European "Common Market" Economic Commission (EEC) in Brussels. I have mined these sources for statistical data and other information, but this book is not intended to be a compendium of such sources or to compete with them and other texts as a complete catalogue of statistical data, other information, and their exhaustive analysis about the world or any of its parts or processes. Moreover, the cutoff date for the use of current material necessarily varied from one book and chapter to another, although I have updated them as explained above.

Finally, I believe there is some further method in this madness of so laboriously—and it is that unless one can rely on an institutional clipping service—reading through, discarding the chaff and selecting the grain, of clipping, filing, evaluating, and using this information from the press. It shows that, despite all of the many indisputable limitations and failures of the press, it is possible to mine it for hidden golden information, if one is mad enough to work out—and systematically work through—a method to smelt and refine these bits and pieces of golden information out of masses of ore and to compare and cross-check them before combining them as in a jigsaw puzzle, until a picture emerges that more or less objectively reflects reality. In short, much of what is recorded in the following pages is the result of an often maddening but hopefully useful exercise in methodical newspaper reading. For the historian—be it of the past or of the present, or for that matter of the future—reading "yesterdays' newspaper," contrary to the old adage, need not be "out of date."

It is a pleasure and an honor to be able to acknowledge gratefully the institutional and financial support of several organizations and the personal help and encouragement of friends associated with the same. When this work began in Chile, I was at the Centro de Estudios Socio-Económicos (CESO) of the University of Chile; several of my then colleagues and political compañeros have continued to encourage me although they are themselves now in exile all around the world. For the winter semester 1973–1974 I was at the Lateinamerikainstitut of the Freie Universität Berlin, where my interest in the crisis continued to grow. Between May 1974 and July 1975 I had the privilege of being a Visiting Research Fellow (Freier Wissenschaftlicher Mitarbeiter) at the Max-Planck-Institut in Starnberg, West Germany. The Institute's administrative and scientific councils and particularly its director, Professor Carl-Friedrich von Weizsäcker, extended continuing generous support to me and my research, including full financial support for a year, without asking for—or receiving—any tangible or visible return. The staff of the Institute library, like Ms. Mundorf and others, especially Ms. Karen Friedman and Ms. Ulla Enders, were of incalculable help in supplying me with research materials; particularly since they have tried to bridge the 450-kilometer distance that has physically separated me from the Institute since mid 1975. Folker Fröbel, Jürgen Heinrichs, and Otto Kreye, to whose project at the Institute I was formally attached, have extended me their completest personal friendship and scientific and practical help as well as their indispensable moral support, to work on "the crisis," even though in their own book (Fröbel et al., 1977) from which I have copied so much, they started out denying that there is any crisis at all.

From May 1975 to April 1978, while still formally a guest at the same Institute in Starnberg, I received generous full-time financial support for my research from the Deutsche Gesellschaft für Friedens- und Konfliktforschung (DGFK), for my proposed research project on "Capital Accumulation, Economic Crisis, Social Conflict and International Relations." At the DGFK I had the friendly support of the chairman of its Research Commission, Dr. Karlheinz Koppe, as well as that of other members like Dr. Dieter Senghaas and Mr. Kreye, who were burdened with reading my interminable "progress" reports. Dr. Humberta Wienholz, Mr. Norbert Ropers, and Ms. Ursula Semin-Panzer of the DGFK administrative staff good-naturedly put up with my frequent appeals to straighten something out for me (that I had usually twisted myself). I am most grateful to all of them for their support and confidence, as well as this long financial support, particularly since they were still extended when it already became apparent that I would not be able to fulfill all of the perhaps unrealistic promises that I had held out in my original research proposal. For the three months from May to July 1978, I gratefully acknowledge the supplementary financial support of the Berghof-Stiftung and its scientific director, Dr. Senghaas, and board member, Dr. Heinrichs, which permitted me to complete the original draft of this study after I should already have finished it, and particularly to write the chapters on the economic and political crisis in the industrial West. For editorial help (to eliminate some of my many errors, confusions, and inconsistencies) and for typing I am particularly grateful to Ms. Yolanda Broyles, Ms. Barbara Wraight, and Mr. Matthias Fienbork.

Since August 1978 as professor at the University of East Anglia in England, I have enjoyed the institutional support of my School of Development Studies (DEV) and the financial support of its Consolidated Research Fund. I have taken advantage of both to use the invaluable services of Ms. Jill Hodges and Ms. Leyla Strutt for the copy editing and reproduction, respectively, of individual chapters on these books as DEV discussion papers, of Ms. Jackie Spray and again Ms. Barbara Wraight for retyping them, and of Ms. Corinna Chute and most especially Ms. Sheila Pelizzon in managing the extremely laborious tasks of clipping, filing, and retrieving the innumerable press clippings and other current sources that I have drawn on to update these books in 1979 and 1980. At Holmes & Meier, I am grateful to my publisher, Max Holmes, for his extraordinary confidence in me and his interest in my project; to my editor, Nathan Laks, for his very intelligent and useful editing and general supervision of these books under the pressure of time; and to the copy editor, Margaret Willig, for the responsible but vast improvement once again of the style and readability of this book, which merits the thankfulness of both the author and the readers.

Last but certainly not least I am grateful for the personal, moral, and political support of my wife, Marta Fuentes, whom I superexploited to do bibliographies, clip newspapers (and then find them again) and varied other dirty work on this book as well as in our home where I worked, and my sons Paulo and Miguel, whose personal and political appreciation of my "work on the crisis" have helped me maintain the hope, which may be an illusion, that there may be some sense to the work it has cost me and the very great sacrifices it has cost them. Though in one or another fit of temper I have now and then been tempted to blame one or another of the above named for some minor shortcoming in my work, deep down I realize and gladly acknowledge publicly that the major shortcomings in this book, of which I am overly aware, are my own or the results of my own crisis. And for the latter I can only offer the partial explanation—and plead for partial dispensation—that it is *the* crisis that engulfs us all.

A.G.F.

Frankfurt, 17 July 1978
Norwich, 6 March 1980

Chapter 1

Postwar Boom (1945–1970): Boon for the West, Bust for the South

The developed nations of West and East command a spectacularly and increasingly disproportionate share of the fruits of the world economic system. From World War II to about 1970 burgeoning world trade benefited the West and East rather than the South, and the terms of trade shifted to the disadvantage of primary commodities other than oil. The West's multinational corporations control a growing share of world production and trade. In the nations of the South, staggering and often worsening poverty stems from mass underemployment and intra-national inequality, revealing the need for revolutionary change.

The present economic system has served the world well.

Henry Kissinger, 1975

The Present Economic System: Some Highlights

Thirty developed countries with less than 30 percent of the world's population now, and foreseeably only 20 percent of the population in the year 2000, account for approximately 90 percent of world income, financial reserves, and steel production, and 95 percent of the world's scientific and technological production. Eight of these countries alone have 80 percent of the world's nonmilitary manufacturing exports (West Germany, 21 percent; United States, 17 percent; Japan, 14 percent; Britain, France, and Italy each about 8 percent, and Canada, 4 percent). Thirty percent of the world's population, living in thirty developed capitalist and socialist countries, produce 60 percent of the world's agricultural output and consume over 60 percent of the food measured in wheat-equivalent consumption or 40 percent of the world's dietary energy. They consume 50 percent of the world's cereal production, of which 60 percent—that is, 30 percent of the world's total cereal production—is consumed through meat. The livestock that produces this meat consumes 370 million tons of cereal annually, equaling the total cereal consumption of the more than 1,200 million people of China and India (Vajda 1971: 204–205 for general data; Abercrombie 1975 for agriculture and nutrition; Clairmonte 1975 for manufacturing exports).

Some further measure of how well "the present economic system has served the world" is that average daily calorie consumption in the developed countries is 3,100 and 2,200 calories in the underdeveloped countries. In terms of food weight this is 800 kilos (1,760 pounds) per capita annual consumption in the developed countries, of which only 90 kilos (198 pounds) is direct consumption, the remainder being indirect consumption through livestock and its food consumption. Annual consumption of food in the underdeveloped countries is 230 kilos (506 pounds), almost all of which is consumed directly (Transnational Institute 1974–1975). Average per capita cereal consumption in 1972 to 1974 in the United States was 1,850 pounds; with the Soviet Union, 1,434 pounds; European Economic Community, 1,000 pounds; Japan, 620; China, 430, and in the underdeveloped countries, 395 pounds. The *increase* of cereal consumption (almost all through livestock) in the United States and the Soviet Union since 1964–1966 alone is more than half the total consumption in the underdeveloped countries (Schertz 1974). Averages, however, particularly in the underdeveloped countries, hide the absolute depths of the low-income receivers. Calorie deficiency estimates by income group are 25 percent higher than average levels by country of calorie consumption. Based on consumption levels by income category, the World Bank estimates that 670 million people, or 46 percent of the population of the underdeveloped countries, suffer from a deficiency of more than 200 calories a day less than the "minimum daily requirement" and another 450 million, or 30 percent, have a deficit of under 200 calories (World Bank 1975: 3, 22, 27). Ernest Feder (n.d.a) estimates that one half of the population of the underdeveloped countries consume no more than 1,500 calories per day and one half of these consume less than 1,000 calories. It need hardly be added how much—that is, how little— of the world's manufactured goods the underdeveloped countries consume. During the postwar period, and even more so for the foreseeable future, the trends in world growth and distribution have been and are likely to aggravate this pattern.

During the postwar decades between 1952 and 1972, the gross product of the developed capitalist countries combined rose by U.S. $1,820 billion from $1,250 billion to $3,070 billion. This increase alone was 3½ times the aggregate gross product, $520 billion, of the capitalist underdeveloped countries in 1972. While per capita real income in the underdeveloped countries rose from $175 in 1952 to $300 in 1972—without thereby increasing the income of the poorest income levels in their societies, which probably declined still further—the per capita real income in the developed capitalist countries rose from $2,000 to $4,000. As a result, the developed capitalist countries with one fifth of the world's population now enjoy two thirds of the world's income, while—excluding China—the half of the world's population in the underdeveloped countries make do with one eighth of the world's income. The poorest underdeveloped countries with one third of the world's population receive one thirtieth of the world's income, that is, one tenth of their proportionate share (UNCTAD 1976a:4).

Postwar Trends 1950–1970: North-South

In the postwar period from 1950 to 1970, the world population increased one and a half times (46 percent), total and industrial production increased nearly three times (GNP, 170 percent; industry, 180 percent), and world trade expanded four times (exports rose from U.S. $61 billion to $312 billion in current prices and by 285 percent in constant prices). But these increases were very unevenly distributed in favor of the industrial developed countries and to the particular disadvantage of the underdeveloped countries. By major world regions the trends were as follows:

TABLE 1-1
World Population Production and Trade by Regions 1950–1970
(1950 = 100)

Region	Population	GNP	Industrial Production	Exports
World total	146	270	280	385
North America	137	210	250	295
Europe	118	260	310	470
Soviet Union	135	435	700	740
Latin America	175	250	300	195
Asia	152	325	820	440
Africa	159			305

Source: Pinto & Knakal 1973:16.

The apparently relatively high expansion rates for production and trade in the underdeveloped countries are, however, doubly misleading: while their total production rose more than that of the developed countries (an average of 5.0 percent annually in the underdeveloped countries compared with 4.7 percent in the developed ones), because of their higher rates of population growth their production per capita rose more slowly (2.5 percent in the former and 3.5 percent in the latter). Furthermore, the developed countries started from a base in 1950 so much larger than the underdeveloped countries, that their rates of expansion made them greatly outdistance the latter in absolute production and trade as well as in their relative shares of total world production and trade. Thus, the relative shares of world trade accounted for by the developed capitalist, socialist, and underdeveloped capitalist countries over this postwar period were as follows:

TABLE 1-2

World Trade Shares 1938–1970
(in percentages of total exports)

Category/Region	1938	1950	1960	1970	1976
Developed	65	61	67	72	66
Socialist	10	8	12	11	10
Underdeveloped	25	31	21	18	24
Including					
Non-oil producing		24	14	12	14
Oil producing		7	7	6	10
Latin America	7	12	8	5	
Asia		13	9	8	
Africa		5	4	4	

Source: 1950–70, UNCTAD 1972a: 32–3; 1976, UNCTAD 1977c: 18.

It may be seen that while the developed countries' share of world trade increased in both postwar decades from 61 percent to 72 percent of world trade, the socialist countries' share increased in the first decade—reattaining the region's prewar share—and then remained roughly stable; and the underdeveloped countries' share declined through both postwar decades from 31 percent to 21 percent—below their prewar share—and then to 18 percent. Since then their share has fallen still further, to 17 percent, and then risen again in value terms because of the increase in the price of petroleum. Excluding petroleum trade, whose share remained roughly stable until 1970, the share of the underdeveloped countries in world trade declined by half from 24 percent to 12 percent and, within that, Latin America's share declined by even more than half, from 12 percent to 5 percent of world trade.

The pattern of world trade as expressed in exports from developed, socialist, and underdeveloped countries within the same category and to each of the other categories and to the rest of the world as a whole, changed over the two postwar decades as shown in Table 1-3.

Table 1-3 shows a large and clear shift in trade patterns: not only did the share of the developed countries in total world trade increase (line 1) as is shown in Table 1-2, but the share of world trade among the developed countries themselves (line 2) rose from a third to more than a half, while the shares of the underdeveloped countries' trade with the rest of the world (line 9), the developed countries (line 10), and among themselves (line 11), declined sharply. In the postwar decades world trade increasingly bypassed the underdeveloped countries. In the 1970s (see chapter 2 and TW) this

TABLE 1-3

World Trade Patterns by Regional Categories 1950–1969
(in percent of total exports)

Trade Direction	Total Trade		Primary Commodities Trade	
	1950	1969	1950	1969
1. Developed to World	58	71	41	43
2. Developed to Developed	34	54	32	35
3. Developed to Underdeveloped	22	14	8	6
4. Developed to Socialist	1	3	1	2
5. Socialist to World	1	11	11	11
6. Socialist to Developed	1	3	3	4
7. Socialist to Underdeveloped	1	2	1	1
8. Socialist to Socialist	0	7	7	6
9. Underdeveloped to World	39	18	48	41
10. Underdeveloped to Developed	27	14	35	32
11. Underdeveloped to Underdeveloped	11	4	11	8
12. Underdeveloped to Socialist	1	1	2	2

Source: Sideri 1972:369.

pattern was modified partly in fact and mostly in appearance: the increase in the price of oil raised the absolute and relative dollar value of the underdeveloped countries' total exports and imports and some countries also increased their manufacturing exports. Moreover, increased imports by OPEC countries stemmed the decline in world trade during the recession in 1975 and increased the underdeveloped countries' relative share of trade. Of course, these modifications have been concentrated in a few underdeveloped economies.

The socialist countries (examined in greater detail in chapter 4), quite apart from their distributive successes and their supposed productive failures, have made very substantial economic progress in the postwar period—especially when compared with the underdeveloped countries—both in internal economic development and in foreign trade. According to the Council for Mutual Economic Assistance (CMEA) Statistical Yearbook 1974 (cited in UNECE 1975c), national income measured as net material product rose at annual rates of 7.1 percent in the Soviet Union and 6.5 percent in Poland, the German Democratic Republic, Czechoslovakia, Hungary, Bulgaria, and Romania (an average of the rates of each of the six countries) during the period 1961 to 1970, and 6.1 percent in the Soviet Union and 7.7 percent in the six Eastern European countries in 1971 to 1975 (1971–1974 actual and 1975 planned growth). With a relatively low rate of population growth, this growth of national product left per capita increases of 4.7 percent annually in the Soviet Union and 4.6 percent in Eastern Europe for the period 1961 to 1965, accelerating to 6.8 percent and 6.7 percent (averaged) respectively for 1966 to 1970. Industrial production rose at annual rates of 8.4 percent in the Soviet Union and 8.7 percent in Eastern Europe (the average of the six countries' rates) in 1961 to 1965 and 8.7 percent and 8.4 percent respectively in 1966 to 1970. For 1971–1975 annual growth rates, except in two instances, exceeded 6 percent (UNECE 1976:2). Recently, however, these growth rates have declined drastically (see chapter 4). As a sustained trend until recently, these growth rates were far higher than those in the capitalist developed and underdeveloped countries. Agricultural production in the Soviet Union and Eastern Europe, as we have observed, also increased at a far higher per capita rate.

Following a period of politically imposed autarchy between 1948 and 1953, in which only intrasocialist trade grew, foreign trade of the socialist countries has expanded rapidly since 1953, especially with the capitalist countries, and that despite a U.S. trade embargo against them. In 1938 foreign trade of the region now comprising the socialist countries of Eastern Europe and the Soviet Union had been 74 percent with the West and only 13 percent within the region. By 1953 this ratio was reversed, with 80 percent of the region's foreign trade being among each other and only 14 percent with the West. Since 1953 East-West trade has again expanded to 25 percent of socialist foreign trade in 1966–67 and 30–38 percent in 1974–75, while the share of intrasocialist trade in total socialist foreign trade has fallen from 80 percent in 1953 to 62 percent in 1966–67 and 32–35 percent in 1974–75 (1974–75 data from GATT 1976: 171 are not entirely comparable to earlier data). While between 1953 and 1967 world trade as well as intracapitalist and intrasocialist foreign trade expanded at annual rates of 7 percent, 6.2 percent and 5.6 percent respectively, East-West trade grew at an annual rate of 13.3 percent and was exceeded only by East-South trade between the socialist and the underdeveloped countries, which grew at an annual rate of 16.1 percent. East-West trade between the now socialist Eastern Europe and Soviet Union and the West had been 6 percent of world trade and 10 percent of Western trade in 1938 and had fallen drastically during and after World War II. By 1950 socialist foreign trade with all regions (East-East, East-West, and East-South) had recovered to 8 percent of world trade; it has been between 10 and 12 percent since 1960. Of this about 4 to 5 percent is accounted for by the Soviet Union, little more than 1 percent by China and other Asian socialist countries, and the remaining 5 to 7 percent by Eastern Europe (UNCTAD 1972b:32–3).

The postwar period witnesses a certain degree of regional concentration or even de facto formation of trade blocs despite—and in part because of— policies to promote free trade, convertibility of currencies, and common markets or free-trade associations. Tables 1-2 and 1-3 as well as the above discussion of capitalist and socialist trade trends indicate the growing tendency during this period for international trade to have been concentrated in industrial products among the capitalist industrial countries and the high but declining concentration of trade among the socialist countries. The creation of the European Common Market in 1960 and its subsequent expansion from six to nine countries had "trade diverting" consequences that contributed to the regional concentration of foreign trade in that area, albeit in part with production emanating from firms with substantial extraregional ownership. Preferential trade increased from 10 percent of total foreign trade in 1955 to 17 percent in 1961 and 20 percent in 1964 to 24 percent in 1970. While nonpreferential foreign trade under the "most favored nation" clause increased from U.S. $58 billion to $175 billion over this same period, preferential trade increased proportionately much more from $6 billion to $56 billion (GATT 1972:9).

However, in part through institutional arrangements of "associate" status, trade conventions, and currency pegs, and in part without them, significant shares of international trade in the postwar period occurred within de jure or de facto trading blocs between certain industrial capitalist countries and particular regions of underdeveloped countries. These de facto blocs become visible in the following pattern of imports and exports between developed and underdeveloped capitalist countries.

TABLE 1-4

Trade Block Patterns Between Developed and
Underdeveloped Capitalist Countries
(in percent of exports and imports)

	Percent Shares of Imports by					
	United States		Western Europe		Japan	
	1960	1971	1960	1971	1960	1971
Coming from						
Latin America and Canada	41	39	18	9	10	13
Africa and Middle East	6	3	28	18	10	18
Asia and Oceania	6	10	10	5	21	26

	Percent Shares of Exports to					
	United States		Western Europe		Japan	
by						
Latin America and Canada	50	55	32	26	3	6
Africa and Middle East	9	5	64	64	4	12
Asia and Oceania	17	26	46	26	15	22

Source: Sideri 1973.

Note: Underline indicates trade block pattern.

Table 1-4 suggests that de facto preferential block trading (underlined in the table) persisted between pairs: the United States with Latin America and Canada; Europe with Africa and the Middle East, and to a lesser but growing extent Japan with Asia and Oceania. This bloc pattern appears when measured by the share of each industrial economy's imports that come from its "preferred" underdeveloped "backyard" region and even more so when measured by the amount of the mostly underdeveloped peripheral regions' exports that go to the same industrial center. That is, the relative degree of dependence on these bilateral relations is even greater for the underdeveloped periphery's exports than it is for the industrialized center's imports.

Despite the underdeveloped countries' legitimate demands for reduced tariff barriers against their manufactured exports in the industrial countries, each underdeveloped region in fact sends a greater percentage of raw materials than of manufactures to its "preferred" center, and the industrial countries, particularly of Europe, concentrate their purchases of raw materials in particular underdeveloped regions more than they do their much smaller purchases of manufactures (Sideri 1973). Therefore, when the trade in raw materials becomes more important than manufactures, trading blocs become more important and their formation is strengthened. Moreover, the preferred backyard peripheries or neocolonies of each industrial center offer a captive market for its manufacturing exports, less likely to be lost than other developed and underdeveloped regions, so that in a recession in which demand declines the share of the industrial center's exports going to its own backyard rises. Indeed, in recessions the proportion of an industrial country's sales to underdeveloped countries as a whole also rises, but less so than sales to its own backyard region. The trading blocs thus offer something of a cushion to the industrialized countries in difficult times, and during these times the formation of economic blocs tends to strengthen.

"National" comparisons of production, productivity, and trade in the postwar period must be partly amended by considerations arising out of the rapid growth of direct foreign investment, particularly by multinational or transnational corporations, beginning especially with American ones but more recently including those of some other countries as well. By 1969, American foreign direct investment (book value of equity and long-term debt of U.S. enterprise in those cases where the U.S. enterprise holds 25 percent or more of the equity) was U.S. $67 billion dollars, of which nearly a third ($21 billion) was invested in Canada and another third in Europe. This concentration of U.S. foreign investment in other industrial capitalist economies (except for investment of $18 billion in the petroleum industry) reflects the predominance of $29 billion—or nearly half of the investment—in manufacturing industry. Indeed, $21 billion of this U.S. foreign investment in manufacturing was even more concentrated in Canada ($9 billion) and

Europe ($12 billion) of which half again was in the European Economic Community still excluding Britain.

The importance of these U.S. transnational firms abroad may be partly gauged by their percentage share of sales (in 1964) of all manufacturing establishments in some countries or regions: in Canada, 22 percent; Europe, 3 percent; Latin America, 7 percent (Vernon 1971:22). Of course, these overall sales percentages lend less than due emphasis to the real impact of the multinational corporations in these economies, societies, and polities as a whole or in particular industries, such as automobile manufacturing in Canada, where their share of industry sales is 100 percent. The sales of multinational corporations abroad have been variously estimated at U.S. $200 billion for U.S. multinationals and $450 billion for all multinationals (BW 19 December 1970; Judd Polk in testimony to the U.S. Congress, cited in Dos Santos 1975: 148). The latter figure would be about one sixth of world GNP, and the former, as is frequently observed, makes the U.S. multinationals abroad "the second biggest economy" of the capitalist world.

While U.S. manufacturing exports increased from $15 billion to $35 billion between 1961 and 1970, foreign sales of U.S. multinationals increased from $25 billion to $90 billion (Dos Santos 1975: 153). Roughly 75 percent of their sales are destined for the national markets of the countries they operate in, and the remainder is exported— increasingly so—to neighboring or other countries and also increasingly back to the United States market itself (Vernon 1971:103). This pattern converts the multinationals into increasingly important and powerful factors in international trade as well. Fully 40 percent of "Latin American" manufacturing exports in 1968 were in fact exported by U.S.-owned subsidiaries in Latin America; U.S. multinationals also account for a very appreciable share of "British" and other countries' exports (Vernon 1971:102–10). At the same time, while American foreign capital was increasing its penetration of the Canadian and West European economies both absolutely and relative to its investment in the underdeveloped world (where American investment increased in absolute terms but decreased relative to its expansion elsewhere), West European and later Japanese capital were increasingly investing in the underdeveloped countries and especially in Latin America, which took from 20 percent to 40 percent of the foreign investment of Germany, Italy, and Japan.

During the postwar decades and before the 1970s, world trade was increasingly concentrated among the developed countries largely as a reflection of the increasing importance of the industrial products, which they produced and traded. Only the increase in the price of oil and in manufacturing exports from the Third World has begun to alter this pattern in the 1970s (examined in TW, chapter 3). The trend in world trade differentiated by categories of production was as follows:

TABLE 1-5

Shares of Industrial and Other Products in World Trade

(in percentages of total exports)

Product	1955	1970
Machinery	18	19
Chemical products	5	7
Other manufactures	26	29
Fuels	11	9
Raw materials and foodstuffs	38	24

While in 1955 the first three categories of industrial products and the last two categories of raw material commodities had equal shares of 49 percent of world trade, only fifteen years later in 1970 the former already accounted for 65 percent or two thirds of world trade and the latter had fallen back to 33 percent or one third of world trade. Both the production and the trade of the former was preferentially in and among the developed industrial countries, though, albeit starting from a low base, the socialist countries achieved an increasing share of this trade among each other and with the rest of the world. The underdeveloped countries, despite important localized increases of industrial production, did not until recently even maintain their participation in this trade.

However, as the last two columns of Table 1-3 show, the underdeveloped countries' share of world trade declined not only in and because of trade in industrial commodities but also because they experienced a declining share of the world's trade in primary raw material commodities. The underdeveloped countries lost a part of their shares of trade in primary commodities, albeit a lesser one than of other trade, to the developed countries. This share declined in trade between underdeveloped and developed as well as among underdeveloped countries, and therefore in the world as a whole. This happened despite the expansion of petroleum production and export by some of these countries. The decline in the underdeveloped countries' share of exports of raw materials was due to an *increase* in the developed industrial countries' share of world trade in primary commodities as well as of other commodities. While the share of fuels in world trade remained roughly stable before the increases in the price of oil in 1972, the share of mineral and agricultural commodities declined sharply.

The underdeveloped countries' share of world mineral production remained stable at 32 percent (as against 45 percent in the developed and 27 percent in the socialist countries) from 1950 to 1970, but has declined since then due to production increases in Canada, Australia, and the socialist countries. Compared to their 32 percent of world production, the underdeveloped countries themselves consumed only 6 percent of the world total and accounted for 41 percent of world mineral exports in 1970. The socialist countries consumed 26 percent and exported 5 percent of the world total; and the industrial-developed capitalist countries, which produce 45 percent of the world's total, themselves exported 54 percent—significantly more than the underdeveloped countries—of the total and consumed 69 percent of the world mineral supplies (Hveem 1975:36).

Compared to the production of industrial commodities and other raw materials, the production of foodstuffs has lagged, particularly in the under-developed countries. While the overall amount of foodstuffs in world trade declined, the share of the underdeveloped countries' exports of foodstuffs declined still more drastically. Many underdeveloped countries that had been net exporters of foodstuffs or large exporters of particular foodstuffs, es-pecially of some grain, began to import these commodities from the devel-oped countries and especially from the United States. The following is an overview of food production by major world regional categories:

TABLE 1-6

Food Production by Major World Regional Categories 1950–1970
(1963 = 100)

Regional Category	Total Production			Per Capita Production		
	1950	1960	1970	1950	1960	1970
World	67	93	119	86	99	104
Developed (capitalist and socialist)	69	94	119	81	97	110
Socialist alone	62	99	134	74	103	125
Underdeveloped	66	92	121	90	99	101

Source: UNCTAD 1972:170.

Thus, while total world food production nearly doubled (+78 percent) in the two decades and increased 21 percent per capita and—contrary to popular impression—rose appreciably faster (116 percent) and over three times more (69 percent) per capita in the socialist countries, total food production in the underdeveloped countries rose 83 percent or about as much as total world production but only half as much (12 percent) as the world production per capita. Moreover, while in the developed capitalist and socialist countries the rate of increase declined somewhat during the second of these decades, in the underdeveloped countries the rate of increase per capita almost stagnated in the decade 1960–1970. Since then food pro-duction per capita in the underdeveloped countries has declined altogether (see TW, chapter 2).

The declining amount of trade in raw materials and the reduced share of the underdeveloped producers in world trade during the postwar period is particularly accounted for by the decline in the terms of trade of raw material commodities relative to industrial products. Before the increase in the price of oil, which improved the terms of trade for the few oil-exporting countries but further depressed them for the vast majority of underdeveloped countries that import oil, the terms of trade declined by about one third at an average annual rate of 1.6 percent for raw materials excluding petroleum and at an annual average rate of 2.2 percent including petroleum over the period 1952 to 1972. Primary commodity terms of trade as calculated by the imperialist handmaiden World Bank declined a bit less from 122 in 1953 or 137 in 1954 to 89 in 1971 or 87 in 1972 with 1963 = 100, while the same terms of trade as calculated by UNCTAD, which is more at the service of the under-developed countries, show a somewhat greater decline from 126 in 1953 or 138 in 1954 to 86 in 1971 or 84 in 1972. An appreciable decline shows up in both indices, which moved in the same direction in every year but two. The terms of trade declined significantly for 23 commodities out of the 28 indexed by UNCTAD and for petroleum as well (UNCTAD 1976b; Clairmonte 1975). In 1972 this decline in the terms of trade represented a loss of some US $10 billion or 20 percent of the underdeveloped nonoil-export earnings from primary commodities. Had raw materials maintained their relative prices, they would of course have accounted for a higher relative share of all traded commodities than they did even at the recorded levels of production—and more of them would have been produced because at higher relative prices it would have been relatively more profitable to produce them. The commodity price boom of the 1970s (examined in detail in chapter 2) made *no* essential change in this pattern or trend except for oil.

Third World Poverty and Unemployment

Further measures of how well the present economic system serves the majority of the people living in the Third World are the amount of pro-ductive employment it affords them and the poverty to which it condemns them. In recent years the problems of poverty and employment/unemploy-ment in the Third World have received widespread official and scientific attention in readily available sources (Turnham 1971 for OECD; ILO 1976, Bairoch 1973 for ILO; Chenery et al. 1974 for World Bank; Jolly et al. 1973, and many others). Therefore, we may here limit ourselves to sum-marizing and quoting some of their findings.

In his report, entitled *Employment, Growth and Basic Needs: A One-World Problem,* delivered to the Tripartite Conference on Employment, Income Distribution and Social Progress and the International Division of Labour, the Director General of the U.N. International Labor Organization, Francis Blanchard, giving due emphasis to (un)employment and (mal)dis-tribution of income, summarized the problem:

> Today, in spite of the immense efforts that have been made, both at the national and international levels, a significant proportion of man-kind continues to eke out an existence in the most abject conditions of

material deprivation. More than 700 million people live in acute poverty and are destitute. At least 460 million persons were estimated to suffer from a severe degree of protein-energy malnutrition even before the recent food crisis. Scores of millions live constantly under the threat of starvation. Countless millions suffer from debilitating diseases of various sorts and lack access to the most basic medical services. The squalor of urban slums is too well known to need further emphasis. The number of illiterate adults has been estimated to have grown from 700 million in 1960 to 760 million towards 1970. The tragic waste of human resources in the Third World is symbolized by nearly 300 million persons unemployed or underemployed in the mid-1970s. . . . In 1972 some 1,200 million people in the developed market economies (67 per cent of their population) were "seriously poor," and 700 million (39 per cent) were "destitute" and suffering from severe malnutrition. By each of these standards, the proportion of the poor in the total population is greatest in Asia (although Africa comes a close second), and some 70 percent of the total are in Asia. . . .

The crux of the employment problem in the developing world thus lies in the high proportion of the labour force earning inadequate incomes. These persons are classified as underemployed . . . [and are] approximately the same as the proportion of the population classified as "destitute." Thus, problems of employment and poverty are inseparable. The labour force of the developing market economies is now around 700 million . . . about 5 per cent of this labour force is openly unemployed. . . . About 36 per cent is underemployed, the proportion being less in urban and more in rural areas. Of the total of unemployed and underemployed, about 80 per cent are rural. Thus the employment problem, like the poverty problem, is largely a rural phenomenon. . . . What is more, there is no doubt that the numbers of the poor have increased, in spite of the rapid economic growth in most developing countries. . . . There is also considerable evidence, although often fragmentary and circumstantial, that the material conditions of life for large numbers of people are worse today than they were one or two decades ago. In a very few countries average levels of living have fallen (ILO 1976:3, 17–23).

Nonetheless, another ILO study suggests that:

Growing poverty is not necessarily associated with growing unemployment. Indeed it is noteworthy that in none of the empirical studies of Asia was unemployment cited as a prominent cause of poverty. In broad terms unemployment is, first, an urban phenomenon and, second, a phenomenon of the middle class. The very poor cannot afford to be unemployed; they must obtain a source of livelihood even if it implies pitifully low earnings. . . . Thus most of the poor are not unemployed and most of the unemployed are not poor (Griffin and Khan 1976:I 38–40).

In India, for instance,

> In 1972–73 "the unemployment rate estimated from labour time disposition of person days according to current activity status was 7.83 per cent for rural areas." By contrast, according to the Central Statistical Organisation's estimates for 1973–74 the number of people living below the poverty line was between 42.7 per cent and 59.5 per cent of the total population. Poverty, it is concluded from these figures, is a more pervasive and far graver phenomenon that unemployment . . . . The extreme poverty among landless labourers and small peasants seems to go hand in hand with relatively low unemployment rates in many parts of the country (EPW 14 Jan 78: 33, quoting the Deputy Chairman of the Planning Commission).

The problem of poverty is also a problem of inequality. In most developing countries the richest 10 percent of households typically receive about 40 percent of personal income, whereas the poorest 40 percent receive 15 percent or less, and the poorest 20 percent receive about 5 percent (ILO-WER 26 March 1976). A major ILO study on *Poverty in Asia* finds:

> In the last quarter century, or roughly during the period when most of Asia achieved its independence, the number of the rural poor has increased and their standard of living has tended to fall. . . . There is at least a strong presumption that the standard of living of the poorest groups in rural areas has deteriorated over time. . . . In most of the countries in Asia the incomes of the very poor have been falling absolutely or the proportion of the rural population living below a designated "poverty line" has been increasing, or both. Similar things almost certainly have been happening elsewhere, in Africa and parts of Latin America, for the mechanisms which generate growing poverty in Asia are present in much of the rest of the underdeveloped world. . . . Growth, even quite rapid growth, has produced not only greater inequality but an absolute impoverishment of a substantial section of the rural population. . . . In most of the countries for which measurements could be obtained either real wages [for agricultural laborers] remained constant or there was a significant downward trend. . . . At the same time . . . the proportion of agricultural labourers below the poverty line increased precisely during the period when real wages are claimed to have risen. If one is to believe both pieces of evidence, then there must have been a change in the occupational distribution of wage earners [due to more capital intensive farming]. . . . The continuation of the highly unequal ownership of land during a period of rapid demographic growth has resulted in increased landlessness and

near-landlessness. . . . In the last two decades in almost every country for which we have data, the cost of living for the lower income groups has increased faster than the general cost of living. The reason for this is that the prices of food and other wage goods have increased faster than the average.

False Answers

It is certainly not the case that the increasing poverty of the poor is due to general stagnation in Asia, or, worse, economic decline. On the contrary, all but one of the seven countries surveyed has enjoyed a rise in average incomes in recent years, and in some instances the rise has been quite rapid.

Only in Bangladesh . . . where average incomes have fallen, the rich still managed to become richer while the incomes of the poor have fallen faster than the average. Excluding Bangladesh, between 1960 and 1973, GNP per capita increased between 1.3 per cent a year (in India) and 3.9 per cent (in Malaysia). That is, during this period, the level of income, on average, increased about 18 per cent in India and 65 per cent in Malaysia. Yet the incomes of the poor fell in both countries, as well as in those which experienced intermediate rates of growth . . . .

Equally untenable is the claim that the growing poverty of Asia is due to a world food shortage or a failure of food production in Asia to keep up with expanding population. . . . It is sheer nonsense to think of the earth as an overcrowded lifeboat in danger of sinking from the weight of the emaciated Asian multitudes, and it is wicked nonsense to describe the plight of the poor in some Asian countries as "international basket cases." When the poor starve, it is not because there is no food but because they do not have the wherewithal to acquire food . . . .

We are in agreement with those who argue that "the nutrition problem is . . . primarily a *poverty* problem: a problem of ineffective demand rather than ineffective supply." . . .

The answer to why poverty has increased has more to do with the structure of the economy than its rate of growth. One structural feature common to all the countries studied is a high degree of inequality. . . . The richest 20 per cent of households typically receive about half the income, whereas the poorest 40 per cent receive between 12 and 18 per cent of total income. The bottom 20 per cent fare even worse, of course, receiving about 7 per cent of the income in the least inegalitarian country (Bangladesh) and merely 3.8 per cent in one of the most inegalitarian countries (Philippines). . . . The basic causes are the unequal ownership of land and other productive assets, allocative mechanisms which discriminate in favour of owners of wealth and a pattern of investment and technical change which is biased against labour. . . . The statistical evidence for China . . . is even more convincing in demonstrating that rural inequality and poverty have been reduced enormously (Griffin and Khan 1976: xv–xvi, 2, 6, 7, 10, 14, 19, 20, 22, 27, 28).

The ILO estimates that there were 300 million unemployed or underemployed people in the Third World in the mid-1970s, *more* than the labor force of about 280 million or the 265 million employed (with over 5 percent officially unemployed) in the developed OECD countries (OECD Economic Outlook 1975 and 1976). The greater extent of rural unemployment and underemployment in the Third World (80 percent of the total) is a reflection of the larger rural population, particularly in Asia and Africa. Rapid urbanization, however, in increasingly shifting this problem to the cities, both absolutely and relatively. In Latin America, which is already more urbanized than Africa and Asia, rural and urban underemployment are nearly the same. In Latin America:

> Only 20 per cent of underutilization can be attributed to open unemployment according to available figures; thus it is clear that four-fifths of the problem remains hidden when it is approached through the more traditional estimate—a veritable iceberg. The submerged part of the iceberg can be divided roughly half-and-half among rural and urban forms of underemployment. This means that broadly three-fifths of the employment problem in Latin America is presently concentrated in the towns and cities (PREALC 1976:13).

In his ILO study of *Urban Unemployment in Developing Countries* Paul Bairoch found, *without* regarding underemployment:

> In one-third of the countries, the urban employment rate exceeds 15 per cent, while, in nearly two-thirds of them, it exceeds 8 per cent. These proportions would probably be even larger if the statistical data were more comparable. For ten of the countries, the urban unemployment rates refer to the capital cities; but : . . unemployment rates are generally lower in the capital cities than in other urban centers. . . . The number of unemployed in urban agglomerations of 20,000 or more inhabitants has grown as follows; 1950: 6 to 8 million; 1960: 11 to 13 million; 1970: 20 to 24 million . . . when urban regions are given the broader definition . . . the estimated number of urban unemployed in 1970 [rises] to between 25 and 32 million. . . . Owing to the lower rate of female activity, the number of unemployed females is obviously smaller than the number of unemployed men; but, in most cases, the unemployment rate is higher among women. . . . In nearly every case, the unemployment rates in the 15–24 age group are equal to, or more than, double the rate for the population as a whole. . . . It appears from fragmentary data that unemployment is mainly medium-term in duration (Bairoch 1973:51–60).

However, according to the Chief of the Technical Secretariat of the ILO World Employment Conference, Dharam Ghai:

> There are many more persons seeking jobs than the numbers currently unemployed. . . . With an estimated urban population in the developing countries of around 630 million in 1970, this would yield estimates of urban unemployed varying between 60 and 90 million persons. These figures would of course be considerably higher if we add to them the numbers who are underemployed (Ghai 1975:5–6).

Bairoch goes on to examine underemployment and concludes that "both at the personal level and at the level of society as a whole, rural underdevelopment is to be preferred to urban overunemployment" (Bairoch 1973:82–3).

Industrial growth is evidently far from offering adequate employment opportunities. Between 1960 and 1972 labor-intensive light industries, particularly the textile industry, lagged behind more capital-intensive heavy industry in providing employment. The metal products and machinery industry—producing mostly durable consumer goods—provided substantially higher rates of employment growth of about 5 percent per year, compared to the 1 percent annual increase in the textile industry and an average of about 3 percent in all manufacturing industry. More employment was generated by heavy industry because its output grew at rates of 8 to 10 percent compared to 5 percent in light industry (UNIDO 1974:14–16). Employment in heavy industry increased faster than in light industry in about two thirds of the Third World countries, but part of this registered increase in employment in the "organized manufacturing sector" merely represents the replacement of unregistered artisan employment which was put out of business (UNIDO 1974:90). Moreover:

> There exist substantial amounts of underutilized industrial capacity in developing countries, not infrequently as much as one half of the installed capacity. . . . Calculations of the employment effect of eliminating underutilization of capacity completely in four particular Latin American countries indicate that 40 to 100 per cent of modern sector unemployment in these countries could be eliminated in this way. Optimistic as these estimates may be . . . (UNIDO 1974:117).

Underutilization of capacity, like unemployment of labor, is after all a chronic structural feature of capitalism, particularly in the Third World; and neither more industrial capacity or greater utilization, still less by international capital, will eliminate this structural unemployment. The following report from Bangladesh offers a graphic illustration for one sector of the unemployed, the educated:

> A sector corporation also very recently had to sort out about 3,000 applications for selecting only a dozen candidates for different clerical jobs. The applicants, to mention here incidentally, included at least one

hundred post graduates. A nationalized banking institution received, in response to an advertisement for filling up a few clerical posts, five thousand applications until recently. The Public Service Commission . . . received in all about 30,000 applications only the other day for filling 132 executive posts in government service. . . . As of 1973–74 forty per cent of the educated labour force . . . in Bangladesh are unemployed. The situation as the recent trends indicate, must have deteriorated further by now (HOL 26 December 1976).

It has been estimated that between now and the year 2000, more than a thousand million jobs will have to be created in the developing countries alone if an end is to be put to unemployment and poverty. The contribution which multinational enterprises can make to this immense task would not appear to be decisive, since at present they employ only an estimated two million people—0.3% of the working population of these countries. In the manufacturing sector, in spite of a rapid growth of investments—in the metallurgical and chemical industries, for instance—the number of jobs created is still very small when compared with the rest of the economy. Multinational enterprises often employ less than 10% of the workers in manufacturing compared with a share of 30% in investment (ILO-WER 12 April 1976).

Thus agriculture, in addition to absorbing a substantial backlog of underemployment, will have to continue to provide employment for new entrants to the labour force for a long time to come if rural-urban migration is to be slowed to a rate commensurate with the creation of non-agricultural jobs. . . . This state of affairs is likely to continue in the developing countries as a whole until the beginning of the second decade of the next century. This broad conclusion is likely to remain true even if non-agricultural employment were to expand much more rapidly (ILO 1976:19).

But with the proletarianization of peasants increasingly converted into landless laborers and particularly the invasion of capital-intensive and land-extensive agribusiness in Third World agricultures, rural and agricultural unemployment and poverty are also likely to accelerate (Feder 1977c). Thus the prospects for future employment and raised average income are very bleak—for the poorest sectors literally disastrous—as long as capitalist development persists in the Third World. Discussing its projections to the year 2000, the ILO remarks:

There is, however, no guarantee or even likelihood that the needs of the poor are satisfied when average needs are met. Furthermore, any shortfall in achieving average basic needs targets will mainly hit the poor. . . . Unless income distribution changes significantly, the basic needs of the [poorest 20 percent of households] target groups can only be met, according to the model, within one generation by rates of growth which are nearly double the already rapid rates achieving in recent years. There are two major exemptions to this generalization: China and the oil-producing countries. In the rest of the developing world the achievement of basic needs would demand, under the model, a combination of roughly doubling the rate of growth and rapidly reducing the rates of growth of population. It is unlikely that either, let alone both, of these conditions could be achieved. . . . Nevertheless, on balance, the projections may be too optimistic rather than too pessimistic in their assumptions. . . .

Conclusions

All these calculations, tentative though they may be, strongly suggest that in many countries minimum income and standards of living for the poor cannot be achieved, even by the year 2000, without some acceleration of present average rates of growth, accompanied by a number of measures aiming at changing the pattern of growth and use of productive resources by the various income groups; in a number of cases these measures would probably have to include an initial redistribution of resources, in particular, land (ILO 1976:40–43).

In words other than the minimum common denominator of the Tripartite—government, employer, and labor representatives—Conference on Employment, Income Distribution and Social Progress and the International Division of Labor of the International Labor Office and its diplomatically worded *Employment, Growth and Basic Needs: A One-World Problem,* massive unemployment and abject poverty in the Third World cannot be eliminated "by measures changing the pattern of growth and use of productive resources by income groups" unless all of the Third World obtains an effective *monopoly* on oil production (which is not possible, and, even if it were, would be eliminated by imperialist military force and technological progress—and has not eliminated poverty even in the few OPEC countries that have substantial resources) or until the Third World does as China did: make revolution. This conclusion is a measure of how well the present economic system has served the world.

Chapter 2
The New Economic Crisis in the West

Since 1967 the industrial West (including Japan and Australasia) has entered another long crisis of overaccumulation of capital, analogous to the great crisis of 1873 to 1895 and the long crisis from 1913 to the 1940s, which included the Great Depression of the 1930s, fascism, revolution, and two world wars. The new economic crisis is marked by excess productive capacity and a decline in the rate of profit, which militate against new investment except to reduce costs of production by making workers redundant at home and moving production sites to cheap labor areas elsewhere. Major investment in technological innovations and new leading industries cannot take place again until the profit rate is raised again through political action. Recessions in 1967, 1969 to 1971, 1973 to 1975, and since 1979–1980 have become more frequent, deeper, and increasingly coordinated throughout the industrial capitalist countries. Unemployment in these countries has risen from 5 million in the first of these recessions to 10 million in the second and 15 million in the third recession. Unemployment continued to rise to over 17 million in the "recovery" from 1975 to 1979. The recession in 1980 is threatening to raise unemployment to still higher and more dangerous levels. At the same time, recession and unemployment have been accompanied by—and indeed seem themselves to have generated—more and more inflation. The oil price hike has become the scapegoat for these problems, whose real sources are to be sought in the structure and development of capitalism itself and whose consequences are aggravated by economic and political policies, which are examined in chapter 3.

Uneven Accumulation and Long Economic Waves

Capitalist development and capital accumulation have always been and continue to be temporally uneven and spatially/sectorally unequal. A quarter century of expansive boom in the industrialized countries has led many people to forget these inherent features of capitalism—some even deny them altogether. As late as 1970, economics Nobel prize laureate Paul Samuelson, speaking at a conference honoring the National Bureau of Economic Research and its work on the business cycle, claimed that the business cycle had been so well analyzed and counteracted as to have practically gone out of existence—a prewar dinosaur turned into a postwar lizard (Samuelson in Zarnowitz 1972: 167, quoted more extensively in Frank 1978c). Ilse Mintz suggested at the same conference that "the time has come, therefore, to adjust the tools of business cycle analysis to the moderation of the cycle[s]" and call them "growth cycles" instead (in Zarnowitz 1972: 40 ff.).

The claim to realism of economic forecasting has been a complete farce, and the economic policy based on it a dreadful failure (Frank 1978 c, d, e). The hard reality of the growing economic crisis of the 1970s has demonstrated the complete inadequacy of economic forecasting and policy to the man and woman in the street, to business and government, and to economists themselves. According to a public opinion poll, Americans rank the forecasting ability of economists on a par with that of astrologers (FOR January 1976), and even that is an insult to the latter (Frank 1978e).

Commenting on the December 1977 meetings of the American Economic Association, *Business Week* notes that economics has become a "niggardly old-maidish science increasingly concerned with arranging and rearranging old furniture," and that "the economics profession faces intellectual bankruptcy." Government statements about the economy have become so vague as to take on the character of the prediction of a Greek oracle (BW 16 January 1978: 120, 29).

The same crisis in the economy and bankruptcy of economics are also generating new historical, theoretical, analytical, and empirical studies of uneven accumulation, economic crisis, and of the present crisis in particular. Ernest Mandel's *Late Capitalism* (1975a) is a milestone. Wallerstein (1974) and the present author (Frank 1977a, 1978a) among others have been returning to the study of historical roots and nature of the entire process. More and more books on the contemporary crisis have been appearing, among them those of J. Kolko (1974), Amin et al. (1975), Castells (1976), URPE (1975, 1978), Annual Register of Political Economy (1978), and Frank (1977c). The participation of the Third World in this uneven accumulation and unequal development is analyzed in TW, chapter 1, and elsewhere in this book.

Several writers suggest that the world capitalist economy has again entered into a downswing, "B," depressive, or crisis phase of a long cycle or wave, a conception widely associated with the name of N. D. Kondratieff (1935, 1944), but which was also studied by Parvus, Kautsky, Trotsky (collected in Parvus et al. 1972), van Geldern (reviewed in Mandel 1975a), and Schumpeter (1939). The most forceful argument of this thesis is that of Mandel (1975a). Shuman and Rosenau (1972) envisioned a downswing phase in the 1980s (but not the 1970s) in *The Kondratieff Wave: The Future of America Until 1984 and Beyond.* The present author argued as much since 1972 for the period beginning in the mid-1960s (Frank 1977c, chapter 1 and ff.). David Gordon (1978) advances the same argument. On the political right, which tends to play down economic crises and the long "Kondratieff" downswing in particular, W. W. Rostow (1978) believes in their existence, but claims that we are now in an expansive upswing phase! On the other hand, Jay Forrester, who became famous through his work on *The Limits of Growth* for the Club of Rome, now claims that we are headed for a Kondratieff depression (FOR 16 January 1978: 145 ff.).

Nonetheless, the thesis which postulates the existence of long waves and argues particularly that we have entered into one such depressive downswing phase at the present time is a "controversial" position, defended by only a small minority of people, both from the right and the left. However, Forrester suggests, "as the evidence becomes more clear, I think economists will take the existence of a Kondratieff wave more seriously" (FOR 16 January 1978: 145). By mid-1978 even that most austere and respectable of institutions, the Bank for International Settlements (the so-called central bankers' central bank) in Basel contemplates the "possibility of a slowdown of the 'Kondratieff' type" (BIS 1978: 8). GATT (sometimes called the rich man's trading club) finds that "events force us seriously to contemplate the possibility of the world moving along a less than full capacity growth path for a prolonged period, during which cyclical upswings would be brief . . . while cyclical downswings would be steeper and more extended than in the earlier period" (GATT 1979b). The fiftieth anniversary of the Wall Street crash of Black Thursday and Black Tuesday on November 24 and 29, 1929, was universally commemorated by the press and all around the capitalist world with the greatest of interest and alarm as another world economic crash appeared more than plausible and the fifty-year interval more than a coincidence.

Here, we review a number of historical manifestations and implications of the thesis of long waves, without trying to enter into a major theoretical debate as to their existence (which Mandel [1975] has already done excellently). Nor will we debate their internal or self-reproductive cyclical dynamic (which Mandel following Trotsky seems to doubt, and which we suspect is significantly greater than they believe—enough to justify calling these long fluctuations not just "waves" but also "cycles").

Those who see any historical pattern at all of long economic waves agree, subject to some controversy, that there was a long "Kondratieff" upswing beginning with the industrial revolution around 1790, followed by a more controversial downswing lasting from 1816–24 to 1848. Representatives of French historiography (Simiand 1932, and Labrousse 1932), now joined by Wallerstein (1974), Gordon (1978, 1979), and *Review* (1979), however, speak of long, apparently cyclical swings lasting one or two centuries in preindustrial times, and beginning as early as the twelfth century in Europe. We have argued elsewhere (Frank 1978a) that the industrial revolution itself was the outgrowth of a crisis of capital accumulation—or downswing—during the years 1762–1789. The more general argument, however, postulates that since the industrial revolution there have been several long waves, each of about a half century in duration, and each marked by an upswing followed by a downswing (or vice versa, depending on the theoretical question of which generates which) lasting about a quarter of a century.

In the half-century-long cycles since the industrial revolution, upswings have been characterized by increasing prices (according to the French school and its more recent adherents), production (Kondratieff), technological innovation (Schumpeter), and profits (Mandel). The long downswings have correspondingly been marked by deflation, lower growth rates, cost-reducing invention (Frank 1978a), and declining and lower profits. Most importantly, downswings have exhibited certain political/economic transformations that have made a recuperation of profits possible, thereby stimulating innovative major new investments and then expansion of production in the next upswing. Schumpeter (1939) placed technological innovation during the upswing— that is, investment in the economic application of cost-reducing technical invention (which we believe is generated by the preceding low-profit crisis, as argued in Frank 1978a), at the heart of this process. But we must agree with Mandel (1975a) that the determinant factor, not incorporated into Schumpeter's theory, is the decline in profits. Profits decline after the organic composition of capital has risen too much, or the capital/labor ratio has become too high in the boom. This leads to lower levels of investment; a preference for cost-reducing rationalization and invention; and the recuperation of the rate of profit, importantly through political defeats of the working class in the class struggle. This renewed increase in profits then stimulates investment and Schumpeterian innovation all over again.

The industrial revolution built on and innovated the technical invention of power-driven machines during the 1762-1789 crisis. As Mandel (1975a) argues, the first long wave since the industrial revolution was associated with the hand manufacture (literally) of textile and other machinery and the steam engines to drive such manufacture. The resulting upswing lasted from 1790– 1793 to 1816–1825 (according to different interpretations), and the downswing until 1847–1848. The defeat of the revolutions of 1848 signified a political and economic blow for the European working classes, and created the political/economic conditions for another long expansion from 1849 to 1873. This boom was associated with the revolution and expansion of transportation through the steam-powered railroad and ocean shipping. This was indeed the only time when *Pax Britannica* and free trade were realities— a time during which the technological gap between the now-industrialized and now-underdeveloped economies became quantitatively, qualitatively and, so far, irrevocably great (Frank 1978b; Hinkelammert 1970).

The crisis year 1873 is generally considered the turning point for another long downswing until 1893–1895, a period often referred to as the first "Great Depression." Conservative economic historians now challenge the supposed "Myth of the Great Depression 1873–1896" (Saul 1969). However, there is substantial agreement that, whatever its nature, this period was followed by another major expansion lasting until 1913, just before the First World War. The prewar upswing was characterized by the relative decline of Great Britain and the initial advance of the United States, Germany, Japan, and Russia. Competitive capitalism gave way to monopoly capitalism, and the quarter-century interregnum of free trade ended with the rise of classical imperialism and colonialism after 1873 (Frank 1978b; Amin 1970). The new expansion was associated with the innovation—which Mandel (1975a) calls the second technological revolution—of the automobile internal combustion engine, electrical motors and lighting, and the vast investment in infrastructure and related industries associated with both (Gordon 1978). The following downswing took hold from 1913–1919 (before or after World War I) to 1940–1945 (before or after World War II). It included the "Great Depression" of the 1930s, following the Wall Street financial crash of 1929; with regard to production, however, the signs of the depression were already visible since 1927. The Great Depression was followed by the postwar upswing until 1966, associated with further expansion of the automobile and the airplane, of petrochemical industries based on cheap oil, and with the beginnings of the electronic and nuclear "third" technological revolution. Since 1967 the capitalist world economy appears to have entered into a new downswing, or economic crisis period.

The Depression and Wartime Basis of the Postwar Boom

Before we examine the contemporary world economic crisis—which is the purpose of this chapter—it might be useful to review briefly the last great crisis of capitalism. The earlier crisis may serve as a historical point of reference, even if "history does not repeat itself," and a number of significant differences between then and now may illuminate our analysis further along. To begin with, it should be remembered that the last crisis was marked not only by the Great Depression of the 1930s, but also by a series of far-reaching and deep-going political transformations: two world wars; the Soviet October revolution of 1917, which apparently removed a large portion of the earth's population from the domain of world capitalism (see chapter 4 below); the Chinese revolution and the establishment of People's Democracies in Eastern Europe after World War II, involving over one fourth of mankind; the breakup of the British empire and the seeds of decolonization; the rise and fall of fascism in Europe as a direct response to economic crisis; and the development of state capitalism in the Western democracies—also in response to crisis conditions—under New Deal, Popular Front, and Labor governments. Does the contemporary world crisis of capital accumulation portend analogous political transformations? Does the current downswing represent the antechamber, motor, or transmission belt of further capitalist development, or the revolutionary transition to a postcapitalist era? Whatever the answer—which depends on the course and outcome of the class struggle—the last great depression and subsequent war involved a number of further political/economic ramifications, which we would do well to recall when examining the present world economic crisis.

The Great Depression of the 1930s fulfilled the usual function of depressions in the capitalist cycle of capital accumulation: it eliminated some capital and capitalists for the benefit of other capitalists, in whose hands capital became increasingly concentrated. The intervention of fascist state power, on the one hand, and of reformism on the other, respectively destroyed or paralyzed the organization of labor and depressed its wages. Particularly in the continental European countries and Japan, the war perpetuated this process and, after the military defeat of the Axis (especially German) challenge to the economic and political ambitions of the United States, American capital was left economically, politically, and militarily dominant in the postwar world. Although the war destroyed some capital stock—and some capital—principally in transportation and housing facilities, the same war also stimulated considerable state-subsidized investment in new technology and productive facilities. Such new investment occurred not only in the United States, which was thereby enabled to emerge from the depression, but in Europe as well. The United States strategic bombing survey after the war found that physical destruction of industrial productive facilities was far less extensive than the Allies had hoped, even in Germany, and much less than the mythology would have most people believe. Thus, in fifteen European countries including West Germany, industrial production in 1946 had fallen to 72 percent of the 1938 level, rose to 83 percent in 1947, and reached 96 percent in 1948. Excluding Germany, where industrial production had dropped to 29 percent, 34 percent, and 51 percent of the 1938 level respectively in the same years as above, industrial production in the other fourteen European countries had fallen to 88 percent of the 1938 level in 1945, reached 100 percent already in 1947, and went on to 113 percent in 1948. Agricultural production was relatively lower (Armstrong et al. 1976: I.23). In 1945 capital stock exceeded prewar levels in most European countries and, with relatively little investment, could be made to produce again quickly.

Unlike capital, with its minor losses and quick recuperation period, labor had suffered desperately from depression and war, and would continue to do so during the first decade of the postwar period, with the exception of the American working class. In Germany, fascism had raised the rate of exploitation of the working class to a level 300 percent above that of the Weimar republic—the West "German miracle" was preprogrammed in the course of the "thousand-year Reich." Real wages in 1948 were at 70 percent of the 1938 level (Altvater et al. 1974). In Italy, real wages in 1946 had fallen to 58 percent of the already depressed 1938 level, and in Japan, to 25 percent of the 1936 level (Armstrong et al. 1976: III.10, 13; IV.11; V.13). In France real wages in 1946 reached only 77 percent of the 1938 depression level, and would fall to 64 percent in 1947 (Armstrong 1976: II.6). Only in Britain did average real wages in 1946 exceed 1938 by 6 percent, but they would then fall continuously, only to reach the 1938 level again in 1951 (Armstrong 1976: VI.31). At the same time, labor's organizations—both unions, and political parties—had been completely destroyed, and would continue to be suppressed for the time being by American occupational forces in Germany and Japan. In other cases, labor's postwar revolutionary militancy would be completely sold out by its reformist-revisionist Communist Party leadership in alliance with the local bourgeoisie for whose benefit it launched a "battle for production"; Communist leadership followed in the footsteps of Stalin's reactionary foreign and class policy, and was further impressed by American blackmail tactics—the United States threatened the use of military power to suppress any possible revolutionary movement or government in Western Europe. (For excellent analyses see Fernando Claudin 1970; Gabriel Kolko 1968; and Armstrong et al. 1976.) Accordingly, the working class suffered a historical political defeat, and was totally domesticated by the end of 1948.

Only then, with industrial and political peace assured, profitability enhanced, and prewar levels of industrial production largely reattained and surpassed, did the United States government launch the Marshall Plan. In this way, American capital would "reconstruct" Western Europe for its own benefit and that of its then-dependent European capitalist junior partners. In 1949, the United States and Great Britain—which devalued the pound—were in the throes of the first postwar recession; many feared that another depression was in the offing. The Cold War, officially started along with the "Truman Doctrine" by Winston Churchill in 1947 in Fulton, Missouri, flared up increasingly, and turned into a hot war in Korea in 1950. Both were employed to press American rearmament into high gear. The Korean War fed the process of recovery and accumulation, particularly in Japan, but also elsewhere in the capitalist world; rearmament in the United States and profitable American investment in European cheap-labor economies fed the expansion and accumulation of American and then European and Japanese capital. Much of the success of these economies, particularly of German capital, was based not on cheap labor alone—in which case low wages could not afford to buy much—but on exports abroad, where wages were higher and demand was supported by American rearmament. Thus, the state had already intervened with political, military, and economic force in the formation of state monopoly capitalism during the depression and the war; the state insured its timely salvation in the immediate postwar years.

The depression, the war, the "permanent war economy," the neoimperialism of the multinational corporation, cheap wages, the disciplining of the labor force and, perhaps not least, the ideology of the "ever bigger and better American way of life" and "limitless growth and development"—all contributed to the maintenance of the rate of profit and thereby to the nearly continuous pace of accumulation during the two decades of the postwar period. After this period had drawn to a close, and under the title "All Systems Stop . . . Goodbye Boom," the conservative London *Economist* (28 December 1974) looked back and observed:

The long boom was due more to good luck than good management, the happy coincidence of three vital factors: (1) After the war, the world propensity to invest rose relative to the world propensity to save, creating adequate effective demand in place of interwar deficiency. Reconstruction was followed by rearmament and the birth of consumerdom. Public spending, raised in wartime, never returned to pre-war levels. Keynesian demand management policies gained worldwide acceptance. (2) Technological progress, and ample reserves of under-utilized labour in backward primary sectors, provided for rapid expansion in supply to meet booming demand. Growth was most rapid in countries with the greatest labour reserves. It was least rapid in the mature economies, principally Britain and America. After the collapse of the Korean War's commodity price boom, industrial countries benefited from ample supplies of fuel and raw materials at stable or falling prices. Poor producer countries were the losers, and the gap between some of the rich and most of the poor widened. (3) The world financial system absorbed the strain of differing growth rates because the oldest rich countries were relative losers.

The *Economist* also offered further explanation of part of its point (2):

> An ample reserve of underutilized labour is one of the basic ingredients for fast growth. A large and backward agricultural sector is the best source for it. . . . Snowflake diagrams illustrate the link betwen fast growth and ample reserves of labour in agriculture. The share of employment in each major sector of an economy is plotted along different axes. Immature economies have rounded snowflakes, but as an economy matures its snowflakes become star-shaped. . . . The more star-shaped a country's snowflake was as it entered the period of post-war growth, the slower its growth in the boom. . . . Fast growing economies are more competitive and so can secure the export orders upon which their fast growth depends. Fast growth also provides the resources for high investment and exports without there being any need for severe restraint on the growth in personal living standards. This is the virtuous cycle which countries like Japan and Italy and France enjoyed during the great boom. Germany had a smaller agricultural sector, but imported immigrant workers for its manufacturing industry (ECO 29 December 1974).

Germany imported labor not only from Southern Europe as *Gastarbeiter* in the 1960s, but even before then as impoverished, very low-wage immigrants from the agricultural and urban sectors of Eastern Europe, including East Germany. With regard to the interests of these workers and for other migrant workers elsewhere, as well as for those whose wages were kept low in part through competition from migrant labor, however, the *Economist* exaggerates a bit in saying that there was no need for severe restraint on growth in personal living standards. In chapter 1 and in TW we examine the role of the underdeveloped, poor producer countries; the underdeveloped sector provided ever cheaper raw materials and capital outflows and, through the brain drain, even supplied substantial amounts of "human capital" to contribute to the capitalist process of capital accumulation in the imperialist center.

Relative Productivity and Differentiation in the West

The postwar period witnessed not only increasing North-South polarization between the developed and underdeveloped capitalist countries (see chapter 1), but also accelerating differentiation among the developed industrial capitalist economies themselves. Over the 1950–1969 period in the United States, GNP and industrial production grew at a moderate annual average of 3.6 percent and 4.1 percent respectively; in Europe these grew more than one and one half times as fast, at rates of 5.5 percent and 6.7 percent; and in Japan the growth rates were 10.3 percent for GNP and 13.8 percent for industry—that is, twice as fast as in Europe and three times as fast as in the United States. Between 1960 and 1975, the real growth of GNP reached 37.5 percent in the United States, 60 percent in the European Economic Community, and 203 percent in Japan (IHT 4 December 1976).

Growth rates in labor productivity diverged still more among the major industrial capitalist countries. This divergence is particularly important insofar as it significantly influences interimperialist competitiveness, with resulting currency devaluations and other competitive measures in the continuing capitalist battle for the world market. Table 2-1 reproduces some estimates of productivity growth rates for the major industrial countries. (Growth rates, however, are not entirely comparable from one country to another.)

These data suggest that in the 1950s and early 1960s, labor productivity grew twice as fast in France and Germany, and three times as fast in Japan, as it did in the United States. In Britain, "the sick man of Europe," productivity grew even more slowly. Much the same pattern continued through the end of the 1960s; however, growth in productivity slackened somewhat in Germany, accelerated in France, and rose three and one half to four times faster in Japan than in the United States.

Expressed differently, labor productivity in the United States grew 35 percent more slowly than in Europe and 60 percent more slowly than in Japan between 1950 and 1965. Then, between 1965 and 1969, the 1.7 percent annual increase in the United States was 60 percent lower than the 4.5 percent growth rate of labor productivity in Europe and 84 percent lower than the 10.6 percent annual increase in Japan. By 1968, 64 percent of American metalworking machines were more than ten years old; and still by 1973, only 33 percent of American machinery was less than ten years old— the lowest rate of renewal since the 1940 end-depression yearly rate of 30 percent (Melman 1974: 183, 82). In the United States, productivity increased at an average rate of nearly 3 percent a year during the 1950s and most of the

TABLE 2-1

Differential Growth Rates of Labor Productivity in Major Industrial Countries
(in percent per annum and total increase for various periods 1950–1976)

	1 1950–64 Economy	2 1960–69 Economy	Industry	3 1963–69 Economy
United States	2.4	2.6	2.9	14
Britain	2.2	2.3	3.3	17
France	4.6	4.9	5.2	35
West Germany	5.4	4.8	5.4	34
Japan	7.8	8.9	9.1	72

	4 1969–73 Economy	Industry	5 1970–76 Economy	6 1977 Economy	7 1978 Economy
United States	1.6	3.4	17	1.4	−0.3
Britain	2.7	3.9	17+	1.2	3.0
France	4.4	5.0	37	3.5	2.9
West Germany	4.2	4.4	42	2.7	2.8
Japan	8.1	7.5	40	3.8	4.4

Source: 1. annual rates, Dos Santos 1978c: 159 from U.S. Department of Commerce data; 2. annual rates, McCracken 1977: 147; 3. total increase, Busch et al. 1971: 79; 4. annual rates, McCracken 1977: 147; 5. total increase, IHT 30–31 July 1977; 6. and 7. F&D March 1979 for 1977–1978.

Note: For the decade 1967–77, the percentage increases of productivity in manufacturing were United States 27, Britain 27, Canada 43, Italy 62, Germany 70, France 72 and Japan 107 (IHT 1 August 1978). In 1978 the economy-wide changes in productivity in these countries were: United States −0.3, Canada 0.1, Britain 3.0, Italy 1.4, Germany 2.8, France 2.9 and Japan 4.4 (F&D March 1979: 24).

1960s. "In the years after 1968, the trend dropped to half that rate. Since late 1976, it has been almost flat" (IHT 1 August 1978 and OECD Economic Surveys, United States 1979: 24).

In the 1970s the growth of productivity slackened everywhere except in Britain (where it was nearly flat already). Productivity growth rates fell particularly in the United States, less so in France and Germany where it now grew two and one half times as fast as in the United States; and productivity fell back in Japan to a rate comparable to that of Europe. Of course, these overall rates mask important differences from one industry to another. For instance, in the steel industry, crucially important not only in its own right but because of steel's significant contribution to so many other productive branches, by the 1970s labor productivity in Japan reached a level twice as high—480 tons per worker per year compared with 240 tons— as in the United States (ICP 6 February 1977: 132). These differential changes in productivity have placed the United States and Britain, at least tendentially and potentially, at a competitive disadvantage, with the continental Western European economies and especially the Japanese in an increasingly advantageous competitive position. Changes in relative productivity and potential competitiveness, however, did not have very serious consequences as long as the United States maintained an absolute advantage in certain important industries and the competitors as a whole still enjoyed high profits in an expanding market. However, these "advantageous" conditions have proved shortlived, and their disappearance—and with them the pegged parities between the dollar and other currencies—has brought the significance of the productivity differential to the fore.

The growth of productivity has declined in all the major industrial countries since 1973, even with negative growth rates in some years in the United States and Britain. This development has generated much research and insistent debate in the latter countries to determine the causes and possible remedies for this decline. One of the two most renowned American experts on the measurement of factor productivity, Edward Denison, investigated seventeen possible causes for the post-1973 decline in American productivity, and finds about two thirds of the three percent decline from 1948–1973 to 1973–1976 (with later calculation up to 1978) "unexplained." Denison writes in the United States Department of Commerce *Survey of Current Business*: "That I do not know why the record suddenly turned so bad after 1973 must be obvious, because the effects of all the determinants of . . . [productivity] that I could measure continuously are excluded from the residual" decline that remains unexplained (Denison 1979: 5 and passim). The other major American authority on productivity, John Kendrick, summarizes the main causes among Denison's explained factors as advances in applied productive knowledge, changes in labor quality (chiefly due to shifts in age-sex composition), and volume-related factors. Kendrick largely agrees with this analysis, but goes on to attribute another significant part of the decline to "the negative impact of governmental regulations." Commenting on these and other attempts at explanation, William Fellner, writing under the auspices of the conservative American Enterprise Institute, attributes "the political-institutional suspects" and "the political subordination of long-run economic efficiency to other objectives." The implications and obvious political purpose of this part of the exercise must be seen as an attempt to turn the political process to the right (Fellner et al. 1979: 5–6 and passim). The socialist Paul Sweezy refers to the "productivity slowdown: a false alarm," and argues that such a slowdown is merely the reflection—the "logical correlation"—of the slowdown in production during the last recession and weak recovery. Moreover, from 1967 to 1978 real wages increased only 2 percent, far less than the already slowed rate of productivity, which rose 16 percent (MR June 1979: 3 and passim). According to Denison, Kendrick, and others, however, the "volume changes" of slower or even negative growth in production only account for a relatively small part (about one fourth for Kendrick and even less for Denison) of the decline in productivity, most of which remains

GRAPH 2-1
The Growth of Labor Productivity and Gross National Product: Deviations from 1960–73 Trend

Labor productivity ——   ═══ Gross national product

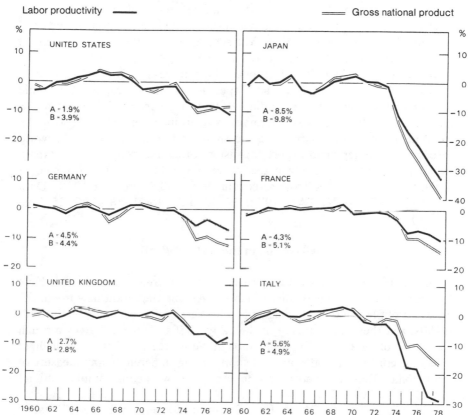

Note: Inset figures equal 1960–73 growth rates of (A) overall labor productivity (i.e., national product divided by total employment) and (B) gross national product.
Source: Bank for International Settlements 1979: 27.

"unexplained." Nonetheless, the fact remains that, with the onset of the 1973 recession, productivity began to decline rapidly not only in the United States but in all the industrial economies, including Japan. Indeed, productivity declined to such a degree in the entire industrial sector that the gap in productivity growth has again narrowed between the United States and Britain on one side and the rest of the capitalist world on the other. These recent productivity declines are shown in Graph 2-1.

These changes in production and productivity have also been reflected in the industrial countries' participation in foreign trade. Foreign trade as a percentage of GNP rose from 4.4 percent to 6.8 percent between 1950 and 1970 and to 8.3 percent in 1978 for the United States; from 15 percent to 26 percent between 1950 and 1970 and to nearly 30 percent in 1978 for the European Economic Community countries; and from 8 percent in 1950 to 14 percent in 1970 and 14 percent still in 1978 for Japan. (Contrary to popular impression, Japan still exports only half as much of its production as Germany, Britain, and Italy, and one third as much as the Netherlands and Belgium.) As a share of total world trade, American exports have declined from 21 percent in 1950 to 20 percent in 1960, 19 percent in 1970, and 12 percent in 1978. The West European share increased from 33 percent in 1950 to 44 percent in 1970 and, specifically, the European Economic Community's share (still excluding Britain) rose from 15 percent to 28 percent. The share of West Germany rose from 4 percent in 1950 to 12 percent in 1978, thus surpassing the share of the United States in world exports. The other rapid export expansion, of course, took place in Japan, which increased its relatively modest share of world exports from 1 percent in 1950 to 3 percent in 1960 to 6 percent in 1970, and 8 percent in 1978. (Data for 1950–1970—UNCTAD 1972: 32–33; data for 1978—IPC 25 June 1979.)

The Decline in the Rate of Profit

In the meantime, however, several other new trends and changes have emerged in the world capitalist economy. As one important new trend, the rate of profit began to decline again—at first gradually, beginning in the mid-1960s, and then more steeply in the early 1970s. Table 2-2 gives a rough indication of the decline in profits, though the source warns that "in the light of all the conceptual and statistical shortcomings inherent in any measure of profitability, these estimates must be interpreted with considerable caution" (McCracken 1977: 304).

The "Report to the OECD by a Group of Independent Experts" headed by Paul McCracken (1977), who compiled estimates mostly from official data issued by the governments of the countries in question, summarizes:

> The figures for the gross rate of return in Table A 20 [summarized in our Table 2-2 above] seem to indicate a trend decline in the United Kingdom, the Netherlands, Germany, Italy and the United States. These figures are subject to relatively clear cyclical fluctuations which, however, do not mask the gradual lowering of the gross rate of return over successive cycles in these countries. . . . In the United Kingdom, the declining trend seems to have commenced early in the second half of the 1960s, and it may have accelerated towards the end of the observation period. In Germany and Italy, the gross rate of return began to fall later, towards the end of the 1960s, but the fall has been continuous since then. In the United States, the gross rate of return reached the peak in 1965 and then followed a moderate declining trend. . . . For Japan and France, it is more difficult to draw a definitive conclusion as to whether there has been any trend decline. . . . Time

TABLE 2-2

Rates of Profits in Major Industrial Countries
(as percent of assets or equity 1960–1975)

	United States Gross	United States Net	Britain Gross	Britain Net	France Gross	West Germany Gross	Japan Gross
1960	15.3	8.5	5.8	2.1	9.5	13.1	
1961	18.9	12.9	5.4	2.9	9.3	12.6	
1962	17.0	10.5	5.2	2.7	9.0	12.1	
1963	17.4	11.0	5.6	3.3	9.1	11.6	12.5
1964	18.1	11.9	5.5	3.4	9.5	12.0	12.8
1965	18.8	13.1	5.4	3.1	9.2	11.7	11.9
1966	18.7	12.7	6.1	2.7	9.6	11.4	12.4
1967	17.6	11.1	4.8	2.1	9.6	10.9	14.0
1968	17.1	9.7	4.7	1.9	10.0	12.5	14.7
1969	15.6	7.6	4.2	1.5	10.4	12.9	14.3
1970	14.2	5.3	3.6	1.4	10.0	12.4	14.7
1971	14.7	6.1	3.7	1.6	10.2	11.7	14.2
1972	15.5	7.2	3.5	1.5	10.3	11.3	13.0
1973	14.7	5.0	3.1	1.3	9.6	11.5	10.9
1974	13.2	2.5	2.2	1.0	8.2	10.9	11.9
1975	13.5	3.5	2.0	0.9	5.7	10.6	13.0

Note: "Divergent definitions of the denominator in the calculation of profit rates would invalidate inter-country comparison of levels of profitability" (McCracken 1977: 306).

Source: McCracken 1977: 305, 307.

series on the net rate of return, which are available for the United States and the United Kingdom, bring out even more clearly the apparently falling trend (McCracken 1977: 306).

The OECD (EO Special Supplement July 1976: 143) has also found declining rates of profit in its major industrial enconomies. Independent investigators have found the same downward trend since the mid-1960s for particular countries; these studies include Glyn and Sutcliffe (1972) for Britain, the Sachverständigenrat (1974) for Germany and, most notably, Nordhaus (1974) for the United States. Nordhaus's major study, however, has recently been challenged by Martin Feldstein as overestimating the decline of profits in the United States (IHT 10 May 1977). Additionally, these studies suggest on the one hand that absolute rates of profit are higher than those registered by official institutions from data supplied by the corporations themselves. On the other hand, it has been widely suggested that real rates of profit are lower than those registered for the 1970s, because corporate bookkeeping and inventory control no longer take adequate account of the erosion of real values through inflation. Andrew Glyn summarizes and concludes:

The fact that rates of profit in the U.K., France, Italy and most probably Japan fell, by 1974 and 1975, to less than one third of the level of the early sixties, and in the case of Germany and the U.S.A. to about two-thirds of the earlier level, shows the depth of the crisis with which the capitalist class is faced on a world scale (Glyn n.d.: 5).

However, the net profit rates shown in Table 2-2—after the deduction of depreciation, financial costs, and taxes— demonstrate the falling trend more clearly, as our source points out. In examining these data, we can see a decline to even less than one third of the 1960s peak in the United States as well. We have divided these time series at 1966–1967 to highlight the apparent trend reversal toward lower profits at that time. (Nonetheless, the German and Japanese data suggest a still stable level of profits at the end of the 1960s and the French data seem to reflect a temporary recuperation of profits after the defeat of the French working class following the events of May 1968.) The break between 1972 and 1973 in the time series reflects the sharp downturn of gross and net profits in all the industrial countries during the most severe postwar recession to date, between 1973 and 1975 (to which we shall return below). Of course, the decline in profits is not uniform. It differs from one industry to another; it affects particularly the more competitive industries, whereas firms with more monopoly power and/or international operations have been better able to resist the decline in profits and, in some cases such as the oil companies, even to increase them.

Cyclical Recessions and Incipient Crisis since 1967

The business cycle seems to fluctuate alongside or on top of this declining trend in profits without, however, masking it, as noted in the McCracken report. On the contrary, with each succeeding cycle and recession, the rate of profits seems to have declined further. Moreover, recessions have become more frequent, lengthy, deepgoing, and more internationally coordinated. That is, recessions have become more general for all the industrial economies. These fluctuations and trends manifest themselves through (statistics on) gross national or domestic product, and even more through (rates of) industrial production, investment, and unemployment. We may review some of these indices for the major industrial countries.

The most important economy, that of the United States, experienced relatively mild recessions, with lower growth rates but no absolute declines in gross national product (GNP) in 1949, 1953–1954, 1957–1958, and 1960–1961. However, these recessions were not particularly coordinated with the other important capitalist economies, which mostly continued to grow and/or had unrelated cyclical downturns. The next incipient recession in 1966–1967 was cut short in the United States by massive government spending on the war against Vietnam, feeding the "Kennedy-Johnson boom." In the same period, West Germany suffered its first serious postwar recession at a time when the Germans believed that recessions were no longer necessary or possible in their country. Britain, France, and several other industrial capitalist economies, excluding Japan, also experienced relatively mild recessions. American spending on the Vietnam war, however, only postponed the underlying recessionary problem, and aggravated it in a variety of ways in the long run. By 1969–1970, recessionary conditions returned to the United States, despite the high and increased military spending of that period. The Nixon administration did all it could through expansive monetary and fiscal policies, price and especially wage controls, and international measures (see below) to prime the pump for a speedy recovery before the 1972 election. In the meantime, however, other major industrial capitalist economies, this time including Japan, were also visited by recession in the years from 1970 to 1972. Recessions were becoming more frequent and more coordinated and general, to say the least. Table 2-3 reflects such recessions and their increasing coordination among the major industrial capitalist economies through growth rates of GNP for each half year.

The cyclical economic fluctuations and the underlying recessive or depressive trends since the mid-1960s is, however, much more importantly visibly expressed through the rates of growth *and decline* of industrial production.

The annual growth rates of industrial production were as follows:

	1964	1965	1966	1967	1968	1969	1970	1971	1972	1973
United States	8.0	8.3	9.4	2.3	5.3	5.1	−4.1	0.7	9.9	8.6
Europe	8.0	4.7	5.4	0.8	7.6	9.4	5.7	2.7	4.6	8.2

Source: U.N. Statistical Yearbook sources cited in MD April-June 1975:64.

Although fluctuations in the growth rates of industrial production were not yet completely coordinated, the bunching of lower growth rates or absolute declines does appear clearly in 1967 and again in 1970–1971.

Graph 2-2 (on page 41) shows clearly how industrial production in the major and several minor capitalist economies has deviated downward from its historic postwar trend in nearly all of these countries since the mid-1960s. (Note the first heavy line between 1965 and 1966.) The growth of industrial production rose to a new peak in 1973, on or below the trendline and substantially *below* the peak reached before the mid-1960s. Then, industrial production fell off sharply during the 1973–1975 recession (after the second heavy line). Among major countries, however, Japan and Germany were exceptions in that their deviations from trend did not decline until the 1970–1972 recession. France is exceptional in that its decline does not appear until the 1973–1975 recession. (However, France has historically been "regularly exceptional" in that its cycles always seem to lag behind those of the rest of the world.)

TABLE 2-3

Growth of Real GNP/GDP[a] — Seven Major OECD Countries

Percentage changes from previous half year, seasonally adjusted at annual rates

	1960 I	1960 II	1961 I	1961 II	1962 I	1962 II	1963 I	1963 II	1964 I	1964 II	1965 I	1965 II	1966 I	1966 II	1967 I	1967 II
United States	4.9	−1.6	2.5	6.8	6.7	3.0	3.4	6.0	5.7	3.6	6.3	7.3	6.6	.3	1.8	4.0
Japan	13.9	12.2	17.1	11.4	6.1	4.8	10.6	15.4	14.9	7.8	3.2	6.8	10.1	12.3	12.8	13.7
Germany	(11.0)[c]	10.0	3.9	1.8	6.1	3.7	−1.9	12.4	4.5	5.3	6.7	3.6	4.6	−2.4	−0.8	3.6
France	8.7	8.3	4.5	5.3	8.6	6.4	2.8	11.2	8.5	2.9	4.9	8.0	5.8	3.8	6.1	5.3
United Kingdom	4.1	2.9	5.6	−0.7	1.6	1.1	3.6	7.8	6.0	3.6	0.8	3.1	1.5	1.9	4.7	−0.5
Canada	2.5	2.3	0.5	8.2	7.0	5.2	4.0	7.3	7.3	5.1	7.4	6.7	9.3	2.6	4.2	2.4
Italy	(11.5)[c]	10.5	3.8	8.8	6.1	3.9	4.9	8.5	2.2	−1.9	4.5	5.7	5.2	7.0	6.8	7.5
Total[b]	(7.0)[c]	2.9	4.7	6.4	6.3	3.5	3.6	8.4	6.7	4.1	5.5	6.5	6.5	3.8	3.6	5.0

	1968 I	1968 II	1969 I	1969 II	1970 I	1970 II	1971 I	1971 II	1972 I	1972 II	1973 I	1973 II	1974 I	1974 II	1975 I	1975 II	1976 I
United States	4.5	4.4	2.6	0.6	-1.2	0.5	4.2	3.0	6.6	6.7	6.9	1.5	-1.9	-3.1	-4.8	8.0	6.4
Japan	12.9	14.0	9.9	9.4	12.9	9.2	6.4	7.6	8.2	11.6	13.0	2.0	-5.1	3.7	0.7	4.8	8.8
Germany	6.3	9.6	6.4	9.2	4.4	5.6	3.0	1.8	4.5	3.6	8.1	0.4	1.8	-3.0	-5.5	4.5	7.6
France	-1.2	15.7	5.0	4.8	7.6	5.8	4.7	6.6	5.2	4.8	6.9	4.9	6.6	-2.1	-6.7	2.4	10.1
United Kingdom	5.8	2.9	-0.7	4.1	1.0	3.4	-0.2	7.1	0.3	2.8	12.0	-2.2	-2.8	4.3	-3.9	-2.9	3.7
Canada	6.3	8.4	4.4	4.3	1.9	2.0	7.4	9.2	4.9	5.7	9.8	5.0	5.4	-0.9	0.5	4.3	7.8
Italy	4.4	9.0	7.0	0.0	9.1	2.1	0.8	2.5	3.1	3.8	6.1	11.8	5.0	-5.2	-4.8	0.8	9.0
Total[b]	5.3	7.2	4.2	3.2	2.6	2.8	4.8	2.7	5.9	6.5	8.4	2.3	-0.6	-1.3	-3.8	5.2	7.3

[a]Gross National Product/Gross Domestic Product
[b]1970 GNP/GDP weights and exchange rates for 1960–71; 1976 GNP/GDP weights and exchange rates for 1972–76.
[c]OECD estimates.

Note: *United States:* GNP at market prices. *Survey of Current Business*, Department of Commerce, Washington, D.C.; *Japan:* GNP at market prices. *Economic Statistics Monthly*, Bank of Japan. Tokyo; *Germany:* GNP at market prices. *Statistical Supplements to the Monthly Reports of the Deutsche Bundesbank*, Frankfurt; *France:* GDP at market prices. This aggregate excludes value-added by general government, financial institutions, and domestic servants among others. Institut National de la Statistique et des Etudes Economiques (INSEE), Paris; *United Kingdom:* GDP at market prices. *Monthly Digest of Statistics*, Central Statistical Office. London; *Canada:* GNP at market prices. *Source:* National Income and Expenditure Accounts. Statistics Canada. Ottawa; *Italy:* GDP at market prices. *Source:* Instituto Nazionale per lo Studio delia Congiuntura (ISCO), Rome.

Source: *OECD Economic Outlook*, December 1977:124.

Differences in growth rates for some years (sometimes quite substantial, as for Japan 1974) shown in the two tables may be due to differences in weighting procedures (as explained in note[b] above and[a] below) used by OECD in constructing their tables.

TABLE 2-3 (continued)

Growth of Real GNP/GDP—Seven Major OECD Countries

(Percentage changes from previous half year, seasonally adjusted at annual rates)

	1961		1962		1963		1964		1965		1966		1967		1968	
	I	II	I	II	I	II	I	II	I	II	I	II	I	II	I	II
United States	2.5	6.8	6.7	3.0	3.4	6.0	5.7	3.6	6.3	7.3	6.6	3.3	1.8	4.0	4.5	4.4
Japan	17.1	11.4	6.1	4.8	10.6	15.3	15.0	7.7	3.3	6.8	10.0	12.4	12.8	13.7	12.9	14.0
Germany	3.7	2.2	5.9	3.7	-1.8	12.2	4.8	5.1	6.8	3.6	4.6	-2.4	-0.8	3.6	6.3	9.7
France	4.5	5.3	8.6	6.4	2.8	11.2	8.5	2.9	4.9	8.0	5.8	3.8	6.1	5.3	-1.2	15.7
United Kingdom	5.2	0.0	1.6	0.8	3.7	7.9	6.9	2.7	1.9	3.1	1.0	3.1	3.5	-0.9	6.4	2.8
Canada	0.5	8.2	7.0	5.2	4.0	7.3	7.3	5.1	7.4	6.7	9.3	2.6	4.2	2.4	6.3	8.4
Italy	9.8	8.8	6.1	3.9	4.9	8.5	2.2	-1.9	4.5	5.7	5.2	7.0	6.8	7.5	4.4	9.0
Total[a]	4.1	6.1	6.3	3.4	3.5	8.0	6.5	3.7	5.6	6.5	6.3	3.7	3.3	4.6	5.2	7.0

	1969		1970		1971		1972		1973		1974		1975		1976		1977	
	I	II	I	II	I	II	I	II	I	II	I	II	I	II	I	II	I	II
United States	2.6	0.6	-1.2	0.5	4.2	3.0	6.6	6.7	6.9	1.5	-1.9	-3.1	-4.5	7.5	6.3	3.0	5.7	5.1
Japan	10.0	9.4	12.9	9.2	6.5	7.5	8.4	11.6	12.9	2.2	-2.2	7.0	-2.0	6.7	7.4	4.1	6.9	4.0
Germany	6.3	9.3	4.3	5.8	2.8	2.1	4.2	4.1	7.0	1.5	1.1	-2.2	-4.5	4.0	6.9	2.8	2.5	2.5
France	5.0	4.8	7.6	5.8	4.2	7.6	5.2	4.8	6.8	5.0	6.3	-1.9	-7.0	2.8	9.6	1.8	3.6	2.9
United Kingdom	-0.3	4.4	1.3	2.2	1.0	6.3	-1.5	3.3	13.7	-3.5	-1.7	4.9	-5.2	-4.1	8.1	3.1	0.8	3.2
Canada	4.4	4.3	1.9	2.0	8.2	9.2	4.9	5.7	9.8	5.0	5.0	-0.6	1.1	3.7	8.9	0.8	3.7	2.5
Italy	7.0	-0.1	9.1	2.1	0.8	2.5	3.1	3.8	6.1	11.8	5.4	-4.8	-4.9	1.0	9.1	5.4	2.3	-1.8
Total[a]	4.0	3.1	2.4	2.7	4.2	4.3	5.7	6.5	8.3	2.3	-0.1	-0.8	-4.1	5.2	7.2	3.0	4.7	3.8

[a]GDP weights: centered three-year moving average. For 1977, 1977 weights.

Note: *United States:* GNP at market prices. *Survey of Current Business*, Department of Commerce, Washington, D.C.; *Japan:* GNP at market prices. *Economic Statistics Monthly*, Bank of Japan, Tokyo, *Germany:* GNP at market prices. *Statistical Supplements to the Monthly Reports of the Deutsche Bundesbank*, Frankfurt; *France:* GDP at market prices. This aggregate excludes value-added by general government, financial institutions, and domestic servants among others (INSEE) Paris; *United Kingdom:* GDP at market prices. *Monthly Digest of Statistics,* Central Statistical Office, London; *Canada:* GNP at market prices. *National Income and Expenditure Accounts,* Statistics Canada, Ottawa; *Italy:* GDP at market prices. ISCO Rome; From 1976 II, figures are based on the same definitions as those presented in the country tables on demand output and prices, which are described in the Technical Annex.

Source: OECD *Economic Outlook*, July 1979: 148.

The deviation of industrial production from postwar (1955 to 1974) annual growth trends in the major industrial countries since the recession appears even more clearly and dramatically in Graph 2-2. The same trend and fluctuations may be expressed in numbers by looking at the highest and lowest quarterly weighted deviations from the historical trend of industrial production in the seven largest industrial capitalist economies—the United States, Canada, Britain, France, Germany, Italy, and Japan, with the addition of Holland and Sweden, in Table 2-4.

TABLE 2-4
Industrial Production Expressed as Deviation from Trend
(in percent for nine industrial capitalist countries)

	1965	1966	1967	1968	1969	1970	1971	1972	1973	1974	1975	1976
1) Highest deviation	4.3	4.4	0.1	0.1	0.4	−2.6	−6.6	−0.7	1.5	−1.0	−9.3	−3.2
2) Lowest deviation	3.7	2.3	−2.0	−2.0	−1.5	−7.2	−7.1	−5.3	0.9	−8.6	−14.7	−7.9

Source: McCracken 1977:339.
Note: Line 1 is the maximum growth rate in each year, expressed as percentage deviation from the historical trend. Line 2 is the minimum growth rate expressed as its deviation from the trend. Minus signs (−) signify that "growth"—that is, decline—was that many percentage points below trend.

These fluctuations, ever longer recessions, and increasingly deep declines of industrial production in the major capitalist economies of the West are also reflected in the duration of the recessions (as measured in quarters of a year), and in the percentage decline of industrial production in each recession as compared with the previous peak. These are shown in Table 2-5.

TABLE 2-5
Length of Recessions (in quarters)
and Declines of Industrial Production (in percent)
From Previous Peaks in Various Industrial Countries

	1957/59		1960/63		1966/67		1969/71		1973/75	
	Quarters	%	Quarters	%	Quarters	%	Quarters	%	Quarters	%
USA	5	12	4	7	2	1	5	7	7	13
Britain	4	3	10		5	2	5	4	4	9
Germany	3	—	2	1	5	6	4	2	7	11
France	4	4	—	—	3	—	2	—	5	12
Japan	4	8	2	2	—	—	1	1	5	20

Source: IPW Forschunghefte 1976: 9, 10; (—) means zero or negligible.

GRAPH 2–2
Industrial Production in Relation to Prerecession Trends

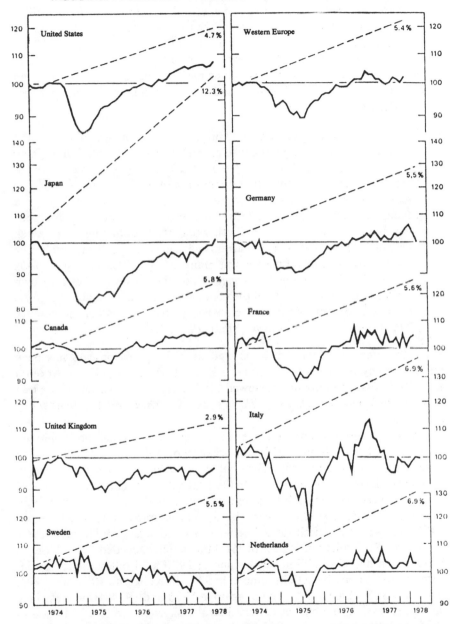

Note: Monthly indices (fourth quarter 1973 = 100) and log-linear trends based on quarterly data for the period 1955–74. The inset figures represent the average annual growth rates implicit in these trends.

Source: Bank for International Settlements 1978: 13.

Credit Creation to Prolong the Boom

When the underlying productive cycle turns downward and profits decline, the business "community" and its state try to extend the boom through the creation of paper money and other forms of credit. Writing in the mid-1770s after more than a decade of depressive conditions, Adam Smith observed in his chapter on "Money" how banks in his native Scotland and England, and particularly the Bank of England, had been creating and lending paper money, backed up by nothing at all.

> The over-trading of some bold projectors in both parts of the United Kingdom, was the original cause of this excessive circulation of paper money. . . . They had over-traded a little, and had brought upon themselves that loss, or at least that diminution of profit. . . . Many vast and extensive projects, however, were undertaken . . . without any other funds to support them besides what was raised at this enormous expense. . . . Those traders and other undertakings having got so much assistance from banks and bankers, wished to get still more. . . . The banks, however, by refusing in this manner to give more credit . . . took the only method by which it was now possible to save either their own credit, or the public credit of the country. . . . In the long run, therefore, the operations of this bank increased the real distress of the country which it was meant to relieve (Smith 1937: 228–300).

Since the time of Adam Smith, as well as before, this process has been repeated many times over; and Charles Kindleberger, who likes to write on timely subjects, has only just reviewed the history of these fluctuations in a book entitled *Manias, Bubbles, Panics and Crashes and the Lenders of Last Resort.*

As the underlying productive situation and the crucial profit picture worsened in the 1960s and 1970s, the creation of credit and debt accelerated again with increasing intensity. The United States federal government budget deficit itself has grown enormously. In the 1950s deficits (and some surpluses) ranged between $1 and $3 billion, except for the $13 billion deficit in 1959 after the 1958 recession (followed by a small surplus in 1960). Between 1961 and 1967, the deficit ranged between $3 and nearly $9 billion in 1967 (except for $1.6 billion in 1965). In 1968 the deficit exceeded $25 billion. In 1969 Nixon had a $3 billion surplus and in 1970 a $3 billion deficit again. After the recession, the deficits jumped to $23 billion in both 1971 and 1972, and fell to $15 billion and $5 billion again in 1973 and 1974. However, since the last recession, the budget deficits literally skyrocketed to $45 billion in 1975, and then grew to over $65 billion in 1976 and in the years since then (USN 28 February 1977). The cumulative budget deficit for the eight years from 1969–1977 was over $247 billion (USN 24 January 1977).

In 1974, *Business Week* devoted a special issue to "The Debt Economy," and even won a prize for it. In the United States, the amount of debt doubled in the fifteen years preceding 1960 and again in the ten years prior to 1970; it has probably doubled again since then. Corporate debt, mortgage debt, installment debt, state and local government debt—all at least tripled between 1960 and 1974; the debt of United States federal agencies jumped by more than 1,000 percent (BW 12 October 1974).

There is nearly $8 of debt per $1 of money supply, more than double the figure 20 years ago. Corporate debt amounts to more than 15 times after tax profits, compared to under 8 times in 1955. Household debt amounts to 93% of disposable income, compared with 65% in 1955. U.S. banks have lent billions overseas through Eurocurrency markets that did not exist in 1955. And there are signs of tension everywhere: corporate debt-equity ratios and commercial bank loan deposit ratios way out of line, consumer installment-debt repayment taking a record share of disposable income, the huge real estate market in desperate trouble despite all the federal government has done to save it. . . .

The numbers are so vast that they simply numb the mind: $1-trillion in corporate debt, $600-billion in mortgage debt, $500-billion in U.S. government debt, $200-billion in state and local government debt, $200-billion in consumer debt. . . . It is an ominously heavy burden with the world as it is today—ravaged by inflation, threatened with economic depression, torn apart by massive redistribution of wealth. . . . Two critically important questions must be asked about the U.S. economy today: Can the debt now outstanding be paid off or refinanced as it comes due? Can the economy add enough new debt to keep growing? . . . Barry Bosworth of the University of California [formerly President Carter's Director of the Council on Wage and Price Stability] warns: If we have a major recession, firms may not have the cash flow to meet their debt payments and may not be able to roll over their short-term debt. Because of the current financial structure, the system cannot withstand a recession as well as it could in the past. . . ." And then there is the most pessimistic view of all: the specter of a chain reaction of defaults by borrowers and failures by lenders, thrusting the world into deep depression. . . . The dangers are greater than in the 1930s. The amounts at risk are greater, and so is the leverage here and abroad. . . .

It is not just a company here or there whose ability to repay is in question but that of the developing lands that borrow heavily and of such powers as Italy, which borrowed $10-billion from the private financial markets of the world. This is money owed to banks whose liquidity is all to often stretched dangerously thin. Should a colossal borrower such as Italy default—and the threat is very real—it could possibly send big banks toppling faster than central banks could respond. . . . In the end the world may very well escape disaster, but there is no way it can escape change (BW 12 October 1974).

Four years later, *Business Week* returned to the same problem with even greater alarm, and devoted another special issue to The New Debt Economy:

> Since late 1975 the U.S. has created a new debt economy, a credit explosion so wild and so eccentric that it dwarfs even the borrowing binge of the early 1970s. True, the heaviest borrowers of the original debt economy are not today's worst offenders. In the three years of the new debt economy, corporate debt has risen 36% to slightly more than $1 trillion, and state and local government debt has increased just 33% to $295 billion, while total debt in the economy has risen 42% to $3.9 trillion. More ominous is that consumer installment debt is up 49% to $300 billion, residential mortgage debt has soared 54% to $750 billion, and the borrowing of the U.S. government, including the Treasury and federal agencies, is up 47% to $815 billion. Overall, for every $3 owed in 1964, the U.S. now owes $4, a growth in debt far faster than the growth of the U.S. economy, even when inflation is counted in economic growth. What is so worrisome is that the biggest borrowers now are the consumers whose ability to repay has been stretched razor-thin, and the federal government whose borrowing is the most inflationary of all. And now business is joining in, again borrowing heaps of short-term money, while the equity markets remain shut to most corporations. The problem only threatens to get worse. "The only time that debt will go down is when the economy crashes, a recession or a depression" (BW 16 October 1978).

Some major industrial corporations threaten to come crashing down. During the 1970–1971 recession, in the United States the Penn Central railroad went bankrupt. The Chrysler Corporation and Lockheed nearly failed, and had to be saved by the banks—partly in their interest—and by the United States government.

These major corporations had been negatively affected by declining American defense purchases. When the British Rolls-Royce Engines Division went into liquidation, was taken over by the British government, and could not deliver engines for some of Lockheed's airplanes, Lockheed faced financial crisis. Lockheed was saved by the United States government after negotiations; we cite the following exchange before the United States Senate Banking Committee on 8 June 1971 between the then-Secretary of the Treasury, John Connally, who has defended many "defense causes," and Senator William Proxmire:

> SENATOR PROXMIRE: I would remind you in a subsidy program it is different, there is no *quid pro quo*. . . . In this case we have a guarantee and there is no requirement on the part of Lockheed to perform under that guarantee. A guarantee of $250 million, and no *quid pro quo*.
> SECRETARY CONNALLY: What do you mean, no benefit?
> SENATOR PROXMIRE: Well, they don't have to perform.

SECRETARY CONNALLY: What do we care whether they perform? We are guaranteeing them basically a $250 million loan. What for? Basically so they can hopefully minimize their losses, so they can provide employment for 31,000 people throughout the country at a time when we desperately need that type of employment. That is basically the rationale and the justification (U.S. Senate Hearings quoted in Melman 1974: 55–56).

Lockheed survived to be the subject of worldwide scandals of bribery and corruption; and part of the Chrysler Corporation has since been salvaged by subsidies from the British government to its plant in England. The British government was also obliged to save Rolls-Royce (aircraft engines) and the entire British Leyland truck and automobile combine, and yet the latter continues to be a lost cause. The Chrysler Corporation—the tenth largest industrial corporation in the United States—lost over $250 million in the first half of 1979 (more than in all of 1975), and is anticipating further losses as the economy, and particularly the automobile industry, enters recession. Chrysler first asked for $1 billion but may need up to $2 billion in government and bank aid (IHT 23 October 1979). To justify such government intervention, United States Treasury Secretary William Miller argued that Chrysler's bankruptcy would cost the government $2.75 billion in the next two years, and would cause 12 percent unemployment in parts of the Midwest (FT 8 November 79). The prospect of this bankruptcy also has the banks trembling and bickering with each other about how to share the loss.

In 1975, American banks held $3 billion of uncollectable bad debts, representing 2.5 percent of their outstanding loans. This was 50 percent more than in 1974 and three times as much as in 1973. However, one fourth of these debts were held by the eight largest banks, with three and one half times more bad debts in 1975 than in 1974. The Federal Deposit Insurance Corporation (FDIC) disbursed money to small depositors in banks that had failed in 1975 at a rate ten times the average of the previous forty-one years since its founding during the 1930s depression (*Time* 16 January 1976). The failure of the few medium-sized banks—Herstadt in Germany and Franklin National and San Diego in the United States—made headlines and sent tremors through the international banking system. The central and other big banks were able to come to the rescue this time, and prevented a domino-like, chain-reaction crash from spreading through the entire international banking system. Nonetheless, everybody asked what might happen if the next time one of two major banks are forced to close their doors after a country or several corporate clients go bankrupt. Since 1975, the debts and debt crises of several countries, including Italy, have grown enormously, and the debt/equity as well as liquidity ratios of the corporations have become more dangerous.

In 1977 Paul E. Erdman published a "truth is stranger than fiction" bestseller entitled *The Crash of '79*, in which an unsuccessful attempt to bail out

Italy is followed by the withdrawal of Saudi Arabian money from New York; an Iranian nuclear attack on the Arab oil fields makes them, and accidentally the Iranian ones as well, radioactive; and these events are succeeded by a not-so-fictional crash on American money markets on March 19 and 20 of 1979. In actuality, President Carter has frozen Iranian dollar assets, effective within the United states and attempted outside, in response to Iran's holding of American Embassy hostages; Iran in turn has refused to accept dollar payments, as the United States gave the Shah asylum for so many months. These developments have made some financial circles extremely fearful, inasmuch as the action involved might provide precedents for further interference in the operation of the world financial system and/or for the withdrawal, sudden or otherwise, of OPEC funds out of dollar markets. Even the *Sunday Times* (2 December 1979) has not failed to draw the parallel with Erdman's fictionalized scenario.

Whether or not the world will "escape disaster," great changes have already taken place; and these credit operations have already "increased the real distress . . . which it was meant to relieve," as Adam Smith put it. By 1974 the world debt load had risen to some $10 trillion, with $2.5 trillion in the United States alone (BW 12 October 1974). Since then, the world debt pyramid has been built still very much higher and faster, particularly through the Eurocurrency market and in the Third World. We shall examine these phenomena further in chapter 4 of TW.

"The trouble began under Johnson" (BW 22 May 1978 headline). It all began with the American war against Vietnam, as the McCracken report seems to recognize in its first subtitle, "The Vietnam War and the European Wage Explosion" on page 44, in its analysis of "The Origins of Present Problems" and "What Went Wrong?" Lyndon Johnson had campaigned for the presidency in 1964 against the conservative Barry Goldwater, promising to stop the fighting in Vietnam, a position directly opposed to that of Goldwater. Instead, certainly spurred on by demands for increased military spending during the incipient 1966 recession, President Johnson escalated the war until he had 500,000 men in Vietnam. To finance this war effort he went on a massive spending spree, "covered" all the while by federal budget and balance of payments deficits. This "cover" worked, because Americans and non-Americans alike accepted the dollars that Mr. Johnson was printing and pumping into the world economy; all concerned believed that the dollar was "as good as gold," for which the United States Treasury maintained a standing offer to exchange the dollar at a fixed rate of $35 per ounce since 1933. Lyndon Johnson's successor, President Nixon, continued this expansive and "generous" policy, except for a brief interruption under Friedmanian "monetarist" influence in 1969. One fine day, however, on 15 August 1971, Nixon showed that the dollar was not as good as gold after all by breaking its link with gold and instituting a "New Economic Policy." In fact, the United States had increasingly lacked the amount of gold necessary to cover potential foreign-owned dollar claims against it. Excepting Charles de Gaulle, who cashed in France's dollars for gold, foreign owners of dollars avoided pressing their claims, preferring to force the dollar to devaluate, perhaps to precipitate a world financial and economic crisis. Moreover, they agreed to put their dollars into U.S. Treasury securities, creating what has been called a "U.S. treasury-bill standard," to replace the gold or gold/dollar standard (Hudson 1977: 17); they thus expanded their own currencies, using these U.S. treasury bills as their "reserves."

Competitive Devaluation with Trade and Payments Deficits

These financial policies—in combination with the relative decline of American productivity, the falling rate of profit, and increased international coordination of business cycles, all in turn affected by these policies—had several further consequences. All these developments evolved simultaneously, but we must unfortunately consider them successively.

The international consequences of the policies in question on the world economy have been enormous. Just as a portion of American military expenditures was financed through a federal budget deficit, so were all of the America military expenditures abroad "financed" by a balance of payments deficit of approximately equal size. This was a way of "financing America's wars with other people's money" (Hudson 1972: 208). Others received dollar IOUs which have been used by "American monopoly capitalism to buy up as much of the capitalist world as it pleases—raw materials, factories, mines, labor power, governments, anything and everything—and to pay not with real commodities but with paper, with dollar IOUs. This in turn requires that foreign governments and central banks should continue to add American money to their international reserves" in "the weird world of international money" (Morris 1975: 8). Thus, the United States achieved "power through bankruptcy" (Hudson 1972: 231). To finance its war, it printed dollars, and used these to buy war matériel and assets—"foreign investments"—abroad. Other governments re-lent their dollars to the United States Treasury for bonds, and used these as reserves to support the expansion of their own currencies and credit. Capitalists in Europe and then all around the world put their dollars into a burgeoning "Eurodollar" and then "Asian-dollar" market, from which dollars were lent again to private and public borrowers in the "first," "second/socialist," and "third/underdeveloped" worlds. (For further analysis, see chapter 4 of this volume and TW, chapter 4.

The "Eurodollar" market soon became a "Eurocurrency" market, in which anybody lent any convertible currency to anybody else, on the basis of reserves and guarantees; these ultimately were no more than other debts floating around in an unending circle—and in a potentially inflationary spiral. No government, international institution, or monetary "authority" retains any control whatsoever over the continuous creation of credit on the basis of someone else's credit in the Eurocurrency market. Here, predominantly bond issues are backed by hardly any currency at all, unless it is the "international reserve" currency of the dollar, thrice devalued since 1971. What *Business Week* says about the American debt economy is all the more true of the world debt economy, and especially its volatile Eurocurrency market.

Increasing strains produced a crisis in 1971. As long as the world economic pie had been growing moderately, the various capitalist interests and their states had been able to reach relatively amicable agreements on how to divide the pie up among themselves under the moderately bullying pressure of the Americans. However, the 1970s witnessed the substantial increase of West European and especially Japanese productivity relative to that of American capital and the decline in the rate of profit in most of the major capitalist countries. All the while, American capital still drew the lion's share of the benefit from the "weird world of international money." These changes made the increasing strains more and more difficult to bear. Then, the 1970 recession hit most major capitalist economies simultaneously, and even forced down the rate of profit in Germany and Japan.

The continuous deficits in the American balance of payments were making it more and more impossible for the United States government to honor real and potential claims on the dollar. Then, for the first time in 1971 and even more in 1972, not only the American balance of payments on goods and service, including financial, account, but also the balance of trade on merchandise account alone, fell into deficit. The United States could no longer even pay for the goods it imported with the goods it exported. The strain and the drain on the dollar had become too great; and President Nixon threw all previously orthodox economic theory and policy overboard on 15 August 1971, declaring the dollar no longer convertible against gold. He forced other major currencies, especially the German mark and the Japanese yen, to revalue upward in relation to the dollar, in effect devaluing the dollar without wishing to say so. Simultaneously, he imposed a special 10 percent surtax on imports into the United States, violating all GATT rules and customs, until the Japanese in particular agreed to play by the new American rules of the economic game. The Japanese called this the "Nixon shokku."

Domestically, Nixon also imposed a "New Economic Policy" (curiously called NEP, like the policy introduced in the Soviet Union in 1922 by Lenin). Through NEP, he imposed "wage and price" controls, designed and operated to control wages far more than prices, in order to help the rate of profit recover for capital. Nixon's administrator of the wage freeze, Arnold Weber, later revealed that business "had been leaning" on the administration "to do something about wages. . . . The idea of the freeze and Phase II II was to zap labor and we did" (quoted in Gordon 1975: 34; also see Frank 1978d).

Mr. Nixon destroyed the world financial system, erected on the basis of the American dollar at the Bretton Woods Conference in 1943, in one fell swoop on 15 August 1971. However, since the productive shifts and financial manipulations reviewed above had been undermining this financial structure for several years, Mr. Nixon only provided the *coup de grâce*. "Pegged" or fixed exchange rates between major currencies and, through the dollar, between such currencies and, through the dollar, between such currencies and gold had reigned throughout the postwar period, except when the United States forced one of its partners to devalue or revalue by "agreement." These fixed rates were now abandoned. Currencies were "unpegged," and started to float up and down against each other and gold. Except for the British pound, whose weakness reflected that of the entire British economy, industry and profitability, most of these currencies floated upward; and relative to them, the dollar was in effect devalued. In January–February 1972 Mr. Nixon called a world monetary conference at the Smithsonian Institution in order to put the world financial Humpty-Dumpty together again by fixing new currency parities in relation to the dollar. Mr. Nixon called the Smithsonian Agreement the most important financial arrangement in history. Nevertheless, all of Emperor Nixon's men at home and abroad were not able to put Humpty-Dumpty together again; and by the summer of 1972 the Smithsonian Agreement was in complete shambles. Floating exchange rates had become a new fact of life in the world. Far from discouraging speculation against fixed exchange rates (in anticipation of changed pegs), the floating rates oiled the speculative fever that has since been further fed by common recessions, repeated balance of payments deficits, and different rates of inflation.

Since mid-1972 every official announcement of a bigger balance of payments deficit for any country has been immediately followed by a speculative decline in the value of its currency. The larger the deficit, the greater the devaluation. Since the oil crisis, the United States balance of payments reached massive deficits, not uniquely related to its oil imports. In 1973–1974 and again since 1977, the balance of merchandise trade has been in deficit to the tune of over $30 billion in 1977, 1978, and 1979 respectively. The United States has accepted the repeated "speculative" devaluation of the dollar with satisfaction, most cynically so by President Carter's Secretary of the Treasury Blumenthal with the sharp decline of the dollar in early 1978, and again by his successor William Miller during the decline in late 1979. A cheaper dollar improves American competitiveness abroad; it makes foreign exports to the United States more difficult, because imports into the United States become more expensive. For the same reasons, European countries and Japan have supported the dollar against their own currencies, buying dollars in the open market as long as they could to prevent their own currencies from rising in value too fast or too far— largely in vain. The German mark, the Swiss franc (particularly beloved for speculative purposes), and the Japanese yen have continued to rise against the dollar and against most other currencies. In response, the German government is continually trying to establish a "fat snake" or "stabilization fund" or "European Monetary System" (EMS) of European parities to include not only the French franc but also the British pound to float jointly against the dollar—the devaluation of the franc and the pound against the mark has been giving non-German capital competitive advantages.

These currency realignments have also translated into dollars and cents the underlying differences in industrial productivities which had been falling in the United States relative to Europe and Japan. When calculated in dollars at present exchange rates, labor costs in many German and certain other European industries are now higher than those in the United States. For this reason German and other capital has reversed the postwar trend where American wages were high and others low; foreign capital is now investing more in—and exporting more jobs to—the United States than vice versa. Among other factors contributing to this trend reversal, the purchase of plant and equipment, as well as speculation with agricultural land, with marks and other highly-valued currencies has become cheap and attractive.

In the late 1960s and early 1970s wages had been rising in most industrial capitalist countries, however calculated; and their governments, with varying degrees of success, had been trying to put a brake on wage increases through wage and "price" controls and "incomes" policies of various kinds (chapter 3). The increase of wages and prices, fed by the flood of dollars and then other currencies, was ringing alarm bells in company boardrooms and government cabinets. This brings us to the problem of inflation.

Inflation and Stagflation

With ever greater insistence, inflation is being called "public enemy number one" by economists, businessmen, political leaders, and the press at their service. Two major theories and supposed explanations of inflation have been making the rounds. These are being propounded with equal conviction by these same spokesmen for essentially the interests of capital as against those of labor.

The first of these theories is one of "demand pull," according to which the growing supply of money, particularly to finance government expenditures through deficit spending, generates too much demand; this demand pulls prices up as "too much money chases too few goods." This "quantity" of money theory of prices was first expounded when gold and silver from Spanish America (a bit like dollars in recent years from North America) arrived in Europe and helped generate an inflationary "price revolution" in the sixteenth century (Frank 1978a). Despite various modifications and refinements, particularly by Irwin Fisher in the 1920s and by Milton Friedman in the 1950s and 1960s, the "monetarist" quantity theory of inflation has remained controversial ever since; and there can be no hope of resolving the controversy here and now. There is substantial consensus, however, on one point made by proponents of this theory—namely, that insofar as there is more money available, more money can chase goods. There is also substantial agreement on one part of the explanation for the persistent inflation of recent years:

> While liberals and conservatives differ sharply over the cure for inflation, they have, surprisingly, reached a consensus that the present inflationary predicament was partly caused by the political sins and policy errors of the 1960s and '70s that were linked to President Johnson's conduct of the Vietnam war and President Nixon's obsessive effort to obtain a huge plurality in the 1972 election [through massive deficit spending]. . . . Memoirs of the time make it abundantly clear that Johnson felt obliged to lie about the cost of the 1965–66 Vietnam buildup . . . [and] to hide the cost of the Vietnam war from the American public (BW 22 May 1978: 113, 108).

These American war expenditures, as we have observed, flooded the world and exported much of the inflationary potential abroad. This money—and the additional money created on the basis of it elsewhere—may have provided much of the fuel for the subsequent inflationary fire. This money, however, was not necessarily the underlying cause or even the spark for this fire.

The alternative and sometimes complementary major theory of inflation argues that rising wages force prices up through a "cost push." For the moment, we shall not examine the scientific merits or demerits of this explanation; its validity seems doubtful, particularly where wage costs are a relatively small component of total costs. Its political/economic implications are, however, clear: halt the rise in wages and push them down again. The political/economic attractiveness of the wage cost push argument to capital and its spokesmen has given this supposed explanation of inflation so much circulation in political circles and through the mass media in recent years that it is hardly necessary to document it further here.

The two explanations and their implications for political/economic policy are complementary, insofar as greater money wage payments can also generate a larger demand pull. In turn, smaller supplies of money and/or fewer government expenditures have a deflationary impact on the economy in general and on employment in particular; this reduces labor's bargaining power to push wages up. Thus, both theories of inflation, sometimes innocently and often intentionally, serve to defend the interests of capital against labor.

Like others on the left, we have argued all along that neither the monetarist demand pull nor the labor cost push theory of inflation is scientifically, let alone politically, correct or satisfactory (Frank 1976a, 1977c, 1978d; Blair 1974; Edwards 1975; Sherman 1976 a,b; Schui 1976). Instead, we propose a profit promotion or profit push explanation of inflation. Briefly put, the thesis states that inflation is caused by monopoly capital, which marks up prices to protect or improve its profits. We say "capital," because it—and not labor—sets the prices; "monopoly," because the sector of capital ruled by the big corporations has the monopoly power to do so; and "profit," because its decline is the reason and occasion for price increases. Studies by the aforementioned authors, among others, support this thesis with considerable statistical facts.

Since 1972 worldwide inflation has been more severe precisely in those industrialized countries in which the rate of profit declined the most. In Britain, Italy and Japan, inflation reached a yearly rate of 25 percent. Among the underdeveloped countries the most severe inflationary takeoffs have occurred where capital suffered the greatest decline in profits and the crisis of accumulation had become most severe. Similarly, as between industries in particular countries, price rises are most marked in industries that are most monopolized. Howard Sherman (1976: 32–33) showed that in the American recession years 1953, 1958, and 1969 competitive prices declined 1.5 percent, 0.3 percent, and 3.0 percent respectively, while monopoly prices rose 1.9 percent, 0.5 percent, and 5.9 percent respectively. In 1948, when the degree of monopolization was not yet as strong, competitive prices had fallen 7.8 percent and monopoly prices also went down, but by much less, only 1.9 percent. This inflationary behavior of monopoly prices compared to competitive prices occurs despite the fact that in the recessions between 1947 and 1965 profits in monopolized industries only declined 26.7 percent on the average, while in competitive industries they declined 51.7 percent and in the smaller industries with less than $250,000 in assets, they had fallen on average by 82.7 percent. According to John M. Blair:

> The weighted average price change in the recession of December 1969–December 1970 by concentration category for the 296 products . . . [shows that] the average *increase* for products with concentration ratios of 50 percent and over (5.9 percent) was nearly as great as the *decrease* for products with ratios of under 25 percent (−6.1 percent). Those in the intermediate group (for example, with ratios of from 25 to 49 percent) registered an intermediate change, declining −1.0 percent. . . . Obviously, the concentrated industries were more successful in translating higher costs (and perhaps other factors) into higher prices (Blair 1974: 457–8).

This was true in Germany, as well as Herbert Schui summarized in his study of the 1974–1975 recession:

> Industries in which a few big firms have a large share of the sales increased their prices significantly more in 1974/75 than industries in which the largest firms do not have an above average share of the market. The mirror image of the foregoing is that production declines in the highly concentrated industrial branches (those with the highest rates of inflation in the recession) significantly more than in the industrial sectors with only little concentration (Schui 1976:5).

Writing from the perspective of Argentina, Victor Testa observed:

> Full employment contributed to the ability of many groups to obtain
> additional increases in wages and salaries through their own efforts, and
> it contributed to spurring on the labour union militancy that was born
> out of the political process of these recent years. At the same time it is
> undoubtable that this position of force of the working class drives the
> bourgeoisie to renew the inflationary process in order to recuperate
> their profit levels through price rises. Inflation as an answer to salary
> increases was a clearly applied policy in France in 1968, in Italy in
> 1969 and in Chile in 1970–73, and it could not but turn up also in
> Argentina. What makes Argentina resemble France more than Chile is
> that the wage increases were obtained through worker action and not
> through official policy: what is similar in the three cases is that the
> answer of the bourgeoisie is the rise in prices and the inflation, which
> transfers the bid for income from the factory interior to the general
> economic front (Testa, n.d.)

Roger Bratenstein wrote:

> It seems remarkable that none of the [eleven underdeveloped] coun-
> tries with a steady uptrend of the national product in the review period
> . . . suffered from prolonged severe inflation. In contrast, the countries
> which experienced large prices increases (Argentina, Bolivia, Brazil,
> Chile, Uruguay) were without exception hit by severe setbacks (Braten-
> stein 1974:322).

Remarkable indeed—that he would suppose setbacks in growth to be
caused by inflation and steady uptrends to be possible only where inflation
was absent. His correct correlation is not remarkable at all because the
"setbacks" in growth he registers are associated with recessionary declines in
the rate of profit to which capital and its dutiful governments (even in
Allende's 1970–1973 Chile) respond by increasing prices—and political
repression.

Thus, all around the Third World as well, inflation has followed economic
and profit crises during or after which capital sought to recoup losses by
raising prices. In these profit promotion inflations, wages have not led, but
rather lagged behind prices in time and in quantity. Monetary and state authorities have, of course, collaborated with capital in the promotion of
inflation by supplying the financial fuel to maintain the inflationary fire, and
by using the economic and political force of state power to help keep labor
"in its place."

Beyond this statistical evidence, the theory which postulates profit promotion as the cause of current inflation has received some "judgmental" support
from certain surprising sources, which are difficult to impeach. Thus, the
voice of American big business, *Fortune* (August 1974: 25), wrote: "In
recent months, however, the real push behind these prices has come from

businessmen straining to restore their profit margins" during the 1973-1975 recession. If we may jump ahead to early 1979 for a moment, in the United States "businessmen find that they can easily fatten their profits by marking up their prices. Many are not resisting this temptation" (ECO 24 March 1979). Commenting on "the mild recession of 1970-71 . . . and the 1972-73 boom," the McCracken report notes with hindsight that "a number of shocks led to an outburst of world-wide inflation almost unprecedented in peacetime, driven primarily not by wage increased but by price increases. . . . It is clear that initially the 1972-73 inflationary outburst was attributable to strain in goods markets rather than in labor markets. But it was natural that at some stage there would be pressure for wages to catch up" (McCracken 1977: 51, 64). This "pressure" has evidently been insufficient, however, since real wages have generally fallen, and have not "caught up" since then.

The august members of the McCracken Commission include a former chairman of the United States Council of Economic Advisers, Paul McCracken; the former governor of the Bank of Italy and then president of his country's confederation of industries, Guido Carli; and a former member of the German Council of Economic Advisers and one of his country's five economic "wise men," Herbert Giersch. These gentlemen and many others like them complained long and loudly in the boardrooms of business, in the halls of government, and through the press all these years that it was labor which was driving up prices and that this must be stopped, which it was. It is therefore welcome news that the McCracken Commission now consents to set the record straight about the innocence of labor as the culprit for inflation. Unfortunately, this verdict appears only on a couple of pages buried in a 341-page report that the public certainly has not read; for the most part, only the 52-page, separately issued summary was cited by the press when the report was published. This summary contains the more guarded statement: "In contrast to the 1960s, this bout of inflation originated less in labor markets and more in product markets, both national and international" (McCracken 1977 summary: 16).

However, the McCracken Commission and countless other institutional and individual analysts and publicists still seem to subscribe to the other variant of a cost push theory, which attributes much of the inflation to an "external supply shock" in the raw materials market in 1972-1974, and especially from oil since 1973. This equally fallacious view seems to ignore completely the simultaneous *deflationary* impact of increased oil prices as higher expenditures for oil have the effect of *withdrawing* purchasing power in the developed consumer countries; partially "sterilize" it in OPEC surplus accounts; and/or "recycle" it substantially to the underdeveloped countries. Since this widespread "oil shock" or "crisis" theory of inflation has been voiced by every political leader and newspaper in the developed capitalist world and most of its professional economists, it is particularly heartening to find a GATT Report—better late than never—explaining:

> Considerable confusion reigns about the immediate macroeconomic effect of the oil price increase in the importing economies. . . . It is thought that, when the recent petroleum price increases have passed through the prices of final products, they will simply be added to the average price increase that had been expected before the event. This implies taking all other prices as given, that is to say, as rising at some predetermined, unalterable rate. Indeed, recent publications abound in theorizing about an underlying, "bedrock," "ingrained" or "basic" rate of inflation to which "exogenous" inflationary impulses must be added. There is no basis for such an assertion, which—if true—would amount to an abdication of government responsibility in the face of inflation. In the Federal Republic of Germany, the Bundesbank [Central bank] has explicitly challenged the view that the trend of other prices can be taken as given when a particular import price rises: "It must also be borne in mind that consumers' extra spending on petroleum products will necessarily lead, in view of their limited income, to certain quantitative reactions among other consumer goods, which will narrow the scope for price increases there" (GATT 1979b:17–18).

As we argued above, these "quantitative reactions among other consumer goods" will be concentrated among nonconsumers with the most "limited income," and among goods produced by the most competitive industries, whose prices are likely to be forced down, while monopoly prices rise. (For further discussion of inflation since 1972, see p. 65 ff.)

What particularly distinguishes the worldwide inflation of the 1970s from the 1960s and earlier times is that it does not alternate with, but accompanies unemployment and stagnation. Hence, the new word "stagflation" and more recently "slumpflation." In the United States a certain amount of unemployment and inflation had risen together in the years following the 1957–1958 recession, but now the simultaneous sharp increase of unemployment and prices has become worldwide. The spokesmen of capital have thus had occasion to invent a new, mystifying explanation of unemployment as being pushed or pulled up by inflation. Their conclusion: combat future unemployment by controlling present inflation through immediate deflationary policies that increase unemployment right now! The mystification, however, is only partially intentional. To a considerable extent it is simply the reflection of the total bankruptcy of both economic theory and policy in the face of simultaneous unemployment and inflation. To this extent, it is easy to agree with the judgment of *Business Week* cited on p. 21.

Neoclassical economic theory and policy assume that inflation occurs when there are additional expenditures and no unemployed resources (in theory always!); therefore, additional monetary demand—along a vertical supply curve of all goods—can only drive up prices. The Keynesian theory, developed during the Great Depression of the 1930s, held, on the other hand, that with unemployed resources—and a horizontal supply curve—increased government or market demand would generate more commodity production at the same prices. The post-Keynesian-neoclassical synthesis became widely accepted during the postwar era, excepting such recalcitrant neoclassical economists as Friedrich Von Hayek and Milton Friedman. This synthesis combined the two views into the following compromise solution: with a relatively large amount of unemployment—and a supply curve that barely slopes upward from southwest to northeast—additional demand can call forth much more output with only small increases in price; and at relatively full employment—and a supply curve that rises more steeply— additional demand can generate only slightly more production and must drive prices up faster and farther. However, neither neoclassical nor Keynesian theory nor their synthesis can contemplate or admit the simultaneous steep increase of both unemployment and prices. Nor can they offer any policy to combat both at the same time; their respective favored medicine of increasing demand can only heat up unemployment, and decreasing demand can only cool down the inflationary patient.

Since it is impossible to increase and decrease spending at the same time, these remedies cannot cure the sick man of both his attacks, much less the causes, of simultaneous economic shivering with fever. Paul Samuelson, long the high priest of Keynesianism in America, now observes: "Whatever government policy does to help handle the 'flation' part of our stagflation inevitably worsens in the short run the stagnation part of the problem. That stubborn reality will not go away. . . . Likewise, whatever government policy does to help handle the 'stag' part of stagflation will ineluctably worsen the inflation part of stagflation" (AEI April 1979: 6). It is no wonder that the *New York Times* arrives at the practical conclusion that government should do neither: neither deflate to combat inflation nor reflate to combat unemployment. The alternatives are either paralysis, or worsening stagnation.

Both theories and their synthesis, as well as all the economic policies associated with them, presuppose that they are dealing with a competitive economy; in fact, the structure of the economy has become more and more monopolistic, such that the monopolies can and do reduce output and employment, simultaneously increasing prices. Moreover, bourgeois economic science has never yet developed a theory that synthesizes microeconomic monopoly price theory—which only refers to the behavior of particular firms—with macroeconomic income and employment theory— which refers to the economy as a whole, but on the supposition that it is competitive and not monopolistic. Theory and policy are faced with the dilemma of growing unemployment with rising inflation, which everybody sees and feels; but they are politically unwilling and scientifically unable to admit the crucial importance of monopoly today. Therefore, bourgeois economic theory and policy retreat to the reactionary, *déja vu* "explanations" and policies of a Friedrich von Hayek and a Milton Friedman. Both have recently received the Nobel Prize in economics. Von Hayek received it after more than a generation of virtual inactivity, and Friedman after two decades of crying vainly into the wind, while many still believed in the post-Keynesian synthesis.

Now that the stark reality of the 1970s has exposed the previous folly of the post-Keynesians, Messrs. von Hayek and Friedman can and do say "I told you so." Even so, they have nothing better to offer themselves other than to return to the theories and policies that were in vogue before the Great Depression of the 1930s—or indeed in the nineteenth century—and to press for their invocation during the new capitalist crisis of capital accumulation. "I had become one of the best-known economists in my 30s, but then two things happened—the complete counter-review of Keynes succeeded and I discredited myself. . . . [The Nobel Prize] was a symptom of the recovery of my reputation." "Paul Samuelson . . . once said that Prof. von Hayek at one time wanted to return to the 19th century days of limited Whig government. 'That's correct,' Prof. von Hayek said. . . . 'The current drive toward a welfare state to create a "just economy" is nonsense. Only individual action can be just. . . . My task is to make politically possible what is not yet politically possible by changing public opinion,' he said. The change in public opinion is occurring, he noted" (IHT 12 March 1979). And now, *faute de mieux,* these old reactionaries are finding willing listeners and enthusiastic disciples all around the world. (For the application of Friedman's theories and policies by General Pinochet's military junta in Chile, see Frank 1976a.) As the *Financial Times* observes, "the world goes monetarist" (FT 13 October 1979).

Unemployment and the 1969/70–1971 Recession

"Full employment" in the United States used to be considered employment with up to 4 percent "normal," "structural," or "natural" unemployment. During the 1950s, indeed the official American unemployment rate fluctuated between 3–5.5 percent, only rising to 6.8 percent during the 1958 recession. During the first half of the 1960s the rate of unemployment in the United States hovered over 5 percent, and in the second half of the 1960s it remained a bit under 4 percent. In Western Europe, unemployment, variously defined and measured, remained at one or less percent in Germany, France, and Holland; at about 2 and 3 percent in Belgium and Britain; and at over 3 percent in Italy. The 1967 recession raised unemployment by one point or more percentage points in most countries for 1967 and 1968. This was the first time since the war that such a rise happened in a more or less coordinated fashion everywhere except in the United States. In Japan, which offers a regime of "guaranteed lifetime employment"—which, however, only applies to part of the labor force—official unemployment hovered uniformly around one percent (ILO YLS 1975).

The 1970–1972 recession increased unemployment even more uniformly and further, as Table 2-6 demonstrates. In the United States the number of unemployed rose from less than three million or 3.5 percent in the late 1960s to nearly five million or over 5.5 percent in 1971 and 1972. In the nine countries which now compose the Common Market of the European Economic Community, unemployment rose from 1.9 million in 1969 to 2.6 million or about 2.5 percent in 1972. (These data were taken from the not quite comparable national definitions and measures of unemployment in ILO YLS 1975.) In Britain it passed 4 percent. Unemployment also rose to 6.3 percent in Canada, to 2.3 percent from an earlier 1.5 percent in Australia, and to 1.4 percent from 1.1 percent in 1969 in Japan. For the industrialized countries of the OECD as a whole, unemployment had been 5.5 million in 1965, 6 million in 1967, and 5.8 million in 1969. Then, it rose to about 7.4 million in 1970, 9.6 million in 1971, and 8.9 million in 1972 (see Table 2-6).

Thus, during the 1970–1972 recession, total unemployment in the industrialized capitalist countries rose by more than 50 percent. Moreover, during the subsequent but shortlived 1972–1973 boom, total unemployment fell back by only about half a million, and most of this reduction was in the United States. In other words, during this recovery unemployment failed to regain its lower levels of earlier years. As it turned out, this failure foreshadowed what was to come with a vengeance during the next cyclical recession in 1973–1975 and in the 1975–1979 "recovery."

Before proceeding to examine these developments, however, it is necessary to comment briefly on the meaning of the official data on unemployment. More often than not, they hide more than they reveal. Frequently, armies of employment statisticians spend hundreds of hours trying to figure out how to hide real unemployment in their official statistics, since unemployment figures are so politically sensitive, as are those for inflation. The higher real unemployment is, the greater is its official statistical obfuscation. Since the percentage rate of unemployment is a simple ratio, the resulting figure depends on what the statisticians put into and omit from both the numerator of those not working and the denominator of the potential work force. For instance, if unemployment rises and persists such that a man is discouraged from looking for a job and no longer even registers his unemployment at the employment office; if he tells the census taker that he did not actively look for a job during the immediately past census period; then that man is not registered as unemployed, because he is too much unemployed! If a woman is not working outside her home in periods of high unemployment, the employment statistician calls her a "housewife" who does "not work." If a youth cannot find his first job, he can be said not to have even entered the "labor force" yet, thus reducing the denominator but proportionately to an even greater extent the numerator of the unemployment ratio. If people migrate out of the census district and return home because they can no longer find employment, they simply disappear from the statistics and cease to "exist" altogether.

TABLE 2-6
Unemployment
(in millions and percentages)

	1 USA millions	%	2 EEC millions	%	3 Industrial millions	%
1965	3.366	4.5	1.5		5.7	
1966	2.875	3.8	1.6			
1967	2.975	3.8	2.15		6.2	
1968	2.817	3.6	2.1			
1969	2.831	3.5	1.9		5.8	
1970	4.088	4.9	2.1		7.4	
1971	4.993	5.9	2.25		9.6	
1972	4.840	5.6	2.5		8.9	
1973	4.304	4.9	2.6(1)	2.5	8.3	
1974	5.076	5.6	3.8	3.7	10.4	
1975	7.830	8.5	4.7(1)	4.4	15.0	5.5
1976	7.288	7.7	5.4(2)	5.2	15.2	5.2
1977	6.865	7.0	6.04(2)	5.7	16.3	5.4
1978	6.000	6.0	5.50	5.5	16.2	5.3
1979, 1st half	5.900	5.7	6.00	5.6		5.2

Notes and Sources: From official and press sources and our own estimates, put together in the following rather unsatisfactory way: USA for 1965–1976 from ILO YLS, for 1977 UN MBS May 1978. EEC refers to all nine member countries. For 1965–1972 from ILO YLS by adding up individual country data. For 1973 from IHT 2 Aug. 1977. For 1974 from FAZ 22 Feb. 1975, FT 19 Feb. 1975. For 1975 from IHT 2 Aug. 1977; for 1976 from IHT 2 Aug. 1977; for 1977 from IHT 26 Oct. 1977. (1) indicates first and (2) second semester of the year. The highest published figures for the year are entered in the table. These figures are higher than those computed from the above-cited official statistical sources (not entered in the table) in part because unemployment in Italy was underestimated by about half a million until 1977, when it was redefined in the official sources and jumped from 0.7 million recorded in 1976 to 1.5 million recorded in 1977. The FAZ source for 1974, however, already gave 1.01 million for 1974 while the official sources only indicated 0.56 million for that year. For the industrial countries, unemployment was estimated until 1974 by using the figures for the USA and EEC above, adding those (from ILO YLS) for Canada, Australia, and Japan, and rounding up to the next decimal to account (inadequately) for the smaller industrial countries. For 1975–1977 the total OECD unemployment figures published in *Economic Outlook* were used; and they are comparable to those that would be derived by our "adding up" method. Again, the highest published figures for each year are entered in the table. For 1978 and 1979 approximations were constructed by the author from data in *Economic Outlook* Dec. 78 and Jul. 79, FT Jan. 79, BIS 1979, OECD Economic Survey, United States 1979, and other sources. There is a small discrepancy in the published unemployment percentage figures for these years. The substantial underestimation of unemployment totals is discussed in the text.

TABLE 2-6 (continued)
Unemployment Rates[1]

Countries	1957–73 highest average annual rate		1975 December	1976 December	1977 December	1978 June	1978 December	1979 April
			in percentages					
United States	6.8	5.0	8.2	7.7	6.3	5.8	5.9	5.8
Canada	7.1	5.5	7.0	7.5	8.5	8.5	8.1	7.9
Japan	1.5	1.1	2.0	1.7	2.1	2.4	2.3	2.1[2]
Germany	3.7	1.4	4.9	4.4	4.5	4.4	4.1	3.9
France	2.7	1.6	4.2	4.3	5.2	5.2	5.8	6.0[2]
Britain	3.8	2.2	5.0	5.6	6.0	5.7	5.5	5.5
Italy[3]	8.2	4.0	3.5	6.8	7.1	7.1	7.4	7.4[4]
Belgium	6.3	3.7	8.7	9.8	11.0	9.9	11.1	11.0[2]
Netherlands	2.7	1.5	5.5	5.2	5.1	5.1	5.3	5.1[2]
Sweden	2.5	1.5	1.6	1.5	1.8	2.1	2.1	2.0
Switzerland	0.0	0.0	0.9	0.6	0.4	0.3	0.4	0.4

Source: Bank for International Settlements 1979: 47.

[1]As a percentage of the civilian labor force (in Belgium the insured labor force). Seasonally adjusted series except for Belgium, Sweden, and Switzerland.

[2]March.

[3]New series as from December 1976.

[4]February.

The full-time real unemployment equivalent of hidden and part-time unemployment in the United States has been estimated as follows in Table 2-7:

TABLE 2-7

Official and Real Unemployment
(in the United States in percent)

	Official	Official Full and Part-time	Official, Estimate 1	Part-time, and Hidden Estimate 2
1967	3.8	4.8	5.3	5.8
1969	3.5	4.4	4.8	5.2
1971	5.9	7.1	7.7	8.0
1975	8.5	10.0	10.9	11.2

Source: Du Boff 1977: 17.

Another estimate for 1975 arrives at a still higher rate of "real" unemployment for April 1975, just before the May 1975 9.2 percent high point of official unemployment; for instance:

Official unemployment	8.2 million	8.9%
Wanting a job but not counted	3.1 million	
Adjustment for involuntary part-time	1.7 million	
Total estimates "real" unemployment	13.0 million	13.6%

Source: MR June 1975: 11.

Similar underestimation of unemployment by official agencies occurs elsewhere. This has been confirmed to this writer by an official of the Ministry of Labor of France for that country, as one example. Union leaders in Britain claim that 1975 unemployment there was closer to 2.5 million than to the official 1.5 million (EPW 21 February 1976: 315). In Japan, according to an "Employment Status Survey," real unemployment in 1974 was twice as high for men and *ten times* as high for women than officially recorded unemployment, raising the total from the official 730,000 to 3,276,000. The last figure excludes over two million part-time employed who wished to work longer, and another two million who were discouraged from looking for work (Mitteilungen aus Arbeitsmarkt and Berufsforschung, No. 1, 1978: 34–49). Moreover, both the absolute and relative underestimation of the officially recorded—compared to the real—number of unemployed tend to grow rapidly, the deeper the recession and the higher the level of unemployment.

According to the German Metal Workers Union, IG Metall, the official 1.06 million unemployed in Germany in early 1977 should be raised by another 614,000 to account for workers who were forced into untimely retirement, among others. Even then, another 1.5 million, or a total of 3 million jobs, would have to be created, according to IG Metall, to reestablish full employment, if account were to be taken of two significant factors: the jobs that have been "transferred" abroad through "runaway" factories; and the immigrant "guest" workers, who returned to their countries of origin since Germany and other European countries imposed restrictions in 1974 on hiring new workers from outside the Common Market (FR 23 March 1977). "Month for month the Federal Labor Office in Nuremberg [Germany] manages to bring off a computational miracle of a special kind. They divine the most varied rates of unemployment without even knowing the number of people who are able to work that live in the Federal Republic" (FR 23 December 1975). Nobody knows how many "guest workers" left the country and went home when they could no longer find a job, or because without one their residence permits cancelled.

In the meantime, the following headlines further illustrate the trend: "Italians Who Return Home Now Outnumber Emigrants. World Economic Crisis Is Believed Cause" (IHT 27 April 1977); "A Reversal of Urban Trend: Joblessness [is] Forcing Italians to Move Back to the Farm" (IHT 28/29 May 1977). (The little more than half million figure for unemployment in Italy in 1974 and 1975 cited in the ILO Statistical Yearbook used in Table 2-4 may vastly underestimate total unemployment for Italy, given as over one million for 1974 by FAZ (22 February 1975), and 1.1 million for 1976 and 1.7 million for 1977 by other sources. We have therefore raised our estimates—but not quoted data—for EEC unemployment by half a million to account for this discrepancy in the data on Italy.)

All the numbers cited above, however, including estimates of "real" unemployment, are only averages. Further, all statistical averages necessarily hide the real variation and differentiation between them. For instance, 8 million official and 11 to 13 million estimated "real" unemployed cited for the United States in 1975 involved over 21 million real people, or over 21 percent, who were unemployed sometime during that year. Of these, 43 percent were unemployed for fifteen weeks or longer before they found another job (Du Boff 1977: 21). Moreover, as early as 1974 three out of four workers who had exhausted their unemployment benefits were still unemployed and/or had dropped out of the labor force four months later, according to a Department of Labor study (IHT 7 March 1976). Thus, the total number of people who really suffered unemployment was three times higher than the official "unemployment figure" in 1975, as well as in most other years (Du Boff 1977: 21–22).

Additionally, it is important to break down unemployment averages by sex, race, age, and other social groups among which rates of unemployment are very much higher than the average. Unfortunately, the data available for these groups are breakdowns of official unemployment statistics; therefore, they still do not reveal the true level of unemployment afflicting these most discriminated-against groups.

A clear pattern and trend emerge: the rate of unemployment is between one and one half and two times as high for female as for male heads of households—and for blue- as for white-collar workers, not included in this table. Registered unemployment is also systematically nearly twice as high for nonwhite (Afro- and Spanish-American) workers as for white ones. Unemployment increased for all categories of workers from the 1960s to the early 1970s, and then again sharply in 1975. This trend can be seen in Table 2-6 for all workers, and appears again in Table 2-8 for each category of workers. Table 2-8 clarifies the additional pattern and trend that the group of workers with the highest rates of unemployment—that is, women, nonwhites and, as we shall see, the young—do not become reemployed as fast as do most workers when employment conditions improve. Thus, when employment rose from 1975 to 1977, unemployment among discriminated-against groups declined to a relatively lesser extent than that of male and white workers.

These high and persistent rates of unemployment are much more serious still among teenagers, whose overall registered unemployment rate of about 20 percent is three times higher than the national average. However, the recorded unemployment of nonwhite teenagers is twice again as high as that of all teenagers—and of young whites—or six times as high as that of workers in general. Moreover, the 20 percent registered unemployment of teenagers in 1975 has persisted at almost the same high level through the recovery until

TABLE 2-8

U.S. Unemployment by Sex, Race, and Age
(in yearly or average percentage rates)

	1967–69	1971–74	1975	1977	1978
Male, household head	2.1	3.8	6.3	4.3	
Female, household head	3.7	5.1	8.2	7.0	
White	3.2	4.9	7.6	6.7	
Nonwhite	6.4	9.7	13.7	12.5	12.3
Teenage	12.6	15.6	20.7	20.0[b]	16.6
White			18.4	18.1	
Nonwhite			39.0[a]	36.1	38.4

Source: U.S. Bureau of Labor Statistics data cited in the following: for 1967–1975, APHA 1975, Figures 14–20 (except for teenage 1972–74 cited in URPE 1975: 70–71); for 1977, USN 21 Feb. 1977: 55; for 1978, IHT 19 June 1978.

[a]Black only.

[b]Estimate.

Note: 1967–1974 averages computed from yearly data. 1975 data are for first or second quarter.

1977 and even 1978; and the 40 percent registered nonwhite unemployment of the 1975 recession has remained stable or even increased during the last few years. That is, teenage unemployment, especially among nonwhites, seems to have become "permanent" for the foreseeable future. Indeed, it has been estimated that the "real" rate of nonwhite teenage unemployment is not 40 but more nearly 80 percent, since "great numbers of young Blacks have simply dropped out of the labor force in despair" (ICP 1975). We may recall that the other category breakdowns are all based on official figures. The real numbers are much higher for these other categories of unemployed as well. The *New York Times,* in an editorial concerning issues in the 1976 election in which American black voters heavily supported Jimmy Carter and gave him the winning margin, observed:

> During the third quarter of 1975, black unemployment rose above 3,000,000 [double the official figure cited above]—counting those workers who are discouraged and no longer looking for a job, because they cannot find full-time employment. This unofficial but accurate picture of black unemployment remained at about 26 per cent during 1975. . . . Cities are also filled with jobless young people whose futures look even more bleak than their pasts, who have no marketable skills, no stake in society, and thus little reason to adhere to prevailing cultural values and norms (IHT 5 April 1976).

The evidence is visible in the crime-ridden, drug-filled nonwhite ghettos, where up to 80 percent of the young compose a permanent army of unemployed.

The situation is not (yet?) as bad in Western Europe, but the pattern and tendencies are similar. Unemployment is greater among blue-collar than among white-collar workers; among registered, not to mention unregistered, women than among male blue-collar workers. Unemployment has grown much more in the formerly labor-exporting countries of Southern Europe— probably to more than one million each in Spain and Portugal—than in the previously labor-importing ones of Northern Europe, and among nonwhite immigrants, especially in Britain and Holland. Most important, unemployment in Europe is very much higher than the average for the young, who cannot find their first or second job, cannot even find apprenticeship, and face unemployment as far as they, the economists, and the politicians can foresee.

The social and political consequences of this unemployment are only just beginning to be generated by the world economic crisis. Moreover, the 1970–1971 and 1973–1975 recessions—and to some extent, except in the United States, the recession of the mid-sixties and the following brief recovery— raised the unemployment rate sharply. The following 1975–1979 recovery did not lower it again to the prerecession level; thus, each recessionary increase of unemployment has taken off from a higher residual unemployment base inherited from the previous recession. Nonetheless, as we shall examine below, economists and politicians—and perhaps the buying and still working general public—still regard inflation, not unemployment, as "the enemy number one."

On the other hand, economists tend to lag behind the times. Sometimes, however, they catch up very quickly; sometimes, the imperatives of capital's interests and the exigencies of its political representatives require economists to fashion new ideological weapons that masquerade under the disguise of scientific economic theory. Then, "fashions in economic thought change with remarkable suddenness," as *Fortune* (September 1976) accurately notes. We may recall that "normal" unemployment in the United States used to be considered 4 percent, though real unemployment tended to be higher. Thus, Milton Friedman—responsible for so much reactionary ideology masquerading as ecoonomic theory, earning him the coveted Nobel Prize—suddenly invents a "natural" rate of unemployment, inevitably a much higher percentage than the earlier "normal" one. "For many years, economists thought that this point was around 4 percent—a figure that got to be called the 'full employment' rate of unemployment. It now turns out that 4 percent is much too low. *In fact, it has been too low for the past twenty-eight years* . . . and has gradually risen to between 5.5 and 6 percent in the last few years" (FOR September 1976: 100. Emphasis in original). Since real unemployment has been even higher, however, a mere 6 percent unemployment still seems "unnatural" to some faithful servants of capital. It is with good reason that the *New York Times* can ask: "How Full Is 'Full Employment'? It used to be 4 percent jobless rate . . . [but] the Conference Board, a business-financed research organization, suggested . . . that an acceptable figure would be 5 percent unemployment. Herbert Stein, who was President Nixon's chief economic adviser, argued in a deliberately provocative article in the Wall Street

Journal a few days ago, that it should be 7 percent" (IHT 4 October 1977). Further, "some economists argue that 8 percent unemployment is now 'normal,' or only slightly above an acceptable rate" (NYT editorial, in IHT 10 November 1976. For further quotations and discussions see Frank 1978d and the remainder of this chapter).

The "scientific" argument behind this discovery of a supposedly old error is that at lower rates of unemployment, spending inevitably leads to inflation. Hence, this new ideological twist functions as a pseudo-scientific defense for the reactionary political policy of reducing expenditures "to fight inflation," and for the priority of inflation over unemployment in general.

We have seen that unemployment rose significantly as a consequence of the 1970–1972 recession, during which profits declined, GNP and industrial production stagnated in some countries—these even declined absolutely though modestly in the United States—and the rate of bankruptcies and other business failures increased. Among such failures were the above-mentioned bankruptcy of Penn Central railroad and the near failure, saved only through emergency bailing out by the U.S. government and the banks, of Lockheed and the Chrysler Corporation. Along with a number of underlying productive and competitive tendencies, the exacerbation of the deficit in the United States balance of payments and then the development of a trade deficit generated the series of world financial crises, beginning in 1971. "Indeed the breakdown of the pegged-rate [currency] system was inevitable, given the way it had been working" (McCracken 1977: 101).

The 1972–1973 Boom and the Oil Crisis

The 1972–1973 boom may be conveniently summarized by quoting the lead sentences of its review in the McCracken report:

> The 1972–73 Boom. Business confidence was rather weak in 1971; an it dropped sharply after . . . the United States measures of 15th August. . . . The rapidity of the upswing . . . was fueled by expansionary monetary policy. . . . The upsurge in food prices arose from a complex of factors. . . . The raw materials boom came a little later. . . . But prices of manufactures also started to rise fast. . . . It is clear that initially the 1972–73 inflationary outburst was attributable to strains in goods markets rather than in labour markets. . . . Two major countries were experimenting with prices and incomes policy at this time. The United States [began in August 1971]. . . . The United Kingdom started in November 1972. . . . Unemployment persisted even at the height of the boom. Thus, the unemployment rate in the United States at the cyclical peak of activity—4.6 per cent—seems to have been at least 1 per cent higher . . . and in several major European countries it was about ½ per cent higher . . . than at the point of comparable demand pressure in the previous business cycle. . . . The theme for our second period seems, in summary, to be the failure of the downturn in

1970–71 to make much impact on increasing inflationary tendencies. . . . Perhaps the most important lesson we draw from this period is the crucial importance of international linkages" (McCracken 1977: 58–65).

The 1973–1973 period brought a very rapid recovery accompanied by various booms. "With the benefit of hindsight we would judge that the shift of policies,particularly monetary policies, in 1971 to settings which were effectively 'all-systems-go' in many countries simultaneously was the most important mishap in recent economic policy history. It contributed to an extremely rapid and synchronized boom" (McCracken 1977: 51). In 1972 there were major elections in the United States, Canada, Germany, Italy, and Japan, and in early 1973 in France. These countries account for about 80 percent of the GNP of all industrialized countries; and in all of them, national governments pursued highly expansionary monetary and fiscal policies to counteract the recession, with a view toward the forthcoming elections. The American deficit made such policies easier to implement both in the United States and in other countries which were "awash with dollars" (McCracken 1977: 52). Nonetheless, "even without the errors of policy induced by the breakdown of the pegged-rate system and the large United States external deficits on current account which accompanied it, there would probably have been a strong upswing in 1972–73" (McCracken 1977: 56).

During the boom, the United States attempted to counteract its deficit and get competitive mileage out of its devaluation of the dollar. (Devaluation had been undertaken in the first place with the following expansion in view.) America then launched a major commercial export drive, particularly of agricultural commodities, no longer restraining agricultural production with quotas or giving away "Food for Peace" (see TW, chapter 2); export of military weapons was also stepped up (see TW, chapter 8). The export of these two commodities, rather than of other industrial goods in which the United States had lost its competitive advantage, jumped to fill the trade gap. At the same time, the Soviet Union and other parts of the world experienced a disastrous crop year, driving the prices of wheat and other crops sky high.

In addition, the short industrial boom drove up prices of raw materials to their highest levels since the Korean war boom. There was a $47 billion increase in world expenditures on raw materials, excluding fuels, during the 1972–1974 price boom; of this amount, $32 billion—or two thirds—accrued to producers in the developed industrial countries, with $20 billion to food and feed producers in the United States and the EEC countries. Only $11 billion, less than one quarter of the gains, accrued to the Third World countries that exported minerals and agricultural raw materials. Even this 35 percent increase in the dollar value of Third World exports only amounted to a 16 percent increase if defaulted by the higher prices of their manufacturing imports; it represented only a 2.5 percent increase if further deflated by the volume and price increases of their commodity imports—mostly food—

during the approximate year and a half of world food shortage (see TW, chapter 2) and commodity price boom (UNCTAD 1974, TDC 174). By 1975, commodity prices had again fallen by 50 percent from their 1972–1974 maximum to their preboom 1970–1972 level.

The other boom, of course, was in petroleum prices. Between January 1970 and October 1973, now all but forgotten, the price of Arab oil increased 70–94 percent, depending on the type of oil and its origin (Sebord 1977: 154). Then, between October 1973 and early 1974, OPEC increased the price of oil another fourfold, bringing the total increase since 1970 to 547–607 percent (Sebord 1977: 154). The reasons for this remarkable price increase with its many worldwide repercussions have been equally widely and still inconclusively discussed. (Some of these ramifications are examined in TW, chapters 3 and 4.) Some argue that the major oil companies, which have certainly benefited vastly, were behind this move in coalition with the oil-producing countries. Others note that the United States government's economic and political position had declined relative to its allies in Western Europe and Japan; America thus deliberately aided and abetted the increase in the price of oil, since the other industrial countries import much more than does the United States with its own supplies. In fact, since 1974 American hegemony over Western Europe has increased again, manifest through numerous international conflicts and discussions between the United States and its allies in recent years.

Others argue that although both Presidents Nixon and Carter have made efforts to reduce American dependence on imported oil, the share of imports in American consumption and resulting drain on the country's balance of payments have in fact increased significantly; this price increase therefore cannot be in the American interest. On the other hand, it was Henry Kissinger himself who insisted that there must be a minimum floor under the price of oil, such that its price would make profitable the exploration and production of more expensive offshore and shale oil, as well as the development of alternative sources of energy from coal, nuclear power, the sun, and so forth. Profitable it has been, though not yet to the extent perhaps hoped for in 1974–1975; the general rate of profit must also rise enough to make massive new energy technology and investments profitable. This has not happened—yet.

It is also argued that the strengthening of OPEC and the petroleum price rise constitute either the cause or the consequence—or both—of a new drive by the Third World to establish a New International Economic Order (NIEO) where it would occupy a more privileged role and place. Our doubts about this thesis are expressed in our discussion of NIEO and its prospects in chapter 5. After the price of oil was raised to about $12 a barrel in 1974, its real value was eroded again by inflation and the devaluation of the dollar to approximately $7—that is, the price floor proposed by Mr. Kissinger. The price was subsequently increased again to $24—worth about $11.50 in 1972 dollars (as FT 18 December 1979 points out)—and then to $30 and more in 1979. However, one thing is certain. The higher price of oil has brought only very limited benefits to the populations of the oil-exporting countries of the Third World (TW, chapters 3 and 4); it has brought considerable additional costs for the oil-importing Third World countries and their populations, which are in the vast majority (TW, chapter 4). On the other hand, capital in the industrial countries has made very handsome profits from its exports to the *nouveau riche* oil-exporting countries (which now buy more West European exports than does the United States). The OPEC financeial surpluses (limited to four OPEC members) are now "recycled" back into the metropolitan banks and through them into their and other Third World economies (TW, chapter 4). All in all, the real impact of the OPEC increase of the price of oil represents more sound and fury than substance.

The 1973–1975 Recession

Meanwhile, the "oil crisis" became the convenient scapegoat for the real crisis, and particularly for the renewed cyclical recession beginning in 1973. Business, labor, governments, politicians, publicists, and the public everywhere blamed all their troubles on the Arab "oil sheiks"; the Arab headdress became a symbol of evil, making the rounds of political cartoons and masquerade balls. This political masking of the real crisis and its causes continued for nearly two years into 1975 before the hard evidence, particularly of steeply rising unemployment, obliged some statesmen to tell people the truth of the matter. (Some economist ideologues still repeat their scapegoat litany about the oil and food crises.)

For our part, as early as 1972 we already argued that "since 1970 but with roots that go back earlier, there exists a new system wide crisis of capital accumulation in the imperialist camp"; and in 1974 we continued "to insist that the crisis was much deeper and had another origin, and that the petroleum crisis was just another consequence, and not the cause, of the general crisis" (Frank 1977c). Indeed, we pointed out that even the 1973 cyclical recession had begun *before* the oil price increase in October. In view of the many contrary claims by responsible statesmen throughout that period, it is welcome if belated news that the "independent experts" of the McCracken Commission now write: "We have suggested that 1974 was likely to be a recession year even without the oil crisis," and "a big rise in the oil prices was no doubt 'in the cards'" (McCracken 1977: 70, 101). Interestingly enough, the report suggests that the recession began in 1974, when in fact it began in the summer of 1973 in the United States, Germany, Britain, and even in the usual laggard, France.

 The 1973–1975 recession, by far the deepest, longest, and most universal of the postwar period so far, began during the second or third quarter of 1973. The three most important features of this recession—low investment and high unemployment as well as inflation—have, however, persisted until the present, and are destined to continue into the foreseeable future. This scenario is all the more likely as another recession has begun.

Gross national product had been growing at rates averaging 2½ percent during the last quarter of 1972 and the first quarter of 1973 in the major industrial countries—the United States, Canada, Britain, France, Germany, Italy, and Japan (ranging from 2.1 percent in the United States to 3.6 percent, and 4.8 percent in the first quarter of 1973, in Japan). In the second quarter of 1973 the GNP growth rate suddenly dropped to 0.1 percent in the United States, to 0.0 percent in Germany, to −1.8 percent in Britain, and only 1.4 percent in Japan, for an average of 0.4 percent in the seven major industrial countries. Very slight recoveries in some countries, along with a further decline to a growth rate of 0.1 percent in Japan, left the overall GNP growth rate in all seven countries at little more than 0.5 percent annually for the three quarters from April to December 1973. In the first quarter of 1974 GNP began an *absolute decline* of −1 percent in the United States and −0.8 percent for all seven countries. This decline accelerated to rates of −1.9 percent for the Unied States and −1.3 percent for the seven countries in the last quarter of 1974, and −2.4 percent and −2.0 percent respectively in the first quarter of 1975. Therefore, after decelerating growth in three quarters of 1973, GNP declined absolutely during six quarters of 1974 and 1975 in the industrial countries. Over the entire recession, GNP declined about 9 percent in the industrial countries as a whole (*IPW Forschungshefte* 2,1976: 20), and 8 percent in the United States alone (WK December 1975: 12). The GNP loss, in the seven major industrial countries plus Holland and Sweden, comparing actual with potential output as estimated by the OECD, was about 2 percent in the last half of 1973, about 5.5 percent in 1974, 10 percent in 1975, and still over 8 percent in 1976 (McCracken 1977: 339).

Industrial production declined very much more than GNP. In 1975 alone industrial production declined about 5 percent. Counting from the previous peak to the 1975 trough, in sixteen OECD countries production declined 10 percent or more. In nine of these countries the decline was more than 15 percent and in four of them it exceeded 20 percent. The absolute decline of industrial production in the three most important industrial capitalist countries amounted to −13.8 percent in the United States, −12.7 percent in West Germany, and −22.8 percent in Japan. In France, Italy, Belgium, and Switzerland, industrial production declined between 16 and 19 percent, according to the West German *Wirtschaftskonjunktur* (WK December 1975). (The East German *IPW Forschungshefte* 2, 1976, makes somewhat lower estimates of decline from the previous peak: −13.1 percent for the United States, −10.7 percent for West Germany, −19.9 percent for Japan, −14.8 percent for Italy, and −11.9 percent for France.) The lowest rates of decline were registered in Britain (−9.2 percent according to WK, −9.0 percent according to IPW), perhaps because generally depressed Britain had hardly experienced any boom in 1972 and hence had less far to fall. These absolute declines of industrial production are graphically reflected in the deviations from "long-term trend" in Graph 2-2, which also shows that this coordinated sharp decline of production is unprecedented in recent history.

The 1975/76 GATT report offers a more global perspective:

Economic developments in 1975 [and 1974] were shaped by the deepest recession of the post-war period in the industrial countries, the effects of which were felt only with a time-lag in other parts of the world. . . . Total world production (excluding services and construction), which had increased by only 3 per cent in 1974—as compared with the record of 8.5 per cent in 1973 and 5 per cent annual average during the 1960s—declined in 1975 by about 2 per cent. This decline, the first since the 1930s, resulted entirely from the fall of about 6 per cent in production in the developing countries. . . . The largest declines in world output in 1975 were in mining and manufacturing, which fell by 4 and 5 per cent respectively. . . . In the developing areas and the Eastern [socialist] trading area output continued to grow, by some 2 and 5 per cent, respectively, both rates being markedly lower than in the preceding year (GATT 1976: 1).

World trade measured in dollar unit values increased 25 percent in 1973 and 40 percent (with some help from higher petroleum prices) in 1974, but only 10 percent in 1975. The dollar value of world exports increased 5 percent in 1975, but when adjusted for inflation, the real volume of exports *fell* by 5 percent. Imports of the industrial countries declined 8 percent in volume (GATT 1976: 3–4). OECD overall exports fell by 6 percent in 1975; their exports to OPEC countries increased 60 percent, but actual trade among the OECD countries themselves declined by a full 13 percent (McCracken 1977: 72). A time lag tended to slow the more far-reaching effects on the industrial world. The advanced countries maintained their exports and world trade in 1974, and were still able to export heavily— indeed more than ever—to the socialist countries and the Third World, where production and import demand remained stable through that year. (The importance of such trade for maintaining Western and world production and trade during the recession and the subsequent "recovery" of trade with the socialist countries is examined below in chapter 4 and of trade with the Third World in chapter 5). In 1975, however, the entire world—"first," "second," and "third"—was hit by the deepest, longest, and most universal recession to date in the contemporary capitalist crisis of capital accumulation: and the first world also reduced its imports from the other two.

This crisis and recession manifested themselves very notably in the realms of prices, employment, and investment.

Inflation skyrocketed to over three times the earlier rate, from an average of 5 percent per year in the OECD countries—and 4 percent in its seven major ones—in 1972–1973, to 13.5 in both groups of countries in 1974. In some of these counties inflation reached much higher rates still: over 24 percent in Japan, 19 percent in Italy, and 14 percent in Britain (OECD EO December 1975: 113). McCracken (1977: 70) refers to peaks of 30 percent inflation in Japan and Britain. It became popular to blame the OPEC oil price increase for this spurt in inflation, although the weight of oil and its additional price in the "basket" of all goods could make only a very small impact on the general price index of goods. Indeed, it could be argued that by initially drawing purchasing power out of producer and consumer hands and temporarily concentrating and sterilizing it in Arab hands, the oil price hike was in fact deflationary. This analysis, incidentally, forms an essential part of the argument that the oil price rise was responsible for the recession.

Referring to similar events in late 1978 and 1979, GATT writes: "The evidence forecloses the dangerously wrong view that the petroleum price increase was a major causative factor behind the resurgence of inflation and the expected rise in unemployment" (GATT 1979b.)

In 1975 the rate of inflation receded slightly to about 10 percent for the OECD area and its seven major countries (but rose in Britain). This derived from the decline in demand pressure, due more to the 1975 recession itself than to any success of anti-inflationary monetary and fiscal measures. Nonetheless, professional economists as well as working and consuming people everywhere noted with bewilderment that prices continued to rise at the same time that unemployment was growing to proportions unknown and hardly remembered since the Great Depression of the 1930s.

We may recall (as Table 2-3 shows) that unemployment grew during the 1970–1972 recession to a level over 50 percent above that in the 1960s: from under 3 million to nearly 5 million in the United States, from 1.9 million to 2.6 million in Western Europe (EEC), and from under 6 million to nearly 9 million in the OECD countries (excluding Spain and Turkey) as a whole. The short 1973 recovery reduced the latter total again by only about half a million, most of it accounted for by a decline of unemployment to 5 percent in the United States. European unemployment remained near its prerecovery recession level, at a modest 2.5 percent. The 1973–1975 recession sharply raised this level by over 50–100 percent. Unemployment rose from 4.3 million or 4.9 percent to 8.6 million or 8.5 percent—and to a maximum of 9.2 percent in May 1975—in the United States. It rose from about 2.6 million or 2.5 percent to about 4.5 million or 4.4 percent in Europe (EEC) and from 8.3 million to 15.2 million or 5.5 percent in the OECD countries as a whole. Again, these estimates are based on official figures, and real unemployment—as suggested above on pages 62–65—undoubtedly rose up to one and one half times the amount indicated.

In some countries, unemployment increased even more sharply, from 1.1 perent in 1972 to 4.4 percent in 1975 in Germany, for example, and even more after 1975, not counting the foreign immigrant workers who returned home. Fifteen million officially registered unemployed workers, on the average supporting a family of four including themselves, actually translate as 60 million people in the industrialized countries directly affected by unemployment. This number at least equals the population of any of the major West European countries. Since real unemployment has been very much higher in actuality, the number of people directly affected amounts to the combined populations of one of the major and several of the smaller European countries put together. Unemployment on this scale had not only been unknown, but had come to be considered as completely impossible since the Great Depression.

Moreover, these levels of unemployment have not turned out to be temporary, but are now apparently structural and persistent in many countries. A cyclical pattern in the growth of persistent unemployment had established itself from recession to recovery in the earlier recessions of the contemporary crisis; this pattern returned with a vengeance in the 1973–1975 recession and 1975–1978 recovery. During the recovery, unemployment declined in the United States, but remained above 7 percent in 1976, fell to 6 percent for part of 1978, and reached a floor of about 5.5 percent in 1979 before rising again. Elsewhere, however, officially recorded unemployment continued to increase during the recovery to over 8 percent in Canada, over 6 million or 5.7 percent in the EEC—and 7 million in all of Europe—and to 1.3 million or 2.4 percent in Japan. These increases in unemployment more than compensated for the decline in the United States, such that total

TABLE 2-9
Discomfort Index
(in seven major industrial countries)

	1 Unemployment percent	2 Inflation percent	3 (= 1 + 2) Discomfort Index
1959–1963	3.2 - 3.8	1.2 - 2.3	5.0 - 5.5
1964	2.9	2.0	4.9
1965	2.7	2.6	5.3
1966	2.5	3.2	5.7
1967	2.8	2.8	5.6
1968	2.7	4.0	6.7
1969	2.6	4.9	7.5
1970	3.1	5.6	8.7
1971	3.7	5.0	8.7
1972	3.7	4.4	8.1
1973	3.2	7.7	10.9
1974	3.7	13.4	17.1
1975	5.4	11.1	16.6
1976	5.3	8.1	13.4

Source: McCracken 1977: 42. The index range for 1959–63 is taken from the sum of the unemployment and inflation rates for each individual year, and not from their ranges that are summarized here.

unemployment in the OECD countries *rose during the recovery* to 16.3 million or 5.4 percent in the second half of 1977. The ILO figures, which include the Mediterranean countries of Europe, indicate an official total of 17.1 million unemployed in North America, Western Europe, Japan, and Oceania in 1977. The discomforting simultaneity of unemployment and inflation has given rise to the invention of the "discomfort index," which is the sum of both. "The 'discomfort index' represents a shorthand technique which highlights, in terms of the central dilemma facing economic policy-makers, the deterioration of economic performances in recent years. It is of course a crude indicator" (McCracken 1977: 42n).

This "crude indicator" suggests that discomfort fluctuated around an index of 5 in the early 1960s and about 6 to 7 in the late 1960s. Then, the index rose to about 8-9 in the 1970–1972 recession, and increased to 11 in the 1973 recovery boom, which registered a new high in inflation. Then, during the 1974–1975 recession, the index jumped up to 17 before it declined again, but still remained above its previous peak in the following years.

Interestingly enough, the "discomfort index" fell during the deepest period of the last recession, with maximum unemployment in 1975 and in 1976—unemployment failed to recede during the recovery; and the rate of inflation had declined more than the rate of unemployment had risen. In this regard, the "discomfort index" is not at all crude, but rather, a good reflection of the discomfort of the economists and economic policy makers who invented the index. For these economists, inflation is public enemy number one, and far more discomforting than unemployment. In their view, unemployment has graduated from being merely normal to being natural as well; for business and certain politicians, unemployment has become not only natural, but downright desirable. This being so, economists have had to catch up with the times.

Excess Capacity and Lagging Investment in the 1975–1979 "Recovery"

The real causes for the employment and unemployment of labor lie in the utilization or underutilization of productive capacity, and in the amount and kind of new productive investment. Additionally, political/economic policies of government, particularly in and through "improductive" service sectors, also influence employment. Low rates of productive capacity utilization—seen also as high rates of underutilization or excess capacity of production—and low rates of investment in both recessions *and* "recoveries" have become increasingly common during this new capitalist crisis of (over)accumulation of capital. Indeed, this weakness in the utilization of existing capacity and the consequent reluctance to invest in the expansion of new productive capacity are the principal marks of all capitalist crises of overaccumulation.

The OECD recently devoted a "Special Section [to] capacity utilization in manufacturing," since this has become a major issue:

Although difficult to measure accurately, the level of capacity utilisation in manufacturing is extensively used as one of the factors
explaining the behavior of a wide range of significant macro-economic
variables including prices, productivity, investment and output. . . .
Inherent in all concepts of capacity is an often unspecified idea of
normal operating conditions. . . . The variety of techniques used to
measure capacity utilisation—surveys, production functions, input-
output ratios, output peaks—and the lack of uniformity in the frequency of capacity estimations further compound the difficulties arising
from differences in definition (EO July 1977: 35).

In one word, estimates of capacity utilization, underutilization, or excess
capacity are hard to come by and even more difficult to rely on. This OECD
analytical discussion does not, however, provide any data on capacity utilization. Table 2-10 presents some estimates assembled (not very satisfactorily, as the notes to the table explain) from other OECD sources.

Ernest Mandel cites the following figures for production in manufacturing
as a percent of installed capacity in the United States: 1966–92, 1967–88,

TABLE 2-10
Manufacturing Capacity Utilization
(in percent)

	1964–73	1974	1975	1976	1977	1978	1979, first quarter
United States	85	80–70	70–66	80	82	84	86
Canada	89	93–86	86–83	82	83	86	90
Germany	86	85–78	78–75	80	81	81	83
France	82	85–78	78–69	83	83	84	84
Italy	78	78–72	72–68	74	73	73	76
Japan	96	98–82	82–77	84	84	86	92
Britain	45	50–30	40–20	25	32	35	38

Notes and Sources: For 1964–1973, 1976–1979 (first quarter) from OECD
Economic Outlook, July 1979: 25. For 1974 and 1975 from OECD *Main Economic Indicators,* April 1978: 129–146, using charts on cyclical indicators and
entering in the table first the yearly high and then the yearly low point on the graphs
for capacity utilization (in order better to reflect the 1974–1975 recessionary decline).
The OECD's data are from the respective country sources, which use different
definitions and measures of capacity utilization. For Britain throughout the measure is
the percentage of firms operating at full capacity and is not at all comparable with the
other measures, which in one way or another reflect the percentage of installed
capacity or technically potential output that is actually used or produced. (Curiously,
but perhaps not accidentally, none of the standard OECD statistical sources give
capacity utilization figures for the years 1974 and 1975.)

1968–88, 1969–87, 1970–78, 1971–75, 1972–79, 1973–83, 1974–78 (ICP 16 January 1975: 7). The excess capacity that is standing idle, unused, or underutilized is the difference between these figures and a rate of 100 percent utilization—8 percent in 1966 and 22 percent in 1974. The editors of *Monthly Review* cite 25 percent of manufacturing capacity as unused in 1975 (and in some industries, over 35 percent) in the United states, but argue that if existing capacity were used at maximum rates as utilized during World War II, then real capacity utilization in 1975 would have been more nearly 50 percent (MR April 1976: 1,8). For 1976, manufacturing capacity utilization in the United States was 82, 77, or 74 percent, according to different sources cited by Mandel (IPC 11 November 1976). Of course, if a very substantial share of installed productive capacity were not used for military production, the underutilization rate would be much higher still. For 1977:

> Highly unreliable figures have become even more questionable . . . the figures are terribly slippery. Officials may be right that factories are operating, on the average, at 80 per cent of capacity. But they may be wrong, too. The true rate could be many percentage points higher or lower than 80 per cent. . . . A recent sampling found that various operating-rates estimates range from a low of 67 per cent to a high of 86 per cent (IHT 12–13 March 1977).

Two important trends and patterns—paralleling those we have found in regard to unemployment—emerge from these figures, however inaccurate they may be in detail. One is the apparent increasing tendency of manufacturing capacity to stand idle in the decade since the mid-1960s. The other pattern is that, after the utilization rate had naturally fallen during each recession, the succeeding recovery did not again raise capacity utilization to the previous prerecession high. A residual underutilization of plant—and corresponding residual unemployment of labor—remained in each recovery, thus reinforcing the tendency of capacity to remain idle. This increasing tendency toward residual excess capacity already appeared in the 1968–1969 recovery, where the utilization rate remained almost stable, and in the 1972–1973 boom, during which the utilization rate remained 5 percentage points below the previous high. It happened again in the recovery after the 1973–1975 recession at least through 1978, before the apparently brief increase in utilization rates in late 1978 and early 1979.

The McCracken report (1977: 158 and passim) remarks on the "low levels of capacity utilization" in the OECD area as a whole; and the OECD notes with respect to the present recovery:

> The enormous amount of slack built up in the OECD area since the beginning of the downturn will not start being reabsorbed over the forecast period: the margin of unused resources would at best stabilize in the course of 1976. To put the present degree of slack in perspective . . . OECD economies could, on average, expand at something

like 6% a year until the end of the decade before regaining high employment conditions (EO December 1975: 20).

In fact, during the "recovery" OECD economies have grown at about half that rate; and the slack has not been stabilized, much less reabsorbed. Particularly hard hit has been the steel industry, but also the steel-using shipbuilding industry, which entered a severe crisis of overproduction and excess capacity in 1974. This trend continued through 1978, and promises to persist for some time to come. Thus, the London *Financial Times,* for instance, headlined: "The steel industry world demand begins to slacken off" (29 July 1974); "Western steel near stagnation" (22 January 1975); "Decline 'without parallel' last year, but record steel output expected" (27 January 1975); "The crisis in steel" (3 April 1975); " 'Gloomy year' for EEC steel" (9 April 1975); "The French steel industry. A deep depression" (19 November 1976). Still two years after the "recovery" began, the *New York Times* (23 May 1977) reported: "From Lancashire in Britain through Belgium and the French Lorraine to the German industrial heartland of the Ruhr, Europe's steelmakers are now experiencing their worst crisis in living memory" (cited in MR November 1977: 3). EEC steel production in 1978 "was still 15 percent below the production levels enjoyed in Europe pre-1974" (FT 7 February 1979); "Steel recession entering sixth year, producers say" (IHT 23 May 1979).

The same is true also in the United States and in Japan. In America, *working* steel mills have been operating at about 75 percent of capacity, even after some of the biggest American steel companies closed down several of their plants altogether during the "recovery." After three years of recovery, steel production in 1977 in the United States, EEC, and Japan put together was still 13 percent below its 1973 peak, and at least 6 percent below it in 1978. In the United States steel output remained below its 1965 level, before the contemporary crisis had begun (MR November 1977: 2–7). Japanese steel production has dropped by more than 30 percent, and one third of its blast furnaces have been idle (HOL 18 December 1977). According to the EEC, in 1977 steel production as a percent or capacity was 59 percent in West Germany, 68 in Italy, 66 percent in France, 70 percent in Britain, and 59 percent in the Benelux countries, amounting to 64 percent in the EEC as a whole. The number of steelworkers declined from 760,000 in December 1975 to 704,000 in January 1978 (FR 12 July 1978).

This "depression" and "recession" in the industrialized countries' steel industry occurred during the general economic recession and subsequent recovery. With the renewed decline into another recession in 1979–1980, the Western—including Japanese—steel industry is faced with a complete tailspin. "Steelworkers [have been] laid off in Northern France," and "British Steel plans to axe 52,000 jobs . . . [or] as high as 60,000— . . . the loss of a third or more of the workforce . . . to reduce liquid steel output" in the face of a £300 million loss last year (FT 1 December 1979). In the meantime, however, steel production has been increasing in the socialist countries and the Third World.

Unused excess productive capacity naturally discourages industry from investing to expand capacity still further. Accordingly, low investment and the failure to recover during "recoveries" are major characteristics of this crisis, like all others. The McCracken report (1977: 158) notes "the weakness of the recovery of investment demand already during the 1972–1973 boom." However, even this weak investment recovery became the high watermark, albeit a low one, of investment since then. During the 1973–1975 recession, investment of course declined again, in some cases very drastically. More significant still, investment has again failed to recover in the "recovery" since this deepest of postwar recessions. This investment gap below the previous trendline is clearly illustrated in Graph 2-3.

In the United States, capital expenditures for fixed investment (measured in constant 1972 dollars) reached a peak of $193 billion in the first quarter of 1973 and fell to a trough of $149 billion in the second quarter of 1975. After two years of "recovery," capital investment still amounted to only $184 billion, 5 percent below the previous peak (MR November 1977: 8). The volume of nonresidential fixed investment declined 2 percent in 1974 and 13 percent in 1975, while residential construction declined 25 percent in 1974 and then a further 15 percent below that in the following year (SCB). The modest increase in nonresidential, and even the larger one of residential fixed investment in 1976 and 1977, as well as a brief spurt of investment in late 1978, did not recover previous rates of expansion and, of course, were not able to fill the gaping hole left by the large recessionary decline. In Europe, the situation was similar. In the United States, surplus capacity installed during the boom years of the 1960s has discouraged large-scale capital investment since then, as have low profit levels and high prices for capital goods.

> There was a sharp decline in capital spending during the most recent recession and only a sluggish pickup since then. The drop in such spending during the latest recession was almost 18 per cent, the sharpest in the postwar period, while the upturn in the first year of the recovery was a mere 0.3 per cent. . . . And no one disputes the fact that capital spending for new capacity has not increased during this economic recovery period—to this point at least—by the same degree that it usually does after a recession (IHT 9 August 1976).

At the end of 1975, the OECD observed and predicted for its member countries in general:

> The weakness of the recovery and uncertainties regarding the future course of final demand are expected to make for a particularly poor performance of business fixed investment. . . . In the current cycle, business investment is expected to stop falling only towards the end of

GRAPH 2-3

The Real Growth of Nonresidential Fixed Investment*
Annual and quarterly indices: 1970 = 100 (semi-logarithmic scale)

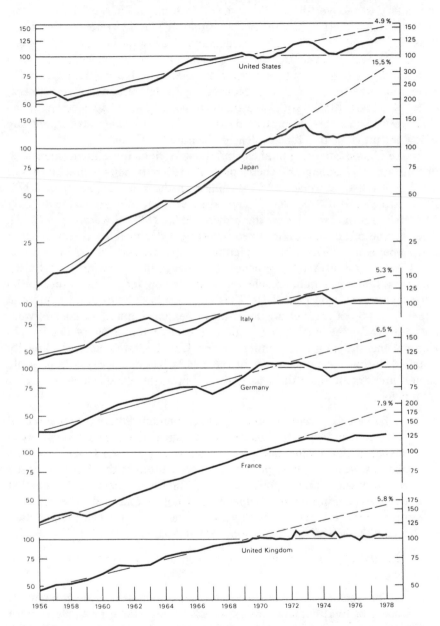

Note: Includes public-sector investment. Trend lines relate to the years 1955–1973.

Source: Bank for International Settlements 1979: 28.

1976. Even with some recovery in profits, the low rates of capacity utilisation, possibly less easy monetary policy, and the high cost of capital replacement may well discourage additions to capacity. . . . In Japan, business investment is forecast to be running at a rate of about 20 per cent below the last peak, with no significant pickup expected. . . . In Europe, productive investment is forecast to continue falling in 1976 in spite of measures of support in France and Germany (EO December 1975: 28–29).

These somber expectations were fulfilled by the 1976 "recovery." *Business Week* observed on 14 September 1976 under the title "Where is the Capital Spending Boom?":

In the US capital spending is still running some 9% below the peak reached more than 2½ years ago, in the second half of 1973. In Japan capital spending is some 24% below the rate of this late 1973 period. In the four major countries of Western Europe—Germany, Britain, France and Italy—the shortfall is some 11%. And if the US seems to be mounting the most successful capital spending recovery of any of the advanced countries, growth in it is still slower this year than in any of the five earlier postwar recoveries (cited in IPC 11 November 1976: 6).

This lag of investment recovery behind and below what had been usual in previous postwar recoveries—that is, during the long expansionary upswing and at the beginning of the new crisis of accumulation—has continued. The McCracken report notes that in 1977,

the problem of a deceleration in investment has extended for several years (particularly in the United States, Germany, Italy, the United Kingdom and the Netherlands). It is difficult at this stage of the cycle to determine how serious the past short-fall in investment has been, but the OECD Secretariat has calculated that if productive investment had grown between 1971 and 1976 at the same rate as between 1965 and 1970, the capacity output from the resultant capital stock would have been roughly 5 per cent higher in 1976 for the seven major OECD countries combined (McCracken 1977: 160–161).

In 1977, the EEC still noted "the lack of buoyancy of fixed investment, the volume of which has been below the peak of three years ago. Capital spending is again inhibited by poor profitability and by uncertainty" (IHT 12–13 March 1977). Later in 1977, the EEC Commission observed that "slow growth cannot generate the investment flows needed to restore and develop productive capacity in the medium-term. . . . This year, the share of capital spending in the EEC's GNP will probably be under 21 percent while it should reach about 23 percent under the EEC program for a better employment situation by the end of this decade" (IHT 16 September 1977).

In fact, investment is nowhere near this goal. Although capital investment, adjusted for inflation, in 1977 increased 8 percent, Administration economists note sadly that this spending was concentrated on such short-lived equipment as cars and trucks, rather than on machinery and plant. More worrisome, most private forecasters expect capital investment this year to increase by only 6% to 7%, even with an expanded investment tax credit retroactive to the start of the year. And even this may be optimistic, since the latest Commerce Dept. survey of investment plans shows a 4.5% increase for the year (BW 23 January 1978).

Under the title "The Economic Outlook for 1978," the December 1977 semiannual OECD review and forecast still observes:

> Trends in . . . particularly business fixed investment have also been hesitant. . . . The prospects for a significant boost from productive investment remain poor. Lack of confidence concerning future sales prospects and low levels of capacity use have served to keep business capital outlays weak in most countries. In general measures to stimulate investment have not put investment and overall expansion on a self-sustaining course (EO Dec 1977: 3,23).

However, there was a "surprisingly strong outturn in the second half of last year [1978], the strongest of the present upswing. The causes of the under-estimate of the strength of investment in the last *Economic Outlook* may . . . to some extent be found in special factors, but in part, there was a straightforward failure to detect the underlying buoyancy of private business investment . . . encouraged by rising capacity utilization rates . . . [and] helped by strong rises in profits" (EO July 79: 22–23). Nonetheless, *Business Week* (2 October 1978) reports, "Capital spending: Going nowhere in '79," and a McGraw-Hill Publications Economics Department survey of American companies predicted that "capital spending by business in the U.S. is likely to fall next year [1979] and in 1980 in real terms" (FT 6 November 1978). By the second half of 1979, investment did begin a renewed decline.

It may be remarked in passing that all this excess capacity and these poor prospects for investment give the lie to the supposed impediment to investment through lack of investible funds often bemoaned by business and its press. Far from suffering a "capital crisis" of 4 trillion nonexisting dollars of credit, as *Business Week* (22 September 1975) and other business spokesmen frequently argue, both private and business savings have risen enormously during and since the recession, and banks are having trouble finding creditworthy borrowers. The "capital crisis" thesis is largely an ideological "money veil" covering the real crisis of capitalism and, of course, an appeal to get more capital through higher profits. Moreover, in the short run, there is no reason to believe that increased profits would necessarily flow into more productive investment. Profits can also flow into speculative financial "investments," capital flight, "rationalizing" investment, or simply into consumption, as the increase in luxury demands of yachts and the like suggests.

Beyond the low rate of investment, its place and type are important determinants of economic activity, including employment. "In the 1970s, it seems probable that exchange rate movements have had a depressive impact on investment activity in Germany (as well as the Netherlands, Switzerland and Austria) and encouraged a shift to capital-deepening by effectively raising the real wage" (McCracken 1977: 159). High relative wages prevailed in these countries, not so much because real wages rose as because their currencies appreciated in value relative to others and particularly to the dollar. This has indeed led to more investment in productive plant and equipment elsewhere in an attempt to reduce costs of production. Moreover, the decline of the dollar has made foreign investment in the United States attractive, particularly for German capital arriving with highly valued marks. Canadian, European, and Japanese investment in the United States have risen sharply in recent years (FR 8 April 1976, 4 October 1977; *Der Spiegel* No. 52, December 1978; NYT 30 July 1979; SCB August 1978). "Karl Otto Pöhl, vice president of the Bundesbank says ... prospects for higher profitability are inducing West German companies to "shift capacity" to other countries, especially the United States, spurred by 'turbulence' in foreign exchange markets that make goods produced in West Germany less competitive in world markets. There has been a 'big flow' of investment capital, measured in hundreds of millions of dollars, from the country...." (IHT 18 March 1978).

Of course, European, Japanese, and also American investments have also shifted significantly to the Third World (see TW, chapter 3) and to the socialist countries (see chapter 4 below). To some extent, this investment serves to shift existing productive capacity (closing down old plants and opening up new ones); this trend on the part of the industrialized countries, with so many investments abroad instead of at home, reduces real or potential employment in the capitalist sector from which this foreign investment comes. Moreover, goods are "banned at home—but exported" (BW 12 June 1978) to circumvent domestic consumer safety regulations; and to "avoid U.S. safety [and] pollution rules 'dirty' industries export plant.... Many hazardous and polluting U.S. industries are 'exporting' manufacturing operations to Third World countries to avoid high cost of worker and environmental protection standards in the United States and other industrialized nations" (IHT 30 June 1978). This is a particularly dominant pattern between Japan and Southeast Asia.

To name another and related measure to reduce costs of production, with still more far-reaching impact on employment in the industrial economies: "rationalizing" investments produce the same amount of goods with lower (labor) costs, but do not expand the capacity to produce more goods.

There does seem to have been a fall in the share of investment going to extensions of capacity and a corresponding increase in replacement investment. Because of the low rate of return on capital there is not enough investment; and what investment takes place is mainly directed to saving labour and reducing costs rather than expanding capacity and providing additional jobs. As cyclical unemployment falls, a more persistent form of structural unemployment will, on this view, emerge, because of a mismatch between the stock of capital and the supply of labour" (McCracken 1977: 159,24).

Business investment in 1977 had barely reattained its 1973 peak, which, we may recall, was itself a low peak resulting from the "weak" 1972–1973 investment recovery; further, of the little investment made during this past half decade, much has been "replacement investment," and has "rationalized" jobs away. Thus, in West Germany new investments for expansion of productive capacity have fallen drastically, and have given way to investments for rationalization and replacement as shown in Table 2-11.

TABLE 2-11
New and Rationalization Investment in West German Industry
(in percent)

	Expansion	Rationalization	Replacement
1970	55	34	11
1971	45	38	17
1972	40	42	18
1973	41	42	17
1974	36	43	21
1975	22	54	24
1976	12	58	30
1977	15	49	36
1978	17	47	36

Source: Deutscher Bundestag, Drucksache 7/5902, Bonn 1976; Rationalisierung and Mitbestimmung (Hg.IG Chemie), Hannover 1976; Handelsblatt, Düsseldorf, 8 Nov 1977. Cited in IPW 1978. Many replacement investments also have rationalizing components.

Correspondingly, there has been an increasing number of strikes to protect jobs that industry is trying to rationalize away; but with high business costs, low profits, and high unemployment, labor is not in a very good position to bargain on this score. Moreover, business makes appeals for support to the general public, arguing that "labor is trying to stop progress." Various estimates suggest that half or more of the jobs that have been lost in recent years have been sacrificed to the progress of these rationalizing investments within each of the major industrial economies.

On the other hand, the growth of real expenditures for research and development (R&D) in the United States, which still accounts for nearly half of the OECD total, grew at the rate of 12 percent per year between 1953 and 1964 and only 3 percent per year between 1964 and 1971. Between 1971 and 1975, however, expenditures on R&D stopped growing altogether (McCracken 1977: 147). The share of R&D expenditures in GNP has fallen from 3 percent in 1964 to 2 percent in 1978 (OECD 1979: 23). The industrial capitalist countries' output in the machine tool industry—which is a particularly significant component and sensitive reflection of investment—still declined in 1976, and rose in real terms by only 2–3 percent in 1977. "In most of Western Europe's industrial nations, the demand for machine tools remained light owing to the continued lack of capital spending, especially in the capital goods industries" (UBS Industry Studies, Machine Tool Industry, June 1978). Capital or investment goods are supplied maninly by industry—and significantly by the construction industry, which has also been in the doldrums in part for the same lack of spending. Low investment has, of course, also contributed significantly to keeping industrial output low. Through 1977, to the extent that industrial production recovered at all, the recovery was based on demand derived from sectors other than that of capital goods.

Only in 1978, beginning especially in the second half of the year and in part continuing on into the beginning of 1979, was there some recovery in private investment. Such investment contributed more dynamically than did consumer spending to the prolongation of the recovery.

This and other developments in 1978 were quite contrary to OECD and other "expert" expectations:

> Economic growth in the world's non-Communist industrialized nations next year [1978] is expected to be well below previous expectations. . . . The experts reportedly expect an overall growth rate of 4 per cent or less from the OECD area as a whole next year, compared with 5 per cent targeted at a ministerial meeting last June. The sharp downturn is expected to be pronounced in the second half of 1978, when the growth rate of the gross national product is likely to settle at an annual rate of about 3 per cent, the sources said (IHT 19 November 1977).

Instead, in the first half of 1978 the growth of GNP remained broadly unchanged from late 1977 at a 3.5 percent annual rate in the OECD area as a whole and at 4 percent in the seven major countries (EO December 1978). Then:

> The earlier situation of fast growth of demand in the United States but slower growth in most other countries, which characterized the two years to mid 1978, has changed in three important respects. First, a generalized acceleration of GNP growth occurred in the second half of

last year [1978]. . . . In the United States, private consumption grew rapidly. . . . In Japan, strongly expansionary fiscal policy. . . . In Germany, unexpected large declines in import prices led to higher real wages, and profits also rose, as only part of the price decline was passed on. . . . The OECD area as a whole experienced a terms-of-trade gain which probably added a full percentage point to the rate of growth of area income. . . . Second, the latter part of last year saw the strongest recovery of private nonresidential investment since the 1974–1975 recession . . . influenced by increasing capacity utilization and higher profits. . . . Third, the geographical pattern of the demand expansion has changed markedly. Domestic demand is now expanding much faster in Japan, Germany, and some other OECD countries than in the United States (EO July 1979: 17–19).

Therefore, the United States economy, which had experienced a much stronger recovery from mid-1975 to mid-1978 than the other OECD economies, is now much more threatened and exposed to the aggravation of another recession than are Japan and the major European economies. The exception would be ever-sick Britain, where the more recently expansive recovery remains more resistant to another recession. The development of another recession is examined below.

Before we discuss another recession, it is important to review some essential elements in—and reasons for—the long recovery in the industrial capitalist countries since 1975, as seen from a worldwide perspective. In a review of "the main features of 1976/77," GATT observes:

In the industrial countries, the recovery of demand was due essentially to a rise of roughly 2½ per cent in private consumption, substantial [inventory] restocking, and a rise of about 11 per cent in the volume of exports. . . . Compared with the previous peak in 1973, the rise in world output stemmed directly from the increase of industrial and agricultural output in developing countries, of industrial output in the Eastern trading area, and of agricultural output in the industrial countries; industrial output in the industrial countries and agricultural production in the Eastern trading area stagnated. . . . In most industrial countries, the recovery in employment has generally been less pronounced than in production. . . . In most Western European countries, as well as in Japan, employment actually declined for the third consecutive year. In the United States, manufacturing employment recovered by about 3 per cent in 1976, but remained below its 1973 and 1974 levels (GATT 1977: 2–4, also cited more extensively in chapter 5).

Moreover, the Director-General of GATT, Olivier Long, has observed:

To a large extent, it is to the developing countries that we owe the continued growth of world trade through the recent difficult period. both in 1977 and 1978, the exports of industrialized countries grew faster to

developing countries than to one another. For all the major industrialized countries, trade with the developing countries is of growing
importance. . . . (GATT 1979a, quoted extensively in chapter 5).

According to the United Nations Economic Commission for Europe:

> The most dynamic market for West European exports over the past
> year has been China, exports doubling to $1 billion in the first half of
> this year (FT 22 November 1978).

Another Recession and Forecasting Confusion Worse Confounded

The Guru Speaks

> Whenever I get worried about the economy, I go up to the top of the
> mountain to see the Great Exalted Economists. . . . "Oh, Master," I
> said, "please tell me what is going on with the economy in this country
> at the moment. . . . Blessed Guru, what is the answer?"
>
> "The only solution is to bite the bullet. . . . But while biting the
> bullet, we should not throw the baby out with the bath water. We must
> hold our hand firmly on the rudder until the storm blows over, keeping
> all options open even it it means tightening our belts."
>
> "I knew you would have the answer, Exalted One," I said with tears
> in my eyes. . . .
>
> He turned to go into his cave to boil his steak. The last words he said
> to me were, "Then again, I could be wrong" (Art Buchwald, IHT
> 8 June 1978).

The most exalted guru of them all, Paul Samuelson had long displayed his
confidence in economics through successive editions of his multimillion
selling *Economics* textbook; his confidence in the economy as late as 1970
was still evident in his statement that the prewar business cycle dinosaur had
evolved into a postwar growth cycle lizard. In 1978 Samuelson was persuaded by a "surprise press conference of President Carter on November 1"
that 1979 would not witness the mere growth recession that most economists
like him were expecting, but "an outright recession" (FT 30 December
1978). By April 1979 Mr. Samuelson said that "economics is so inexact a
science and the future is so unpredictable that it is an act of arrogant folly to
try to specify. . . ." (AEI April 1979:6).

Economic forecasting these days and economic policy making based on
such forecasts are well summarized by Samuel Brittan in the *Financial
Times* (19 December 1978) as "lies, damn'd lies and forecasts . . . no better
than the toss of a coin"; by Joseph Kraft writing in the *International Herald
Tribune* (6 June 1979) as "economic double-think. . . . Thus there is, by
Secretary Blumenthal's own account, a basic contradiction in the administration's economic forecast"; by *Business Week* (16 January 1978) as

"facing intellectual bankruptcy" and "so vague as . . . a Greek oracle"; and two years earlier in 1976 by the American public as "on a par with that of astrologers (FOR January 1976). For instance, Treasury Secretary Blumenthal said in March 1977 that "the upturn won't last," and in April that "there are at least 3 years of prosperity ahead" (IHT 3 March and USN 4 April 1977).

In 1979, the forecasting confusion only became more confounded: "The Great American Recession Debate, Who Is the Judge and Timer?" (IHT 17 May 1979).

> The signals are hard to read. Conflicting indicators. The recession that refuses to arrive on schedule. Perhaps not since the onset of the severe 1974–75 recession have forecasters and businessmen who rely on their projections been in such a state of uncertainty. The economic outlook is so clouded and the signals the economy is giving off so contradictory that economists can find evidence for virtually any economic scenario—from continued strong growth well into 1980 to a recession that is already under way. . . . The present confusion has opened up a widening credibility gap regarding the reliability of economic projections (BW 2 April 1978).

> [Let us examine] why the forecasters are off course in plotting monetary policy. . . . They simply do not know how much the rate of growth in "true" transactions money has decelerated. . . . Deceleration . . . is not 8.3% to minus 2.5% but more like 8.3% to minus 1%. . . . Forecasting has therefore become a guessing game for the monetarists. The result is total confusion (BW 7 May 1979).

> The Federal Reserve Board is facing renewed political criticism of its tight money policies this week in the wake of the embarassing $3.7 billion error in the calculations of the money supply this month, which it admitted last Thursday (FT 29 October 1979).

> The way economists have been falling on their faces lately in their predictions for the U.S. the idea of forecasting for the entire world seems as prudent as using a computer printout as a hangglider (BW 9 April 1979).

The economic forecasting and policymaking double-talk and double-think of which Michael Blumenthal was past master (see Frank 1978d on Economic Astrology) have been "clarified" by Mr. Blumenthal himself in "his law" since he left the United States government: "The people running the major economies of the world don't know what they're doing. . . . Of all the economic projections we got on growth and unemployment—and we consulted a wide spectrum—not a single one turned out to be right" (FT 19 October 1979). Assuming the truth of these statements and given the wide spectrum of official, business, academic, and press sources which we have consulted, a certain lack of clarity in the discussion of the 1979–1980 turn from recovery to recession is explainable and perhaps even excusable. At the end of 1978, remarkably broad consensus emerged: "1979 Outlook: Recession. But it will be short, mild and help curb prices, say *Time*'s economists" (TIM 25 December 1978). "A survey taken in December [1978] . . . shows how solid is the consensus that there will be a slowdown in 1979. Of forty-five economic forecasters . . . forty-four expected that the rise of real output . . . [and] the demand for output . . . would also rise less. . . . And forty-five out of forty-five thought that the average unemployment rate would be higher in 1979 than in 1978": (AEI January 1979: 1). "Business forecast: A year of slowdown and inflation. . . . Economists now anticipate sluggish business conditions at best, recession at worst (at some point during the year), rising unemployment, and continued inflation. They also expect some retrenchment in corporate profits. . . . It is quite remarkable to find such a close-knit consensus in forecasts as economists exhibit today. None of the recessions of the past three decades was spotted in advance by forecasters as a group" (BW 25 December 1978). "Fears of a world recession next year, as a direct result of President Carter's recent anti-inflation package, will cast a shadow over the two-day meeting of the OECD's high-level Economic Policy Committee, starting here tomorrow" (FT 16 November 1978). By April 1979, however, "Slow News Is Good News, But Is U.S. News True? . . . There simply is no smell of recession in the U.S. business atmosphere" (IHT 26 April 1979).

The American index of leading economic indicators, widely used to "predict" economic trends and changes, has mostly fallen and pointed downward since late 1978. By March 1979 it had fallen in four months out of five, and in April it showed the largest single monthly drop ever, 3.3 percent. In the meantime, some previous drops were recalculated into rises of the index, and the sharp April drop was revised to only a 2 percent drop (IHT 1 May and 30 June 1979). During the remainder of 1979, not only the "leading" index itself but its constant later revisions as well have gone up and down like a yo-yo, making these virtually useless for the purposes of analysis, let alone forecasting. This and related other circumstances have substantially aided in the constant fudging of the condition and outlook of the economy by political leaders and others. Just after the subsequently-revised "largest single month drop ever" in the index of leading economic indicators in April 1979, President Carter said, "I think our economy is very stable. I don't think we will have a recession. And none of my economic advisers think we will have a recession" (IHT 7 May 1979). Treasury Secretary Blumenthal said the same thing in May (IHT 3 May 1979), and repeated it in June (FT 4 June 1979). However, a few days after Blumenthal's statement, "the non-partisan Congressional Budget Office . . . unofficially warned Congress to expect a fullfledged recession later this year and through most of 1980" (IHT 11 June 1979). By the end of June President Carter was saying that OPEC oil price increases would "make a recession much more likely than it was before" (IHT 2 July 1979).

The administration itself and congressional (joint and Senate) budget committees had been playing leapfrog in their estimates and forecasts since the beginning of the year, and would continue to do so through the summer. Each source tended to revise its own and others' estimates in the direction of increasing pessimism although, as usual, the administration continued to cling to the most optimistic—and unrealistic—position. "The Senate Budget Committee was considerably more pessimistic than the Administration in its own forecasts last January, but not nearly pessimistic enough, it concluded in July" (NJ 25 August 1979: 1396). The leapfrogging of economic forecasting is illustrated by the accompanying Table 2-12.

TABLE 2-12

Differences Among U.S. Government Economic Forecasts in Early 1979
(in percentage rates)

Forecast Source and Date	Growth		Inflation		Unemployment	
	1979	1980	1979	1980	1979	1980
Administration January	2.2	3.2	7.4	6.3	6.2	6.2
Administration July 12	−0.5	2.9	10.6	8.3	6.6	6.9
Congress Budget Committee July	0 to −2	2.9	10.9		6.9	7.2
Senate Budget Committee July	−1.0	2.9	10.9	8.9	6.9	8.9
Administration Confidential July 27				8.8		9.2

Source: NJ 25 August 1979: 1396; NYT 12 July and 2 August 1979.

In July the Congressional Budget Office was announcing "a mild recession" which was "less pessimistic than those of three private economic consulting firms but more pessimistic than the figures the Administration is expected to publish tomorrow in its midyear review of the economy" (NYT 12 July 1979). "Recession starting, White House says, revising forecasts. Mild, brief slump expected" (NYT 13 July 1979). Subsequently, and to President Carter's express dismay, there was an unfortunate leak from his own administration:

> The Government's senior economists, in a confidential revision of the Administration's July 12 economic forecast, predict a deeper recession this year and "an anaemic recovery" in 1980 that will cause the national unemployment rate to climb to 8.2 per cent at about the time of the November [1980] Presidential election. In the forecast prepared for public distribution as part of the July 12 midyear review ... the

Administration forecast that the unemployment rate would climb to 6.9 per cent in the autumn of 1980 (NYT 2 August 1979).

Optimistic economic forecasts by the White House are an old, and bipartisan, story. But to the Carter Administration's embarrassment, the pronounced optimism of Administration's midsummer forecast for 1979 and 1980 has been impeached in only three weeks. In the past, it usually took a little longer. . . .

The disclosure of the admittedly "more pessimistic" July 27 forecast raised a number of questions. First, how realistic was the July 12 exercise? More generally, how candid can any Administration be when it expects business conditions to deteriorate? And more pointedly, are White House forecasts colored by policy considerations? (NYT 3 August 1979).

In the meantime, speculations abound elsewhere about the possible effects of an American recession on the rest of the capitalist world and about economic prospects in Western Europe and Japan per se.

[There is] a gloomy long range weather forecast. . . . The City has been circulating rumors of oil company projections . . . [of] growth in the developed world down to zero or less well into the 1980s. The crisis is here, but not the policies to meet it. The possible recession seems to remain relatively low on the agenda. . . . Inflation is seen as a far more urgent problem (FT 23 June 1979).

In aggregate, OECD GNP forecast is to slow down from 3¼% growth (at an annual rate) likely to have been realised in the first half of this year, to around 2¾% through the period of mid-1980, largely because of developments expected in the United States (EO July 1979: 6).

However, in two unnumbered pages added to the front of the just-quoted publication, the OECD revised its estimates

in the light of decisions taken by OPEC in Geneva and the Summit in Tokyo. . . . As a result, OECD's inflation will be higher, growth lower, and current accounts in smaller surplus or larger deficit, than forecast in the present *Economic Outlook*. The extent of the changes cannot be forecast with precision. . . .

GNP growth . . . is likely to be reduced to 2%, rather than the 2¾% forecast. Because of the terms of trade loss, real income is likely to grow even more slowly, at around 1½% (EC July 1979: n.p.).

Similarly, the annual report of the International Monetary Fund, issued in September 1979, predicts a "long and hard world wide recession starting early next year as a consequence of the weakness of the American economy." However, at the annual meeting of the IMF in Belgrade in late September 1979, the IMF amended its forecast for 1980 further downward, and said that "world economic growth will be lower than the percentage in the annual report" (as reported in *El Pais*).

Also, OECD growth forecasts, lowered still further, are even more pessimistic than those published by the OECD's six-monthly economic outlook last July (FT 9 November 1979).

On the other hand, "Global Recession Doubted . . . five leading West German economic institutes forecast today in a joint annual report" (IHT 23 October 1979). Even so, in Britain "output [is] flat as economy nears turning point. . . . The all-industries index of production fell by 4 per cent. between July and August . . . while manufacturing output dropped by nearly 6 per cent in the month" (FT 16 October 1979). "Bank Issues Gloomy View For Britain" (IHT 21 June 1979).

"CBI [Conference of British Industries] expects industrial decline to get worse" (FT 29 October 1979). "FT Business Opinion Survey Confidence at two-year low. . . . Companies are starting to cut back heavily on investment plans. They also expect a sharp cutback in employment" (FT 5 November 1979).

"Short but severe recession forecast for next year . . . by Cambridge Econometrics" (FT 29 October 1979). Former Chancellor of the Exchequer "Healy predicts deepening recession" (FT 21 November 1979). "Forecast of 2 million jobless by 1982" (FT 16 November 1979). "Gloomy Treasury forecasts 1–2% fall in economic activity" (FT 14 November 1979).

> "Frightening" economic forecasts confirmed . . . using the Treasury's own model. . . . Gross domestic product was shown as 3.7 per cent lower in the first half of 1980 than a year earlier, and 4.2 per cent down in the second half. the 1981 declines were 1.2 per cent in the first half and 0.3 per cent in the second (IHT 13 September 1979).

> There will be a fall in Britain's manufacturing output of around 5½% between now and end-1980 if Sir Geoffrey Howe aims. . . . Unemployment, on the model's reckoning, may be up to 9½% of the labour force by end-1981, and manufacturing investment down to 85% of its inadequate 1978 level. There would be a point in this recession if it were used (a) sharply to bring down Britain's appalling price inflation . . . (b) to shake out resources from inefficient uses and free them for profitmaking ones. But everybody knows that his "recession is not on course to do any such thing" (ECO 20 October 1979).

Elsewhere, the situation at the end of 1979 and the prospects for 1980 are also dim. A *Financial Times* (17 December 1979) survey of Europe is eloquently suggestive in its headlines, review, and forecasts about major industries and countries:

> Economic growth in the European Community is expected to fall from just over 3 per cent this year to only 2 per cent in 1980 (the lowest

since 1975) . . . according to the European Commission. The Community's balance of payments is now well into deficit and deteriorating after a substantial surplus in 1978, while Community-wide unemployment is likely to rise from 5.6 per cent this year to 6.2 per cent in 1980. . . .

The present EEC jobless total is around 6.5m. . . . Within five years it could rise to 15m. Yet one adult in two in the Community already has personal experience of unemployment during the period 1975–78; 13 per cent of those interviewed by European Commission researchers had themselves been unemployed, while a further 36 per cent had known someone . . . who had been jobless. The proportion of those with personal experience rises significantly to two-thirds in the 20–29 age groups. . . . Of the 9,000 questioned more than one in five said they felt threatened by unemployment during the next two years. Among young people aged between 15–24 the proportion rose dramatically to 46 per cent . . . while among people who had already had a taste of being unemployed 48 per cent were worried by the prospect of shortly being yet again without a job. . . .

Pressures [exist] to improve industrial efficiency. . . . Governments sures are at work. . . . [There is an] engineering exports battle. . . . If there is one over-riding theme that dominates engineering . . . it is that international competition will become even tougher. . . . Both Germany and Britain, however, have been losing market share in the world export league in engineering. . . .

Shipyards face steady loss of business. . . . Textiles need survival kit. . . . Steelmakers face a difficult year . . . expecting steel consumption in the EEC to fall by perhaps 2 per cent in 1980 . . . while . . . exports from the Community to third nations will fall by 4m tonnes to 28m tonnes. . . . That is likely to mean an overall decline of some 6m tonnes in Western European steel production from the expected 1979 levels of some 140m tonnes. . . . The market is turning sour all over Europe. . . . Order levels among the leading European steelmakers have fallen away badly since September. . . . Chemical sector worried . . . [and] only just beginning to emerge from a long period of overcapacity, weak prices and poor profitability . . . [as] the European industry faces the threat of growing competition from the U.S. in the form of cheap imports . . . largely based on low Government-controlled oil and gas prices in the U.S. . . . But with the threat of increasing competition in base chemicals—not just from the U.S. but from Middle East producers and from the Eastern bloc countries . . . what the European chemical industry could see over the next 10 years is a thorough-going rationalisation—and not just in the usual euphemistic sense of closures and disinvestments, although both of these are in the cards . . . [but also] a move towards specialties and away from basic chemicals (FT 17 December 1979).

Only "developments in electronics" and "big spending in communications" are seen as escaping the general industrial downturn.

The same *Financial Times* (17 December 1979) survey of Europe displays some variations in economic trends and prospects among different countries. Among major countries, the least threatened by economic downturn is West Germany, where it is hoped that "a sharp recession can be avoided," although "a fall in demand in key partner countries like France, Britain—and perhaps the U.S.—would be hard to compensate for," and where the balance of payments, for the first time in fifteen years, is in deficit and likely to remain so in 1980. For France, "the outlook for 1980, while not brilliant, is far from disastrous as the country is "entering the 1980s in a chastened but by no means pessimistic mood." Even so, French unemployment may double by 1985 to 2.5 million (FT 30 October 1979). Austria displays an "impressive best all-around economic performance in the Western World—but the prospects for 1980 are for a marked slowing down of expansion." Finland experienced an upsurge—not a boom—in 1979, but unemployment may rise again in 1980. Norway is in an "improved competitive position . . . [after] fifteen months of a stringent price and incomes freeze." In Sweden a "mini-boom was started by the devaluation of the krona in August 1977 and sustained by a moderate two-year wages settlement in 1978." According to another survey (FT 11 December 1979), however there are now "worrying trends in the economy . . . [as] the inflation rate and other financial indicators are all moving in the wrong direction. Many companies are also holding back on investment plans."

Elsewhere in Europe, economic trends and prospects appear much worse. Except for North Sea oil, "in almost every other respect, Britain is at a disadvantage. The country suffers from low growth, poor productivity, high inflation and an alarming propensity to import. . . . The economic forecasts are bleak. The Treasury's own model suggests a fall in GNP next year of 2 per cent." "The Belgian economy is often a sensitive barometer for economic conditions and trends in neighboring EEC countries. . . . Lately the mercury has been dropping at the same dramatic rate as it rose during the first half of 1979. Next year is set to be a lean time for the Belgian economy, with real growth forecast . . . at 2 per cent."

For Denmark there are "Gloomy New Year prospects. . . . There will be nil GNP growth, and private consumption will fall by about 2½–3 per cent." For the Netherlands "private forecasts for the early years of the next decade indicate another downturn," and GNP growth is forecast at 2 to 2.5 per cent for 1980, down from 2.75 per cent in 1979. For Switzerland "slow economic expansion" is foreseen for 1980 after a 1979 growth of probably less than one per cent. Domestic demand "remains sluggish" and exports may suffer from recession elsewhere. "The recession deepens [in] Spain [which] faces another year of sluggish growth . . . at an even slower pace than the current year of 2 per cent growth . . . with stagnant domestic demand, a continued lack of investment confidence." Italy "is now anticipating a growth recession next year in a climate of intense inflationary pressures." GNP is expected to grow by 1.5 per cent in 1980. The Turkish economy has been in sharp recession which, by all indications, will continue unabated in the early 1980s" (FT 17 December 1979).

The least unfavorable situation and prospects are still reported from Japan: "Japan's income statistics indicate encouraging but also uncertain factors" (FT 26 October 1979 advertisement); "Japan's domestic demand is proving firm despite many uncertain factors" (FT 26 November 1979 advertisement). With recession elsewhere, however, especially in the United States, prospects for Japanese exports are dim as well. In particular, "Japan's car industry must reappraise its world-wide role" (FT 29 October 1979).

The OECD *Economic Outlook* published in December 1979 forecasts for its seven major countries and for the area as a whole a GNP growth rate of .5 percent for the first half and of 1.5 percent for the second half of 1980. This averages out to 1 percent growth for the year as a whole, compared to 3.25 percent in 1979. For the United States, the OECD forecasts a sharp decline of −2.75 percent for the first half of 1980, followed by a hope for .5 annual growth rate in the second half, averaging to a −2.5 percent decline for all of 1980. For Britain the forecast is a −2.75 percent decline in the first, followed by a continued −.5 decline in the second semester. By contrast, for Germany, France, and Italy, the OECD forecasts a declining growth rate from 3 to 4 percent in 1979 to 1.75 percent during the first half of 1980 followed by a further slowdown to 1.5 percent growth in the second half of 1980. For Japan the OECD forecasts are 4.5 and 3.75 percent growth in the two halves of 1980.

> A recession on the scale of 1974–75 is unlikely because there is less cyclical synchronisation of demand in the OECD economies and because the magnitude of the oil price shock this time is only about two thirds as large as in 1973. There are, however, important risks that the out-turn might be worse. . . . The supply and price of oil . . . and unforeseen depressive effects from the widespread tightening of demand management, including higher interest rates (FT 20 December 1979).

However, like other institutions all throughout 1979, and like the OECD itself six months earlier in its July 1979 *Economic Outlook,*

> the OECD was obliged to update the already grim predictions for 1980 in its bi-annual economic outlook on the very eve of the report's publication today, to take account of the most recent increases in the price of oil. . . . The area's gross national product was likely to increase by no more than 0.3 per cent next year, instead of the original forecast in the report of 1 per cent (FT 20 December 1979).

The entire industrial capitalist automobile industry is again facing a severe structural crisis as the industrial countries move into another recession. The threat of bankruptcy by Chrysler—the world's third largest automobile firm—during the 1973–1975 recession and even more so now is merely the most visible tip of the iceberg of overcapacity in the world automobile industry. Chrysler lost $250 million in one year during the last recession, and already over $300 million in the first half and perhaps $700 million to $1 billion in all of 1979. To get cash, it has sold its operations in France to Peugeot-Citroen (recently merged) and in Brazil to Volkswagen. Not only Chrysler, but all producers and sellers of automobiles in the United States did "battle with '79 backlog" and "face[d] '79 inventory jam" during the summer of 1979 (NYT 31 July and 29 August 1979). Sales of the new 1980 models began in October 1979 with a decline of 17 percent over October 1978, so that production plans were reduced to 20 percent below those of the previous year. In Japan, 1979 production is expected to be one percent below 1978, due largely to reduced exports; 1980 production is projected to fall by a further 5.5 percent and exports by 8 percent (FT 29 October 1979). British Leyland is again facing bankruptcy, and has even threatened to stop production. Even the most stable of automobile industries, that of West Germany, finds output leveling off in 1979 (with 2 percent growth during the first ten months), and anticipates a 10 percent decline in domestic new registration for 1980 (FT 13 September and 26 November 1979). Indeed, world automobile production, which grew 43 percent between 1970 and 1978, is expected to increase only 8 percent between 1978 and 1985 (FT 2 July 1979, citing Economist Intelligence Unit). Productive capacity in Europe alone was 12 million vehicles in 1979, and is anticipated to grow to 13 million by 1982–1983, while 1979 European sales were only 1 10.5 million (ICP 19 November 1979, citing Eurofinance), and 8.9 million in the EEC (FT 17 December 1979).

This renewed recession and decline in the automobile industry—even more extensive than in industry in general—arrive on top of a very uneven recovery from the last recession. Production in West Germany in particular, France, and only just recently in Japan increased over previous maximums in 1973; but in the United States and notably in Britain and Italy, production never again reached pre-1973–1975 recession high points. In *no* industrial capitalist country—except in Sweden, just barely in France, but including Japan—had *employment* in the automobile industry reattained its prerecession maximum by 1977. In the United States, where it had fallen to 80 percent of its 1973 level in 1975, employment only reattained 90 percent of its previous level. Instead, productivity had risen about 20 percent everywhere, and over 30 percent in Japan, except in Britain and Italy (FT 4 December 1979). The latter two, particularly, are now facing drastic declines and reorganization. The American and European automobile industries are now proceeding in the production of "European" and "world" cars through integrated production and exchange of components among plants in various countries. For the Italian Fiat, these include Italy, Spain, Brazil, *and Poland*; for Volkswagen, participating countries are Germany, the United States, Brazil, Mexico, and soon perhaps China (FT 17 December 1979). Moreover, reorganization and resiting are also imperative for the Japanese automobile industry, which is especially dependent on exports (thirtyfold increase from 1965 to 1977) to American and

European markets; these markets themselves are declining and increasing their protectionism, especially against Japanese imports, which have additionally suffered from the rising value of the yen, at least until recently.

Because of the importance of the automobile industry for the steel, rubber, and other input industries—and for the "automobile society" in general—recession in the automobile industry has economic and social effects are beyond its direct structural weight in the economy. For the major European countries this weight of the automobile industry is suggested by the following figures:

Country	Number of Workers	Percent of Total Workforce	Percent of Production	Industrial Exports
France	250,000	5	5.9	10
W. Germany	600,000	8	6.9	12.5
Britain	480,000	6.3	5.9	10
Italy	200,000	4	5.2	10

Source: ICP 19 November 1979: 1136 quoting LM 3 July 1979.

The automobile industry includes over 1.5 million workers, or from 4 to 8 percent of the workforce producing 5 to 7 percent of industrial production and 10 percent of industrial exports, that are directly employed producing automotive vehicles; about another 2 million produce automotive parts, and some 1.8 million sell and service them (estimated by the author from above total and proportions of ancillary workers and employees in 1975 in ICP 19 November: 1166 citing FR 30 December 1976). Therefore, even a mild recession, let alone another depression or resurgence of the structural crisis (see pp. 96–97), in the atuomotive industry is bound to have the most widespread consequences. (These are examined in greater detail under the titles, "Crisis in the West European Automobile Industry" in MR September 1979 and "Big Shake-out Nearing for World Auto Industry" in ICP 19 November 1979.)

Moreover, there are other substantial reasons to anticipate that the coming recession may in many respects be even more severe than the one of 1973–1975. One reason is that this recession is much more welcome (on which more in chapter 3 below) and "needed" than the previous one. The earlier recession did not drive enough capital into bankruptcy to clean up the capitalist house sufficiently, and did not successfully break the back of labor organization and militancy. Therefore, the capitalist states will do even less to combat this recession domestically than they did in the last one. The Debt Economy, as *Business Week* aptly calls it, has grown spectacularly in an attempt to keep the wolf from the door; thus, a further acceleration in the growth of debt threatens to increase the possibility of a crash of the already excessively unstable financial house of cards; this has made worried bankers even more prudent, and reinforces economic conservatism. At the same time, the financial and institutional resources formerly available against the spread of recession—such as the development of speculative Euro- and Asian currency markets and, to counteract them, the introduction of flexible exchange rates and international economic coordination through economic summit conferences and the like— have already been substantially exhausted, or have failed outright. Internationally, moreover, the safety valve or net that the socialist and OPEC countries offered capital through increased demand for Western exports is already significantly exhausted, and much less likely to be available during this new recession. After their last expansion, the limited capacity to pay for and/or absorb imports of these economies has already had to be restricted; these economies are not likely to come to the rescue of Western capital again as they did after 1973.

> As for the OPEC market, the virtual disappearance of Iran as a customer for European machinery and other products has been a serious blow. Other Middle Eastern countries have been adopting a more cautious approach to industrial development, while Nigeria, too, has sharply reduced its purchases. . . . Competition for the available business is intense, not only from the United States, but from Japan and from developing countries like South Korea and India. Hopes that China would replace the Middle East as the growth market for European exporters have been disappointed during the past year. . . . More orders will certainly be placed during 1980, but on nothing like the scale that had seemed likely two years ago (FT 17 December 1979).

Thus, there would seem to be significant limits to consumer, investment, and export demand during this new recession.

The new recession begins at a level of unemployment, particularly in Europe and Japan, that is vastly higher than that prior to the 1973–1975 recession, and a level of investment that has only just reattained its 1973 level. The serious "scientific" projections from official and institutional forecasters seem unable or unwilling to take due account of these factors in the preparation of their generally overoptimistic forecasts; therefore, in considering the rise of real unemployment from the present registered 17 million and the decline in investment from little more than the 1973 level—as well as the constraints on world trade during this new recession—we must leave much to the imagination for now, to be reviewed in the future. In brief, we are again facing the prospect of a recession which may be even more severe than that of 1973–1975. It comes at a time when the economic, social, and political manifestations and consequences of the last recession have not by any means been overcome. This sobering circumstance is itself a mark of deepening crisis.

What Went Wrong?

This question was raised by the McCracken commission, clearly speaking for many others who had thought that recession, let alone crisis, was a thing of the past. This general question may be broken down into three immediate questions—in increasing order of importance—to which most economists have virtually no answers: when will another world recession start, or has it begun already? What will happen to investment? And what is the reason for all these economic problems and uncertainty?

With regard to the timing of a new recession and how long and how deep it might be, we have already emphasized earlier in this chapter the limitations and pitfalls of astrological exercises in economic crystal ball gazing (see also Frank 1978c, d, e). *Business Week* (22 May 1978) again reminds us that "this—as already demonstrated—is not a time when much reliance can be placed on economic forecasts, even for the immediate future." Nor was there ever such a time, for any future.

Then what about investment? With lower growth rates and the possibility, if not likelihood, of another absolute decline of industrial production, GNP, and trade in another recession, the medium-term prospects for investment are, of course, not very bright. More important still, there is an essential problem concerning investments that most analysts, publicists, and politicians are not willing to face, at least publicly. If—as we argue—the world capitalist system has again entered a long crisis of overaccumulation in which the previously leading industries, like automobiles, must give way to new industries based on new technology, then major new investments must flow into such new directions. One of these includes new sources of energy, among which nuclear power seems to be of particular interest to capital. Another comprises new sources and methods of processing raw materials from the oceans, the earth's poles, the moon, and in outer space, as well as pollution control in the industrial countries. A third may be the development and use of new genetic and biological processes and forms of life. At another level, there is pressure toward increasing automation of production and services through new generations of computers and information processing, using new electronic technology. However, the first of these new areas, and particularly nuclear power, has arrived at an essentially economic—that is profit—impasse. The generally low profits and frequent losses in the nuclear power industry have impeded the technological solution—through greater safety of the present fission reactors—to the environmental problems that are deservedly causing increasing public concern. The other new technologies, except the electronic area in part, are still in the process of incipient development. All of these technological developments and the investment in them and in related areas cannot take place until it again becomes profitable to do so.

This is confirmed by a survey made by the Union Bank of Switzerland. After noting that "today it is increasingly [but erroneously] assumed that the current sluggishness in capital spending is due mainly to a long-term weakness in technological innovation," the bank goes on to observe that although

> the number of inventions commercially utilized by industry has been declining since the early seventies, this should, however, not be ascribed to stagnation in technological research and development but rather to the fact . . . that the environment for commercial exploitation

is not always favourable. Major factors in this respect were the drop in demand for capital and consumer goods due to the recession, lower utilization of production capacity, pressure on prices and yields, the higher risks involved in the practical application of technological innovations, the currency unrest as well as diminished self-financing capability of many companies. Scientific and technological development itself has not slowed down. . . . No general shortage of innovations need be feared for the future (Union Bank of Switzerland 1978b: 5–6).

Before it becomes sufficiently profitable to make such major innovations and investments on a larger scale, a number of important changes have to take place: much more existing excess capital will have to go bankrupt, be written off, and/or be destroyed. Costs of production will have to fall, and technological as well as labor processes of production will have to undergo far-reaching and deep-going changes. To make these changes possible, labor costs and wages in turn will have to decline or be forced down; and the spatial and sectoral distribution of production will have to be modified throughout the world. In short, the rate of profit will have to be raised through massive social and acute political transformations involving the widening and deepening of the class struggle between capital and labor. If world capitalism has again entered a major crisis of accumulation, as we believe, another major capitalist investment boom cannot take place until capital has succeeded in reorganizing capitalist production on a new basis—either with the willing collaboration of labor, or by obliging labor to accede against its will. The other alternative is that capital might fail to reorganize itself and labor, because it may not be able to overcome the latter's resistance. In that case, there would not be another capitalist boom following the present crisis, and the crisis would lead to the replacement of world capitalism by another economic, social, and political system. The next recession, no matter when it comes, would only be another but not yet final part of this process.

In view of these circumstances, the third question posed above, relating to the fundamental reasons for all these political/economic problems, can certainly not be answered in terms of the "policy errors" characteristic of the arguments of conventional bourgeois economists, publicists, and politicians. The McCracken commission is an example.

"WHAT WENT WRONG?" the McCracken report asks in capital letters (McCracken 1977: 12, summary: 11), and adds in smaller letters, "and why?" (p. 11, summary p. 9). Their answer includes the following:

Going back to the 1960s, in the United States [there was a] failure adequately to finance the war in Vietnam and major new social programmes. . . . In Europe demand fluctuated around a high level. . . . 1972 was an election year. . . . The 1972–73 boom was exacerbated by the fact that bottlenecks appeared earlier than expected. . . . One reason why the 1974–75 recession was so severe was that, when the oil crisis came, the world economy was already beginning to respond to restrictive policies put in place in 1973. . . . The recovery which began in the middle of 1975 was intended to be moderate but sustained. It has so far proved rather fragile. . . . What lessons can be learned from this experience? There has been a severe deterioration in the short-run trade-off between activity and inflation. . . . In the last few years this deterioration was sharply accelerated by a series of shocks—the harvest failures and explosive rise in oil prices. . . .

To sum up, the immediate causes of the severe problems of 1971–75 can largely be understood in terms of conventional economic analysis. There have been underlying changes in behaviour patterns and in power relationships internationally and within countries. But *our reading of recent history is that the most important feature was an unusual bunching of unfortunate disturbances unlikely to be repeated on the same scale, the impact of which was compounded by some avoidable errors in economic policy.* . . . Adverse expectations born of recent experience will be with us for some time. But there is no fundamental reason why, in more favourable circumstances and with improved policies, they cannot be reversed. . . . This conclusion may sound sanguine (McCracken 1977: 12–14, summary: 11–17, emphasis in both originals).

In the face of this "reading of recent history" and its understanding "in terms of conventional economic analysis," it is hard to know whether we should laugh or cry. Perhaps, before we decide, we should look for better explanations elsewhere.

Experts Still Seek Cause of 1973–75 Slump

U.S. economists in business, government and the academic world are still arguing about the causes of the unusual 1973–75 recession, believing that an understanding of causes is essential to a cure for some lingering problems. The recession debate involves a variety of issues: What caused the inflation? Did the Nixon administration's wage-price controls make matters worse? What was the role of the various major surprises—the food price explosions, the oil embargo and the quadrupling of oil prices? Was the Federal Reserve on balance a help or a hindrance? . . . Others disagree about the impact of controls, but economists generally agree that the pace of 1971–73 business boom was excessive. . . . Otto Eckstein, Harvard economist and president of Data Resources, cites these major "external shocks": The food price explosion of early 1973, the oil embargo of November 1973 and the quadrupling of oil prices, the second food price explosion and the ending of wage-price controls in 1974. . . .

What has been learned from the 1973–75 experience? One expert says . . . "the real end of the ball game is real GNP. . . ." Prof.

Friedman sticks to his opinion that the Federal Reserve should concentrate on expanding the money supply at a steady rate. Data Resources and Arthur D. Little, the consulting firms, say . . . "We need to know more about how industries operate, how they deal with the customers." "We need to learn more about the impact of external shocks" (IHT 19 August 1976).

External shock indeed. An unusual bunching of unfortunate disturbances! The august members of the commission, headed by Paul McCracken, the former chairman of the U.S. president's Council of Economic Advisors, are using conventional economic analysis indeed. The experts, economic consulting firms, and economics Nobel Prize winners—all have the same answer to "What went wrong?" and "What has been learned?"—nothing! Nonetheless, it is revealing that "the *recession* debate involves a variety of issues: what caused *inflation?*" Another former chairman of the Council of Economic Advisors, Walter Heller, was certainly right in December 1974 (with by then some 6 million recorded unemployed in the United States and 12 million in the OECD) when, in his presidential address to the American Economic Association, he told his colleagues that "inflation is surely Economists' Enemy Number One." He was still right even after official unemployment had risen by a further 50 percent. In conversation with the present author (in October 1976), yet another former chairman of the president's Council of Economic Advisors, Gardner Ackley, regarded "the crisis" as synonymous with "inflation," without any regard for unemployment or anything else. He said that he was directing a worldwide collaborative effort to find the causes of both. What final answers did Mr. Ackley think this major study would provide? Answer: "the external shocks of price increases in food and oil"! Did not the financing of the Vietnam war initiate this inflation? No, answered Mr. Ackley. In this regard, Mr. Ackley has a legitimate difference of opinion with those who succeeded him as chairman of the Council of Economic Advisors; for Mr. Ackley was chairman when President Johnson started the inflationary "failure adequately to finance the war in Vietnam"! Subsequent events may have led Mr. Ackley to become more conscious about the existence of recessions; however, the causes of such recessions still remain equally external to him. Mr. Ackley testified to the United States Congress on 7 February 1979: "We will continue to have recessions in the future as in the past, as the result of exogenous events and of mistakes of private and public policies. But there is no temporal inevitability about recessions. . . . It is conceivable that there might be occasions when we would wish deliberately to produce a recession" (AEI February 1979: 2). Even granting these acts of policy, McCracken concedes: "The most important events we would classify under the head of *shocks* are the food and oil price explosions and the breakdown of the system of pegged exchange rates. . . . It would be false to regard these shocks as entirely accidental or as something exogenous to the economic system as a whole" (McCracken

1977: 101). Thus, we may admit that it advances our understanding to recognize failures of policy, and that the "shocks" were not quite external or accidental at all. Unfortunately, however, in conventional economic analysis they still remain an "unusual bunching of unfortunate disturbances unlikely to be repeated"—that is, an accident after all! These "shocks" are not considered as subjects to be accounted for or explained—let alone managed or even prevented—by conventional economic analysis or by those who formulate political economic policy based on it. It is certainly easy to agree with *Business Week* when it observed, after the meeting of the American Economic Association, that "economic science is bankrupt," and that government statements are so "vague that they had the character of a Greek oracle" (BW 16 January 1977). Nonetheless, is *Business Week* itself any better? In its "Special Report. Jobs. A Look at the Nation's Most Nagging Problem," *Business Week* can do no better than to ask and answer "Why many young people can't find work: competition . . . lack of skills . . . high pay rates . . . unions . . . seniority rules . . . automation" (BW 21 February 1977). In its "Special Report. The Great Government Inflation Machine," it can do no better than to inform us that "the real villain is the federal government. . . . Government itself bears the prime responsibility for the high underlying rate of inflation" (BW 22 May 1978). In a word, the bankruptcy of conventional economic and political analysis is total, also at *Business Week*.

It is more than sanguine, if not naive—perhaps false innocence?—to attribute the crisis to external shocks, unfortunate disturbances unlikely to recur, and errors of policy response. Nonetheless, policy—and particularly state policy—does have some bearing on the development of the crisis; and it is important to examine this policy in the context of the class struggle of which it is an integral part.

Chapter 3
The Political Economic Response to Crisis in the West

Capital and the states under its influence in the West have responded to the deepening economic crisis through political policies of deliberate unemployment in order to weaken labor unions and to reduce labor's wages in particular and to impose belt-tightening austerity measures "in the national interest" on the population in general. These measures are defended as supposedly "necessary to combat inflation as public enemy number one," while Keynesian economic theory and policy is giving way everywhere to the advance of "monetarism," led by Milton Friedman, and to the resurrection of Friedrich von Hayek, both of whom have been awarded the Nobel Prize in economics. In each country, the motto is welfare: farewell as "productive investment" (unabashedly beginning with increased military expenditures) takes priority, along with reduced costs of production to maintain or increase the ability to compete on the world market. International coordination and control of these policies remain beyond grasp, however, which further limits the applicability of Keynesian theory and policy, and which threatens the income and welfare of most people through austerity in each country without significantly improving the competitiveness of any country. The initial attempt to impose these economic policies has been through reliance on social democratic measures, parties, and governments with the willing or grudging support of organized labor and of Communist parties, where they are significant. However, as this support wears thin and social democracy becomes less effective as a means to organize voluntary participation in or at least compliance with these crisis policies, the political center of gravity shifts increasingly to the right. Political repression is increased and institutionalized, threatening an Orwellian 1984, so that the growing economic crisis increasingly poses a serious political and ideological crisis for all concerned.

The Class Struggle through Strikes, Unemployment, and Wages

As we have tried to show in the previous chapter, "natural" unemployment in the Friedmanian sense indeed exists; it is also "natural" in the course of capitalist capital accumulation that under certain circumstances there be unemployment and inflation, recurrent cyclical recessions, as well as new major crises of capital (over)accumulation. These "natural" developments, which are in the "nature" of capitalism, are in turn determined by business and labor action—that is, by the course of the class struggle between the two. This class dynamic also determines state political/economic policy and action. Therefore, to continue our analysis we shall examine how these two classes have been participating in and contributing to the development of the crisis and how they have sought to resolve it. The history of previous capitalist cycles and crises suggests that it is "natural" for real wages to rise toward the end of a recovery or boom, and to continue to do so for a short time after the downturn from the peak. Explanations vary, but tend to argue that wages rise as the organic composition of capital rises during the upswing; the higher capital/labor ratio gives labor relatively more power to bargain for higher wages. Boddy and Crotty (1976a, b) have argued that there was a "wage push" in the United States, and Glyn and Sutcliffe (1972) that there was one in Britain and other major industrial capitalist countries, which created a "profit squeeze" in the late 1960s and early 1970s. Howard Sherman (1979), working theoretically, and Thomas Weisskopf (1979), working both theoretically and empirically, have individually and in collaboration examined and tested these two explanations, as well as the "underconsumptionist-realization crisis" thesis, for business cycle downturns in the United States. Sherman and particularly Weisskopf tentatively conclude that the decline in the rate of profit was due only in small part to changes in the organic composition of capital and to worse conditions of realization. According to these authors, the thesis that the rate of profit declined because of an increase in the strength of labor received far more empirical support than either of the other two explanations. Both authors emphasize, however, that their conclusions are highly tentative owing to their failure to take account of various relevant factors, the most important of which is the role of the state.

The class struggle and policy conflict are reflected by rates of profit, wages, unemployment, and strikes. (It is unfortunately extremely difficult to get reliable data on any of these, presumably because they are so politically sensitive.) We observed in chapter 2 and Table 2-2 that the rate of profit has tended to decline since the mid-1960s. During the first part of this period, the decline of profits was accompanied by a simultaneous increase in worker militancy, reflected in the strike rate. (Some argue that labor militancy actually caused this decline, at least in part.) The wage rate too was partly (some argue wholly) pushed up by this militancy. Table 3-1 shows that work stoppages due mostly to strikes (lockouts are not listed separately) in the

TABLE 3-1

Strikes

Workdays Lost Through Strikes and Lockouts in Seven Industrial Countries
(in millions of wordays per year)

Country	1965-66	1967-69	1970-72	1973	1974	1975	1976	1977	1978	1979[e]
USA	24.3	44.7	47.0	27.9	48.0	31.0	38.0	35.8	39.0	34.2[e]
Canada	3.7	5.6	5.7	5.8	9.3	10.9	11.7	3.3[e]	7.5	7.6[e]
Britain	2.7	4.8	16.1	7.2	14.7	6.0	3.3	10.1	9.4	11.0[e]
France	1.8	52.0	3.3	3.9	3.4	3.9	5.0	3.7	2.2	2.1[e]
Italy	10.7	18.5	18.4	23.4	19.5	23.7[e]	22.1[e]	14.5	8.9	13.9[e]
Germany	—	0.3	1.5	0.5	1.0	—	0.5	—		
Japan	4.4	2.7	5.0	4.6	9.6	8.0	3.2	1.5		
Total	47.7	128.6	97.0	73.3	105.0	83.5	83.8	68.9*	67.0	68.8[e]

Notes and Sources: For 1965–1974 from ILO Yearbook of Labour Statistics 1975, except France. 1967–1969 from OECD Main Economic Indicators, Historical Statistics, which gives 150 million for May–June 1968. 1975–1976 from OECD Main Economic Indicators April 1978. 1977–1979 from OECD Main Economic Indicators Nov 1979. (e) means estimated by the author, for 1979 by extrapolating available quarterly or monthly data to a yearly basis, for Italy by dividing total numbers of hours lost by 8 to approximate the days lost, which is the measure for other countries. Japan 1975–1977 from ILO Yearbook 1978. 1978 and 1979 totals exclude Germany, which is negligible except for 1978, and Japan. (—) means negligible.

*Excluding Japan.

seven major industrial capitalist countries taken together rose from some 48 million workdays annually in 1965 and 1966 to 128 million in 1967 to 1969. Strikes increased in almost every country individually, beginning with the 1967 recession and particularly in France and Italy. (The high three-year average includes the estimated 150 million workdays lost in France during the "events" of May–June 1968.) Excepting France, the strike rate remained stable or increased in other countries during the 1970–1972 recession for an annual average of 97 million workdays, more than double the 1965–1966 rate, in the seven countries put together. Unemployment, we may recall, also increased since the mid-1960s, but still remained at relatively moderate and "acceptable" rates, except in the United States and Britain.

It is very difficult to obtain reliable data on real wages. The official statistics always seem to show a rising ratio of money wages to prices, even in those years when all other indications suggest that real wages have declined. However, there seems to be general agreement that real wages on the whole did rise during the 1960s. According to Glyn and Sutcliffe (1972: 76, 166) the share of wages and salaries in national income rose during the 1960s in every major industrial country. In the United States this share of wages rose from 64.0 percent in 1965 and 1966 to a maximum of 68.5 percent in 1970 (URPE 1978: 344).

The 1970–1972 recession and 1973 inflation helped slow or halt the rise of real wages and of the wage share in national income in some of these countries. Unemployment rose, but not enough to stop worker militancy or to force wages back down. In the 1972–1973 recovery, unemployment declined somewhat, and worker militancy fell off again, perhaps with the subsequent rise in wages.

The 1973–1975 recession and following "recovery" seem to have brought major modifications with them. Unemployment rose by 50 to 100 percent (Table 2-6), and remained high. Thus, unemployment has become a constant threat to labor and an efficient instrument with which capital can discipline labor's militancy, wage demands, and the work performance of individual workers. We shall observe below how state austerity policy has generally sought to maintain this high rate of unemployment, and has refused to, or refrained from, pursuing expansionary policies under the pretext of "combating inflation." Labor militancy and the strike rate declined very notably in 1975 and/or 1976 in the seven major industrial countries put together and in several of them individually; and the strike rate seems to have remained low or declined further since, although in 1978 it took a sharp upturn in West Germany.

There is substantial, though incomplete, evidence that real wages have fallen again as well. The share of wages and salaries in national income in the United States has fallen from 68 percent in 1970 to 66 percent in 1976 (URPE 1978: 344). Real wages seem to have declined in the United States, Britain, and Japan in 1974 (FAZ 21 September 1974), and in the United States, Britain, and West Germany in 1975 (LM 23 December 1975).

Scattered indications suggest that some real wages continued to fall as well during the recovery years of 1976 and 1977. In Britain, real wages fell in 1976 and 1977, rose in 1978 and the beginning of 1979, and started to fall again in mid-1979 (FT 15 November 1979). According to the United States Bureau of Labor Statistics, average weekly real earnings in the United States fell from $96.64 in 1972 to $95.73 in 1973, $90.97 in 1974, and $90.53 in 1975. In 1976 and 1977 they rose to $91.76 and $93.77 respectively, but still remained substantially below their 1972 and 1973 levels (IHT 9 February 1978). Indeed, average weekly real earnings (adjusted for inflation) of nonfarm workers in private industry only rose 1.2 percent from 1967 to 1970 and another 1.2 percent from 1970 to 1978—after dropping below their pre-1967 level during some years in between. While labor earnings rose less than 2.5 percent, labor productivity increased 16 percent since 1967 (MP June 1979: 3). The conservative Bank for International Settlements in Basel offers estimates of changes in nominal (money) and real earnings in industry for various countries (but note the differences in their own estimates for some years such as 1977), reproduced in Table 3-2. These estimates also suggest that real earnings declined in the United States, the United Kingdom, and several of the smaller industrial countries; in the other major countries, wages apparently continued to rise, but at significantly reduced rates than before.

Outside of the United States,

> weak labour market conditions in nearly all countries, and incomes policies in a few, have contributed to a substantial moderation of nominal wage increases in 1978. As consumer prices have decelerated less, real wage gains have declined—in line with or even below productivity increases—in a number of countries. . . . In Japan . . . real wages rose slightly less than productivity. . . . In Germany, real wages in 1978 also rose less than productivity. . . . Real wages grew broadly in line with productivity in France. . . . In Canada real wages fell by almost 3 per cent in 1978. . . . The United States was the main exception to this . . . trend . . . [and] the only country, among the seven largest, experiencing a swing to wage incomes during 1978. . . . [However] with the area experienced favourable terms-of-sale developments, 1978 witnessed . . . raised national income relative to GDP [Gross Domestic Product produced within the OECD countries] (EO December 1978: 31–43).

"The OECD area as a whole experienced a terms-of-trade gain which probably added a full percentage point to the growth of area income" (EO July 1979: 17).

In the United States, with unemployment reduced in 1978, real wages seem to have increased. The OECD observes "that the restraining influence of unemployment on rates of pay increases has been diminishing. The results vary from sector to sector." In high wage and unionized sectors, wages keep

TABLE 3-2

Nominal and Real Earnings in Industry

Countries	Nominal earnings[1]						Real earnings					
	1969–73 average	1973–77 average	1974	1975	1976	1977	1969–73 average	1973–77 average	1974	1975	1976	1977
							changes from December to December, in percentages					
United States	6.7	7.6	8.7	6.8	7.0	7.8	1.4	−0.1	−3.1	−0.2	2.1	0.9
Canada	8.5	13.3	16.6	13.4	12.4	10.0	3.4	3.7	3.6	3.6	6.5	0.5
Japan	18.7	15.0	25.6	14.5	11.2	9.3	8.9	3.6	3.0	6.3	0.7	4.3
Germany	12.5	9.6	16.4	6.5	7.2	9.3	6.2	4.8	9.9	1.0	3.2	5.6
France	*12.3*	*15.5*	*20.3*	*14.8*	*15.1*	*12.1*	*5.3*	*4.1*	*4.4*	*4.7*	*4.7*	*2.8*
Italy	*18.9*	*23.8*	*24.0*	*20.2*	*28.7*	*22.9*	*9.3*	*4.9*	*−1.0*	*8.2*	*5.8*	*7.0*
United Kingdom	13.0	17.5	27.6	20.7	12.3	11.1	3.9	−0.2	7.1	−3.4	−2.4	−0.9
Austria	9.7	10.1	15.3	10.4	7.2	4.4	3.3	3.0	5.1	3.4	0.0	−0.2
Belgium	14.1	14.9	24.4	16.2	9.5	9.1	8.0	4.3	7.5	4.7	1.8	2.6
Denmark	15.9	14.3	22.0	13.9	11.4	10.2	7.3	3.7	5.6	3.9	−1.5	−1.8
Finland	15.4	15.9	24.6	17.2	14.0	8.8[2]	6.8	0.9	6.6	−0.8	1.5	−3.9[2]
Netherlands[3]	14.8	12.5	16.6	13.9	8.0	9.5	6.9	3.8	5.3	3.5	−0.6	3.9
Spain	18.4	28.1	31.3	26.5	31.1	21.6[3]	8.2	7.2	11.4	10.9	9.4	−5.0[3]
Sweden	10.3	13.0	13.7	18.7	11.0	8.9	2.8	2.1	1.9	9.0	1.3	−3.4
Switzerland	*8.8*	*5.6*	*13.0*	*7.7*	*1.6*	*2.1*	*1.0*	*2.2*	*5.0*	*4.2*	*0.3*	*1.0*

SOURCE: Bank for International Settlements 1978: 22.

[1]Monthly, weekly, or hourly earnings, except for figures in italics, which refer to wage rates.
[2]September.
[3]October.
Note the differences between the tables here and on page 108 for recent years and especially for 1977. These differences provide greater evidence of how difficult it is to get reliable data on changes in real wages.

TABLE 3-2 (continued)
Nominal and Real Earnings in Industry

Countries	Nominal earnings*					Real earnings				
	1974	1975	1976	1977	1978	1974	1975	1976	1977	1978
	changes from December to December, in percentages									
United States	8.6	6.1	7.7	7.4	9.3	-3.2	-0.8	2.8	0.6	0.3
Canada	16.6	13.4	12.7	9.6	6.8	3.6	3.6	6.5	0.1	-1.5
Japan	25.6	14.5	11.2	9.3	7.0	3.0	6.3	0.7	4.3	3.4
Germany	16.4	5.9	7.2	9.3	5.7	9.9	0.5	3.2	5.6	3.2
France	*20.3*	*14.8*	*15.1*	*12.1*	*12.6*	*4.4*	*4.7*	*4.7*	*2.8*	*2.6*
Italy	*24.0*	*20.2*	*28.7*	*22.9*	*16.1*	*-1.0*	*8.2*	*5.7*	*7.0*	*3.8*
United Kingdom	27.6	20.7	12.3	11.2	15.0	7.0	-3.4	-2.4	-0.8	6.1
Austria	15.3	10.4	7.2	4.4	4.7	5.1	3.4	0.0	0.2	1.0
Belgium	24.4	16.2	9.5	8.7	6.3	7.5	4.7	1.8	2.3	2.3
Denmark	22.0	13.9	11.4	10.2	9.7	5.6	3.9	-1.5	-1.8	2.4
Finland	24.6	17.2	14.0	7.9	5.7	6.6	-0.8	1.5	-3.6	-0.2
Netherlands	*17.1*	*13.1*	*8.4*	*6.5*	*5.0*	*5.6*	*3.7*	*-0.1*	*1.2*	*1.1*
Spain	31.3	26.5	29.8	27.0	26.1	11.4	10.9	8.3	0.5	8.2
Sweden	13.7	18.7	11.0	8.9	6.1	1.9	9.0	1.3	-3.4	-1.2
Switzerland	13.2	6.2	1.1	2.1	3.7	5.2	2.7	-0.2	1.0	2.9

SOURCE: Bank for International Settlements 1979: 46.
*Monthly, weekly, or hourly earnings, except for figures in italics, which refer to wage rates.

up with inflation to a far greater extent than for the majority of wage earners, 80 percent of whom are now nonunionized.

One of the remarkable developments in the first half of 1979 was the moderate behaviour of wages against a background of worsening inflation. . . . This experience pointed to some effects of the voluntary wage standards, and a similar restraining influence is anticipated from next year's program. . . . Rapid rates of inflation and stagnant employment are likely to entail declines in real disposable incomes over the year to mid-1980. It is this sustained decline in real purchasing power and the corresponding fall in real consumer outlays which is primarily responsible for the forecast drop in real GNP growth. . . . Given the extent to which the rise in wages has lagged behind the rise in prices, there must be some risk that wages will catch up. It must be a major objective of policy to counter this tendency. If [only] a catch-up of wages could be prevented. . . . (OECD 1979: 25, 52, 53, 58).

The administration's senior economic advisors, convinced that the risks of a severe recession will increase if organized labor tries to catch up with inflation, are searching for ways to persuade unions to hold back on wage demands. Treasury Secretary Michael Blumenthal; Charles Schultze, chairman of the Council of Economic Advisers; Alfred Kahn, the president's top adviser on inflation; Barry Bosworth, director of the Council on Wage and Price Stability; and Labor Secretary Ray Marshall are united in fearing a catch-up wage policy (NYT 18 June, IHT 19 June 1979).

This major policy objective to push down real wages and keep them from catching up with inflation, not only in the United States but throughout the West, is examined in the remainder of this chapter. (The similar policy objective in the Third World is examined in TW.)

Wage rates, of course, apply only to those who are working. Those who are fully or partially unemployed have suffered an even greater decline in income—even with unemployment insurance payments, which are paid by the state and not by business. Moreover, even if wages and salaries in particular job categories were to remain the same, unemployment has been forcing millions of people to downgrade themselves and accept less skilled jobs for lower pay. In West Germany, 30 percent of those who have found employment after being unemployed regard their new jobs as "below" their former ones (FR 10 March 1976). Technological "progress" seems to involve "de-skilling" in many other ways as well (Braverman 1974).

On the other hand, "moonlighting" in the United States, or "black" work in Europe—that is, taking on a second or third job—has become a mass trend. From the point of view of the workers, "regular" jobs now provide inadequate earnings. From the point of view of the employer, this development offers a way of "avoiding high social welfare costs" through illegal employment. Additionally, in this "black market" employers pay salaries in quick cash at less than accepted or even legal rates (IHT 9 September 1977). Such work is, of course, concentrated among the least qualified, most discriminated, youngest, and worst paid workers. A 1973 survey in France showed that 95 percent of young workers worked over forty hours a week, 32 percent of boys aged sixteen to twenty-one worked over forty-eight hours a week, and 15 percent of workers aged seventeen to twenty worked over seventy hours a week, all of course at extremely low pay (LM 10 December 1975).

These and other modifications in wages, employment, and "work processes" suggest that exploitation is increasing in the industrial capitalist economies as a result of the crisis and the "anti-crisis" policies of capital and the state. Other indications, instruments, and consequences of increased exploitation include the near-universal "speed up" of assembly lines, elevation of work norms for piece work, and rising accident rates. Precise data are difficult to find, however. For instance, with the increase in unemployment in West Germany, workers reported fewer work accidents and took fewer cures in hospitals and rest homes since the onset of the recession, because they now fear for their jobs, not because they suffer less from accidents or sickness. On the contrary, they probably suffer more. The ILO data on industrial accidents are not very current or useful, and other more recent figures on accident rates are difficult to find. In the United States the rate of industrial accidents increased by 30 percent during the 1960s (NACLA 1978b: 5). The recent heightening of interest in industrial accidents, perhaps reflecting an increase in the accident rate itself, has been generating more serious studies (APHA 1975, URPE 1977, NACLA 1978b). Hopefully, these will soon show whether the accident rate has increased as a consequence of the economic crisis and anti-crisis policy in the industrial capitalist countries, as it is increasing in the Third World (see TW, chapter 5). Certainly, labor has staged a growing number of strikes for better working conditions, or rather against their deterioration and the cutback of workers' physical and financial protection against industrial health hazards. These factors partly motivated the 1978 coal miners' strike in the United States. In this connection, United Mine Workers President Arnold Miller had earlier complained about mine accidents and inadequate protection of the workers.

The counteroffensive of capital and the state extends over a very broad front. The OECD convened an International Management Seminar on "Collective bargaining and inflation: New relations between government, labour and management." Its final report contains some revealing passages:

> Labour unrest, often of an ideological type, was causing employers to think more than heretofore in terms of joint solidarity.... It was pointed out by many participants that employers ought to institute (or improve existing) arrangements which would help them collectively to resist pressures for inflationary wage claims.... For these reasons we

consider the lock-out to be one of the most important factors for per-
suading people in a pluralistic society with different views on wage
policy to agree to explore possibilities of compromise. . . . The conclusion here is that the introduction of socially responsible wage policy
requires strong, well organized employers' organizations as well as
equally strong trade unions. . . . "Left wing radicals are constantly
opposing peaceful and balanced solutions." In blunt terms, delivery of a
socially responsible wage policy is not possible if unions and employers
have different views about fundamental social and political objectives.
It would appear that unions in the United States, Japan and the Federal
Republic of Germany were freer than most from such fundamental
disagreements. . . .

A stronger employers' organization and an increase in bargaining
power means that high profits can be achieved *and* inflation will be
realigned. . . . The employers' organizations in centrally bargained
systems . . . appear to have utilized their already strong and sophisticated organization to steer government anti-inflation wage policies in a
way more helpful to the needs of business and industry. . . . The
introduction of a socially responsible wage policy, which is expected to
be more than a brief and exceptional interlude in what is regarded as the
normal course of free collective bargaining, leads to a tendency of
strengthening the central representative organization. . . . There was a
general acceptance of the need for employers, both individually and
collectively, to take a strong part in the vital task of reducing inflation in
line with the 1976 OECD scenario (OECD 1976a: 17–27, emphasis
in original).

This OECD scenario (quoted on pages 122–123) projects a substantial
redistribution of income from labor to capital. To obtain this shift of income,
capital has solicited the increasingly willing cooperation of the state and of
one political party after another in the imposition first of "incomes" policies
and "wage and price" controls; "austerity" policies; and now the "anti-
inflationary," deliberate maintenance or increase of mass unemployment.

State Austerity and Deliberate Unemployment Policies

A first important policy response by the capitalist states to rising wages
and falling profits was to try to impose income policies and/or wage and price
controls. These represent attempts to restrain the increase in wages and
supposedly to keep this increase in line with the growth of labor productivity
that might "justify" it. Incomes policies and controls were imposed in most
industrial capitalist countries in the late 1960s and early 1970s with varying
degrees of success and failure. The London *Economist* (21 September 1974)
pointed out that "it is a popular misconception that wage controls produce
more strikes. The reverse is usually true." In the United States and Britain,
incomes policies and wage controls have generally resulted in fewer strikes.

The wage and "price" controls which Mr. Nixon introduced with his "New Economic Policy" on 15 August 1971 did in fact succeed in reducing both strikes and real wages. However, British Conservative Prime Minister Heath's attempt to force his "industrial relations" policies on labor in 1973–1974 resulted in his defeat by the miners' strike and the subsequent election, after which a Labour government was faced with the task of disciplining labor.

As the world economic crisis became increasingly serious, especially with the onset of the 1973–1975 recession, the uncertain success of the incomes policies which had been designed to stem the rise in wages was followed by the switch to outright austerity policies, intended to push down wages altogether and to discipline labor sufficiently to succeed in doing so. We may recall that, "with the benefit of hindsight," the McCracken commission now considers the expansionary monetary policies following the 1970 recession as "the most important mishap in recent economic policy history.... The major error of policy we see was the overly expansionary policy at the beginning of the 1970s" (McCracken 1977: 41, 102). Since then, "policies appear more cautious than during previous recovery periods, with governments determined to avoid repeating the mistakes of the 1972–73 phase of excessive demand" (OECD EO December 1975: 7).

Reviewing "the oil crisis and the 1974–1975 recession," the McCracken report notes that

> there can be no doubt that a slowdown was intended by governments and seen necessary to counter the threat of runaway inflation. Virtually all OECD countries moved into recession.... The oil price increase imported a contradictory impact on OECD economies which governments in the main made little attempt to offset, and in some cases was further reinforced by an intensification of their fight against inflation. The result, as is well known, was a severe recession. There seems little doubt that a substantial recession was intended.... It is indeed possible to point to considerable evidence of the importance of demand restraint in cooling off inflation and expectations in 1974–76 (McCracken 1977: 66, 70, 107).

These august representatives of capital—such as Guido Carli, the president of the Italian Confederation of Industry and former governor of the Bank of Italy—can say quite unabashedly that "a substantial recession was intended." At least therein they are telling the truth. That is, capital and the governments which serve it were determined to make virtue out of necessity, and to turn the recession to good use—if necessary, by reinforcing it in the name of "fighting inflation."

In reviewing recent macroeconomic policy in several industrial capitalist countries, Oscar Braun writes, quoting various official sources and other analyses:

This deliberate policy of recession has sometimes been made explicit. In November 1974, the Chancellor of the Exchequer in Great Britain declared: "if wages rise beyond the limits set by the TUC, the government will be compelled to take offsetting steps to curtail demand. and the effects ... *are bound to lead to unemployment.*" In other words, if the workers ask for higher wages, the government shall take care to leave them without jobs. . . . The policy of "deliberate recession" was not exclusively British; it was worldwide. In the United states "the severity of the current recession can to a large extent be attributed to restrictive monetary and fiscal policies." In France, "by autumn the government's mid-year anti-inflationary measures—combined with the worsening international economic climate—rapidly reduced the pace of expansion." In Germany, "economic policy . . . last year singlemindedly focused on economic restraint." In Italy, "industrial production fell back dramatically largely because of the drastic measures taken to correct the high balance of payments and to slow down the inflation rate." In Japan, "the credit restrictions which were introduced at the end of 1973 . . . contributed significantly to the subsequent fall in output" (Braun 1976: 8–9).

Essentially the same austerity policy of deliberate recession, masquerading behind a fig leaf of "fighting inflation," has since been imposed not only in the major industrial capitalist countries—the United States, Britain, France, West Germany, Italy, and Japan; austerity also arrived, with some leads or lags, in the minor industrial and not-so-industrial OECD countries of Canada, Sweden (with a lag—the crisis did not hit there until 1976), Norway, Finland, Denmark (with a vengeance), Austria, Holland, Belgium, Spain, Portugal, Greece, Turkey, and "far away" Australia and New Zealand.

The economic crisis and the imposition of austerity policies generated political crises and/or changes of government in most of these countries—the United States, Britain, Italy, Japan, Sweden, Norway, Finland, Denmark, Holland, Spain, Portugal, Australia, and New Zealand. If we consider political crises within ruling parties or governing coalitions, resulting in the replacement of more progressive by more conservative ministers and even prime ministers, we can point specifically to Britain, Japan, West Germany, Canada, Portugal, and Greece. "It was no coincidence that leadership of governments all over the world has changed abruptly within the space of a year. From Chile and Canada to Britain and Italy, economics and economic resentment played a big part in the upheaval. . . . You have minority governments everywhere. . . . No one has the strength to do anything" (BW 6 July 1974). They did, however, have the strength to impose austerity, if only by appealing to "the people" to sacrifice in the "national interest," even while the economic resentment and political upheaval continued, and often accelerated, as the crisis developed further.

Capital offers as one of its main arguments that labor must sacrifice wages and the public welfare in the "national interest" "at this time of emergency" so that "our economy" can become more competitive and export abroad "to maintain employment at home." However, when capital everywhere applies this policy and tries to export at the same time, this argument—and its victims—suffers from the fallacy of composition, just as when everybody in a crowd gets on his toes better to see the parade. Nobody gains, and everybody suffers discomfort or lower wages "in the national interest"; everybody, that is, except capital, in whose interest state policy everywhere has coerced labor into accepting competitive real wage reductions and other austerity policies, without increasing anybody's exports, production, or investment. In fact, in 1975 world exports decreased by 5 percent and OECD exports by 9 percent (intra-OECD by 13 percent), and industrial production and investment still have not recovered. Only the wage level dropped and remained lower–and unemployment rose and remained higher.

It is impossible to review this entire political/economic process here and to examine the successive enactment of austerity policies in country after country. Britain may serve as an example, despite variations on the theme of austerity depending on differences in economic and political circumstances from one country to another. Thus, Britain differs from some other countries in that it had long since experienced a crisis of its own. Therefore, and lately aided by North Sea oil, the British post-1973 decline has been less abrupt than elsewhere. On the other hand, a Conservative government was brought down by its inability to deal with the crisis; and a Labour government was faced with the task, until its failure to do so satisfactorily brought on another Conservative government. Of interest also from the point of view of economic theory and political/economic policy, is that a Labour government turned Keynesianism on its head in the birthplace of Keynes.

The British Austerity Policy as an Example

There can be no doubt that the downfall of Prime Minister Heath's Conservative government and his own subsequent resignation from party leadership were caused by labor strike resistance to the Industrial Relations Act and other antilabor austerity measures. The number of days "lost" annually in strikes in Britain had risen from some 2 million in the mid-1960s to 5 million in the late 1960s, and nearly to 11 million in 1970. Then, with a miners' strike reminiscent of that of 1926, this number jumped to nearly 24 million in 1972. In 1973 it declined to 7 million, but in 1974 it rose again to nearly 15 million days lost in strikes. The miners' strike caused a shortage of electricity, and the government imposed a "three-day week" on industry. Heath had to go.

Two weeks before the 10 October 1974 elections, on 27 September 1974, *Business Europe* reviewed the "Business Implications of the UK elections" for its executive readers:

Privately, some British industrialists believe that for the immediate, short-term economic future of the UK, a Labour Government may be preferable, because it would avoid a political-industrial clash with the unions. In view of the openly made threats by left-wing union leaders against a possible non-Labour Government, perhaps this is not such a bizarre attitude (BE 27 September 1974).

Of course, the "left-wing union leaders" were not the only ones who were making "threats." On 5 August 1974, Lord Chalfont had written in the prestigious London *Times*: "Could Britain be heading for a military take-over? . . . Armoured cars at Heathrow [airport]: A rehearsal for a coup?" Rehearsal or not, it did not come. Instead, the London *Financial Times* reported on the day after the Labour victory:

Indeed, some Tories were already arguing yesterday that a narrow Labour win was probably the best outcome of the election given how hard it would be for a Conservative administration to govern through the economic crisis without the closest cooperation of the trade unions. . . . A slender, whippable, Parliamentary majority is ideal for keeping the Left in order. . . . A Government elected on a minority vote and with a bare overall majority in Parliament is less likely to pursue extreme policies and more likely to take the practical steps needed, however unpalatable, to meet the economic situation (FT 12 October 1974).

The newly elected Labour prime minister, Harold Wilson, called for "united action over the economy":

Britain is facing the gravest crisis since the war. . . . Our first over-riding task is to make progress in paying our way abroad. . . . It is vital that we do not imperil this improvement of our balance of payments, by a loss of output through unnecessary disputes or by pricing ourselves out of world markets. Our central problem in conquering this crisis is inflation. . . . Fighting inflation is a matter of national survival. It is the main threat. . . . So we are all agreed—on our national priorities. . . . There can be no opting out. That is what the Social Contract is about (FT 15 October 1974).

The *Financial Times* observed:

Labour spokesmen now seem to have acknowledged . . . the need to ease liquidity and profitability of industry . . . [and] the need to keep both wages and personal consumption under strict control, a role Labour has assigned to the Social Contract (FT 12 October 1974).

A few days later:

A strong appeal to union members to tone down wage demands and improve industrial relations in the interests of stemming unemployment and helping the country's economy was made here to-day by Mr. Jack Jones, General Secretary of the Transport and General Workers' Union (FT 18 October 1974).

Mr. Jones had made his career as the most militant "leftist" of Britain's labor leaders. Subsequently, the number of days "lost" through "unnecessary disputes" declined from 15 million in 1974 to 6 million in 1975 and 3 million in 1976. This "improvement in industrial relations," however, far from being "in the interests of stemming unemployment," was both accompanied and to some extent caused by unemployment. Instead, unemployment more than doubled from 600,000 in 1974 to 1,400,000 in 1977, rising from 2.6 percent in 1974 to 3.9 percent in 1975, 5.3 percent in 1976, and 5.8 percent in 1977. Real wages, of course, declined.

In February 1975, the chancellor of the Exchequer, Mr. Denis Healey, warned "that the social contract is not yet delivering the voluntary wage restraint which is required from trade unions" (FT 25 September 1975). Therefore, "wage cost inflation will dominate Healey's Budget. . . . Mr. Healey said bluntly that wage increases were now the main cause of U.K. inflation" (FT 20 March 1975).

We cite the *Financial Times* editorial under the title, "Ready to be convinced?"

> There is a substantial body of opinion in the country, especially among organized labour and inside the Labour Party, which has come to expect that a Chancellor of the Exchequer should automatically seek to stimulate the level of demand in the economy when unemployment is tending to rise, as it is (even if relatively slowly) at present. To these people, the fact that the Chancellor has chosen to introduce a mildly deflationary Budget will seem like a slap in the face—underlined by the fact that unemployment may reach a million by the end of the year. It will be said—and not altogether without justification, in view of Labour's resistance to direct controls over wage rates—that the Government has lost faith in the efficacy of the social contract and is relying instead on high unemployment to keep wage claims down to a reasonable level (FT 16 April 1975).

Two months later, the "Government acts to arrest slide in sterling. Healey plans 10% pay limit. A rigid ceiling of 10 per cent on all wage increases and strict cash limits on public sector wage bills are the key elements in the Government's proposed measures to reduce the U.K. rate of inflation and restore confidence in the pound" (FT 2 July 1975). Over at the unions, Jack Jones cooperated again, but the pound, of course, then plummeted from 2.30 to 1.70 to the dollar anyway, even while the dollar itself declined.

It was not long before the relatively "progressive" Harold Wilson also had to take his hat and be replaced by a staunch representative of the right wing of the Labour Party, James Callaghan, as prime minister. Denis Healey had done a satisfactory job, and stayed on as chancellor of the Exchequer. The Labour left was increasingly put out to pasture. By the end of 1976, "slowly and painfully, the Cabinet [was] getting round to discussing the terms this country [would] have to accept in order to secure the loan from the International Monetary Fund, a large slice of which [was] needed immediately to repay the central bank credits drawn since last summer" (FT 29 November 1976). Painfully perhaps, but not so slowly, since two weeks later "Britain Slashe[d] Spending by £2.5 Billion in Effort to Win IMF Loan," as the American *International Herald Tribune* (16 December 1976) announced in an eight-column banner, front-page headline. A few days later:

> IMF Board Meets to Approve $3.9 Billion Loan for Britain. Clearance [is] a Formality. . . . The [board] members have already discussed informally an agreement worked out between the IMF staff and Britain. . . . As a condition for receiving the loan—the largest ever made to a single country—Britain agreed to reduce public expenditures by £2.5 billion ($4.5 billion) during the next two years and to limit the growth of domestic credit. Although financial markets initially appeared to regard the conditions as too lenient . . . US Treasury Secretary William Simon said that the United States, which has the largest block of votes in the IMF, would support the loan (IHT 4 January 1977).

Soon Jack Jones and other labor leaders agreed to a flat £6 limit to wage increases, the "same" for everyone.

Half a year later, the *International Herald Tribune* saw Britain, the mother country of John Maynard Keynes and Keynesianism, "abandoning Keynesian policy. £1.9 Billion Deflationary Plan Set By Britain for Next Year":

> Britain's Labour Government today abandoned 30 years of Keynesian policy and announced a stiff £1.9 billion ($3.4 billion) deflationary package at a time of high and rising unemployment. Chancellor of the Exchequer Denis Healey told the House of Commons next year he will slash £1 billion from a wide list of Labor's favorite programs. They range from job subsidies through school lunches to public housing. This, however, had been expected. But Mr. Healey will also slap £900 million tax on business that can be passed on to consumers through higher prices. That was a shock. . . .
>
> The decision on such a tough set of measures is seen here as a triumph for U.S. Treasury Secretary William Simon and conservative international financiers. In public and private, they have been warning Mr. Healey that he could expect no more help for the ailing pound unless he tightened Britain's belts. . . .
>
> Conventional Keynesian economics calls for stimulating an economy with idle resources through tax cuts and increased spending. Mr.

Healey and Mr. Callaghan have turned this doctrine on its head. Just this month, unemployment reached a new high of 1.3 million, or about 5.5 per cent.

The largest cuts will hit the capital spending of nationalized industries, public housing and subsidies to business for holding or creating jobs. . . . The opposition Conservatives have been calling for just such measures and so applauded (IHT 23 July 1977).

The Conservatives were not alone in welcoming the defeat of Keynesianism. The arch-enemy of Keynesian economics (and labor), Milton Friedman, applauded with relish, and gave the Labour prime minister a standing ovation (although, unfortunately, Mr. Friedman like most of us was not present) when Mr. Callaghan "explained" all this to his constituents at their next congress. Mr. Friedman wrote:

To Jimmy From James

Let me urge Mr. Carter to listen instead to what his counterpart in Britain, Prime Minister James Callaghan, said to the Labour Party Conference on Sept. 28:

"We used to think that you could just spend your way out of a recession and increase employment by cutting taxes and boosting government spending. I tell you, in all candor, that that option no longer exists, and that insofar as it ever did exist, it only worked by injecting bigger doses of inflation into the economy followed by higher levels of unemployment as the next step. That is the history of the past twenty years."

That must surely rank as one of the most remarkable and courageous statements ever made by a leader of a democratic government. Read it again. Savor it (NW 6 December 1976: 45).

Perhaps it is only incidental and anecdotal that Milton Friedman himself had visited Britain, and found that country a "horrible example" of the effects of public spending (IHT 25 October 1976); thus, he recommended the same "deflationary" medicine of expenditure cuts to the British that he had already prescribed for Chile, where it was pushed down the people's throats by General Pinochet's bayonets. Perhaps Jimmy Carter did read the "James to Jimmy" message transmitted through the good offices of Mr. Friedman again; perhaps he savored the same medicine—for, contrary to his electoral promises to cut taxes and unemployment, President Carter has also ultimately pronounced "inflation his enemy Number One." In Britain in the meantime, "the unacceptable face of Labour's pay policy [is] the widening gap between rich and poor. . . . A survey reveals a consistent deterioration in the relative earnings of low paid workers in general and of women in particular . . . [while] executives once again drove a coach and horses (or perhaps a company Rover) through the government's pay limits" (*New Statesman* 17 November 1978). "Rank-and-file revolt [brought an] end of an era for Jack Jones and pay policy. . . . The shop-floor has spoken. . . . It has decided that the time has come to take pay bargaining back where it came from. This week saw the first and last big defeat of Mr. Jack Jones's career. . . . The Government is in muddy retreat from Waterloo" (FT 9 July 1977).

Prime Minister Callaghan warned repeatedly in late 1977 and throughout 1978 that such a dissolution of the government-labor "social contract" through labor militancy would undermine the very basis of his Labour movement, and he even threatened to resign to prevent it. Callaghan offered guidelines for pay raises of 5 percent (with inflation passing double that figure), and the workers—often pressuring or even bypassing their union bureaucracies—went for and frequently received 20 percent. However, they had to strike to get it, both in the public sector of schools, hospital ambulances, fire protection, railways, BBC, and so forth, and in the private sector, transportation, and elsewhere. Callaghan was right about his social basis. It is widely believed that the strikes of winter 1978–1979 cost him his job. "What matters most, however, is that at the moment of truth the unions have failed to deliver, yet Mr. Callaghan is left with no alternative. . . . The mood of the country is now against the unions. That is his weakness. . . . Mrs. Thatcher seemed to be winning by default. . . . There was a general feeling that the Government was breaking down and the belief that the election was being handed to the Tories on a plate" (FT 20 January 1979). According to the succeeding and successful Conservative Prime Minister Margaret Thatcher, "millions of British workers go in fear of union power." The electorate and many workers themselves supposedly became disgruntled with labor power and militant action, and voted Labour out of office. Others might say that the Labour government showed itself no longer able to control its labor constituency and the unions, and therefore it had lost its usefulness. The Conservatives offered to cut taxes, cut spending, and cut down union power and labor militancy; and in the May 1979 election they won a forty-three-seat overall parliamentary majority.

Tory Chancellor of the Exchequer "Howe says spending cuts to start at once" (FT 23 May 1979). However, after an initial cut in income taxes, particularly for the rich, "Howe [is] gloomy over chances of large tax cuts next year . . . and stressed that bringing the money supply under control would have priority" (FT 13 November 1979).

> A major shift from taxes on income to taxes on spending, and sweeping cuts in public expenditure, formed the centre-piece yesterday of what Sir Geoffrey Howe, the Chancellor of the Exchequer, called an "opportunity Budget," aimed at widening choice and improving incentives. The economic outlook over the next year, however, remains extremely gloomy. The Treasury forecasts accompanying Sir Geoffrey's speech project a slight fall in both consumer demand and total output during the next 12 months. . . . The absolute benefits will be largest for those on highest incomes. . . . [Howe said] "some check to the growth

of output and employment is unavoidable." Many MPs see it as a big gamble (FT 13 June 1979).

Howe presents his "opportunity budget." Income tax cut by £ 3.5 billion. VAT [Value Added Tax or sales tax] up to 15% [from 8 and 12% previously]. MLR [Minimum Lending Rate of Interest] increased to 14%. The first Tory budget takes risks with an already unhealthy economy—but they may prove justified. Sir Geoffrey Howe's first budget deflates the economy which is already slowing down, and adds 3–4% to retail prices when inflation is already speeding up. The first year of Tory rule will, by its own published reckoning, see 16% inflation and a fall in national output. Bold or foolhardy? The logic is clear enough. . . . This Budget wobbles on the edge of overkill. The changes in the three reciprocal elements—direct tax, indirect tax and public expenditure— are all very large: direct tax and public spending cuts approaching £4 billion, indirect tax rises close on £3 billion. The argument for shock tactics was certainly compelling (ECO 16 June 1979).

It is "monetarist monomania," according to the previous Chancellor, Denis Healey (FT 29 November 1979) "so the British economy will be the testbed for monetarism in practice. It will not work of course. That is the one absolute certainty" (GUA 28 May 1979).

The other main drive is the

Tory pledge to curb union militants. . . . Mrs. Margaret Thatcher warned trade union militants last night that one of the top priorities of an incoming Conservative government would be to curb their powers and the damage they could do to British society. . . . She said "We have got to deal with the chaos caused by some of these militants" (FT 25 April 1979).

The now leader of the moderate wing of the Tories, the former Conservative Prime Minister "Heath backs Tory moves to curb unions" (FT 27 April 1979).

Mr. James Prior, the new employment secretary, is pledged to: stop the spread and minimise the effects of closed shop agreements; outlaw picketing of firms not involved in a dispute; cut social security payments to strikers' families . . . making strikes more expensive . . . provide funds for voluntary union ballots. Steamrollered together, these issues could push the guardedly neutral Trades Union Congress, reluctantly, to the left and into battle (ECO 12 May 1979).

All this, *The Economist* reminds its readers, is "what you voted for" (ECO 16 June 1979).

Austerity Policy During the 1975–1979 "Recovery"

The imposition of an austerity policy in Britain through a social-democratic Labour government, and then continued with a vengence by a Conservative government, was only one example of the general austerity wave. It was similar elsewhere. Again with the benefit of hindsight, the McCracken commission reviews the "cautious re-expansion [of] 1975–77: the fragile recovery" in the OECD industrial capitalist countries as a whole:

> As we write in early 1977, 21 months after the recovery began and nine months after it began to falter, two themes in particular have emerged. The first relates to policy making. It is evident that, this time round, governments have eschewed the "front-loaded" recovery, the early over-expansion, in favour of a more gradual approach emphasizing somewhat longer-term considerations of both high employment and price stability. Our second theme is concerned with the widening differences in performance among individual countries. . . . Some slowing down in the rate of recovery was to be expected. After the 1973 experience governments were understandably inclined to be cautious (McCracken 1977: 75, 78).

This time, however, hindsight was not necessary because, as the McCracken report implies, "governments" themselves had foresight; they did not look forward to "high employment" or to "slowing down the recovery," but rather to keeping both down, right from the start of the recovery. Writing in late 1975 at the beginning of the recovery, the OECD observed:

> Policies appear more cautious than during previous periods, with governments determined to avoid repeating the mistakes of the 1972–73 phase of excessive demand. Thus, monetary policy may continue to be less expansionary, in many countries, than at the comparable stage of past cycles. . . . The most striking aspects of the recovery as here depicted are its slowness (by the standards of earlier recovery periods) and its failure to gather strength in the course of 1976. . . . Such a forecast may seem surprising at first glance, and deserves critical examination. . . . A rather moderate recovery, which would—on past experience—be an unusual occurrence, might not be an unwelcome prospect to the countries concerned (EO December 1975: 7, 6, 5).

Whether or not this "moderation" was welcome to the "countries concerned" is debatable—and has been the subject of political debate; nonetheless, there can be no doubt that "moderation" was the policy of bourgeois governments, representing the interests of capital. To remove the shadow of any lingering doubt, we may also cite the OECD as it looked back a year later, in December 1976:

The fact that the recovery seems to have tapered off significantly and so soon in the countries where strong home demand would be appropriate, has been regarded by some observers as a mark of failure. . . . Such judgment, with its undertones of pessimism for the future, seems highly questionable. It would be truer to say that policies have produced very largely what their authors expected of them. . . . When it came to reflationary action in 1975, governments were intentionally cautious in handing out fiscal stimulus, despite the existence of large slack. . . . Governments were, in most cases, similarly cautious in the monetary policy that accommodated this recovery as it developed because the lessons of the previous revival phase were plain to see. Under these circumstances it was not surprising that, as the effects of fiscal stimulus wore off and the change in the inventory cycle worked itself through, recovery slackened. . . . Given what was at stake, it can be considered a mark of success, not failure. . . . Very quick return to full employment and capacity use is considered a fruitless aim. . . . (EO December 1976: 5–6).

In the meantime, "given what is at stake," this intentionally recessive and deliberate unemployment policy received the collective political stamp of approval at the spring 1976 meeting of the Ministerial Council of the OECD, and was consecrated in its "A Growth Scenario to 1980," published as a special supplement to the July 1976 OECD *Economic Outlook*.

Under this scenario, output would, on average, grow from 1975 to 1980 by some 5.5 per cent per annum. . . . The period from 1973 to 1980 is in many respects a more appropriate interval for considering the underlying trend . . . at just under 4 per cent per annum. . . . For a number of countries unemployment is likely to remain a serious issue over the years to come. . . . The same is, of course, true for inflation. . . . There is indeed a danger that the range of developments in individual countries could be wider than that shown in the scenario. It would, of course, be tempting to consider a more favourable scenario in which full employment of resources was achieved more rapidly without a serious resurgence of inflation and with less divergence in performance between countries. Unfortunately, there are few grounds for believing that this is a realistic alternative unless economic policies prove much more effective than in the past. Attempts to pursue a significantly faster growth rate would almost certainly lead the world back into the 1973–1975 experiences of inflation followed by recession. The central problem for policy common to all countries is the rate of inflation. . . . [not the unemployment that remains since 1973–1975!] A relatively moderate recovery . . . would be preferable to a sharp upturn. Analysis of the present scenario permits identification of some of the key policy problems that might arise. . . . A special effort will have to be made in many countries to restrain the medium-term growth rate of consumption, both private and public, in order to meet two main demand requirements in the period covered by the projections. These are: i) An increase in the share of investment in output. . . . ii) An increased share of exports. . . . The present projections [no longer single scenarios!] envisage implicitly a sizeable shift in income distribution from the OECD to the OPEC area in the international sphere and from labour to capital at home. This is, of course, the counterpart to the shifts in resource allocation towards exports and investment. . . . In the first instance a revival of investment demand depends on strengthened confidence in the likelihood of a sustained rise in sales and profits. In the longer-run, some action may be necessary to ensure that the revival of business investment is not choked off for lack of profit or of equity capital. . . . There seems, however, to be, at least in some countries, a strong apprehension that insufficient profitability and/or highly-geared financing of these investment flows may jeopardize their achievement. . . . This implies a reduction in the growth rates of real wages and hence consumption of the population of the area as a whole, relative to the growth of output—at least over the medium-term. . . . A slowdown in public expenditure . . . is planned in a number of countries (EO July 1976: 129, 134–138).

Here is the evidence, right out of the horse's mouth: to say that "a relatively moderate recovery would be preferable" because "the central problem for policy common to all countries is the rate of inflation" simply means that "the present projections envisage implicitly a sizeable shift in income from labour to capital" "to strengthen confidence in sales and profits" and "to ensure that the revival of business investment is not choked off for lack of profit." In plain English, "although the public argument is framed in terms of the necessity to restrain wage increases and keep down inflation, the real point is to keep [money] wage increases down so that inflation can continue to erode living standards and restore profitability" (Glyn nd: 7). What is more, the point is not only to "keep wage increases down," but to keep up real wage declines and achieve "a sizeable shift in income from labour to capital."

In mid-1979, the OECD would look back and write: "Indeed, as can be seen from the accompanying table, 'The 1976–1980 Growth Scenario for the OECD Area,' the performance of the OECD economy taken as a whole during the period 1975–1980 is likely to prove decidedly less favourable than envisaged in 1975, in terms of output, price stability, unemployment and international payments equilibrium" (EO July 1979: 9–10). The OECD table cited compares the following:

TABLE 3-3

Economic Forecasts and Likely Outcomes

Average annual percentage changes	1980/1975	Likely outcome
GNP/GDP (volume)	5½	3¾
Gross fixed investment	9	5
Labour productivity	4	2½
Employment	1½	1¼
Final year of period		
Unemployment rate	4	5½
Change in GNP/GDP deflator [inflation]	5	8–9
Current balance ($ billion)	7½	−15 to −20

Source: *Economic Outlook* July 1979: 10.

Unfortunately, after preparing and apparently typesetting these more pessimistic revisions of the already pessimistic 1975 projections, the OECD felt obliged, "after this issue went to press on the 11 June," to add two unnumbered pages to the front of the same issue on "The Implications of Recent Decisions": "As a result, OECD's inflation will be higher, growth slower, and current accounts in smaller surplus or larger deficit, than forecast in the present *Economic Outlook*. The extent of the changes cannot be forecast with precision"! (EO July 1979: no page number; quoted more extensively below).

Capital's real intention is not to combat inflation, which is created by monopoly capital and helps all capital reduce real wages. The real point is to increase profits by reducing real wages through various means, including inflation and unemployment. However, to the extent that it is still impolitic to admit to wanting to increase unemployment, it sounds better to say that inflation is public enemy number one. After all, everybody pays higher prices, but not everybody is unemployed. At the same time, capital can even try to make unemployment socially acceptable too. One way to help is by converting a 4 percent "normal full employment" rate of unemployment into a 6 to 8 percent "natural" rate of unemployment, as Mr. Friedman and his reactionary disciples advocate. Of course, this is not simply an academic exercise, much less a scientific one, but rather a political reality. *Fortune* (September 1976) further clarifies this fact while writing in support of the "natural" rate of unemployment:

> When the unemployment rate is pushed below its natural levels by over-expansive monetary and fiscal policies . . . wages are bid up to much higher levels. . . . Unemployment must remain at much higher levels than conventional political rhetoric demands. . . . It would be better to err on the side of conservatism, and stop nudging down the unemployment rate when it gets close to 6 per cent. . . . There is no doubt that the [wage] rate has been pushed down by the high unemployment rates of the last couple of years. . . . The trade-off between

wage increases and unemployment has recently become much more favorable, i.e., a given degree of unemployment has a greater effect in holding down the rate of [money] wage gains. . . . As unemployment continues falling, we could lose some of this benefit (FOR September 1976: 100–106).

For whom, we may ask, has the trade-off become more "favorable"? Who is the "we" that might lose some of this "benefit" when unemployment falls? Capital, of course; certainly not labor or any other sector, except, perhaps, some of capital's intellectual servants who may receive some form of payoff for calculating this "trade-off." Who should "err on the side of conservatism" (sic) and "stop nudging down the unemployment rate"? The state, of course, or "the government of the people, by the people and for the people," as capital still likes to call it, quoting Abraham Lincoln. The voice of American big business, *Fortune,* in the same September 1976 issue—just before the election of Jimmy Carter—also published "the first in a *Fortune* series, 'An Agenda for the New Administration. . . .' To a considerable extent the articles in the series will be prescriptive. . . . There is every reason to believe that an unremitting war on inflation should be our major national priority." The populist Jimmy Carter, however, promised to make unemployment his economic number one, and to combat it first and foremost with an expansive $50 tax cut for everybody. Giving the devil his due, the *New York Times* (5 September 1976) wrote: "Carter Shifts His Emphasis on U.S. Spending. Stresses Inflation Curbs, Balanced Budget." The September 1976 issue of *Fortune* also observed in an editorial entitled "Where Carter Stands on Business Issues" that "there is no real mystery about Carter's appeal to conservatives. On many social issues . . . he *is* a conservative. . . . Even though he calls himself a 'populist,' he doesn't look like a threat to the established order." Once elected, the populist Jimmy Carter still continued to inveigh against unemployment, promising to reduce it to 6.6 percent in a year; just in case, however, he preferred to "err on the side of conservatism," and appointed reliable economic conservatives—reliable until the president had to let his Director of the Budget go in scandal—to all the important economic executive positions. " 'On fiscal matters, Carter is very, very conservative,' says Hamilton Jordan, the President's top political lieutenant" (IHT 8 April 1977). One week after that revealing statement, Jimmy Carter proved it: He reneged on his "most popular electoral promise" (FR 16 April 1977), and killed the $50 tax rebate saying that this stimulus to the economy was "unneeded" (IHT 15 April 1977). As early as January, "the AFL-CIO last night rejected President-elect Jimmy Carter's economic stimulus package assailing it as a 'retreat' from the goals he set in his campaign, in a public break with the man they supported for the White House" (IHT 12 January 1977). Then, it was not long before labor, the poor, and black Americans, who had put "Jimmy" into office, had all turned sour on him; he had broken every economic promise made to them, and disappointed their every expectation. "Black leaders complain the President isn't living up to expectations,

and a labor leader says Carter has done nothing for labor. It's a sad feeling"
(USN 30 May 1977). Among other things, Carter refused to support labor's
demands to raise the minimum money wage from $2.20 to $3.00. Carter
proposed $2.50 to Congress. With inflation, real wages were supposed to
decline. *Business Week* (21 August 1978) noted "labor's rising anti-Carter
mood. The rank and file is angry and militant over wage restraints."

By March 1978, with official unemployment "down" to 6 percent,
"Treasury Secretary Blumenthal was calling inflation, not unemployment,
the No. 1 problem" (IHT 20 March 1978).

> In his April 11 speech, President Carter announced that his Admin-
> istration had elevated the fight against inflation to its No. 1 priority, put
> a 5½% ceiling on wage increases for federal employees [inflation was
> 6.3 percent in the 12 months preceding February 1978] and promised
> intensified efforts to hold down wages and prices in the private sector. . . .
> The speech appear[ed] to touch the public mood (BW 22 May 1978).

Carter said that his new program required "sacrifice for the common good,"
but another interpretation of his speech and program is contained in the
following:

> Carter's real aim, however, is to tighten the squeeze on the living
> standards of working people in order to shore up government finances
> and the deteriorating competitive position of U.S. imperialism. His
> most acute immediate problem is to prop up the U.S. dollar. Otherwise
> he risks a drastic disruption of world commerce. . . . Carter's plan
> includes the following: Strong backing by the federal government to
> efforts of employers to drive down real wages of American workers. . . .
> Support to the employers' campaign to roll back environmental protec-
> tion guidelines and safety standards on the job. . . . A cutback of
> government action to provide jobs for the unemployed. . . . A hefty tax
> hike combined with cuts in projected federal spending. . . . There will
> be no cutbacks in military spending, however. Carter has agreed as part
> of a NATO military buildup to boost armaments outlay by 3% yearly
> in real terms. Thus, the main burden of the cuts will fall on social-
> welfare spending. . . . Wall Street's response to Carter's stepped-up
> anti-labor drive in defence of the dollar was immediate and dramatic. . . .
> The stock-market took off like a skyrocket. . . . Financial capitals
> around the world got the message too (ICP 19 June 1978).

Indeed, "there is no real mystery about Carter's appeal to conservatives." A
major union leader observed that Carter "gave the impression that unemployment would be his principal focus if elected. But this has not been so"
(USN 6 June 1977). Indeed, "the job surge poses a dilemma. The surprising
decline in the unemployment rate to 6% in April [1978] . . . leaves the job-
oriented Carter Administration in the ironic position of hoping that the
improvement in labor markets abates temporarily" (BW 22 May 1978).

The deliberate policy of recession in the guise of combating inflation, which continues merrily on its ascent, has become even clearer in the United States and elsewhere since mid-1978.

"Bad news is good news and good news is bad news," says an economist at the [U.S.] commerce department. He is not being altogether facetious. Mr. Michael Blumenthal, Mr. Charles Schultze, Mr. James McIntyre and other policy-makers who have just had a meeting with President Carter at Camp David want some air let out of the overblown economy because they fear that the alternative is a big bang later. In consequence the administration is, most unusually, reassured rather than worried by those economic statistics which indicate that an early slowing of the growth rate is in prospect.... An unexpected 347,000 increase in employment last month, and a fall in the unemployment rate to its lowest level since August 1974, caused paradoxical dismay (ECO 24 March 1979).

[Mr. Blumenthal] has admitted publicly that in 1977 economic policy, then tailored to the need to reduce unemployment, was unnecessarily expansive, thus spurring inflation. He says he has no intention of making the same mistake again. Since the Administration now speaks much more with one voice—his— it is not hard to believe him (FT 26 June 1979).

The United States must be willing to accept "austere policies (that) run the risk of recession in order to fight inflation," Treasury Secretary Blumenthal said today.... President Carter's top economic advisers agreed that they must risk a deeper recession if necessary to slow the U.S. economy (IHT 11 April 1979).

Republicans have found little to criticize in the Carter budget; indeed, many liberal Democrats claim it could easily have been drafted by a Republican president.... Senator Kennedy has criticized Mr. Carter's priorities as being too harsh on the poor and sick. But that other barometer of public moods, Governor Jerry Brown of California, has decided that further retrenchment is the wave of the future (ECO 17 February 1979).

The budget is conservative on social spending, liberal on defence spending which is raised from $114.5 billion to $125.8 billion in line with America's pledge to NATO to incease it by 3% in real terms.... A retreat is in order from the big spending tradition of the Democratic party that dates back to President Roosevelt's "New Deal" and continued through President Johnson's "Great Society" programmes (ECO 27 January 1979).

Mondale to Push Carter Spending Cuts in Visits to Liberal Democrats (IHT 17–18 June 1978).

The chairman of the Budget Committee in the United States House of Representatives, Robert Giaimo, observed: "it wasn't shouted from the rooftops, but when the fiscal 1980 budget was put together, it was deliberately fashioned to slow the economy down (NJ 25 August 1979: 1397).

> For the first time in living memory, a Democratic President is proposing a budget that contains no spending for new social programs in the coming year. . . . Most economists believe there is little he [Carter] can do to prevent the onset of a recession, and few want him to try. "The government has decided to take a major risk of a recession," says Data Resources President Otto Eckstein. "The question is whether the Administration will admit to itself that it had to create the recession and will then let it run its course. . . ." Orthodox though it may be, Carter's decision to use budget restraint and admit that it may cause higher unemployment is politically dangerous to a President whose hold on his party is less than firm. . . . By preempting the right-center, Carter has put the Republicans in a bind and left the man who seems most anxious to challenge his renomination, California Governor Edmund G. "Jerry" Brown Jr., scrambling for an issue. But he has also exposed his left flank to Senator Edward M. Kennedy" (BW 29 January 1979).

> Now Brown is prepared to confront Carter as a born-again conservative. . . . On the domestic front Brown has maneuvered himself to the right of Carter. . . . Brown's sudden embrace of the balanced-budget concept. . . . Brown is saying he can do it nationally without labor. . . . He's looking to the wider constituency on the right (BW 5 March 1979).

> The feared entry of the liberal Kennedy into the electoral race . . . would some months ago have forced a total change in the economic policy of Carter. . . . [But now] Kennedy, despite his liberal label, has conceded on this point and also favors limits to public spending. . . . [With regard to defense spending] curiously all the candidates seem to agree with slight differences, including the liberal Kennedy. In an interview with *Business Week*, Kennedy already talks of maintaining the present level of defense spending, including the additional 3% increase in real terms, that Carter defends. The three principal Republican opponents favor the same or more (EPA 10 November 1979).

> "If the election is Kennedy v Reagan (or Carter v Reagan) the lefterwing candidate may be an advocate of much harder money than is sensible in a recession, in order to woo what will then be a pretty rightwing just-left-of-Reagan marginal vote" (ECO 13 October 1979).

Under these circumstances, Carter's replacement of Arthur Burns by William Miller at the Federal Reserve and then Miller's transfer to the

Treasury to replace Treasury Secretary Blumenthal and the appointment of Paul Volcker to head the Federal Reserve Board are all logical extensions of this policy, meeting no substantial opposition, to install out-and-out monetarists at the helm of American and world capitalist economic policy making. Volcker still denied the existence and prospects of a recession even when President Carter had acknowledged it, perhaps following his adviser Stuart Eizenstat's advice offered in a secret 28 June 1979 memorandum: "We should not attempt to avoid the obvious, as Ford tried to do, but we should be honest and admit a recession is likely." Carter did admit the probability of recession, although he did not follow Eizenstat's advice to blame it all on OPEC (WP 7 July, *Boston Sunday Globe* 8 July 1979). Volcker insists that recession or not, he would proceed with his deflationary policy. Volcker's appointment was applauded by business and government throughout the industrial capitalist world; the applause rose to a crescendo in some circles when he instituted a new ultra-monetarist policy of holding the supply of money down no matter what, and letting the rate of interest rise instead as far as the market would drive it—which was to 15 percent a few weeks after the new policy was enforced. Some businessmen have expressed fear and even alarm that a tight credit squeeze at high rates of interest would drive them out of business, " 'The standard of living of the average American must fall,' Mr. Paul Volcker, the chairman of the Federal Reserve Board, said recently at a congressional hearing. . . . Mr. Charles Schultze, chairman of the president's council of economic advisers, agreed emphatically" (ECO 27 October 1979).

The big financial and economic powers that be have lent their unqualified support: "BIS [Bank for International Settlements] Urges 'Mild Recession' " for the United States (IHT 12 June 1979), and the *New York Times* wrote as early as May 1979 under the title, "Economic News Analysis: The World Needs a Recession":

> The time to switch from stimulus to restraint appears to have arrived simultaneously in Japan, the United States, Canada and Western Europe, increasing the probability of recession next year throughout the industrial world. . . . Throughout the industrial world, central banks and governments have come to believe that slow is beautiful. But too slow can still be painful, especially to the jobless (IHT 3 May 1979).

In view of the summer and autumn partial upturn in the long since unreliable index of "leading economic indicators," the incredulous are still saying, "a funny thing happened on the way to the recession. . . . So far the much heralded recession is still not in sight" (ECO 27 October 1979); and " 'We arranged a recession, but nobody came' one U.S. policy maker observed ruefully after the October credit crunch had been imposed, as an emergency measure" (FT 13 November 1979).

> Some economists think it will take a severe recession to begin unwinding the wage-price spiral. Conference Board economist Audrey

Freedman says: "The only solution I see is massive unemployment" (IHT 25 September 1979).

These open admissions about the steadfast pursuit of a recession policy apparently have to be counterbalanced and masked behind a welter of confusing statements to the contrary.

In May, several weeks before the sharp increase of petroleum prices in July,

> Stuart Eizenstat, President Carter's principal adviser on domestic policy, said yesterday that if the Organization of Petroleum Exporting Countries continued to raise crude oil prices, there would be a greater threat that the present mild slowdown in the U.S. economy would turn into a recession. Mr. Eizenstat's comment on a television interview program amounted to an acknowledgment that inflation and the administration measures to combat it—primarily restrictive budget and credit policies—might produce not only slower economic growth but also an outright decline in business activity accompanied by a rise in unemployment (NYT 28 May, IHT 29 May 1979).

On 28 June 1979, the same Stuart Eizenstat cynically counseled Mr. Carter in a confidential memorandum subsequently brought to light by the *Washington Post*:

> In many respects, this would appear to be the worst of times. But I honestly believe we can change this to a time of opportunity. We have a better opportunity than ever to assert leadership over an apparently insolvable problem, to shift the cause for inflation and energy problems to OPEC, to gain credibility with the American people. . . . My recommendations for how to do this . . . many of which I have discussed previously with you and separately with Ham[ilton Jordan] and Jody [Powell], are as follows: (1) Use the OPEC price increase as . . . a watershed event. . . . With strong steps we can mobilize the nation around a real crisis and with a clear enemy—OPEC (*Boston Sunday Globe* 8 July 1979).

On June 30 President Carter said, "I think the OPEC decision will make a recession much more likely than it was before," and that it would cost 800,000 jobs (UPI 1 July, IHT 2 July 1979). Presumably after receiving other advice as well, in his memorable "Crisis of Conscience" nationwide televised address of 15 July 1979, President Carter recoiled a bit and did not put all the blame on OPEC after all—perhaps because public opinion surveys told him that two thirds of the American people believed the "energy crisis," including all the gasoline lines, to be a put-up job, mostly contrived by the oil companies. Such a large number of statesmen, politicians, businessmen, bankers, economists, and publicists of all kinds have, however, insisted on confusing the real economic crisis with and blaming it on the "oil crisis" that we scarcely need to cite all of them. One example will suffice.

The "responsible" *Financial Times* headlined: "THE PROSPECTS AFTER THE LATEST OIL PRICE RISE/Growing gloom over the threat to world prosperity" (FT 30 June 1979). The heads of government who met at the 1979 economic summit in Tokyo discussed nothing but the oil crisis, as though it were *the* crisis. The *International Herald Tribune* headlined across five front-page columns: "Seven Nations Vow Oil Limits, Denounce OPEC Increases At Tokyo Economic Summit . . . A major disappointment of the summit was that the concentration on energy pushed all other major world economic topics into the background" (IHT 30 June, 1 July 1979). The July 1979 OECD *Economic Outlook* devoted a special section to "The Oil Situation," and revised all of its analyses "in the light of the decisions taken by OPEC in Geneva and by the Summit in Tokyo." As early as a year before, the Bank for International Settlements had introduced the first chaper of its annual report by saying: "The main threat running through this Report is that the world economy operated last year under the converging influence of three depressive factors: the global oil imbalance, the external payments disequilibrium . . . and the persisting inflationary disturbances. . . . this evaluation of the present state of the world economy might seem rather paradoxical" (BIS 1978: 3). Indeed!

Fortunately, one major international organization—albeit not one that reaches the reading or television-viewing public—clarifies this question less paradoxically and more responsibly:

> Considerable confusion reigns about the immediate macroeconomic effects of the oil price increase in the importing economies. It is widely expected to increase both inflation and unemployment. . . . There is no basis for such an assertion, which—if true—would amount to an abdication of government responsibility in the face of inflation. . . . There is similar confusion of views concerning the potential deflationary impact of the petroleum price increase. . . .
>
> The evidence forecloses the dangerously wrong view that the petroleum price increase was a major causative factor behind the resurgence of inflation and the expected rise in unemployment. . . .
>
> At the outset it is important to stress that the petroleum price increase which occurred in several steps between December 1978 and June 1979 did not *cause* the present resurgence of inflation in the industrial countries nor the recession now beginning in the United States. . . . In both the United States and Western Europe, inflation rates were already rising by the middle of 1978 when the impression that a petroleum glut existed was widespread. . . .
>
> The possibility of a prolonged period of slow growth must be contemplated mainly because conventional demand management policy itself is now obviously in a blind alley, the theory underlying it being incapable of transcending the inflation-unemployment problem. At the present juncture, the conventional approach tends to immobilize policy making. . . .

These events force us to seriously contemplate the possibility of the world economy moving along a less than full capacity growth path for a prolonged period of time during which cyclical upswings would be brief, soon stifled by rising inflation, while cyclical downswings would be steeper and more extended than in the earlier period because of the increased difficulty of subduing inflationary pressures. . . .

The world economy has been stumbling along for most of the decade in a vain effort to recapture the earlier confidence and progress. . . . The risks and tensions inherent in the present trends raise the possibility of cumulative deterioration.

The present unemployment is not due to a failure of aggregate demand but to a failure of coordination within the economy. . . . The macroeconomic policy impasse is due to an analytically ill-founded view . . . [which] rests on the belief that inflation can only be fought by unemployment, and it manifests itself in attempts to calculate the amount of unemployment "required" to reduce inflation by a given amount (GATT 1979b: 12–23).

An isolated instance of sober and sobering analysis, perhaps all the more valuable for its parity, was introduced into the press—albeit on the not exactly popular financial page—by Francis Cairncross, writing in *The Guardian*:

First the oil price rise has been a lot smaller in proportional terms. From before the December oil price rise until a week ago, the oil price rise had been about a third of the 1973–74 rise. . . . As oil prices rise, there will inevitably be a transfer of purchasing power from the oil-importing world to the OPEC countries. Of course, some of that will come back to the industrial West in the form of higher imports by Middle Eastern countries. . . . The net result is likely to be that many countries decide this autumn not to compensate for the deflationary impact of the oil price rise, but to aggravate it by tightening their fiscal and monetary policies. Now whether this adds up to a bad recession or a dreadful recession will depend on other uncertainties. . . . If there is much worse to come then 1980–81 really could turn out to be bleak years. They will be years when unemployment starts to rise . . . from a base which is already worryingly high. It will be unemployment . . . which will emerge again as the industrial world's biggest concern. One problem, however, would temporarily vanish in the throes of a bad recession. That is energy. . . . The slow-down in world economic growth will inevitably cut the growth in demand for oil. At the same time, supplies of oil from non-OPEC sources—the North Sea, Alaska and Mexico—will be building up fast. The result could well be the emergence next summer of another oil glut (GUA 30 June 1979).

Coordinating Policies Internationally Remains Unresolved

Interestingly enough, what Carter and his conservative economic team refused to do at home, they asked Prime Ministers Schmidt in West Germany and Fukuda in Japan to do in their countries: as balance of payments surplus countries in 1976–1978, Germany and Japan were asked to prime the pump, stoke their locomotives, and pull the world economy out of slump. This was the argument at the "economic summit" of the seven major capitalist heads of government in London during May 1977, and in the repeated pressure that President Carter and Treasury Secretary Michael Blumenthal have brought to bear particularly on West Germany. This conflict has been widely debated in the press, with editorials in the *New York Times* (IHT 11 and 26 January 1978) and, of course, the German press (for instance, FR 13 and 15 February 1978). Moreover, West German Chancellor (formerly Economics Minister) Helmut Schmidt and his finance ministers have steadfastly refused to follow the American prescription, which Carter himself was unwilling to fill in the United States. Schmidt argued that his locomotive was too small to pull the world economy, and that spending more in Germany, which exports 30 percent of its GNP and about half its industrial production, would only drive up German prices without helping the world at all. What Schmidt meant was that increased German spending would sabotage his own austerity and wage restraint policy at home; raising German prices would make German exports less competitive abroad. "In West Germany, all three parties no longer believe in Keynesian politics—deficit spending" (BW 15 May 1978; BW agrees with German professor it quotes). Schmidt rejects "vulgar Keynesian economics. . . . John Maynard Keynes dealt with a national economy that was in deep recession for home-made deflationary reasons. Nowadays, there is no such thing as a national economy. The national economies . . . are not suffering from the effects of deflationary fiscal and monetary policies. They are suffering from the medium-term effects of inflationary policies" (interview in BW 26 June 1978: 94). Schmidt's ultra-conservative, "liberal" economics minister Count von Lamsdorf says, "an economy is not a coin machine" that can be operated by spending (ZT 17 February 1978). On the other hand, the head of the West German Trade Union Federation (DGB), Heinz Vetter, observed that "unemployment is planned into [the economy]" (FR 20 May 1978); the Metal Workers' Union, IG Metall, observed that "employers take unscrupulous advantage of unemployment [through] intimidation of workers, increase in the (rat-race) work pace, and pressure for overtime work instead of hiring new workers" (FR 25 April 1977). Moreover, though Britain and Italy have been "forced" to apply austerity by international capital as though they were "banana republics," local capita in these countries and in West Germany and Japan is quite ready to insist on austerity as well, even without foreign pressure and also against it, if need be. For the real goal is everywhere the same: to use austerity to squeeze labor and be "competitive."

These conflicts between the governments of the United States and of its closest allies, West Germany and Japan, demonstrate once again that the intracapitalist contradictions over how to exploit labor and how to divide the spoils are by no means resolved. Competitive devaluations of the dollar and other major currencies (involving forced revaluations of the German mark, Swiss franc, and Japanese yen, which threaten their export capacity); stringent American opposition to West German nuclear business deals in Brazil and French ones in Pakistan; a new wave of protectionism (examined in chapter 5); American attempts to "intimidate and almost to dictate terms" to the Japanese (as the latter are quoted in chapter 5); and other forms of international political/economic competition have again become the order of the day.

In an interview with *Business Week* (26 June 1978), West German Chancellor Helmut Schmidt "answered" the following question: "What are you willing to offer at the summit, and what do you expect from the U.S.?"

> I understand that some participants want to talk about growth or unemployment [referring apparently to the American demand that West Germany fire up its "locomotive" more]. I want to talk about a better balance in the energy equations of the world [meaning the United States should reduce its oil imports to reduce its balance of payments deficit, and thereby take some pressure off the exchange rate between the dollar and the mark]. I want to talk about a better balance in the network of payments, at least among the rich industrial countries [that is, to stop competitive devaluations against the mark]. Third, I would like to talk about our joint interest in preventing protectionism. . . .
>
> At the end of 1973, I personally foresaw a deeper crisis in the world's economy than we experienced in the early thirties. Not only the four so-called summits, but many, many other consultations have helped to avoid "beggar-thy-neighbour" policies which could very well have arisen. I would see the 1978 summit in this context.

As host to the next economic summit two weeks later, Mr. Schmidt perhaps had reason to be so diplomatic—but not so sanguine. If all these consultations had really prevented the implementation of the "beggar-thy-neighbour" policies that the capitalist industrial states have indeed been pursuing, Mr. Schmidt would not have to talk about the three problems he mentions, and still another summit would not be necessary.

After the first summit, the American Secretary of State, Henry Kissinger, observed in a *Business Week* (13 January 1975) interview: "How you, in fact, coordinate policies is still an unresolved problem." It still is. The *International Herald Tribune* speculated:

> Another Economic Summit—But Why Bother? After the Failures of the Last One (IHT 2 February 1978).
>
> The past year has demonstrated that the world economy does not respond much to pronouncements by heads of governments convened

at summit meetings. What might it respond to? That's not clear. But, as the OECD observes, the present slackening trend is not likely to turn around by itself (IHT 3 January 1978).

Neither are these heads of government likely to turn it around, nor have they wanted to, as Schmidt suggests in his reference to growth and employment, even before the summit started; nor have they done so. Indeed, the slack became deeper, and the signs of a new world recession appeared in time to be considered at the next economic summit in Tokyo in June 1979. However, instead of considering this problem, the assembled world leaders devoted 100 percent of their attention, albeit with 0 percent success, to the simultaneously renewed increase in the price and momentary shortage of petroleum. As to the international payments problem, on the one hand, President Carter has so far failed to implement his energy- and import-saving program over the opposition of domestic interests. On the other hand, the international money market and payments "system" has become a multiheaded monster—the multinational corporations, wealthy Arabs, and others shift their money around, or only threaten to do so, in a "Eurocurrency" market, which has seemingly unlimited growth potential and is under no state or other institutional control of any kind. Economic—like military—protection is always bad, and indeed offensive, if the other one is guilty of it; but no one is willing to give up such protection himself, or potential recourse to it. Thus, it is easy to understand that the pious pledges made at the summit in London in May 1977 were already thrown into the wastebasket again in Brussels—both at NATO headquarters and at the Common Market Commission—two weeks later. Nobody had a better tradition of violating international economic pledges than the government of the United States (Frank 1978d).

Of course, capital and its states are trying determinedly to make common cause in confronting and overcoming the economic crisis through the greater exploitation of labor in the industrial countries and the superexploitation of labor in the Third World. Nonetheless, the international conflicts about how to do so remain, and are summarized by Fred Block when he writes of "Contradictions of Capitalism as World System":

> The point is simple: the greater the openness of the world economy, the greater the extent of international economic interdependence and the greater the need for institutions to manage the international economy in the same way central banks and national governments manage domestic economics [God forbid!]. The problem, of course, is how one establishes such an international structure in a world of competing nation states. Three basic solutions to the problem exist: the exercise of this coordinating and managing role by one dominant and responsible power, the development of supranational institutions to which national governments cede important elements of economic sovereignty, and the development of an effective joint partnership among a number of major nations that would coordinate the world economy in their common

interest. The international monetary system has worked best in those periods when one nation had the economic and political power to assure general acceptance of a code of international economic behaviour and could provide by itself adequate quantities of international credit and liquidity. But the continuing U.S. balance of payments deficits indicate that the U.S. no longer has the absolute economic superiority to fulfill that coordinating role. This leaves only the second or third solutions as possible means towards international economic coordination today. . . . Governments would be extremely reluctant to turn over to an international agency the right to defend or improve their country's international position. . . . Joint management would most likely involve significant shifts in U.S. (and other countries') foreign and domestic policies (Block 1975: 10–12).

Capitalist governments are least likely to undertake such shifts and sacrifices precisely during the crisis that makes them most necessary for the "common good." Therefore, the stronger sectors of capital are not likely to sacrifice the profitability of imposing austerity on labor at home and abroad; and the weaker sectors of capital will continue to impose austerity or worse on labor in order to compete better with bigger capital, which in its turn uses economic or political blackmail to oblige weaker capital—as in Britain and Italy—to do so. Either way, competitive austerity seems to be the order of the day. Thus, it is possible to use the International Monetary Fund (IMF) to exert pressure on weaker sectors of capital and, of course, on populations at large in smaller countries, now including Britain and Italy. However, we have not yet arrived at the stage where the IMF and other supranational institutions can be used to resolve the contradictions among stronger sectors of capital and the states under their sway. These states are still unable to coordinate their attempts to impose austerity on their own and others' labor and population. On the contrary, the 1973–1975 recession brought the European Common Market to the brink of an abyss—direct electons to a European Parliament were subsequently devised to offer a measure of legitimacy and salvation. Since then, "the Community's achievements in the past few years have been largely negative," and in 1979 again, "the nine nations of the European Community have come close to the brink of one of the worst crises in the Community's history" (FT 17 December 1979). In a lecture to commemorate the "father of Europe," Jean Monnet, the former European Commissioner from Germany (and now director of the London School of Economics) again suggested in 1979: "We may yet experience the ultimate crisis of a break-up of the European Community, and we may see it happen within the next 12 months," since its institutions are increasingly "irrelevant to Europe's real needs" (FT 27 November 1979).

If there are any limits to inflation and unemployment in the industrial capitalist countries, they are set by economic competition among themselves and by a common political fear of popular unrest and rebellion that might go out of control. Rates of inflation in one industrial capitalist country which exceed those in the others threaten to price that country's exports out of the international market. Excessively high rates of inflation in all or in the most important of these countries can only be sustained through the monetary and credit creation of an increasingly fragile financial house of cards that threatens to crash down with the next unfavorable economic wind. Excessive rates or pockets of unemployment pose political risks that capital and its states may no be willing to run. However, the United States has already experienced very high rates of unemployment among certain social groups without apparently having yet reached the working and unemployed people's threshold of political tolerance. With 6 to 8 percent registered unemployment now considered "natural"; with 20, 40, and 80 percent unemployment in some social groups now actually normal; and with 30 to 50 percent unemployment averages now standard in many Third World countries; there is no telling how far capital and its states may be prepared to go before recoiling from the political threshold of unmanageable social problems.

Welfare: Farewell

Labor is clearly not the only target of the austerity policies. The poor, the minorities, and the public generally are also scheduled for sacrifices, as the British Labour Party's cuts in their own "favorite programs" of social welfare demonstrate. In fact, everywhere in the capitalist world where the welfare state had grown up in industrialized countries (and exceptionally, as in Chile, in the Third World), the new crisis of capital accumulation is imposing the motto—welfare: farewell (for the Third World, see TW, chapter 7).

> Is Inflation Inevitable? U.S. Experts Cite "Welfare State." At the Massachusetts Institute of Technology, Robert Solow, a leading liberal economist, said, "The single most important reason for inflation is that we are a society that has tried to prevent deep recession, to provide income security for people and to help those who suffer. We no longer let big business go bankrupt or people go unemployed for a long time." Many economists to the right of Mr. Solow tend to agree. Milton Hudson, a senior economist with Morgan Guarantee Trust and a former Federal Reserve Board official, believes that inflation results from the "almost universal commitment to the objective of full employment . . . and the welfare-state" (IHT 20 January 1979).

The intended message, obviously, is that to combat public enemy number one, inflation, we should abandon the commitment to full employment, accept the new levels of "natural unemployment" as observed above, *and* dismantle the welfare state.

With the help of Daniel Patrick Moynihan, later Ambassador to the United Nations, President Nixon already began to dismantle Lyndon Johnson's "Great Society" program during the 1970 recession in the United

States. Since then, and particularly with the onset of the major recession after 1973, the "fiscal crisis of the state" (O'Connor 1972a) has become notorious through the systematic cutback of welfare programs of all kinds—especially those for minorities, women, children, education, health, housing, and policy protection (for the people as distinct from political interests) at the federal, state, and local levels. The crisis in the City of New York (for an analysis see Demac and Mattera in ZW No. 2, 1977) is only the most spectacular tip of the iceberg which is freezing out welfare all the way through the body of society. James O'Connor explains:

> The underlying reason for the fiscal crisis is the basic relation—between Big Capital and Big Labor, who, in effect, "export" their conflicts to the competitive and state sectors of the economy. This happens in a number of different ways; first, labor and capital in the monopolistic sector support the growth of state financed [services]. . . . Second, unions and management in monopolistic industries collaborate in the introduction of labor-saving technology. . . . When the state "takes up the slack" by expanding state employment (as opposed to increasing welfare), costs in state industries tend to increase. . . . Third, Big Labor and Big Capital combine to socialize the *social* costs of production, the costs of ameliorating urban decay, reducing pollution and other environmental damage, and so on. . . . Last but not least, both Big Capital and Big Labor are ardent supporters of the military budget. There is one crucial difference between the attitudes of Big Capital and Big Labor. . . . Capital opposes any program that socializes profits (O'Connor 1972b: 33–35).

These conflicts are exacerbated by the general crisis of capital accumulation and by cyclical recession, during which the monopolistic sector "exports" high costs and low incomes to both the competitive and the state sector even more. Both end up in an economic bind, but that of the public sector becomes more politically visible. The populist Jimmy Carter, who promised to "reform" the welfare system in the United States in order to make it more "efficient," is likely to reduce welfare expenditures and benefits and to use any possible improvement in the administration of welfare to emasculate it. Carter's former Secretary of Health, Education and Welfare, Joseph Califano Jr., for instance, proposed to eliminate one tenth of the nearly one million acute-care hospital beds in the United States (IHT 19 September 1977); Califano was dumped from the Carter cabinet essentially because he tried to defend health, education, and welfare too much against the Carter administration's attempts to cut them. We have noted above that the Carter "budget is conservative on social spending," and that "for the first time in living memory, a Democratic President is proposing a budget that contains no spending on new social programs."

Taxpayers' revolts in Denmark and California, which presaged others such as in Britain, are used as political instruments of the will of capital: to cut welfare. For several years already, a "taxpayers' rebellion is closing public schools or cutting back programs in scores of U.S. communities. . . . Classes in still other communities have been cancelled by teachers' strikes after taxpayers' decisions to economize" (USN 20 December 1976). The "Proposition 13" tax cut referendum in California was overwhelmingly supported in a white Los Angeles suburb, but opposed by 75 percent of the voters in predominantly black and poor neighborhoods in Los Angeles (IHT 21 June 1978). "The Proposition 13 movement affects wages first. It causes reductions in numbers and limits the salaries of community workers . . . [and has] hit first and hardest on the wages of workers" (IHT 4 October 1978). If Proposition 13 failed to cut expenditures drastically in California, it was only because the state had a multibillion dollar budget surplus (IHT 7 June 1979). Former California Governor and ultraright candidate for the Republican presidential nomination, Ronald Reagan, interpreted the tax cut vote as a clear sign of the "people's" opposition to excessively high taxes, too much spending, and too much government (radio report 25 June 1978). The liberal Senator McGovern, on the other hand, charged that Proposition 13 had an "undertone of racism," which its sponsor of course denied (IHT 21 June 1978). The American political humorist Art Buchwald, who writes about very serious things, offered a preview: "If Johnny couldn't read before, he's really in trouble now that there is a taxpayers' revolt in the United States. In a couple of years this scene could be played all over the country. Hey Johnny. . . . why aren't you in school? School's closed. . . . Can't [go to the park]. The park's closed. . . . All the libraries are closed. . . . The streets are full of garbage. No one's picked it up. . . . The fire engines won't come any more. . . . The emergency room at the hospital is closed. The police station closed eight months ago" (IHT June 1978). Not only in the United States, but throughout Western Europe as well (and of course in the Third World, as is analyzed in TW, chapter 7), in concert with turning Keynesianism on its head, welfare: farewell has become the crisis response of the present. Capital now wants only to eliminate all "improductive" expenditure and to concentrate state expenditures and other policies in support of "productive" investments, such as in military production.

Speaking about the West in general as well as about Italy, the president of Fiat, Giovanni Agnelli, made the situation crystal clear: "Industry versus social services heavy competition for finance forecast" (FT 16 February 1979). For Britain, the *Financial Times* examines "the government's dilemma over public spending: Cutting back just to stand still":

> The Conservatives inherited a public sector which had already been pruned back on several occasions. . . . By the last financial year, 1978–79, fixed capital spending had dropped by 23% per cent in real (inflation adjusted) terms since 1973–74. Over the same period total current expenditure rose by 16¾ per cent in real terms. . . . Nevertheless, the potential rise in public spending and borrowing seems to have surprised Tory Ministers. The subsequent immediate cuts exercise was

much larger than Tory Ministers had originally planned or than Treasury officials had previously thought possible at such short notice. . . . The result is that the Government has had to seek actual cuts in some programmes. . . . The danger is that roads, hospitals and schools will be allowed to deteriorate. . . . [There are] daily reports of dramatic cutbacks in services—the closure of old peoples' homes, hospitals and even whole universities. Spending programmes are being examined which would have appeared almost untouchable before the general election (FT 27 October 1979).

Employment subsidies [are] discriminately down. Special employment measures, training programmes and job-finding schemes [have been] . . . cut by £172 million this year. . . . The special temporary employment programme . . . is to be cut. . . . The youth opportunities programme is cut. . . . [There has been a] cut in the training opportunities scheme (ECO 16 June 1979).

The Government is considering tightening up on the "available for work" rule which governs unemployment benefits, taxing short-term unemployment and sickness benefits, and reducing state benefits to strikers' families" (GUA 10 May 1979).

In an aggressive speech to Conservative MPs, Mrs. Thatcher declared that the Government's next priority must be what she described the "Why Work? syndrome. . . ." the Cabinet intends to cut public expenditure next year, particularly in the politically explosive area of unemployment benefits (FT 14 December 1979).

But, as *The Economist* reminded, "it's what you voted for" (ECO 16 June 1979).
On the other hand,

Anyone who thought that the Government would honour its pledges about disengaging from business affairs by immediately carving into its spending on industry must now be disillusioned. The changes in spending revealed by yesterday's White Paper are minimal. They reflect the Government's acceptance that it might honour existing commitments and should not demolish grants on which industry's forward plans have been based.

Nationalised industries appear to have escaped almost unscathed from the Government's pruning exercise. In fact, beneath the statistical fog of changed definitions and varying price bases, it looks as if the present Government is actually being more generous than its predecessor to state corporations (FT 2 November 1979).

And under the title, "Public expenditure plans (1980–81)—Political Assessment [of] Tory philosophy firmly put into figures," the *Financial Times* goes to the heart of the matter:

Indeed if one had to pick out a single sentence from the expenditure White Paper to illustrate both the Tory conviction and the strength of the determination to break with the practices of almost the whole post-war period, it would be the following: "Higher public expenditures cannot any longer be allowed to precede, and thus prevent, growth in the private sector." The break with what has popularly come to be known as Keynesianism can rarely, if ever, have been so categorically stated. The accepted economic doctrine of the past 30 years has been stood on its head (FT 2 November 1979).

The only possible amendment is to note, as we did on pp. 117–118, that the Labour government under James Callaghan and Denis Healy had already turned Keynes on his head with the encouragement of the United States government and the IMF; as the Tory ideologue and now minister of Industries, Keith Joseph, explicitly emphasized in an electoral rally which the present author attended, the Labor government had already shown that anti-Keynesian budget cuts can be made (when the IMF told them to, Joseph added), and that the Conservatives only propose to do more of the same!—except, of course, in spending on "defense" and the police, which Britain must raise, if only to meet our obligation to its allies. The Conservative economic analyst, Samuel Brittan, of the *Financial Times* (8 May 1979) warns: "Beware of the Defense Lobby. . . . Conservatives traditionally have been the party favouring high 'defense' (by which they mean military) spending."

Elsewhere, David S. Broder writes under the title, "A 'Cold-War' Drift in U.S.?"

The conservative political trend, which so far has been fed mainly by public resistance to domestic welfare spending and the fears of inflation, would probably be accelerated by a good stiff dose of anti-Communist rhetoric. . . . A demand for increased defense spending to counter the perceived Soviet threat would complicate the already tricky campaign to curb inflation. . . . But, unless the signs are misleading, Carter at this point lacks the personal and political strength to resist successfully the forces that are gathering here and in the other NATO countries to stiffen resistance to what is perceived as Soviet aggrandizement (IHT 17 May 1978).

Pentagon Sees Public Shift on Arms Spending

The Pentagon's new defense budget calls for $123 billion for fiscal 1978 . . . about 10 billion more than for fiscal 1977. . . .

Thomas Halstead, executive director of the Arms Control Association, said: "Apparently there is a major effort under way to recreate the atmosphere of the 'missile gap" days of the 1960s. . . ." Jeremy Stone, director of the Federation of American Scientists, said . . . "the predictable result of the current exaggerated reports of Soviet civil defense and alarms over Soviet missile modernization will be a wholly unnecessary increase in our defense budget—which will be spent aimlessly on irrelevant responses" (IHT 3 January 1977).

It is hardly necessary to document the new challenges to détente and the renewed creation of an armaments gap, this time for NATO as a whole, since capital in all its countries now needs more military spending. Every NATO country has pledged to increase arms expenditures by at least 3 percent each year, despite the universal drive to cut government spending. President Carter, who campaigned on a promise to cut arms expenditures, asks for a 5 percent increase for 1980 and 4.5 percent per year for the next five years. Carter now emphasized rapid deployment of armed forces around the world, and his new stance is described at the White House as "marking the end of the Vietnam complex" (FT 13 December 1979). British Prime Minister Thatcher is keeping her promise to increase *only* military and police expenditures, thus cutting all other government expenditures, especially those on social services, all the more in order to reduce total government spending. On the other hand, welfare and everything that is not directly productive—of profit, that is—must be sacrificed to "the national interest." John Maynard Keynes, the father of modern fiscal policy, and Beveridge, the father of the welfare state, have been disowned simultaneously. One supposed "justification" was expressed in a *Washington Post* editorial: "Social benefits were set up on an assumption that there would be high growth to pay for them. If that assumption fails, a good deal of painful adjustment is going to be necessary. One example here in the United States is the recent social security bill, with its sharp increases in payroll taxes in the coming years to meet pension commitments" (IHT 3 January 1978). "Social Security Commissioner Calls Improvements in Benefits Unlikely. He Says Stress Must Now Be on a 'Decade of Reform,' in Which U.S. Must Make 'Painful Adjustments'. . . . But some of the tightening he talked about would mean smaller checks for some future beneficiaries than the law now permits" (NYT 17 July 1979). In West Germany also, the old age (Renten) security system has entered a "structural" economic and political crisis which, however, is being deliberately managed to justify an attack on welfare in general. The ideological and political offensive of capital to legitimize its new crisis policy is indeed manifold.

The Social-Democratic Response

A first major political response to the growing economic crisis has been the recourse to social democracy. Since the mid-1960s in country after country in the industrialized world, social-democratic parties have led governments, and labor unions have been asked to extend increasing collaboration to impose first incomes and then austerity policies. The social base in labor for social-democratic and labor parties and the discipline imposed by labor unions on their members have been the major means used to achieve the acceptance and legitimation of these policies in broad sectors of the population beyond labor itself. As the participants in the above-cited OECD "Management Seminar" noted with satisfaction, unions—particularly in the United States, West Germany, and Japan—are freer than most "from fundamental disagreements about fundamental social and political objectives" of capital (OECD 1976a: 17). Though unions in Britain are in greater disagreement, we have seen that they also collaborated effectively in imposing incomes and austerity policies, albeit at the cost of some shop-floor rebellions. Indeed, management—as expressed in the above-cited seminar—requires and wants strong unions precisely in order to quell such grass roots labor rebellions; management needs such unions to deliver the consent of the membership (at least in the major industries) in collective bargains for a "socially responsible wage policy," agreed upon by top management and union leadership. "A central function of unions in monopolistic industries is to guard against spontaneous rank-and-file activity such as wildcat strikes and agitation around the general issue of 'managerial prerogatives' and to maintain labor discipline in general" (O'Connor 1972b: 21). This central function and the conflicts it involves were major issues in the recent miners' strikes both in the United States and in Britain. Moreover, even where the big unions still hold out for wage bargains to defend their members against the decline in real wages due to inflation, these unions still collaborate with capital and the state in imposing other aspects of austerity policies in general. "The position held by union leaders on both sides of the Atlantic [is] that their principal responsibility is protection of those on the job, not those looking for one" (IHT 14 December 1976). The McCracken commission notes: "Over a period of years, organized labour may well have moved to a position where it prefers a higher real wage even when this is at the cost of higher unemployment. Much of the burden of the higher levels of unemployment may be borne by people who are not members of trade unions" (McCracken 1977: 159). "In effect, unions are the agents of technical progress and rational manpower planning by monopoly capital.... The result is that the burden of inflation is shifted to workers in the unorganized industries and competitive sector" (O'Connor 1972b: 21–22). "Productivity, absenteeism and efficiency are problems about which the union is concerned" (Bruno Trentin of the Italian metalworkers' union, cited by BE 16 March 1976). Thus, in this regard, Communist labor unions are no exception; on the contrary, *Business Europe* notes with satisfaction:

> Two key labor events in Italy may signal a real breakthrough for foreign investors, with more longterm significance than the resolution of the political crisis. The first is the publication in the newspaper *La Repubblica* of an interview with Luciano Lama, leader of the Communist trade union CGIL. In an unprecedented statement by an Italian labor leader, Lama acknowledged the need to restrain wages in the face

of unemployment and, more importantly, the economic need for companies to dismiss excess labor. [In] the second important development . . . Italy's three largest unions . . . pledge to modify wage demands and accept 'more mobile' labor. . . . Most significantly, Lama did not demand a *quid pro quo*. He said, rather, that labor and wage flexibility would be in the workers' best long-term interest (BE 17 February 1978: 49).

The Lama interview was not just theoretical. It coincided with contract negotiations with Unidal, a giant food-handling firm that was on the brink of collapse. The new labor agreement permitted the transfer of some workers and the dismissal of others. Shortly after the interview, the three labor confederations . . . appealed for reasonable limits on severance pay (IHT 21 March 1978).

The other important collaboration of "big" and "organized" labor is its indirect participation in labor and other social-democratic governments. We noted above that "some industrialists" and "some Tories" in Britain regard a Labour government preferable to a Conservative one, "to avoid a political-industrial clash with the unions." This attitude also found echo elsewhere. *Business Europe* called it "not such a bizarre" one (BE 27 September 1974); and a Union Bank of Switzerland economist later commented: "what is needed is a solid conservative government . . . and labour right now has the better chance of providing that" (IHT 13–14 November 1976). A major reason for this is, as the *Financial Times* (12 October 1974, also quoted above) observed, that "a slender, whippable Parliament majority is ideal for keeping the left in order. A government elected on a minority vote with a bare overall majority in Parliament is less likely to pursue extreme policies." This is all the more the case, of course, if this parliamentary majority is dependent on a "Lab(our)-lib(eral)" coalition, as it was in Britain and still is in West Germany. The liberal FDP party in Germany, with only 7 percent of the vote, has control of four ministries among which are those usually regarded as the most important ones: foreign affairs, interior (politics), and economics; in this last ministry, the FDP imposes a particularly reactionary policy. In West Germany and some other countries (as under the last Labour government in Britain), these liberal parties blackmail the social democrats by threatening the withdrawal of liberal parliamentary votes and delivering them to the right. Indeed, in 1977 there was not a single country in Western Europe with a one-party majority government, and the small coalition parties have since continued to hold the decisive power to swing over to the right opposition at a moment's notice—until the major conservative parties win outright without such help, as in Britain in 1979. That is, the social-democratic parties no longer always have the better chance of providing a conservative government. Now, the conservatives themselves sometimes have that better chance. Moreover, the credibility of Social Democracy depends on its ability to grant reforms to the working class without endangering the reproduction of capital. If it cannot improve workers' living standards it will, eventually, lose its political base as its actions continually give the lie to its rhetoric. A period of crisis is not one of these times though. The central requirement then . . . is an increase in the rate of exploitation (Harrison 1974: 55).

This crisis seems to have caught up with Scandinavian social democracy, which governed for over a generation. "Throughout Scandinavia, there sems to be a gentle groundswell gathering behind the forces of moderate conservatism" (FT 17 December 1979). Now, social-democratic coalition governments are balancing on a razor's edge—like the minority governments in Denmark and in Norway (with a single vote margin in Parliament)—or they have already been voted out of office, as in Sweden. Of course, as some Swedes observe, "this could be for Sweden an historical decline. . . . The fact now is that many of our problems will never go away" (IHT 25–26 March 1976) "and Mr. Unger is convinced that voting for the so-called bourgeois parties made no difference at all. 'I voted for change,' he said. 'I got more of the same' " (IHT 28 March 1978). Those who voted for a change and only got more of the same or worse are even more abundant in Southern Europe and Japan, where Socialist and Communist parties have made the biggest electoral advances.

The Communist Response and Its Acceptance

The electoral advances of Communist parties, first at the municipal level (Tokyo, Rome, and numerous other cities in Italy and France); at the national level, particularly in Italy; and related changes of political line in both rhetoric and praxis by "Eurocommunist" parties in Italy, Spain, France, Japan, and elsewhere have been the subject of the most widespread documentation, analysis, and commentary. (See, for instance, books by Communist Party General Secretaries Marchais 1973, Berlinguer 1977, Carrillo 1977, and their critics Claudin 1977, Mandel 1978, Les Nouvelles Littéraires 1978. For an examination of Eurocommunist theory and praxis, see our critique of Claudin in Frank 1978f.) Here, however, we will limit ourselves largely to the review of a few facts and their evaluation by the business press and other representative of capital.

Business International wrote in 1976 under the title "Why Italy's Future Is Not As Chaotic As it Seems":

> International companies are *not* likely to get caught up in the web of Italian politics. . . . Political instability . . . is far from being as chaotic as most press commentary suggest. . . . This view is shared by many in Italy and accounts, by and large, for the relatively sanguine attitude toward Italian policies by the international business community. . . . In

the unlikely event that the worst scenario comes to pass, i.e. Communist participation in the government . . . opinion in business circles generally holds that government economic policy would not change noticeably. . . . Many Italian and foreign businessmen agree that a broad coalition including the PCI could succeed where the revolving-door regimes of the past decade have failed: particularly in tackling the country's pressing social problems by enacting overdue reforms in such areas as health, transportation, housing, schools and public administration (BI 23 January 1976, emphasis in original).

In short, the PCI would merely tackle Italy's more pressing problems and help administer the government more efficiently. . . . The effects on the business climate could be salutary in certain areas—operating in a politically efficient country, sensible economic planning, and exorbitant wage demands kept in check by the PCI, which presumably would have some leverage over CGIL, the communist union and Italy's largest (BI 9 April 1976).

The sense . . . is best given by the concluding words of veteran PCI leader Giorgio Amendola: "The recovery of the Italian economy imposes sacrifices. But I would not like this to be interpreted to mean that the PCI is ready, in order to enter the government, to barter commitment to seek and obtain from workers what others cannot. If the necessary measures require a united effort by all the democratic forces and by ours, the commitment is a necessary consequence, not a preliminary request for the Italian Communist Party" (BE 26 March 1976).

Enrico Berlinguer, the secretary general of the Italian Communist Party and the chief promoter of the "historic compromise" of "Eurocommunism," clarifies still further:

Our project, I believe, is not aimed at being and cannot be a program of transition to a socialist society. . . .

In whose name are the old ruling groups asking us for help? . . . They say that the sacrifices of the workers serve to attain three objectives of general interest: redress the national economy, accentuate the upturn of production, maintain and extend employment. What response must we give to these objectives? We have no doubt: we answer 'yes' to all three, but we must immediately add something else. . . . What is the most significant fact about the present crisis from the political and class standpoint? It is that the capitalist world . . . [has] been compelled to turn to us—toward the working class, the toilers, the Communists—as a force which has now become indispensable in setting things in order, in making machinery of the economy and the state function, in bringing efficiency to the entire Italian social system . . . This reveals something which is genuinely new from the historic point of view. The old ruling classes and the old politicians are no longer in a position to impose sacrifices on the working class; today they must ask us to do so, and they are asking us (cited in IPC 23 June 1977: 8, 11; also in Mandel 1978).

That is, "the most significant fact about the present crisis from the political and class standpoint" is that to make "the machinery of the economy and the state function" and "to impose sacrifices on the working class; today they must ask us," and the Communists "have no doubt: we answer 'yes.' " The evidence of this policy of collaboration can be found not only in the political rhetoric, but also in the political practice of the Communist Party of Italy: in their effort to make the capitalist machinery of the economy function, "the loudest voices now heard in support of sacrifices and austerity are those of the Communist union leaders" (IHT 21 March 1978). Because the left now agrees to help the repressive machinery of the bourgeois state function, "Berlinguer equates the new left with the fascists" (FR 20 September 1977); "Italy's political parties forge new unity against terrorism" (FR 20 April 1978). There is no doubt that the most stalwart defender of the bourgeois state, and specifically its repressive police action today is the Communist Party of Italy.

Santiago Carrillo, the secretary general of the Spanish Communist Party, writes in his *"Eurocomunismo" y Estado:*

> Already during the war and afterwards, we Communists were criticized for our *moderation;* because we defended the rights of the petit-bourgeois and bourgeois parties to participate in the government and at least in political life with full rights; because we insisted on the defense of the small and medium property owners. . . .
>
> Developed capitalist society carries socialism in its innards. . . . How can the state apparatus be transformed by democratic means? . . .
>
> The strategy of the revolutionaries of today in the developed capitalist countries has to orient itself to turning around those ideological apparatuses, to transform them and use them—if not totally, then partly—against the state power of monopoly capital. Modern experience shows that this is possible. And here is the key . . . to transforming the state apparatus by democratic means. . . .
>
> That means it supposes the coexistence of public and private forms of property for a long period. This way the stage of political and economic democracy that is foreseen in our program takes on its full significance; in this phase, which is still not socialism, and which already is no longer the domination of the state by monopoly capital, the existing productive forces and social services must be preserved at their maximum recognizing the role that private initiative plays in them. . . . If this is so, it is evident that a democratic socialist Spain would have to maintain an open policy towards the foreign investments and the multinationals that are useful for our economic development. . . . I already see the doctrinaire

ones complaining that this is "pure reformism." That does not scare me (Carillo 1977 passim, emphasis in original).

The political praxis of the Spanish Communist Party is even more purely reformist than its rhetoric. "Spanish Communists Champion Moderation. The Spanish Communist Party has been full of surprises since its legalization last month. Each step the party of Santiago Carrillo has taken has been an effort to demonstrate its moderation and add to its vote in the June 15 elections, which could fall short of 10 per cent" (IHT 3 May 1977). It did. The result was that Santiago Carrillo offered Prime Minister Suarez a coalition against the Socialists, who became the second strongest party. Suarez refused. Untiring, Santiago Carrillo took the initiative to propose the Pact of Moncloa (the government house), which the prime minister and the Socialists did accept. This pact was to formulate the extremely severe austerity program—outlined and supported by the Communist Party itself—which the government has since imposed on the Spanish workers, with the cooperation of the Comisiones Obreras, the Communist-led labor unions.

In France, the Communist Party of Georges Marchais has taken an apparently more militant line against the government of Giscard d'Estaing and its socialist allies led by presidential candidate François Mitterand. This apparent hard line, however, was designed principally if not exclusively to break up the Union de Gauche electoral coalition; the Communists succeeded in doing so in September 1977, six months before the elections. As a result, the left was defeated in the elections of March 1978, although opinion polls had given it a substantial majority for over a year. The reasons for this Communist Party tactic and its consequences have been widely debated before and since the elections. The Communist strategy and resulting defeat have now led to a groundswell opposition movement within the party, reflecting substantial rank-and-file disillusionment with what is regarded as a betrayal of the popular cause. A dozen party intellectuals have published long individual critiques everywhere except in the party press, which refused them. (A summary appears in Les Nouvelles Littéraires 5 June 1977.) Nonetheless, one major reason for breaking up the alliance and sabotaging the electoral victory of the left seems obvious in the following: "Happy to Shun Problems of Governing, French Labor Chiefs [are] Relieved by Leftist Split. . . . Leftist labor leaders are most concerned by the prospect that they would not be able to satisfy their workers' demands if their parties took over the national government next year" (IHT 7 October 1977). There can be no doubt that, if the left had won the 1978 elections in France, the tasks of imposing an austerity program would have fallen on it; and if it had failed in this appointed task, it would have been ousted again soon enough. This is what the rightist Gaullist leader Jacques Chirac was waiting for, so that he could enter government to "save" France and pick up the pieces. The (self) defeat of the left has severely hindered or at least delayed the political prospects of the far right, led by Chirac. For now, the task of continuing and deepening the austerity program remains with Prime

Minister Raymond Barre. Before the elections, it was politically impossible to push the "Barre Plan" too zealously. Afterward, however, Prime Minister Barre announed that in the interest of "fighting inflation," he would under no circumstances adopt a reflationary policy (IHT 23 June 1978). Of course, the French Communist Party also defends the armaments industry, the number one export industry, with over 300,000 workers employed in France. President Giscard and Prime Minister Barre represent the interests of big, internationally oriented French and foreign capital, and are trying to impose its policy in France, like everywhere else: austerity at home to make French capital more competitive internationally, and the creation of wider markets through foreign policies of intervention in the Middle East and Africa as well as the enlargement of the Common Market to include Turkey and the Mediterranean countries of Europe. This leaves Gaullist challenger Chirac to defend the interests of nationally oriented capital, the peasants, and certain middle class interests; thus, Chirac has been opposing these Giscard-Barre domestic and foreign policies, and pleading for increased domestic spending for "the people." (For an analysis of the difference between the two policies— excluding this reason for the difference—see Gilbert Mathieu in LM 22 March 1978.) However, if Chirac were to become president or prime minister, he would rapidly be obliged to pursue the same policies as his predecessors, and some of his Gaullist supporters are already critical of his populist stance.

The French Communist Party now suffers from a serious credibility gap in this political/economic area. In another area, however, no such gap exists. The French Communist Party supports the maintenance and extension of the French nuclear "force de frappe," and on this score it leaves little doubt. As the Italian Communist Party has become the strongest supporter of bourgeois state power in Italy, the French Communist Party has become the most enthusiastic defender of the French "nation." The extent to which this political position will compromise the French Communist Party—namely, in the defense of French "national" interests through military intervention in support of reactionary regimes in Africa tomorrow, as in Algeria two decades ago— remains to be seen.

What has now become obvious was earlier expressed in the magazine of American big business, *Fortune*, in 1976:

> Can Communists be democrats? Only a few years ago, the answer would have been—no, obviously not. Today it isn't so obvious at all. . . . It would be foolish to deny the possibility of democratic Communism. There is no inherent reason why Communist parties must be totalitarian. . . . Communists would appear to have some powerful reasons for moving toward democratic positions (FOR March 1976).

It would be foolish to deny that the Communist parties are "making the machinery of the economy and state function" in harmony with the tenets of *Fortune* and *Business International*; and it is obvious that this is why they can now be called "democratic," even though—indeed precisely because—they successfully limit the ability of their popular mass base to oppose this policy through democratic action inside and outside the Communist Parties.

The policy of the Eurocommunist parties was summarized succinctly by the Communist mayor of St. Etienne, the working class Parisian suburb, and clearly appreciated by *Business Europe*, which interviewed him:

> Beyond the rich reserve of trained workers Sangeudolce claims that the strong union movement in St. Etienne has created a disciplined labor force. "To incoming companies, we can offer social peace," says the Communist mayor. And, he quickly adds, "We are sincerely committed to free enterprise" (BE 19 June 1977: 178).

Mr. Luciano Barca, a member of the Politburo of the Communist Party of Italy, observes for his party: "Our proposals will now be much more realistic. We will not be seeking radical transformations of society" (ECO 7 April 1979). Of course, these "realistic" proposals, this offer of social peace, and the commitment to free enterprise do not distinguish the Communists very much from other parties, and do not recommend them highly to the crisis-affected workers who are seeking a real alternative. It should come as no surprise, therefore, that in recent years these parties have suffered electoral decline and significant worker indifference to day-to-day policy. In the May 1979 Italian elections, the CPI's vote declined from the previous 34 to 30 percent of the vote. However, this 4 point decline signified a 12 percent loss in the total Communist vote, which was especially heavy in its working class stronghold cities and among the youngest voters (eligible to vote for the parliament but not the senate). In France, the Communist Party had itself sabotaged the Union de Gauche, and thereby brought on the latter's defeat and its own decline; the party stalwarts have since reacted by "go[ing] back to the ideological ghetto" (GUA 14 May 1979), indicating "that it intends to work alone from now on. This self-imposed return to the political ghetto was accompanied yesterday by a tightening of the organizational screws and an alignment with Soviet-foreign-policy positions. Soviet officials here welcomed the shift as pointing to the end of Eurocommunism. . . . Even the Italian and Spanish Communists have had to start compromising with Moscow" (IHT 11 May 1979). It may also be argued that "the key blow to the Eurocommunist movement has been the divergent strategies. . . . [Therefore] it has faded away as any kind of coherent political force. . . . Whether it never really existed, as some claim, or whether it has been left moribund in the conflicting struggles within and among the Western Communist Parties is a matter of argument" (IHT 17 April 1979).

Similarly, it should not come as a surprise that the *International Herald Tribune* was moved to ponder on the "Last Days of Eurocommunism? . . . Its its unions (Commisiones Obreras) far behind. In view of all these events, it is longer is plausible to Western Europe, or perhaps no longer even a valid aim, and thus that the Socialists all along have been right. But in that case, why a Communist Party?" (IHT 28 April 1979). The *Washington Post* editorializes:

It marks the decline, though perhaps not the demise, of "Euro-communism" as a major force threatening or promising (take your choice) to redraw the political map of Europe and to turn the whole East-West contest practically inside out. It is hard to believe that as recently as two years ago serious people on both sides of the Atlantic, contemplating what seemed to be the inexorable rising fortunes of Communist parties in France, Italy and Spain, were debating nothing less than the ultimate fate of the West (IHT 12 May 1979).

In Spain, the Socialist Party (PSOE) and its trade unions, still virtually nonexistent at the time of Franco's death, have left the Communist Party and its unions (Comisiones Obreras) far behind. In view of all these events, it is not surprising that the secretary general of the French Communist Party, Georges Marchais, felt obliged to tell his party's congress that "Euro-communism has not died," and that the dissident from his party, Jean Pony, hurried to tell a Spanish newspaper that "Eurocommunism has not died, but it is sick" (EPA 9 May, 10 May 1979). It is difficult, therefore, to understand why Faire and Sebord (1973) and still later Sebord (1977) have had such high expectations for a socialist revolution in the near future in "Southern Europe" or "the circum-Mediterranean" region; equally perplexing is Ernest Mandel's suggestion (1975c: 27) that the "most favorable conditions for the abolition of the capitalist system exist in France, Italy, Spain, Great Britain, and perhaps Portugal . . . and in a further category, countries like Belgium and Denmark." Indeed, Mandel's own Fourth International allied *Intercontinental Press* was moved to present the 1979 Communist Party (CP) Congresses under the summary headline "French CP Waves Flag, Italian CP Hails Austerity" (ICP 2 April 1979).

It is not our purpose here to criticize social-democratic and Communist theory, policy, and practice, or to enter the ongoing debate about what differences, if any, remain, between them (but see Frank 1978f). Certainly their actions speak louder than our words. Nonetheless, the extent of the real political/economic ramifications of this theory and praxis perhaps deserves an additional comment here. The social-democratic parties (and this probably includes the French and Spanish Socialist parties, though they have not had the opportunity to prove it in government) have not only accepted capitalism, but also capitalism as it is—that is, monopoly capitalism. The social-democratic parties offer to manage capitalism for the monopolies by disciplining their labor and other constituencies and submitting them to the austerity policies—and ideology—that capital requires. Additionally, social democracy protects capital and capitalism from possible challenges from the left.

Moreover, what challenge does the Communist left really pose? As Mr. Berlinguer flatly states, certainly not socialism or even the threat of transition to socialism. The Communists inveigh against imperialism and "state monopoly capitalism"—particularly against monopoly, since they want to preserve and indeed expand the power of the state. They also want to preserve capitalism. All they want is to eliminate the elements of monopoly and imperialism, at least partially (whereas social democracy has long since accepted these). The Communist parties propose to eliminate monopoly and imperialism, however, as though these represented a benign tumor in the capitalist economic body which could be extirpated without interfering with the functioning of the remainder of the economic body. Indeed, the Communist parties argue that the capitalist body would function better without monopoly. (Curiously, so does one of the staunchest defenders of capitalism, Milton Friedman.) That is, the Communist parties, like the social-democratic ones, want to preserve capitalism, but the Communists want to make capitalism more healthy by eliminating what they regard as its debilitating monopoly disease.

This raises the question of the accuracy of the Communist theoretical diagnosis: to what extent are monopoly and imperialism separable from capitalism today, or to what extent could capitalism function without monopoly or imperialism and their protection by the state today? The evidence suggests that, realistically speaking, to none at all. Thus, the fundamental theoretical strategy of the Communist parties to combat monopoly and imperialism but not capitalism is totally unrealistic, and increasingly places them in the position of defending capitalism as it is, no less than the social democrats. The latter have long since divested themselves of their inconvenient theoretical baggage; now, as in the case of the "dictatorship of the proletariat," the Communist parties are beginning to do the same. Of course, for capital and its spokesmen, including *Fortune, Business International,* and Mr. Agnelli of Fiat, for example, the proof of the pudding is in the eating; and it is Communist praxis which counts more than its ideological recipes. Nevertheless, the more the Communist parties change their fundamental ideological base (including the abhorrence of monopoly and increasingly of imperialism as the alliance with the Soviet Union is breaking down), the easier it will be to accept the Communist parties, like the social democratic parties long since, as "democratic" defenders of the capitalist status quo. What remains to be seen is the extent to which current political praxis and emerging ideological theory will be acceptable to the working-class base of these parties.

Unions and the Capitalist Disciplining of Labor

The respective roles of social-democratic parties and governments and of Communist parties nationally and internationally—as well as of labor unions at the shop floor, factory, industry, national, and international levels—extend beyond their collaboration in the imposition of the incomes, austerity, and deliberate unemployment policies that capital needs to weather its economic crisis. These parties and unions also collaborate, intentionally or inadvertently, with capital in its increasing effort to cut costs of production; to raise profits through rationalization of production and the reorganization of labor or work processes at home; and the "runaway" transfer of industry to areas where labor is cheaper and/or markets are bigger. Additionally, the state with social-democratic support offers very extensive incentives as well as direct financial and other support to capital's growing efforts in the areas of rationalizing and foreign investment.

To cut costs and to maintain and eventually raise profits, capital is introducing measures on a substantial scale to rationalize production and to "humanize" work through "job enrichment." It is no accident that this movement is growing precisely now, with capital increasingly engulfed by a severe accumulation crisis. The "Taylorism" and then "Fordism" of the early twentieth century as well as the "human relations" management following the Hawthorne experiments in the 1930s were also pressed forward by capital in times of economic crisis (Braverman 1974, CSE 1976). "Hence the question: is not job-enrichment an adaptation of Taylorism and Fordism to new conditions of struggle in production, with the aim of preserving the profitability of capital, rather than a radical revolution of the labour process?" (CSE 1976: 63). This question would seem to merit an affirmative answer, and the big labor unions are collaborating in this task again now as they did in the previous introduction of the time-and-motion studies of Taylor and the Ford assembly lines.

> Experiments along these lines have been conducted in the USA in some large multinational firms such as Texas Instruments, Polaroid, Corning Glass, IBM, Chrysler, Ford and General Motors. In Europe, they have been tried at, for example, Volvo, ICI, Phillips, Olivetti and FIAT.... At the Volvo factory in Kalmar, the job recomposition experiment is based on the use of new types of wagon, substituting for the assembly line for the assembly of the Volvo 1964: the wagons perform three functions at the same time:—they convey information to the factories from the computers;—they transport bodies and chassis;—work benches are mounted on them. Industrial job recomposition and enrichment seems to be, then, only an adaptation of labour processes in mass production (Taylorism and Fordism) to new conditions of control of labour power, to new conditions of reproduction of the domination of capital in relations to the conditions of production ... and constitute a new capitalist practice: Neo-Fordism (CSE 1976: 63, 65).

> Union Decries Dehumanization of Jobs. National Protest Day Set in U.S. ... The pressures, the union contends, include compulsory overtime, arbitrary absenteeism controls, computerized scheduling so exacting that it results in what the union derisively calls "timed potty breaks...." Its rallying cry: "We are people, not machines" (IHT 1 June 1979).

The president of Aktieboläget Volvo, Per Gyllenhammar, comments in the *Harvard Business Review* under the title, "How Volvo adapts works to people":

> We wouldn't invest in dock assembly if we couldn't see economic as well as social justification for it. We can already see that it is possible to cut the standard assembly line production time sharply. . . . We couldn't really reorganize the work to suit the people unless we also changed the technology that chained people to the assembly line. . . . In any show of power, the employees today will "win" and management will "lose," though the inevitable result is that everybody loses. Instead of an adversary game, I hope we can rewrite the rules to make business the kind of game in which everybody wins. . . . Instead of people receiving discipline from the supervisor, the new climate emphasizes self-discipline (HBR July–August 1977: 103–112).

In plain English, isn't it the other way around? Capital invests in new technology when it sees economic justification for it, and it adapts people to work now by emphasizing self-discipline. Of course, the workers' own organizations from the shop floor to the national and international level are also called upon to collaborate in this "self-discipline." What is more, the American United Steelworkers Union itself insists on a "commitment by industry to modernize at their existing locations" (IHT 8–9 October 1977).

The political implications of this collaboration of social-democratic labor, Socialist and Communist parties, and labor unions with capital to reorganize capitalist production and bourgeois society both in the short and in the long run are extremely far-reaching—to the right. To begin with, the good advice of one West German labor leader to another that "on the left there is nothing for us to gain" (FR 22 January 1977) seems to be equally applicable in other countries. Simultaneously, in France "the national council of the C.F.D.T. puts the accent on the fight against the leftist currents" within it (LM 3 November 1976). This is all the more noteworthy inasmuch as the C.F.D.T., although linked to the Socialist Party, is the most independent left-wing trade union confederation in France. In Britain, "economic difficulties have brought a sense of realism and moderation. They have made extremists retreat," according to an economic consultant of Barclay's Bank, quoted by the *New York Times* (3 February 1976); the *Times* also observes that there is less talk about public ownership and class warfare in industrial relations because of the increasing success of the "moderates over militant, often Marxist, leaders [as] British Laborites take a new look at ideology." On the other hand, "the centrist revolutionaries" in the Labour Party have been largely defeated, or have used their final weapon—resignation—proving "that you can't beat them by joining them" (EPW 12 June 1976).

According to an article in early 1978 in *Business Week*,

> British politics seem likely to take a right turn. . . . Public-opinion polls and test samples by election analysts indicate that the majority of

the working class . . . now disagree with the basic left-wing socialist tenets upon which the credo of the Labour Party has rested since the famous 1945 election manifesto. . . . Today the polls indicate that many working-class voters no longer believe in nationalization of industry as a panacea, nor, for that matter, in a continuing close relationship between trade unions and the Labour Party. . . . Labour's policies are going to have to change if the party is to survive. . . . If Callaghan wins the general eleciton, Benn and the left still will be on the outside looking in. If Callaghan loses, and the balloting confirms the trend away from Labour Party principles among blue-collar workers, the Labour left wing will be left with a power base that has shrunken to a minority of disaffected middle-class voters and intcllectuals. . . .

Fortuitously, the Tory leader, Margaret Thatcher, has made room for Callaghan in the center of Britain's political spectrum by moving the Conservatives to the right. . . . That kind of shift within the Labour Party would have an enormous effect outside Britain, as well (BW 17 April 1978).

In the 1979 election, the Conservative Party ran on an election platform based on three major promises: to cut taxes, to cut spending, and to cut into labor and especially union power. With this platform the Conservatives won 339 seats in Parliament and, except in Scotland, swept to victory in every former labor stronghold of the Labour Party, which ended up with 268 seats and only 37.8 percent of the popular vote—that is, its lowest share since 1931. The Liberal Party won eleven seats, and other parties seventeen. Fortified by its forty-three-seat absolute majority, the new Tory government immediately proceeded to fulfill at least the last two of its election promises— cuts in government spending, especially on health and education, and attacks union power with a vengeance, leaving the public and labor reeling.

The *New York Times* observes that the "Outlines of [a] New Industrial Society Begin to Emerge in West Europe":

Confrontations between unions and employers are slowly giving way to accommodation aimed at peaceful social changes. . . . The search for alternatives to old conceptions of class conflict is spurred by the fears generated among unions and employers alike by inflation, unemployment and the struggle for export markets. . . . What is emerging is a design in which two-way negotiations over wages and working conditions yield increasingly to three-sided bargains on an economy-wide basis, with governments, unions and industries involved as full partners. . . . This quest for "Social Contracts" stems from a growing conviction among European union chiefs and business executives as well as ranking public officials that any return to unrestricted collective bargaining on the U.S. model is improbable in the foreseeable future. . . . Their belief that some form of incomes policy will be a semi-permanent fact of European life stems from awareness of the interdependence of

all the industrialized countries and of the degree to which that interdependence has been heightened by the long reach of multinational
corporations (IHT 23 July 1977).

But in the United States also there are "new moves to curb inflation
rate. Carter and unions agree on U.S. 'national accord.' President
Carter and the main U.S. trade union federation yesterday announced
British-style 'social contract' to secure the Labour movement's participation in the Administration's flagging programme to curb the surging
inflation rate" (FT 29 September 1979).

Still and all, we may agree with a "Left Eurocommunist" like Claudin
(1977, Frank 1978f) and a Trotskyist like Mandel (1978) when they argue
that it is still premature to make short shrift and write off the European
working class entirely. This mistake was already made, as Mandel points out,
before workers mobilized in the "events" of May in France and the "hot
summer" in Italy in 1968–1969 and in the strikes of 1972 and 1974 in
Britain. Indeed, it may be particularly premature to write labor off completely if and when, to face an ever-deepening crisis of capital, the business
and government "partners" demand even more self-discipline on the shop
floor and even more sacrifices from labor through their mutual "social
contract." What is more, this three-sided bargain among capital, labor, and
the state—which is also spreading to the United States—evidently involved
state power in the "free market" process of wage determination, and therefore makes the essentially *political* nature of that process clear to one and all.
Some may draw political conclusions from this lesson. On the other hand,
past experience, including that since 1968, seems to provide little realistic
justification for hopes of immediate "revolutionary reform" of or within the
Communist parties, as Claudin and others plead and hope for. (Even
Claudin's analysis of these parties shows how realistically hopeless the
situation is, as we argued in Frank 1978f.) Neither does there seem to be the
probability of another but more widespread and successful "May 1968"
under Trotskyist and other "revolutionary" leadership, as Mandel seems to
be waiting and organizing for; or of "autonomous" movements capable of
successfully challenging the labor and party bureaucracies, if the complete
paralysis of the "extra-parliamentary" left in Italy at this time of the
country's most acute political crisis is any guide. Finally, there is also
"Moscow's acute dilemma over Eurocommunism. [West European Communist parties seem] More of a threat than an ally" (FT 6 July 1977).
"Moscow's first interest is to prevent the spread of the Eurocommunist
infection to Eastern Europe and then to the Soviet Union itself. . . . Indeed,
some Eurocommunists suspect that important forces in the Kremlin might
welcome the break-up of the Western Communist movement" (Victor Zorza
in IHT 8 September and 29 June 1977). The mutual disenchantment of
Moscow (and Peking) and the Eurocommunists with each other has, of
course become as plain as day. They also disagree about what to do in
Western Europe. The Eurocommunists want to reform capitalism, and their

Soviet counterparts do not want even that. They prefer the status quo. However, the status quo is highly unstable, and capital and its states are preparing for the eventuality that in a deepening crisis they will have to demand still greater economic sacrifices from labor. It may well become politically problematic to obtain these sacrifices through "social contract" and labor's "self-discipline." In that case, capital will again have recourse to greater force and other powers of persuasion, and it is already preparing to use these.

The Political/Economic Crisis and the Shift to the Right

Capital's concern and preparation was publicly manifested through the publication of the revealing book, *The Crisis of Democracy, Report on the Governability of Democracies to the Trilateral Commission* (1975). This commission subsequently attracted considerable notoriety after some of tis members were elected or appointed president, vice-president, secretary of state and to other high officials in the United States and certain other governments. The director of the Trilateral Commission, who wrote the "Introductory Note" to that report, was Zbigniew Brzezinski, who later became President Carter's national security adviser. The obvious pedigree of the Trilateral Commission lends *The Crisis of Democracy* the aura of political policy at the highest level. Some excerpts speak for themselves:

from Chapter I. Introduction I.
The Current Pessimism About Democracy . . .

What are in doubt today are not just the economic and military policies but also the political institutions inherited from the past. Is political democracy, as it exists today, a viable form of government for the industrialized countries of Europe, North America, and Asia? In recent years, acute observers on all three continents have seen a bleak future for democratic government. . . . This pessimism about the future of democracy has coincided with a parallel pessimism about the future of economic conditions. Economists have rediscovered the fifty-year Kondratieff cycle, according to which 1971 (like 1921) should have marked the beginning of a sustained economic downturn from which the industrialized capitalist world would not emerge until close to the end of the century. . . .

The current pessimism seems to stem from the conjunction of three types of challenges to democratic government. First, contextual challenges arise autonomously from the external environments in which democracies operate. . . . Worldwide depression or inflation . . . may present serious problems to the functioning of democracy. . . . Changes in the international distribution of economic, political, and military power and the relations both among Trilateral societies and between them and the Second and Third Worlds now confront the democratic societies with a set of interrelated contextual challenges. . . .

They arise, however, at a time when democratic governments are also confronted with other serious problems stemming from the social evolution and political dynamics of their own societies.... At the present time, a significant challenge comes from the intellectuals and related groups. . . . This development constitutes a challenge to democratic government which is, potentially at least, as serious as those posed in the past by the aristocratic cliques, fascist movements, and communist parties. In addition . . . a parallel and possibly related trend affecting the viability of democracy concerns broader changes in social values. . . . The new values may not survive recession and resource shortages. But if they do, they pose an additional new problem for democratic government in terms of its ability to mobilize its citizens for the achievement of social and political goals and to impose discipline and sacrifice upon its citizens in order to achieve those goals.

Finally, and perhaps most seriously, there are the intrinsic challenges to the viability of democratic government. . . . In recent years, the operations of the democratic process do indeed appear to have generated a breakdown of traditional means of social control, a delegitimation of political and other forms of authority, and an overload of demands on government, exceeding its capacity to respond. . . .

[In] France and Italy . . . a very sizeable part of the electorate will always vote for extremist parties. . . . A general drift toward alienation, irresponsibility, and breakdown of consensus also exists in these countries and even in Sweden. . . . In Denmark, the netherlands, and Britain, the social democratic consensus is breaking down. . . . The late sixties have been a major turning point. . . .

from VI. Conclusions: Toward a Democratic Balance

Predictively, the implication of this analysis is that in due course the democratic surge and its resulting dual distemper in government will moderate . Prescriptively, the implication is that these developments ought to take place. . . .

Al Smith once remarked that "the only cure for the evils of democracy is more democracy." Our analysis suggests that applying that cure at the present time could well be adding fuel to the flames. Instead, some of the problems of governance in the United States today stem from an excess of democracy. . . . Needed, instead, is a greater degree of moderation in democracy. . . .

In practice, this moderation has two major areas of application. First, democracy is only one way of constituting authority, and it is not necessarily a universally applicable one. . . . The areas where democratic procedures are appropriate are, in short, limited. Second, the effective operation of a democratic political system usually requires some measure of apathy and noninvolvement on the part of some individuals and groups. . . . In itself, this marginality on the part of some groups is inherently undemocratic, but it has also been one of the factors which has enabled democracy to function effectively. . . . "Democracy never lasts long," John Adams observed. "It soon wastes, exhausts, and murders itself. There never was a democracy yet that did not commit suicide." That suicide is more likely to be the product of overindulgence than of any other cause (Trilateral Commission 1975: passim).

This "suicide" of democracy is even more likely with a little help from its "friends" who have discovered the challenges to democracy from a sustained economic downturn and—as Brzezinski emphasizes in his "Introductory Note"—are concerned that "their discussion of 'The Crisis of Democracy' is designed to make democracy stronger . . . and more democratic."

There is widespread and increasing evidence that the Trilateral Commission is not merely whistling in the dark. However, we can convey here only the very smallest—and perhaps most superficial—part of this evidence; our sources include mostly press reports.

Poll Finds Conservative Mood No Move to the Right in U.S.

What many perceive as a groundswell of conservatism in the United States—a new right, as it has been called—may instead be only an expression of extreme dissatisfaction with the federal government, a Washington Post poll suggests. . . . The Post's findings cast doubt on the assertion by rightist groups that the time is ripe for conservative candidates to unseat liberal or moderate incumbents in this year's House and Senate elections (IHT 14 March 1978).

The liberal Washington newspaper certainly sees the smoke, but perhaps it is trying to use its poll to deny that there is any fire. Even so, liberal and moderate candidates performed very poorly in the 1978 primaries and elections.

"[A] conservative tide currently floods the US Congress. . . . There is plenty of evidence of a tide running against the Liberals. Most of the 17 incumbent congressmen who were beaten, went down to strongly conservative challengers and in the Senate liberals . . . all went down to conservatives" (New Statesman 17 November 1978). "But [some] Democrats proved sufficiently adept at assuming classically Republican positions to minimise their losses. . . . The country's mood was clearly conservative, especially on fiscal matters, but also to a lesser extent on social issues" (FT 9 November 1978).

In the judiciary branch as well, there have been

shifting patterns in [the] High Court. . . . The clearest move the Court made in its 1975–76 term was to give the police and courts more leeway in handling criminal suspects and defendants. . . . The Court made it easier for police to search citizens without a warrant. Made it harder for a defendant to plead entrapment, easier for officials to seize a citizen's personal records. Made it more difficult for inmates to challenge disciplinary action (USN 19 July 1978).

The Burger Court Shows [a] Clear Trend with Landmark Rulings. . . . The death penalty [was] upheld. . . . [The Supreme Court has been] restricting the rights of criminal defendants, reinforcing states rights; refusing to expand, and sometimes limiting, privacy rights; and curtailing access to the federal courts. . . . The ruling was almost always in favor of the prosecution. . . . Civil liberties lawyers . . . are shocked and angry (IHT 12 July 1976).

Since then, in its spring 1978 session, the United States Supreme Court ruled in the Stanford University *Daily* case that the police may search the premises and seize testimony, even of citizens against whom there is no suspicion of criminal action or intent. (The police might thus find useful information as they did at the Stanford *Daily*.)

The abuses of civil liberties by the executive branch of the United States government have received substantial publicity through the Watergate scandal and revelations about the actions of the CIA and FBI as well as the repeated perjury of their responsible officials, who deny these continuing actions. Still, these continue, and even increase: "President Carter personally approved secret television surveillance of a U.S. citizen recently. . . . The legal basis for such surveillance is unclear. . . . Attorney General Griffin Bell also approved the wiretapping" (IHT 13 February 1978).

"Carter Seeks Eased Curbs on CIA Missions" (IHT 2 May 1979). Members of Congress and the press have been saying that the CIA's wings have been clipped too much (witness its supposed paralysis in Angola and Iran). Domestically, "Vast Police Surveillance Alleged in U.S. For Political Purposes . . . [it] continues 'on a vast scale . . .' a 3½ year study by the American Friends Service Committee maintains" (IHT 18 April 1979).

In Canada, Prime Minister Trudeau in late 1977 swore that it could never happen here.

"I do not think people suspect the RCMP of conducting themselves as the FBI does." But they certainly should: Buggings, break-ins, mail tampering, an enemies list and other illegal activities of Canada's security forces are coming to light here daily in a flood of revelations confronting Prime Minister Trudeau. The disclosures also include illicit use of medical and income tax records, arson and a variety of "dirty tricks," all contributing to the spectacle of a Canadian version of Watergate (IHT 23 November 1977).

Outside the United States government, in the society at large, "Political 'Decay' in U.S. Worries Scholars" (IHT 7 September 1976). The following headlines reflect various aspects of this "decay": "The trend of the last two decades shows a precipitous decline in voting in large industrial states" (IHT 5 November 1976). "Rightists in U.S. West Reviving Posses to Enforce Their Laws" (IHT 29 September 1976). "Big Arms Cache of

Rightists Unit Found in Calif." (IHT 13 December 1976). "Major U.S. Klan Faction is Armed and Openly Defiant" (IHT 17–18 March 1979). On 3 November 1979 Ku Klux Klan members openly fired on an anti-Klan demonstration and killed five people on the street in Greensboro, North Carolina, in front of the television cameras which relayed the event around the world. The popular rampage that cost an estimated $1 billion in one night (since revised down to $350 million) during New York City's second blackout made some people reflect upon the same "alienation, irresponsibility and breakdown of consensus" that worries the Trilateral Commission. This is "N.Y.C.'s Message for Carter," as conveyed by the *New York Times*:

> [Mr. Carter does not] need yet another commission to discover that half the black and Hispanic youths in his major cities are out of work and out of hope and out of mainstream America. . . .
>
> The need in our cities is for both defense of the society and insurance against the unemployment underclass. That is not a noble way of defining our most urgent human problem, but . . . (IHT 21 July 1977).

What is the solution? If the "measures of apathy and noninvolvement of some individuals and groups" hamper "the effective operation of a democratic political system," as the Trilateral Commission fears, then the solution is "a greater degree of moderation in democracy" instead.

Political Repression on the Increase

In Europe, similar tendencies are emerging. "Holland's Chief of Government fears Rightward Trend in Europe. . . . Prime Minister Joop den Uyl [says] the 'present tendency in all of Europe [is] to restoration toward the right' " (FR 21 September 1976).

> In various political circles and in part of public opinion, the idea is abroad that a general process of a "political right turn" is going through Europe. . . . I believe this is due to three economic reasons. In the first place, and possibly most important . . . [is] a reaction against the levels of tax pressure. . . . Another economic factor that seems to be rejected by the ordinary European is the growing economic intervention by the state. . . . Additionally, I believe, there is a third socio-economic phenomenon that the European citizen rejects: the express power and lack of control of the labor unions (EPA 29 November 1979).

The facts that the writer adduces to support his thesis are that the labor and social-democratic parties have been voted out of office in England and Sweden, where taxes were highest, but have been retained in office in Germany and Austria, where the three factors he cites are at least in evidence. On the other hand, particularly at German initiative, there is taking place: "A European Convention Against Terrorism. The end of the political offense?"

Inspired essentially by Federal Germany, it was to be signed on 22 September at Strasbourg by the Committee of Minsters of the Council of Europe. . . . This text climaxes the repressive legislation put in force in the past few years by the whole of the western countries. . . . If it is ratified, it would establish a sort of federalism of delinquency, especially political. Its purpose: to facilitate extradition. . . . The convention turns its back—to begin with—on the liberal tradition on the European level—and consequently on the national level—of a fundamental distinction of penal law: political offenses and offenses of common law. . . . With this text, therefore, there is no more political offense. . . . This convention denies in brutal fashion one of the principles of the rights of man which has long been accepted by positive law: the right to [political] asylum. . . . Federal Germany is demanding an almost general and automatic procedure of extradition. Who wants to help her fill her prisons? (LM 12 November 1976).

European justice Ministers, meeting in Dublin, have signed a new convention on terrorism designed to get around the reservations of some countries—including Ireland—about extradition. It replaces an original convention which Ireland and Malta refused to sign. The Irish Government claims it has constitutional difficulties about extraditing for 'political' offenses (FT 5 December 1979).

France, which originally held up the signature of this convention, did indeed extradite the German lawyer Klaus Croissant without much ado and in the most scandalous fashion. On the other hand, right before a demonstration by French and foreign opponents of atomic energy at a French nuclear power plant, the West German police sent photographs of West German opponents of nuclear energy ahead to the French police. And they were used. Further, "the West German Interior Ministry said that its close relationship with the Dutch police brought about the arrest last year of two German terrorist suspects . . . and that teamwork displayed by French and Swiss authorities led to [another] capture at a Swiss border post" (IHT 9 May 1978).

In West Germany, "the danger for internal security of the Federal Republic still comes from the 'left-extremists' according to the Verfassungsschutz [the political police]"—not from the "right-extremists" who have received increasing publicity (FR 28 June 1978). Accordingly, political repression against the left has been increased by the Social Democratic government to an extent in recent years impossible to summarize here. The West German weekly pictorial magazine *Stern* (6–12 July 1978; circulation 1,876,444) published an exposé of the "Überwachungstaat" (surveillance state) with photographs of police officers identifying and filming individuals at demonstrations:

These pictures are not out of a Nazi film. These pictures are German reality: West Berlin, 1 May 1978—police officers observe peaceful demonstrators. Freedom 1978—that means, no citizen is safe anymore from being shadowed by the police and the Verfassungs-schutz [political police]. No citizen can escape the computers of the guardians of the state. Millions are already registered. Freedom '78— mobilization against the citizen, prohibition to exercise one's profession and destruction of the democratic state of law. It means more police, better weapons and shooting to kill. . . . A demonstrator whose neck and head are held by the police. Plainclothes policemen photograph him with a police camera for the archives . . . Wherever Germans demonstrate—the guardians of the state are there. No matter whether it is about nuclear power plants, unemployment or slumhousing; whoever makes use of his basic rights is already suspicious for the police.

Nuclear power is a matter of very serious economic concern at home and abroad for big West German business and the state: "A planned, very important German industrial restructuring for the 1980s and 1990s relies heavily on an advanced nuclear industry and its exports" (IHT 29 June 1978). However, the West German nuclear business not only calls forth President Carter's staunch opposition to West German sales of nuclear reactors to Brazil; it also draws environmentalist opposition from urban and rural residents of various political shades at home. Therefore, during demonstrations against nuclear power plants in West Germany, the government closed off superhighways for a full day, searched 50,000 cars and confiscated jacks and tire irons as "potential weapons," turned people back at the borders, stopped and searched trains in the countryside after swooping down on them with helicopters, and beat hundreds of people black and blue. Police raids and "accidental" shootings of innocent people by the police are common occurrences. The government denies that it is holding any political prisoners, and calls them "common criminals" instead. Nonetheless, political prisoners receive uncommon treatment—they are systematically kept in solitary confinement for many months and in specially sound- and sight-treated, all-white cells, designed to eliminate stimulation of the senses. This police action is, however, only the administrative praxis of a series of politically repressive laws and a political climate deliberately created by the most responsible representatives of the West German "state of law."

The Bertrand Russell Tribunal—which previously examined American aggression against Vietnam and military terror and torture in Chile and other countries of South America—limited itself at its third session, in 1978, to examining the "Berufsverbot." Under this decree communists, and even left Social Democrats and conscientious objectors, have been denied public employment, particularly as teachers, after the Social Democratic government passed a "Radikalenerlass" law. Though the number of people who have been denied employment specifically under this decree is about four thousand, the number so affected through various subterfuges is many times greater, and those who have been investigated by the Verfassungsschutz number about two million (*Stern* 6–12 July 1978). Those who have been intimidated by this witchhunt—evidence of which goes right through the society to high school students—are virtually countless.

Furthermore, it was recently revealed that the border police maintained a list of 239 organizations and another of 187 publications ranging literally from A to Z (*Aktion Dritte Welt/Third World* to *Zivilcourage,* also including the foldout of the West German edition of *Mad* magazine). The police regards these as "extreme left," and have been controlling and registering carriers of such publications on computers at airports and other border crossing points (FR 30 May 1978). Moreover, the *Frankfurter Rundschau* (FR 30 March 1978) expresses the following concern: "To read can sometimes turn out to be expensive. How often does the Verfassungsschutz control public libraries and book stores?" For, as it turns out, the political police fills its computers with information on who reads and/or buys what in libraries and bookshops. The Trilateral Commission (1975: 30–31) is very concerned about the "tremendous increase in the number of intellectuals, would-be intellectuals, and para-intellectuals." Evidently, it is not alone in its concern. In October 1977, several leading West German political figures—including the heads of the conservative Christian Democratic (CDU) and Christian Social (CSU) Parties, Helmut Kohl and Franz-Joseph Strauss—made public statements very similar to the following assertion by CSU member of Parliament, Carl-Dieter Spranger:

> Terrorism has only been able to develop as dangerously as it has because numerous left intellectual publicists, politicians, theologians, professors minimized the danger and called it harmless . . . thereby extending the dangerous circle of sympathizers (FR 5 October 1977).

Among the guilty "left intellectuals" Spranger named were Nobel Prize winner Heinrich Böll, writer Günter Grass, and "politician" Willy Brandt, who was chancellor when the "Radikalenerlass" was passed, and who is still chairman of the governing Social Democratic party. The witchhunt, however, has hardly been limited to attacks against "left intellectuals." In 1978, the West German Parliament, with only four left-wing Social Democrats refusing to vote in favor, passed a new series of "anti-terror laws," one of which expressly permits the issuance of a single search warrant for one apartment to be used to search *every* apartment in the same apartment block/housing project as well. That would have been useful at Watergate!

In the meantime, in neighboring Switzerland laws and ordinances are said to allow still wider repression than in West Germany. Further, a certain Ernst Cincera has taken it on himself to organize the "fight against subversion" through the maintenance of a privately financed file and microfilm system of "subversives," some of whose names and activities he publishes in a regular bulletin, "What, Who, How, When, Where" (NZZ 24 November 1976).

The above-cited West German attack against the principle of political asylum in Europe, by denying the political character of political offenses, together with the similar West German initiative at the United Nations for the worldwide combat against "terrorism," are only the most visible signs that the increase of political repression in West Germany is not limited to that country alone, but is calculated to extend far beyond its borders. There is other evidence that West Germany—with the agreement of right-wing supporters and even governing forces in certain countries—is being built up to become the "political gendarme of Europe" to match its increasing economic dominance. The head of the Social Democratic Party, Willy Brandt, intervened in Portuguese and Spanish politics with West German funds; the Social Democratic Chancellor Helmut Schmidt lent money to shore up Italy's balance of payments in reaction to the increasing gravitation of the Italian Communist Party. In Europe, West German economic power and West German political repressions are meant to, and do, go hand in hand. If the West German bourgeoisie keeps its own house in order, the ruling class and its state can intervene elsewhere in Europe more effectively if and when the "need" should arise.

The political right and "democratic" governments elsewhere, however, are not simply waiting for eventual West German help in combatting their "subversion" and "terrorism" at home. The article in the London *Times,* cited above—"Armoured Cars at Heathrow: A rehearsal for a coup?"–went on to give serious consideration to the following in the English "mother of democracies":

> It would be wise to recognize that more and more people in this country, many of them men and women of impeccably liberal instincts, are beginning to contemplate seriously, and not without some satisfaction, the possibility of a period of authoritarian rule in Britain. . . .
>
> [An] officer was writing in a book to which the present Chief of Defense contributed a foreword: "If a genuine and serious grievance arose, such as might result from a significant drop in the standard of living, all those who now dissipate their protests over a wide variety of causes might concentrate their efforts and produce a situation which was beyond the power of the police to handle. Should this happen, the Army would be required to restore the situation rapidly."
>
> It is against this background that the self-styled action groups should be assessed. . . . Those at the private enterprise end of the political spectrum are beginning to organize themselves to fight battles which no political party seems disposed to fight for them. Large industrial concerns are beginning to talk in terms of a coordinated defence against industrial action or wholesale nationalization. The voice of Aims of Industry is becoming more insistent and more extreme (LT 5 August 1974).

Some people, including the British fascist leader of the 1930s, Oswald Mosley, and the American rightist, William Buckley, were expecting a military takeover in 1974, a time which witnessed increasing strikes in

Britain; such a takeover has not occurred. It is not likely now, but the threat remains and could arise again in the future. In the meantime, many "large industrial concerns" are increasing their finance of "coordinated defence." (A major bank through it opportune publicly to deny having contributed to the fund). At the same time, the League for the Defence of Freedom is becoming more insistent and more extreme—to the right. So is the outright fascist National Front. Meanwhile, in British-administered Northern Ireland,

> draconian powers against the IRA—unprecedented in peacetime— were announced. . . . The legislation will also allow a policeman to arrest without a warrant . . . and detaining suspects for up to a week. . . . This particular act, taken together with its subsequent amendments, has already been described by many international jurists as being more draconian than similar legislative provision in any non-Communist country in the world other than South Africa (FT 26 November 1974).

Since then, there have been revelations and denunciations of systematic torture of detainees. The British Army has certainly gathered considerable experience in handling civilian protest in Northern Ireland (as the Americans did in Vietnam). The British armed forces could and would just as well apply such expertise in Britain itself if the occasion arose. According to Mr. Jonathan Rosenhead, an executive of the British Society for Social Responsibility, "there is a rather disturbing parallel between what has been happening in Northern Ireland and what is now happening in England" (GUA 27 April 1979). This consideration should also be assessed against the background of the self-styled action groups elsewhere in the British Isles. Under the Labour government, "Scientists' warning after Southall rioting: Police 'may use gas and plastic bullets . . .' and SPG [Special Patrol Group] officers were being used as 'shock troops to spearhead this new aggressive policy'" (GUA 27 April 1979). The new Conservative government, of course, ran and won on an election promise significantly to increase expenditures and other support to the police and army.

The French army was said to have been extremely interested in the lessons it could derive from the military coup in Chile, and no doubt it has been assimilating the experience of the British Army in Northern Ireland. The French police used one thousand men in the operation to surround and capture one unarmed man, the West German lawyer Klaus Croissant, whom they delivered to the Germans that same night before any court might pronounce a staying order. Similarly, President Giscard d'Estaing refused to stop the reinstitution of capital punishment by the guillotine.

In Italy, authorized denunciations have revealed part of a plot at the highest level of the army and certain political circles to stage a military coup d'etat in 1970—that is, after the "long hot summer of 1969." More recently, such a step seems a less likely response. Nonetheless, in 1977, "Italy Suspend[ed] Habeas Corpus For Terrorists" (IHT 2 May 1977), an act indicating a rightward trend similar to that in the rest of the West.

Italy Uses Crackdown Law, Closes 4 Neo-Fascist offices. . . . The decree used for the first time against the neo-Fascists today permits the police to close down the headquarters of political groups when they are suspected of harboring arms even if there is not conclusive evidence. The decree also enables police to make preventative arrests and to keep suspects for 48 hours. It is the first of several measures intended to give police more power against political groups regarded as subversive. Both the Communists and the Christian Democrats wanted the new law-and-order measures. For the Communists this represented the reversal of a long-held policy (IHT 4 October 1977).

The Italian government has introduced a package of emergency anti-terrorist measures . . . [which] include life sentences for terrorists and wider powers for police forces. Police will now be able to detain and interrogate suspects without charges for 48 hours . . . to intercept telephone calls and search suspect buildings. . . . These measures . . . have been broadly welcomed by the main political parties (FT 17 December 1979).

Indeed, "all parties accepted yesterday that these extraordinary but not exceptional laws are necessary," and they also include "more severe norms regarding the definition of subversive associations" (EPA 14 December 1979).

This Communist Party "reversal" and all party agreement had been very emphatic. The Communist Party of Italy has appointed itself the most zealous defender of "law-and-order," and made the strongest and loudest calls for police repression during the kidnapping of Aldo Moro. Moreover, as we noted above, "Berlinguer equates the new left with the fascists" (FR 20 September 1977), such that the new "crackdown laws" are to be equally used against them. The question remains as to how far "the new left" extends.

In Portugal, after the "roses in gun barrels" liberation from forty years of fascism on 25 April 1975, "now the mood of the country appears to be one of frustration and complaint and most conversations with leftists, rightists or those in between seem to end with the view that the only solution may be another dictatorship" (IHT 5 November 1976). Since then the political center of gravity has certainly continued to move further and further to the right with the increasing deterioration of the economic situation. The failure of the austerity programs obliged Prime Minister Suares to resign, but the economic situation continued to deteriorate further. As a result, the right was voted back into the government in December 1979. On the opposite side of the globe, Chief of the Japanese "Self-Defense Force" Sakata observed: "Fascism or a trend towards fascism is rising in our country" (FER 14 November 1975). Although fascism has certainly not arrived in Japan, the political trend has continued to move increasingly to the right. Harder economic times have resulted in "a subtle shift to the right in national politics" and toward "fiscal moderates" at the local level (IHT 8 May 1979).

In the 1979 municipal and prefectual (provincial) elections, the Socialists and Communists lost all fifteen prefectual governorships as well as Osaka and, for the first time in twelve years, Tokyo to the nationally governing (conservative) Liberal Democratic party, which has been cutting social services. In the meantime, "Japanese Fleet sails on tide of rising militarism" (GUA 11 October 1978); and "Japan Enshrines 14 Top War Criminals" as "Right make[s] Hirohito's dynasty safe" with the wholehearted support of the prime minister and his Liberal Party (IHT 24 April 1979 and GUA 28 April 1979). In New Zealand and Australia also, the political trend has been sharply to the right and against labor: "How Australia Plans to curb the power of the unions. Federal and State governments introduce anti-strike legislation" (FT 31 October 1970).

The Crisis and the Ideological Challenge

In view of the growing economic crisis and the various actions and reactions in the social sphere, on the political level, and not least on the ideological front, a number of people have begun to invoke George Orwell's authoritarian "Big Brother is watching" society in his famous anti-utopia *1984* as a realistic prospect for just about that time (Amin et al. 1975; Amin, Frank and Jaffe 1975; Frank 1977c). Ernest Mandel (1975c) thinks that this "oft-cited 1984 fear complex in half-left, pseudo-left or moderate circles who want to escape from their own responsibilities" should not be exaggerated. Perhaps. However, there are also increasing references to 1984 in other circles: "Text of the Draft of a Federal [German Personal] Registration Law of 6 December 1977. A Law in Anticipation of 1984?" (FR 12 January 1978). "Computer Banks [in USA]. Big Brother is watching" (FT 22 October 1974). These and many similar fears are expressed in the press and elsewhere on the moderate right. Moreover, we can safely conclude that there is some fire behind all this smoke, particularly on the ideological front.

According to the "first global poll of public opinion," taken in the capitalist countries by Gallup International in 1975/1976, in the United States 33 percent, in Western Europe 39 percent, and in the Far East 30 percent of the people thought that "living conditions for people like yourself in this country are better . . . than they were five years ago" (USN 24 January 1977). The remainder, well over half, thought that they were the same or worse. In the United States 49 percent said "worse." Since then, although a minority may still find that "life is improving," hardly anybody anymore considers full employment a realistic prospect for the foreseeable future. In mid-1976, 66 percent of Americans no longer felt that full employment in the United States was a realistic goal. (Interestingly enough, in the same poll 69 percent blamed the government, 65 percent blamed the labor unions, and only 38 percent thought that business should take some responsibility for inflation; USN 13 September 1976). In his major nationwide television speech of 15 July 1979, President Carter observed that most Americans think the next five years will be worse than the last five (which were already worse than those before). The president then went on to analyze the "crisis of conscience," for which, however, he offered no remedy. Certainly, the dream of "ever bigger and better" through the "American way of life" has vanished for most people in the industrial countries, and has turned into a nightmare for many of them. As early as December 1973, *Time* magazine announced that this had been the "last year of the past"—that is, of the postwar era; and it pictured Western Europe as going downhill from then on. Perhaps *Time*'s editors and writers were not aware at the time just how real, steep, and prolonged this descent would be; but a large majority of the West's population has by now probably become aware of it, and this awareness grows with each succeeding recession. This situation poses a most serious problem for capital and the state on the ideological front, where the erstwhile postwar "bigger and better" ideology is increasingly belied by reality—not just by the "intellectuals, would-be intelletuals and para-intellectuals" that the Trilateral Commission cites. What new ideology is to replace the old, to offer the necessary legitimation of the system so as to achieve "social control" over the growing number of people who are "alienated" from the "mainstream" of life in capitalist society? That new ideology and the means to achieve its acceptance are still the subject of insistent search. "A genetic defense of the free market" through sociobiology (BW 10 April 1978) by Gary Becker and other Chicago-trained economists might convince some paraintellectuals, but is unlikely to catch the imagination of the masses. The *Harvard Business Review* (November–December 1975) published an opinion and attitude survey for the United States, and addressed the issue of "individualism" versus "communitarianism." Seventy percent preferred individualism, but only 62 percent thought that it existed in the United States at present. That is, 38 percent thought communitarianism already dominant today. Forty percent thought communitarianism more suitable for solving problems in the future; and 73 percent anticipated that communitarianism would be dominant in the United States by 1985.

> As the survey shows, many believe that we are in the midst of an ideological transition. When a traditional ideology loses acceptance, the community loses direction. Its institutions are no longer legitimate.... A society that ignores ideological change may promote the anarchy that inevitably leads to totalitarian temptations; history is replete with examples.... Ideology II... is becoming the legitimizer for our great and essentially communitarian institutions—Exxon, ITT, First National City Bank of New York, the U.S. government, Harvard University, and the like (HBR November–December 1975: 15).

Thus, it seems that the alternative to "individualism" is less "communitarian" than corporativist.

The extent of the social, ideological, and political problem and the urgency of corresponding countermeasures manifest themselves visibly as the tip of an iceberg. There has been Watergate in the United States and Lockheed and other scandals in Japan, Italy, and elsewhere, all of which have forced the resignation of heads of government or of state. Their successors, like Jimmy Carter and his "I'll never tell a lie" campaign and then his "human rights" campaign, have correctly sensed their principal immediate political task to be the short-term restoration of ideological legitimacy. Though they have had a measure of short term success during the 1976–77 economic recovery, none of them can be sure of its permanence, particularly if another recession—and/or the one after that—is very deep. There are other, less visible, but all the more real, manifestations.

Mental Health in the U.S. President's Study Panel Finds Emotional Stress More Widespread Than Was Previously Believed

. . . and that one-quarter of the population suffered severe emotional stress . . . and that it was probable that about 40 million Americans had diagnosable mental disturbances and were in need of professional care. . . . 16.4 per cent of the populations of North America and Europe could be defined as having "functional psychiatric disorders" (IHT 17–18 September 1977).

Only suicide and homicide, among death rates, rise and fall with unemployment and its familiar consequences during depressions. . . . The most dramatic indicator of the relation between job security and stress is the suicide rate. . . . For men of all labor market ages there is a peak in suicide for each peak in unemployment. . . . Among working-age males, for each unemployment peak there is an ulcer death rate peak . . . with a lag of between 1 and 3 years. Alternatively, one might emphasize the stresses which rise with the boom of the business cycle, such as overwork . . . [which make] heart disease, stroke, cancer, cirrhosis, diabetes, accidents, influenza-pneumonia, and many smaller causes of death such as ulcers rise during the boom with the lengthening of hours of work. . . .

The movement of death rates in the next decade will depend on whether and how capitalism recovers. . . . A recovery can only be produced by extraordinary extraction of surplus from one or more worker groups. If the small cohort is the object of this intensification, its health gains will be lost. If the baby boom children continue to bear the brunt of redistributive measures, the prospective increase in death rates for this group as it moves into maximal risk ages for heart disease, cancer, and cirrhosis will be that much larger (Eyer and Sterling 1977: 9,30–32).

Under the headline "Jobless Youths Worry West Europe. Fears Grow on Crime, 'Unemployables,'" the IHT (14 December 1976) reports:

The blight of jobless youth has fallen over Western Europe [leading

to the] development of a hard-core of long-term unemployed people. . . . As in the United States, it is school dropouts—often from the
least favored strata, often with inadequate vocational training or an
education mismatched with the needs of employers—who get the
hardest hit. In U.S. cities, rising youth unemployment has been associated with increased crime and other violence, suicides, drug addic-
tion and prostitution. An investigation has found fears running deep in
many Western European countries that they may be headed down a
similar path. Economic and social forces are combining to make youths
into . . . a new underprivileged group. . . . There is a danger of making
unemployables out of our employed. . . . There is too much similiarity
for comfort between what happened in the northern cities of the United
States and what is happening here [in London]. . . . Youth unemployment has grown so much in Britain that it is now genuinely reflected in
delinquency, crime and anti-social behavior (IHT 14 December 1976).

But since it is not possible to work to death all those who are employed or
to wait for all those who are unemployed to commit suicide, some other
social and ideological measures are necessary for the quarter of the population that is mentally disturbed and even for the three quarters that is not
(yet). One possibility is the "Big Religious Revival in U.S." and elsewhere as
well. In his triumphant tours of Mexico, Ireland, the United States, and his
native Poland, the very conservative Pope John Paul II drew far greater
numbers of people to hear or see him (3 million in Mexico, 5 million in
Poland, and in Ireland one third of the entire population at a single mass) and
elicited a far deeper response than conventional politicians of all hues put
together ever have. Referring to the estimated 150,000 young sect members
of "substitute religions" in West Germany, the *Frankfurter Rundschau*
(11 July 1978) points out that "common to all these groups is the fixation on
an authoritarian leadership figure with the foundation of a claim to abso-
lutism and total obedience that are tied to a strict submission to the group."

For the first time in nearly two decades, church attendance is up. . . .
Chuch membership is up, particularly in evangelical churches. . . . The
proportion of Americans—39 per cent—who believe religion is increasing its influence on U.S. life "is up sharply in recent months and
has tripled since 1971," Mr. Gallup said (IHT 18 June 1977).

[Church] membership of groups with a fundamentalist or related view-
point has increased steadily, while membership of non-fundamentalist
groups peaked in the mid 1960's and has declined since then. . . . They
seek to alleviate these uncertainties and disruptions by turning toward a
traditional and fundamentalist religious outlook (SA April 1976: 35–
36).

As the above-cited article on "The Science-Textbook Controversies" documents, these fundamentalists have launched a far-reaching campaign against

"the authority represented by scientific dogmatism." But they seek to replace it with far more reactionary political dogmas, such as that of the notorious "Moon" sect, whose ties to the South Korean CIA have been exposed in the world press.

There have been widespread attacks on the liberal and progressive education reforms of the 1960s, such as set theory, which helped children reason in mathematics, and notably also on integrated schooling, in which unequal educational opportunities were reduced somewhat. Reforms in educational content and organization are now on the retreat in the face of a well-financed and organized counterattack from the political right and ultra/right inside and outside the churches in the United States, Britain, West Germany, and elsewhere. The pretext for the attacks everywhere is that "Johnny can't read" or do arithmetic, and that test scores and educational achievements have fallen everywhere in the industrial world. The latter corresponds to fact and is another symptom of the crisis. But the proposed remedy of the economic, political, and ideological right is to cut educational expenditures (as noted above), reduce educational opportunities intended for minorities and the poor (in which they have been backed up by "anti-busing" movements and the Bakke decision of the U.S. Supreme Court), and to give educational content a politically and ideologically reactionary turn to the right.

> After 25 years of trying to follow America's lead in mass education, many nations are finding they have gone too far, too fast, and are trying to pull back. The once widely held idea that education for all would enhance economic progress and serve to equalize social classes is being abandoned in much of Europe and the Far East, and in many "third world" countries. . . . Even the rapid growth of college and university systems is being questioned in many nations. Many educators contend . . . an overeducated and underemployed graduate population. . . . The result has been a sweeping—and some would say regressive—reform. . . . All these suggestions of academic counterrevolution cause little surprise among American educators (USN 8 November 1976).

In West Germany, "conservative professors celebrated the 450th anniversary of the University of Marburg in their own way [with a call for the] return to 'leadership through the best. . . .' The so far most important association of professors . . . asked industry for contributions [and] as "retribution' promised its 8,500 members to help organize the necessary salvation of the German universities from political alienation and blind fanaticism" (FR 27 June 1977). Several right-wing parliamentarians, state ministers of education, and others in West Germany have formed a "Working Group Free Society [which] wants to drive political education into the right corner . . . [and] has taken the counter-offensive against all left—and liberal—enlightening developments in educational guidelines and textbooks"

(FR 4 November 1976). The counteroffensive is in full swing at the local and state or district school-board levels in one country after another.

Another development is "Dwindling Coverage of Foreign News in U.S." (IHT 6 February 1978) as well as elsewhere. At the same time, concerted political and financial attacks from the right are increasing against television programming that is not sufficiently "balanced" or not exclusively conservative. Programming or entire networks in Munich, Hamburg, and Paris have suffered such attacks. In short, the political right has launched a widespread ideological and literally reactionary counteroffensive all around the industrial capitalist world and the Third World. This worldwide counteroffensive includes the visible reactivation—and now international coordination—of fascist groups in the United States (Skokie, Illinois, and elsewhere), Britain (National Front campaigns against "coloureds"), West Germany (the new Hitler wave, local Nazi demonstrations, exposés of Nazi activities in the army), France, Italy, Japan, and elsewhere, which are only a glimpse of the tip of the iceberg.

Three increasingly widespread recent developments on the ideological and sociopolitical front merit special attention. They are the women's liberation movement, the ecological movement, and the revival of nationalist or regionalist movements. None of these are authoritarian per se. On the contrary, each of them, and perhaps the gay and other movements as well, in its own way contains an antiauthoritarian response to existing organized exploitation and/or repression of large sectors of the population, which is to be welcomed by progressives and people of goodwill everywhere. All three of these movements contain important progressive, socialist, and even revolutionary currents. But at the same time, it is possible to point to strong escapist tendencies in these movements and to note that they seem increasingly to be joined and/or taken over by politically right-wing groups. The exploitation and oppression of women is cemented in the social and economic organization of our society, and most socialist and revolutionary movements have done little or nothing to reduce, let alone to eliminate it. Therefore, the more than legitimate formation of women's liberation caucuses in left-wing parties and any progressive leadership in the women's movement are only to be welcomed. But almost everywhere the women's movement seems already to have shed its erstwhile left leadership and increasingly to support the political positions and status quo demanded by the right. The many environmental groups, ecological movements, and "green" political parties that are springing up in the West also represent much legitimate opposition to the reduced "quality of life" that capital is imposing on the population at large. Even more than the women's movement, the ecological movement and the green parties bring together people from a very large range of the political spectrum from left to right. (Many of them have concluded that "left" and "right" have become unidentifiable and/or meaningless.) But even if these social movements and political parties include many people who are subjectively left, the objective political consequence of their joint action is likely to be to reinforce the political movement to the right. They help to divide or otherwise weaken progressive and revolutionary movements and parties on the left, destroy center-left parliamentary coalitions, and throw the elections in this or that country or region over to the parties of the political right. The renewed rise of nationalist and regionalist parties may have similar but even more far-reaching consequences.

The renewed spread and intensification of nationalism and regionalism in the developed countries as well as elsewhere in the world could be the subject of a book in itself. Indeed, many books written by spokesmen of one or another of these movements are appearing (in English, for instance, *The Break-Up of Britain: Crisis and Neo-Nationalism* by Tom Nairn, 1977, and *Scotland 1980: The Economics of Self Government,* edited by Donald MacKay, 1977). Many of these nationalist and regionalist movements have made headlines elsewhere, and they are destined to do so increasingly as the crisis deepens in Scotland and Wales; Euzkadi (País Vasco, Cataluña, Andalusia, and Galicia in Spain; Flemings and Walloons in Belgium; Bretagne and Corsica in France; Sardinia in Italy; the Jura in Switzerland; Quebec in Canada; in Cyprus and elsewhere. Nationalism and regionalism are also becoming acute forces of contention in Yugoslavia, Eastern Europe, the Soviet Union, China, Vietnam, Kampuchea, elsewhere in Southeast Asia, Sri Lanka, various parts of India, the Middle East, and Africa, in many of which the forces of nationalism seem to be mobilizing the masses and pre-occupying the political leadership more than the ideological and political struggle between classes at the regional, national, or international levels. Perhaps the accelerated differentiation of development levels from one region to another, an acceleration generated by the economic crisis, is an important determinant of this nationalist and regionalist response. But the political implications of the ever more widespread appearance of these particular ideological responses also gives cause for further reflection.

Nationalism was already the subject of insistent soul searching by Marxists and others, from Marx and Engels to Lenin and Stalin, between a hundred and fifty years ago. They faced the dilemma of supporting or opposing popular mass movements at a time when many of these nationalist movements, especially after 1870, served political ends manipulated by the most reactionary and imperialist sectors of the bourgeoisie, as Carlton J. Hayes (1941) showed in his classic study. To some extent, notably in Germany, this tendency persisted through much of the twentieth century. But with the rise of the anticolonial and national liberation movements, particularly during and since World War II (except in the socialist countries that were liberated from fascism and where nationalism has often been manipulated for reactionary purposes by outside political interests), nationalism became a cause that Marxists and progressives were able and anxious to support. The present writer and others like him certainly supported nationalist causes all around the globe in writing and otherwise. Particularly after the war against, and the liberation of, Vietnam and other parts of

Indochina, nationalism retains a deservedly large political capital of good-will and support throughout the world.

However, today—not unlike a hundred years ago—it is becoming increasingly important to question whether many nationalist and regionalist movements, independently of the subjective desires of many of their leaders and supporters, are not serving or being manipulated by essentially reactionary interests to divide and conquer popular movements of resistance to capital as it seeks to confront the new crisis of capitalism. The United States playing "the Chinese card" in their global poker game with the Soviet Union, the Soviet Union's sudden abandonment of Somalia and perhaps of Eritrea in favor of Ethiopia in its power play against the West and China in Africa, and the Vietnamese invasion of Campuchea and the Chinese invasion of Vietnam are suggestive of the divisive and unprogressive uses and consequences of nationalism on the global level. But the neonationalism and regionalism that ae growing in many parts of Europe and elsewhere, as well as their flowering in China, Vietnam, and Campuchea, portend the additional danger that popular resistance to the restructuring of the world economy by capitalist capital will be derailed into nationalist protests that are ineffective at best and literally reactionary at worse. While the crisis of capitalism is differentiating the economy and society further and while some sectors of capital are launching dangerous authoritarian counteroffensives, nationalism and regionalism, like fundamentalist religion, may seem to offer ideological escapes for many individuals and another safety-valve for the capitalist system as a whole. The threat is very real that, even when real possibilities for it may exist, socialism may be sacrificed on the altar of nationalism and/or religion.

Of course, mystical, spiritualist, and fundamentalist religious waves; nationalist or regionalist movements; individualist escapes into personal neuroses, drugs, and criminality; as well as other centrifugal ideological responses of escape, offer no more of a solution than the possible instability of multiple political parties each pulling its own direction. Therefore, at each critical moment of the growing crisis, at least at the national levels, some existing or potential political leadership makes increasingly insistent calls for common sacrifice and self-discipline for the national good. There have already been several serious suggestions for the formation of coalition governments of national unity, which would include the broadest if not the entire parliamentary political spectrum. Some of these proposals have come from the political right, but, significantly, the most insistent ones have been made for their countries by the Communist parties of Italy and Spain. So far, the political situation has not yet ripened for such emergency political measures—that is, capital and the right have not yet found themselves obliged to accept or impose them. But the next economic recession or another lagging "recovery" from it, or the next recession after that, may well generate political emergencies in which such governments of national unity may appear as the only or at least the first acceptable political response. Of course, such governments would inherit and incorporate the ideological preparations made in the meantime by the political right (and some by the "left"). But if the crisis persisted or got worse, these emergency governments would have to pave the way for more permanent economic, social, political, and ideological crisis management, which could only select and utilize those aspects of previously centrifugal responses that could be incorporated into a centripetal and systematic crisis management.

The reactionary counteroffensive, like the growth and spread of fascism during the Great Depression of the 1930s, has its roots and raison d'être in the deepening economic, social, political, and ideological crisis of the capitalist world economy. We can—and I believe must—agree with Ernest Mandel when he says:

> Under these conditions, the conclusion is one that we have stressed continually for several years: The possibility of a new period of accelerated growth of the type that occurred during the 1950s and the beginning of the 1960s is, in the final analysis, liked to a radical increase in the rate of surplus value through a sharp compression of the mass of direct and indirect wages. Only such a modification could seriously relaunch the rate of profit and the rate of self-financed investment by the big monopoly trusts (that is, investments that are made without massive resort to inflation). And such a genuine upturn in the rate of profit is indispensable for generating a new era of *capitalist* "prosperity. . . ."
>
> Under these conditions, it is clear that a struggle for a substantial rise in the rate of surplus value—the sort of struggle that has marked the 1970s and will continue to mark the rest of the 1970s and the 1980s, just as it marked the 1920s and 1930s in Europe—has only just begun. . . .
>
> The capitalist world will not be able to pass from its present phase of general social crisis and generalized economic recession to a new phase of lasting and prolonged expansion except by first inflicting a crushing defeat on the working class and by inflicting disasters in the form of appalling famines, new bloody dictatorships, and new murderous wars on all humanity. . . .
>
> Increasingly, tough tests of strength between capital and labor will occur in many imperialist countries. Pre-revolutionary and revolutionary situation will arise in several of these countries (Mandel 1975b: 967–968).

What is not yet clear, especially in view of the political experience of labor and the political policies of its organizations and leadership on the left reviewed and foreseen above, is whether the working class and its allies will be able to take advantage of these "pre-revolutionary and revolutionary situations," or whether capital will "inflict a crushing defeat on the working class" and "bloody dictatorships" on us all.

We are still, then, in a situation of extremely unstable and fragile equilibrium. . . . In this situation, an accident of whatever kind—political, social, economic, or fiscal—can set off either a revolutionary explosion, or a counter-revolutionary, much more aggressive offensive of the bourgeoisie (Mandel ICP 13 May 1978).

In the face of the inevitable conflicts generated during another recession and the one after that (in time for 1984?), which will it be?

Chapter 4

Long Live Transideological Enterprise! The Socialist Economies in the Capitalist International Division of Labor and West-East-South Political Economic Relations*

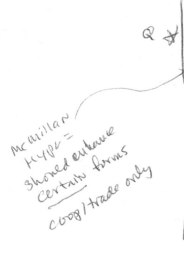

Q ✗

*McMillan
Hype =
showed evidence
certain forms
coop/trade only*

There is only one world market, the capitalist one. The so-called socialist economies, and particularly those of Eastern Europe, are being (re)integrated into this capitalist market as buyers, sellers, and producers at a pace which seems to have been accelerated by the deepening economic crisis in both the West and the East. The socialist East occupies an intermediary place in the international division of labor between the capitalist West and the Third World South. The exchange of raw materials for manufactures and the balance of payments deficits resulting from this unequal exchange between the South and the East are analagous to the similar structure of trade between the East and the West. Nonetheless, important interest groups in each of these societies have significant immediate motives for and derive long-term advantages from promotion of this East-West/South trade. However, the cause of socialist revolution in the Third World is not furthered by, but instead is often sacrificed to, these economic ties and related political interests and obligations. The Soviet Union with its political economic policy supports bourgeois forces and sometimes reactionary states all around the Third World.

The Chinese domestic policy of the four modernizations, especially since the death of Mao, and the foreign policy of "the enemy of my enemy is my friend" have led to Chinese alliances with reactionary forces all around the world. These are particularly flagrant instances of the sacrifice of socialist advance to other interests, including nationalism. In North Korea and in Vietnam since the liberation of the south, international economic engagements may also compromise some socialist domestic and foreign policies.

Some Prefatory Statements on Socialist International Relations

On Orthodoxy

Russian raw materials are necessary for the reconstruction of the world economy. Without them it is impossible—that is economically obvious. Even Keynes . . . admits that. V. I. LENIN

We [The Soviet Union] are in the process of becoming a part, a very particular part, but nonetheless an integral part of the world market. . . . Foreign capital must be mobilised for those sectors of industry that are the most backward. L. TROTSKY

We can admit without shame . . . that so far socialism has found no acceptable concept of its own covering the question of foreign trade and international economic relations. IMRE VAJDA, former president of the Hungarian Economic Association

On Policy

The new economic mechanism should establish a close relationship between internal and external markets. It should increase the impact of influences originating in foreign markets on domestic. . . . CENTRAL COMMITTEE OF THE COMMUNIST PARTY OF HUNGARY

---

*This chapter was written in July 1976 and revised in November of that year, between one and two years before the other chapters of this book. Nonetheless, it seems best to leave this chapter as originally written (and subsequently published in article form), except for minor editorial changes. To take account of some important more recent economic and political developments, especially in China, addenda written in May 1978 and December 1979 have been inserted after the sections on the Soviet Union and Eastern Europe, China and Vietnam, respectively.

The representatives of industry often regard foreign trade as something secondary. This absolutely false point of view must be changed, and the contacts between industry and foreign trade must be strengthened. The importance of a stable division of labour between socialist and developing countries must be stressed.   A. KOSYGIN

On Practice

Because of the broad economic links between capitalist and socialist countries, the ill effects of the current crisis in the West have also had an impact on the socialist world.   L. BREZHNEV

It may be hoped that the crisis which is raging in the West may come to a rapid end, since it affects and creates uncertainties for the Bulgarian economy, which to a certain extent is dependent on trade with the countries of the West.   T. ZHIVKOV,
first secretary of the Communist Party and president of the
Council of State of Bulgaria

On Strategy

The more varied our international relations, the more difficult will it be . . . for our possible opponents to break them. And even if [war or blockade] were to come, we would then be decidedly stronger than we would be under conditions of 'autarky' and the thereby consequent slower development.
                        L. TROTSKY

The key to US strategy towards the USSR has been to create mutual vested interests in the preservation of the international order. . . . Relations [between the US and the USSR] have become so stable that dramatic new departures could no longer be expected.   HENRY KISSINGER

We will be happy if our efforts to better Soviet-American relations help draw more and more nations into the process of detente—be it in Europe or Asia, in Africa or Latin America, in the Middle East or the Far East.
                        L. BREZHNEV

On Ideology

Lev Vasiliev [Director of the Kama River truck plant, the largest industrial project in the world, under construction in the Soviet Union with substantial Western participation] would no more call himself a revolutionary than a czar. . . . He is the leading member of an elite new breed of Red executives—well educated, well travelled, little interested in ideology and rhetoric—on whom the Kremlin is pinning its hopes for a managerial upheaval.   *FORTUNE*

Our foreign policy, today and in the future, is marked by the decisiveness with which it defends the interests of the Soviet people—the protection of the invulnerability of our borders, coastline and airspace, the defence of the dignity of the Soviet flag and of the rights and security of the Soviet citizens.

FOREIGN MINISTER GROMYKO

It is the first time that an arm of the USSR government [the Black Sea and Baltic Insurance Co, a subsidiary of the Soviet state insurance agency, Ingosstakh] has supported the United States government in insuring US private investment [against expropriation] overseas. We hope this is the beginning of similar mutually satisfactory arrangements between the two governments.

BRADFORD MILLS,

president of U.S. government Overseas Private Investment Corporation (OPIC), which insures U.S. private foreign investment against nationalization/expropriation in underdeveloped countries

My congratulations on the occasion of the sixtieth anniversary of the October Revolution. The relations of Chase Manhattan with your country began in 1924 in relation with the importation of U.S. cotton for the expansion of your textile industry. Since then, the international trade of the U.S.S.R. has grown considerably. We at Chase are convinced that the U.S.S.R. will continue to be a factor of growing importance in world trade. Of course, we hope to be able to cooperate with the Soviet Union to help it attain this goal.

David Rockefeller
President, Chase Manhattan Bank
(published in *New Times*,
Moscow, No. 46, 1977)

Two World Markets or One

The epigraphs above imply that the leadership of the socialist world has a deeply rooted history, both past and actual, of maintaining foreign trade and other international economic relations with the capitalist world. This tradition's survival—at least since the early 1920s—is taken for granted and even considered essential for the development of the kind of society envisaged by socialist leadership. In referring to the Soviet Union and the countries of Eastern Europe, the word "socialist" is used herein without the cumbersome quotation marks that would perhaps appropriately reflect legitimate doubt as to the real status of these societies. Indeed, economic integration of the socialist economies into the world capitalist economy (division of labor) and related political compromises have been considered not only a necessary evil, but apparently even a positive good—so much so as to call into question the extent to which the socialist world is separate or different from the capitalist world. Of course, international relations between the socialist and capitalist worlds are far from the only or even the most important side to this question. On the contrary, international relations, real and desired, merely reflect internal relations of production and other conditions in the socialist world, which themselves raise questions about qualitative or quantitative degree of shift over time toward or away from socialism in the part of the world that goes by that name. Opinions on this score vary widely.

There are four points of view: (1) These countries are indeed socialist. This opinion prevails in the so-called socialist countries themselves (except, of course, that the Europeans and the Chinese each deny that label to the other), but is also widespread in much of the rest of the world. (2) The socialist countries are ruled by an ill-defined elite that dominates their peoples. This view is popular with some sections of the capitalist world's bourgeoisie and intellectual elite. (3) The socialist countries, or at least the East European ones among them, are really capitalist, either because they never ceased to be so or because they have already returned to being so. This view holds favor in left intellectual circles in the capitalist world. (Opinion makers and followers in the East European and Chinese centers and those influenced by them at home and abroad frequently level this claim at each other.) (4) The socialist countries are neither socialist, capitalist, nor even a hybrid, but rather they represent some distinct kind of society that may or may not be transitional between the other two. This last body of opinion includes the Trotskyist thesis of "deformed worker states" and several other "new left" views that are less easy to define or label.

It is *not* the purpose of the following pages to analyze the essence of the socialist countries in terms of one of these four views, and even less to offer a clear choice between them. If the present author had to choose—and the reader may wish to know the author's personal inclinations in this regard—he would incline to a variety of the fourth opinion, with the proviso that current socialist society is likely to be transitional to capitalism, and with the emphasis that whatever the category, this part of the world is increasingly in integral part of the capitalist world economy.

The main purpose of the following pages is to document this integration and its cumulative and even accelerating tendency; to offer some tentative explanations for this tendency; and to examine possible consequences thereof for the economic and political process in the capitalist countries, developed and underdeveloped, and for their international relations with the socialist world.

It might perhaps be said that the Stalinist period of building "socialism in one country" was characterized by an increasing degree of autarchy, as foreign trade declined after 1928, regained its previous level in 1946, and doubled by 1950 (Carlo in Jahn, 1975: 84). However, this statement should be doubly qualified. In the first place, Stalin did not disdain foreign trade or the domestic sacrifices made on its behalf. During the depression years the world market price of wheat declined drastically, and Soviet production also declined during collectivization, leading to hunger and death by the millions. Stalin used collectivization to increase the share of the harvest that went to urban centers from 12 percent of the harvest in 1928 to 27 percent in 1931;

he also vastly increased the share destined for exports, from 0.14 percent in 1928 to 7.33 percent in 1931, before both shares declined again somewhat in 1932 (calculated from Ellman 1975: 847). The significant sacrifice of domestic consumption was undertaken to finance imports of industrial plants, machinery, and technology from the capitalist West. This Soviet foreign trade policy was pursued as long and as far as possible; and Henry Ford, among others, actively collaborated with it.

Secondly, Stalinist autarchy, both before and after the war, resulted more from western boycott than from Soviet and, later, East European socialist policy. The American boycott continued for over two decades after the war, and still continues in part through the refusal to grant most-favored-nation treatment or to extend Export-Import Bank loans, both denied on certain political pretexts ("human rights" and Jewish emigration). However, the United States has never successfully imposed its boycott policy on the European capitalists; and European competition, among other factors to be examined below, has increasingly obliged the Americans to make the economic pilgrimage to the East as well (for an account of the boycott, see Adler-Karlsson 1971). In any case, Stalin's later claim that "the single all-embracing world market disintegrated, so that now we have two parallel world markets . . . confronting each other," one capitalist and one socialist, was never true, even in his own time, and would be all the more untenable after his death in 1953 (Stalin 1953).

Growth and Composition of East-West/South Trade

Since 1953 East-West trade and East-South trade (i.e., with the capitalist underdeveloped countries) have grown appreciably. In the late 1960s and 1970s the following tendencies have been particularly marked: East-West/South trade has grown faster than socialist production. The growth rate of East-South trade has exceeded that of East-West trade, and both have grown significantly faster than East-East (intrasocialist) foreign trade. The growth of socialist imports has been faster than that of exports, particularly in trade with the industrialized West. This imbalance has led to an increasing balance of payments deficit of the socialist countries with the West (but a surplus with the underdeveloped countries). This deficit is financed by a growing debt by the socialist to the developed capitalist countries. These tendencies emerge from the following data:

East-West/South trade (defined as trade between the countries that are socialist today and the rest of the—capitalist—world) represented 6 percent of total world trade in 1938, fell to 1 percent in 1953, and rose back to 3 percent by 1967. Since then East-West/South trade has grown still further. East-West trade represented 10 percent of the West's foreign trade in 1938, 2 percent in 1953, and 4 percent in 1967. As a percentage of the now-socialist countries' trade, East-West/South trade was 74 percent in 1938, fell to 14 percent in 1953, and rose back to 25 percent by 1967 and to 32–35 percent in 1974–1975, according to apparently not quite comparable data in

GATT (1976: 171; Wilczynski 1969: 395). Between 1953 and 1967, while intrasocialist trade grew at an average annual rate of 6 percent, East-West trade grew at 13 percent and East-South trade at 16 percent a year (Wilczynski 1969: 55–56). The CMEA (Council of Mutual Economic Assistance [Comecon]) Statistical Yearbook offers somewhat different data, but displays similar trends.

TABLE 4-1

East-West and East-South Trade Growth Rates
(in percent per annum)

Period	CMEA Production Average	USSR	Intra-CMEA Trade	East-West Trade	East-South Trade
1956–60			10.9	13.5	17.6
1961–65	5.4	6.5	9.0	10.1	17.4
1966–70	6.8	7.7	8.8	11.3	11.2

Source: U.N.E.C.E., *Long Term Economic Growth of East European Countries: Objectives, Major Factors, and Patterns between 1960 and 1990* (Geneva: UNECE 1975c).

According to the UN Economic Commission for Europe, between 1966 and 1972 the evolution of trade between the Comecon countries of Eastern Europe with other parts of the world (and with each other) was as follows.

TABLE 4-2

Comecon Foreign Trade with Major Categories of Countries, 1966–1972
(in annual percentage rates of growth)

Trade Partners	Exports			Imports		
	1966–70	1971	1972	1966–70	1971	1972
Soviet Union and Six East European Countries						
Soviet Union	7.2	10.2	18.0	9.0	7.2	4.1
Other East Europe	8.6	8.2	7.5	8.2	10.5	15.3
Asian Socialist	7.4	20.0	−4.6	3.0	24.2	13.8
Western Europe	10.9	11.6	7.6	13.1	6.0	16.1
Other Developed	13.3	8.4	11.1	3.8	28.0	51.6
Underdeveloped	11.0	3.5	3.4	7.9	−0.9	2.0
Six East European Countries Only						
Soviet Union	7.2	10.2	18.0	8.9	7.2	4.1
Other East Europe	9.2	9.6	13.2	9.5	12.0	12.2
Asian Socialist	14.1	15.9	−0.7	8.6	14.9	7.7
Western Europe	11.2	10.1	12.8	12.5	9.1	16.8
Other Developed	12.3	7.3	16.5	7.8	46.1	17.1
Underdeveloped	9.0	9.7	−2.0	5.9	3.2	5.8

Source: U.N.E.C.E., *Bulletin économique pour l'Europe* (Geneva: UNECE, 1974b), 34.

Table 4–3 shows that the average annual growth rates of socialist foreign trade roughly doubled from the period 1965–1970 to the period 1970–1975, though they slowed down again in 1976 and 1977. East-West and East-South trade continued to grow consistently faster than intrasocialist East-East trade, and East-West trade grew more rapidly than East-South trade, except in 1976–1977. East-West/South trade increased from 37.4 percent of socialist Eastern Europe's total (including intrasocialist) foreign trade in 1970 to 45 percent in 1977 (UNCTAD 1979a).

From 1970 to 1977 East-West trade increased 8 percentage points, and East-South trade rose 3 points in the shares of total Comecon trade, while the share of intra-Comecon (East-East) trade fell by a further 3 points, according to CMEA data. However, despite this growth in East-West/South trade, the share of Comecon trade in total world trade fell from 10 percent in 1970 to 9.3 percent in 1977 (FT 12 September 1979). It is important to note that the value of world trade has been substantially inflated during this period—especially by the prices of oil, which accounts for a significant share of world trade.

The growth of foreign trade of the Soviet Union and Eastern Europe with the capitalist developed and underdeveloped countries, as well as among the socialist countries themselves, is detailed in Table 4-3; but these and the above cited CMEA data have not been adjusted for inflation. Therefore, especially during the most recent years, these data substantially overstate the real growth rate, and all exaggerate the difference between East-West/South increases and those within the socialist countries, among which prices were still largely maintained before 1975. Nonetheless, even after adjustment for inflation, growth rates of East-West/South trade have still been higher than those of intrasocialist trade.

We may observe from Tables 4-2 and 4-3, and in the data cited above, that in recent years East-West/South trade has continued to expand more rapidly than intrasocialist trade, but that the growth of East-South relative to East-West trade has fallen off, particularly since 1970. East-West trade has grown very rapidly in recent years (apparently at annual rates of 20 percent, 30 percent and more), yet because of inflation, its real value comes to less than the figures suggest. Nonetheless, for the years 1972–1974 the growth in East-West trade measured in real value is still estimated at nearly 75 percent (UNCTAD, 1975e: 114). After the relaxation of the American embargo—with a 3.8 percent "low" growth rate of imports in 1966–1970 including the Soviet Union—trade with the United States began to pick up. This trend is also reflected in higher growth rates, especially of Soviet imports, from "Other Developed" countries. The 51 percent jump in 1972 imports with the Soviet Union included (compared to 17 percent with it excluded), reflects the latter's major wheat import from the United States that year—sometimes dubbed the "Great Grain Robbery." The important motor force behind recent East-West trade expansion, however, is the Western export/Eastern import of machinery, equipment, and whole plants (e.g., the Fiat plant named after Togliatti in the Soviet Union) embodying advanced technology; the

TABLE 4-3

Foreign Trade of the Socialist Countries of Eastern Europe, 1965–1977
Value in millions of dollars (f.o.b.)
Exports

| Destination | Year | | | | | | Annual average growth rate | | Percentage rate of change over previous year | |
	1965	1970	1975	1976	1977	1965–1970	1970–1975	1976	1977
World	19,939	30,895	75,730	84,743	99,786	9.2	19.7	11.9	17.7
of which:									
Developed market-economy countries	4,052	6,774	19,387	22,775	24,848	10.9	23.5	17.5	9.1
Developing countries	2,772	4,754	12,404	13,363	17,015	11.4	21.0	7.7	27.3
Socialist countries of Eastern Europe	12,443	18,363	42,075	46,416	52,805	8.1	18.1	10.3	13.8

TABLE 4-3 (continued)

Imports

Origin	Year					Annual average growth rate		Percentage rate of change over previous year	
	1965	*1970*	*1975*	*1976*	*1977*	*1965-1970*	*1970-1975*	*1976*	*1977*
World	19,652	30,177	85,632	91,829	100,266	9.0	23.3	7.2	9.2
of which:									
Developed market-economy countries	4,390	7,800	30,580	33,024	32,502	12.2	31.2	8.0	−1.6
Developing countries	2,437	3,493	11,372	11,786	13,328	7.5	26.0	3.6	13.0
Socialist countries of Eastern Europe	12,252	18,393	42,426	45,801	52,781	8.5	18.2	8.0	15.2

Source: UNCTAD 1979b, p. 4.

East pays for these, insofar as possible, with raw materials, fuels, and food exports (but wheat imports), and with the return delivery of manufactures, in part produced through imported technology.

Since 1971 East-West trade has expanded at a particularly rapid rate, but socialist imports have risen even faster than exports, resulting in increasing balance of payments deficits and growing debt with the West. This tendency has been particularly marked for the socialist countries of Eastern Europe; but except in 1973–1974, when high raw materials prices favored the Soviet Union's exports, its foreign trade with the West has also been in deficit. The data are contradictory and not always clear, but a general trend in recent years emerges nonetheless. East-West trade was $2.5 billion in deficit in 1973 for the Soviet Union and Eastern Europe as a whole, including about $0.5 billion for the Soviet Union (UNECE 1974c: 78). Thanks to the rise in prices of raw materials, the Soviet Union reversed its deficit to a surplus of $1 billion in 1974. However, the deficit of the Eastern European socialist countries still continued to increase in both absolute and relative relation to the Soviet Union, so that the global deficit for 1974 still amounted to $2.2 billion (UNECE, 1975a). The cumulated balance of payments deficit of the Soviet Union and Eastern Europe with the industrialized West (excluding Japan) reached $7.6 billion in 1972; the Soviet Union alone showed deficits of $2.5 billion in the same year (UNECE 1974a: 70), $10 billion in 1974, and $12 billion in 1975 (UNECE 1974a: Table 3.14 and p. 43). Because of the capitalist world recession in 1974–1975, Western imports from the East (socialist exports to the West) declined while socialist imports from the West continued to rise. This continued imbalance resulted in a still greater socialist deficit of $6 billion, including a Soviet deficit alone of 3.6 billion rubles or about $4.8 billion, with the West in 1975 (UNECE 1975b; *Le Monde; Peking Review*).

According to more recent reports, the East European socialist countries' deficit, which was on the order of $1 billion for 1972, has risen still more, to $8 billion for 1975 and $9 billion for 1976, concentrated in trade with the United States, France, Japan, and especially West Germany (IHT 18 October 1976). About half of these socialist balance of payments deficits with the West are covered by official and supplier credits; the rest by Soviet sales of gold and increasingly, albeit in unknown amounts, by borrowing on the Euro-currency market. Although the size and rapid increase of the socialist countries' foreign debt are causing sudden alarm in the West (see IHT 18 October 1976 headline, "OECD Chiefs Meet Secretly on East Bloc's Rising Debt"), nobody seems to know for sure just how high that debt really is: "The Eastern managers jealously avoid all documentation of the credit balance. East-West money business are state secrets. A leading functionary of the Soviet State Bank jokes . . . 'we don't want to take a thankful research field away from the western Kremlin astrologers.' So the highest (estimated) figure that is mentioned is nearly double the lowest." The Polish Press Agency, Pap, numbers the total Eastern debt at $19 billion. "[The German] Dresdner Bank estimates the debt at 'a good $30 billion'. . . . The East experts of the Chase Manhattan Bank in New York... around $35 billion. ..." (WW, 1 October 1976: 16). Another German source estimates $22 billion for 1975 and $32 billion for mid-1976, of which $11 billion is owe by the Soviet Union (IHT 17–18 July 1976). For the end of 1976, the IHT (18 October 1976) reports an estimated projection of $38 billion in East European debts to the West. In mid-1976, the socialist countries owed 20 billion D marks ($8 billion), half of them through supplier credits, to West Germany alone (FR 15 July 1976). For later data, see page 229).

An increasing share of this socialist deficit and debt with the West is being settled multilaterally, with a possibly significant portion through East-South and West-South trade. East-South trade between the socialist world and capitalist underdeveloped countries has, until recently, been growing faster than other trade, doubling every four years between 1953 and 1968, and growing at a compound annual rate of 21 percent between 1971 and 1974 (Nayyar 1975b: 3; UNCTAD 1976c: 7). Burgeoning East-South trade has typically resulted in a chronic and growing balance of payments surplus for the socialist countries and a corresponding balance of payments deficit for the underdeveloped ones. Although much of this trade has been conducted on a bilateral basis with nonconvertible currencies, an increasing amount of East-South trade is carried on through the convertible currencies of developed capitalist countries. Significantly, the remaining surplus/deficit in East-South trade, after other attempts at elimination or settlement, is settled in the same convertible currencies. In order to prevent the undue and lopsided piling up of balances (between socialist and developing countries) bilateral agreements stipulate a maximum "swing" allowed in the payments balance. Any excess balances are settled to the end of each six-month period in goods, gold, or convertible currencies at the choice of the creditor (Salvi 1971: 72).

The socialist countries thus partially redress their deficit with the industrialized West through their surplus with the underdeveloped South, whose overall deficit is of course thereby increased still further. Moreover, part of the bilateral commodity payment received by the East from the South is also "multilateralized" and often sold to the West through so-called switch transactions. Salvi explains:

> The mysterious art of switch trading has been described in a nutshell by one writer as: "When the Russians don't wish to take up a consignment of Moroccan oranges to which they are committed under a bilateral trade agreement; they go to a specialist known as a switch dealer in one of Europe's financial centers and he arranges their resale to someone else at a discount. . . ." Export income [of one or more developing countries] can suffer when a bilateral trading partner dumps a part of that crop and so helps bring down the world price for it (Salvi 1971: 73).

Even more significant, at least from the point of view of the chronically deficitary socialist countries in East-West trade, are the "linked export and import arrangements, compensation deals and other types of parallel trading [which] contribute substantially to East-West trade finance by transferring eastern Europe's claims toward developing countries with non-convertible currencies into a means of financing the western import surplus" (UNECE 1974a: 27).

Thus, within the general international division of labor, growing East-South trade represents a positive, if modest, aid to the socialist countries in an effort to reduce their deficit, generated by the growing imbalance in Eastern import surplus/export deficit, with the industrialized countries. For the underdeveloped countries, bilateralism with the socialist world signifies an absolute increase in trading possibilities and a relative decrease in economic and political dependence on the West. However, the growing multilaterality of East-South trade and its inclusion in the international division of labor increases the overall deficit, debt, and dependence of underdeveloped countries.

To summarize the commodity composition of East-West trade, roughly two thirds of the socialist countries' imports include industrial products, and two thirds of the exports with which they pay for these consist of raw materials. In East-South trade the proportions are reversed: two thirds of socialist imports from the underdeveloped countries are raw materials, and two third of socialist exports to the South consist of industrial commodities. That is, as trading partners, the socialist countries are to the developed capitalist ones as the capitalist underdeveloped ones are to them—or vice versa! This pattern, its characteristic trends continuing beyond the dates cited, and some differences between the Soviet Union and the Eastern European socialist countries in this regard can be seen in Tables 4-4 and 4-5.

TABLE 4-4

Commodity Composition of East-West and East-South Trade
(in percent of socialist exports)

| | 1957–59 | | 1965– 66 | |
	Manufactures	*Raw Materials*	*Manufactures*	*Raw Materials*
East-West	33	67	40	60
East-South	60	40	68	32
East-East	57	43	68	32
	Percent of Western exports/Socialist imports			
East-West	68	32	67	33

Source: Wilczynski 1969: 37, 40.

The commodity composition of the socialist countries' trade with each other—two thirds exports of manufactures and one third raw materials—is structurally similar to that in East-South trade. From the developed capitalist West, however, the socialist countries principally and increasingly import industrial commodities, paying for them with raw materials, mostly food-stuffs and fuels. In this regard, however, there is a difference between the Soviet Union and other socialist countries. This difference reflects the pre-dominance of raw materials in the exports of the Soviet Union to other socialist countries and to the world as a whole; also evident is the much greater preponderance of exports of manufactures and imports of raw ma-terials by the socialist countries of Eastern Europe in their trade with the Soviet Union and other countries. Table 4-5 indicates the percentage of machinery and equipment in the total exports and imports of the Soviet Union and the socialist countries of Eastern Europe.

TABLE 4-5
Machinery and Equipment in Socialist Foreign Trade
(in percentages)

	Imports		
	1960	*1965*	*1970*
USSR & Eastern Europe	29	33	35
Eastern Europe only	28	33	36
USSR only			35
	Exports		
USSR & Eastern Europe	26	28	29
Eastern Europe only	33	35	37
USSR only			22

Source: UNECE, *Economic Bulletin for Europe,* XXIII, 2, 16–17; Carlo 1975:94.

Thus, while machinery and equipment account for a similar share of total imports by the Soviet Union and Eastern Europe, they represent a signifi-cantly greater proportion of East European than of Soviet exports. In both cases, however, the share is also rising. Eastern Europe exports substantial quantities of manufactures to the Soviet Union in return for raw materials and fuels, but depends even more on higher technology manufacturing im-ports from the West. Similarly, East European countries export a higher proportion of manufactures to the underdeveloped countries than does the Soviet Union.

With respect to equipment, the Soviet Union consistently imports about 50 percent more than it exports, both in its total and in its intrasocialist trade. Thus, in 1960 equipment comprised 31 percent of total Soviet imports, while representing only 21 percent of total exports. In 1970 the relation was still 34 percent of imports and 22 percent of exports. Of its exports of machinery in 1970, the Soviet Union sent 72 percent to other socialist countries, 25 percent to underdeveloped countries, and only 3 percent to developed capitalist countries. Even in East Germany (the DDR), the most industrialized of the East European countries, where 56 percent of total exports were from the metal-working industries in 1970, only 11 percent of its exports to West Germany (the BRD) came from this sector, while 49 percent of the BRD's exports to the DDR came from metal-working industries (Carlo in Jahn 1975: 95–96).

The same capitalist international division of labor that is reflected in this pattern of commodity composition in East-West/South trade can be further illuminated if we look at the factor proportions involved in the production of the commodities traded:

> On the average, trade between the USSR and the West is intensively capital import biased, between the USSR and the LDC (less developed countries) intensively capital export biased, and between the USSR and the CMEA (Comecon) factor neutral. . . . The direction of embodied factor intensive bias is positively correlated with the level of development of the trading bloc. Thus when the Soviets trade with relatively developed countries, they import capital intensive commodities and export labor intensive goods. When they trade with nations at a similar developmental level, imports and exports embody factors in approximately equal proportion, and when they trade with underdeveloped regions, they export capital intensive and import labor intensive products. The average pattern, however, is only half the story. The time trends are also significant. . . . In just thirteen years (1955–1968) we encounter a factor bias reversal transforming the Soviet Union from a labor intensive to a capital intensive exporter to the West. Similarly, USSR-CMEA trade exhibits a significant factor bias reversal between 1955 and 1963. . . . We could anticipate that sometime in the near future the Soviet Union will demonstrate a capital intensive export bias in its trade with all countries. . . . Soviet policymakers have systematically expanded light industrial imports which have been paid for more and more by natural resource and heavy industrial exports. Since light industrial goods are relatively labor intensive while natural resource and heavy industrial goods are strongly capital intensive, the politically motivated shift in the structure of Soviet commodity trade is undoubtedly correlated with the progressively increasing capital intensity of Soviet exports and the concomitant increase in the labor intensity of Soviet imports (Rosefielde 1974: 673–674, 678).

Although the above analysis perhaps exaggerates the rapidity of this shift, the emerging trends are nonetheless already visible in East-South trade relations. In 1970, 75 percent of East European exports to the underdeveloped countries were manufactures and 70 percent of the latters' exports to the socialist countries consisted of raw materials. The share of light manufactures in the underdeveloped countries' exports to the socialist countries—

TABLE 4-6

Commodity Structure of Trade of Developing Countries with the Socialist Countries
of Eastern Europe, 1965 and 1970–1976 (latest year available)
(Percentage share in total exports or imports)[a]

	SITC	1965	1970	1971	1972	1973	1974	1975	1976
Exports to socialist countries of Eastern Europe									
Food, beverages and tobacco	0+1	43.2	39.7	34.8	32.9	37.0	37.2	40.6	38.4
Crude materials (excluding fuels) oils and fats	2+4	32.7	30.7	28.7	24.8	23.5	23.0	16.7	16.0
Mineral fuels and related materials	3	0.2	1.5	4.2	8.0	9.3	12.2	16.1	18.8
Chemicals and manufactured goods	5+6+8	17.1	22.9	26.6	30.0	24.8	23.1	21.6	20.4
Machinery and transport equipment	7	6.8	5.2	5.7	4.3	5.4	4.5	5.0	6.4
Total	0–8	100.0	100.0	100.0	100.0	100.0	100.0	100.0	100.0
Imports from socialist countries of Eastern Europe									
Food, beverages and tobacco	0+1	9.2	10.1	11.7	9.5	13.8	16.3	11.7	11.0
Crude materials (excluding fuels) oils and fats	2+4	5.3	6.5	7.1	8.5	7.8	9.7	7.6	7.4
Mineral fuels and related materials	3	9.8	7.0	7.7	8.4	8.7	13.2	14.1	15.2
Chemicals and manufactured goods	5+6–8	33.1	31.2	30.7	31.5	28.4	30.1	29.9	26.8
Machinery and transport equipment	7	42.6	45.2	42.8	42.2	41.3	30.7	36.7	39.6
Total	0–8	100.0	100.0	100.0	100.0	100.0	100.0	100.0	100.0

aSITC 0–8

From *Monthly Bulletin of Statistics*, United Nations, March 1971, September 1974 and 1976, May 1977 and June 1978; *Commodity Trade Statistics* (Statistical Papers, Series D), various issues. UNCTAD, *Handbook of International Trade and Development Statistics*, 1969 and 1976. UNCTAD 1979b, p. 10.

Source: UNCTAD 1979b, p. 10.

no less than to the developed capitalist ones—increased from 5 percent in 1962 to 15 percent in 1970; the proportion grew even more rapidly in the early 1970s to 20 percent in 1972 and, with the 1973 raw materials price boom, to 17 percent in that year (Nayyar 1975b: 17–18). With the increased and accelerated Eastern import of Western technology and the Eastern drive to export more arms, machinery, and other industrial products to the Third World in the 1970s, this pattern has been reinforced.

Thus, the underdeveloped countries stand in similar relation to the socialist ones as do these to the developed capitalist countries with regard to both the factor proportions and commodity composition of East-West and East-South trade. In other words, the socialist countries occupy an intermediate position in the international division of labor, in this respect not unlike the most advanced among "subimperialist" underdeveloped countries, such as Brazil. The East imports advanced technology manufactures from the industrially developed capitalist countries, paying for them with raw materials and incurring a growing trade deficit. In exporting less sophisticated manufactures to the underdeveloped countries, the socialist countries run up a trade surplus, part of which they use to reduce their trade deficit with the West, also not unlike the subimperialist capitalist countries.

East-West/South and Tripartite Cooperation in Industrial Production

Beyond simple trade, the East-West/South international division of labor is being extended through long-term agreements for cooperative *production,* distribution and finance. Perhaps the most symbolic—but also real and functional—expression of this recently accelerating trend comes with the opening of a branch office of Rockefeller's Chase Manhattan Bank at Number One, Karl Marx Square, in Moscow. The UN Economic Commission for Europe writes:

> Certain long-term factors were in principle favorable to east-west trade as a whole. . . . There are, first, long-term (10-year) economic, trade and cooperation agreements among east-west European governments. The number of these increased from 93 (out of 119 possible) in the first half of 1973 to 102 at the end of 1974. Also, their nature has been changing. Previously, they had aimed primarily at the liberalization of trade and payments, but now they are increasingly concerned with industrial cooperation, trade in licenses, joint construction of enterprises, joint ventures in third countries, technological transfer, credits, and marketing. They provide also for establishment of joint commissions whose purpose is to stimulate contacts, cooperation and the establishment of foreign representation. Their impacts on industrial cooperation are encouraging. Following these agreements, special measures have been adopted in Poland (1972), the German Democratic Republic and Czechoslovakia (1973), Rumania, Hungary, and Bulgaria

(1974) to encourage domestic enterprise to seek international cooperation: they enjoy special facilities for the supply of capital goods, raw
materials and finance, and they benefit from tariff preferences and help
in management. . . . Particularly for East-European countries other than
the Soviet Union, industrial cooperation is a most promising factor for
the expansion of their east-west trade. There are a number of other
factors which help cooperation. Hungary and Rumania now admit on
their territories mixed corporations with minority foreign capital participation. Four such corporations were set up in 1974 in Rumania and two
in Hungary. . . . The gradual application of the GATT rules to Poland,
Hungary, and Rumania has often been extended to other countries. . . .
In the Soviet Union, there were, in mid-1972, 36 offices of foreign
companies and in mid-1974 over 70 (including 17 offices of Western
banks). In Rumania there are now 126 such offices. . . . Up to mid-1973
about 600 (industrial) cooperation agreements were signed in this field.
In Hungary alone, by the end of 1973, some 300 agreements existed (68
percent of which were in metal-making and metal-using, 11 percent in
other heavy industry, 11 percent in food industry, and 9 percent in light
industry). In 1974 there was an acceleration in their growth. At present,
firms from the Federal Republic of Germany are engaged in about 350
cooperation projects with enterprises and economic organizations in
East European countries (UNECE 1974c: 76-78).

By 1975 the 200 agreements of 1971 and the 600 agreements of 1973 had
grown to over 1,000 such East-West cooperation agreements, of which over
600 were in the metal-using sector (UNECE 1975a: 41).

Several authors and of course the business press, such as Business Inter-
national/Business Eastern Europe, have examined the varied kinds of East-
West industrial cooperation agreements. Hugo Radice summarizes:

EWIC agreements may be categorized loosely according to the extent to
which market relations are suspended. Less close types include licensing
or supply or plant or know-how with payment in resultant product, and
subcontracting. Closer types include co-production or product-line specialization, usually with a net financial balance of flows of parts, sub-
assemblies, know-how, licenses and final products; joint research, development and design work; and joint projects in third countries. Legally,
these agreements are almost always contractual, with the exception of
joint ventures for marketing in the West, and the still limited possibilities
for joint ventures with capital participation in Hungary and Rumania.
Most contracts run 5-10 years, and because of the complexities involved take up to two years to negotiate. . . . It is estimated that
cooperation agreements account for 15-20 percent of engineering exports from Poland and Hungary to the West, i.e., about 2 per cent
of total exports to the West: in other sectors and countries, figures are
probably much lower (Radice 1975).

We should not, however, underestimate the significance of these apparently modest—but rapidly growing—percentages, since they promise far-reaching impacts on the emerging structure of the international division of labor and—as we will observe in what follows—on the structure and relations of production in East, West and South. This impact is already suggested in part by Wilczynski's somewhat more detailed summary:

> Joint East-West ventures assume different forms: (i) The mildest form is the exchange of licenses, designs and industrial trainees. (ii) Cooperation in exporting parts of complete plants to third countries. (iii) Co-production ventures where a Socialist enterprise is usually supplied by a Western firm with initial key equipment and then certain key components, technical designs and perhaps technical advisers. The Western firm is entitled to an agreed portion of the production of the complete article. (iv) Dual production and marketing undertakings where a Socialist enterprise is supplied with similiar assistance as under (iii), but the final stages of production are usually completed in the West ("vertical co-production"). Subsequently the Socialist enterprise undertakes the marketing of the completed article in the Socialist Bloc whilst the Western partner does it elsewhere. (v) A Western enterprise, using its own key equipment, technical know-how, management methods and technical staff, carries on production in a Socialist country. The latter supplies the buildings, raw materials and labour. The Western enterprise is guaranteed an agreed share of production. . . . The initiative in the new drive for joint production and trading schemes has originated primarily from the Socialist side, particularly from the more dynamic Eastern European countries (Wilczynsky 1969: 382–383).

East-South collaboration in the production of manufactures and raw materials and in the processing of the latter is also preceeding apace. As UNCTAD observes in "The scope of trade-creating industrial cooperation at enterprise level between countries having different social systems," (UNCTAD 1975d), the underdeveloped countries often do not have the industrial base or other infrastructure to support agreements like the East-West ventures outlined above. Consequently, some East-South patterns of industrial cooperation are somewhat different. UNCTAD summarizes:

> The supply of (capital) equipment and (related) services with payments in derived or other manufactures may refer to the supply of production lines or complete plants; the supply of equipment or plant for the exploitation of natural resources supplemented by studies of the availability and accessibility of the resources . . . and the supply of equipment on a leasing basis. . . . It is beyond doubt that projects providing for the transfer of complete plants facilitate the incorporation into the relevant contracts of explicit guarantees covering the set-up time schedule, performance of the production line, breakdowns before expiration of the warranty and output quality. . . . Most contracts conform

to the formula of "two-phase" cooperation. . . . During the firm [first?] period, the partner from the industrialized country usually delivers capital equipment incorporation specific technology accompanied by technical assistance. In the course of the second phase . . . the developing country pays for goods and services received by return deliveries which can consist in goods produced through the use of the equipment and knowledge it has received. . . . A typical sub-contracting contract provides that the industrial enterprise in the developing country will produce and deliver an agreed quantity of semi-manufactured finished goods that are generally produced on the basis of documentation, know-how, frequently machinery, and occasionally particular product components, provided by the contracting socialist country. . . . Most contracts have a long-term and hence dynamic character. . . . Subcontracting between enterprises of developing and socialist countries would appear to meet three specific situations in particular. First, the case where the enterprise in the developing country has an economic advantage in the manufacture of certain components of an industrial product owing to a favourable production function (factor mix). Secondly, where the production capacity of the enterprise in the socialist country is insufficient to meet effective demand and new investment is considered uneconomical in view of industrial specialization targets adopted by the country in question. Thirdly, an industrial enterprise located in a developing country might consider that the cost of a new line of production would allow it to be more competitive if . . . part of the transformation process requiring highly specialized machinery and labour is sub-contracted to an enterprise in an industrialized country. . . . Co-production and specialization . . . consists in the specialization by each partner either in the production of certain components or in parts of a final product, which is then assembled by one of the partners or by both, each for the requirements of its own market(s). . . . There are two fundamental forms of joint venture: the equity joint venture and the contractual joint venture. In general, equity joint ventures are the traditional and most common form . . . in developed countries. Contractual joint ventures are frequently used where the laws of the developing country in which the business operations are to be conducted do not recognize the concept of private ownership of property or do not allow for ownership of property by non-residents (UNCTAD 1975d: 8–9).

In other words, with certain variations, East-South industrial cooperation agreements—like East-West ones (and traditionally West-South ones)—range from simple licensing and export of equipment or complete plants, all the way to socialist foreign investment in underdeveloped countries. This investment may take place either through ordinary equity ownership arrangements or, in the less frequent politically inconvenient cases, through some kind of contractual subterfuge. By 1975 the socialist countries of

Eastern Europe had completed or were implementing 2,900 industrial and other projects in developing countries, and had extended 11 billion rubles in credits (Ivanov 1975: 4).

East-South trade, aid, and other economic relations have, as previously observed, expanded more rapidly than trade between other regions. Estimates of total trade and the East European balance of trade surplus for various years appear in Table 4-7.

TABLE 4-7
Growth of East-South Trade, 1952–1972
(in $U.S. millions)

	1952	1956	1960	1964	1968	1972
	East European Trade with Capitalist Underdeveloped Countries					
East European Exports	175	470	880	2100	3070	5080
East European Imports	215	405	950	1520	1940	2820
	East European Trade with Less Developed Socialist Countries*					
East European Exports	860	1213	1767	1122	1717	2180
East European Imports	610	1130	1722	1010	863	1160

Source: Nayyar 1975b: 4.

*China, Cuba, Mongolia, North Korea, North Vietnam. Decline after 1960 reflects the Sino-Soviet break.

The distribution of this trade by continent has been roughly 40 percent with Asia and 30 percent each with Africa and Latin America. Until recently, however, East-South trade has been highly concentrated in relatively few countries in each of these continents. In Latin America, Argentina and Brazil have been the only important trading partners in addition to Cuba. In Africa the major trading partners until recently have been Algeria, Ghana, Guinea, Sudan, Tanzania, and Egypt; the latter, of course, has overshadowed all the others by far. Then, Soviet-Egyptian relations broke down, and economic, political, and military relations expanded with Morocco, South Yemen, Angola, Mozambique, and for a time with Somalia, soon replaced by Ethiopia.

In Asia, beyond the East Asian socialist countries, by far the most important socialist trade-aid-industrial cooperation partner has been India, with more limited economic relations with Afghanistan, Pakistan, Sri Lanka, Burma, Malaysia, Indonesia, Syria, Iran, and Iraq. These countries account for about three fourths of East-South trade and aid. East European economic relations with these countries have preferentially, though not exclusively, concerned their public sector and its enterprises. Some of the countries have received important aid for capital projects, particularly the famous Aswan High Dam in Egypt; the East also provided aid for the Bokara and other steel mills in India, projects whose financing had previously been considered but then rejected by international (World Bank), governmental, and private financial institutions in the capitalist world. Indeed, about 30 percent of socialist East-South aid has gone to India and Egypt alone. Beyond Vietnam and Cuba, and lately Angola, Ethiopia, and Afghanistan, India and Egypt have also been the major recipients of socialist, especially Soviet, military aid. The Soviet Union has not only supplied armaments to India, but has enabled it, for instance, to build Mig jet fighters at home. Most of this trade and aid has taken place thorough bilateral clearing arrangements. Payment for imports and loans from the socialist countries of Eastern Europe have been made primarily with raw materials (e.g., some 30 percent of Egyptian cotton exports). Increasingly however, exports to the socialist countries, especially India, include significant amounts of light manufactures and, more recently, products of heavy or engineering industry, which now account for some 40 percent of India's exports to the socialist countries. One item of agreed-upon Indian export to the Soviet Union, for instance, was ten thousand railway wagons per year for several years (Salvi 1971: 62). However, the *Peking Review* claimed that after India had built some of these wagons, the Soviet Union decided not to pay the previously agreed-upon price and offered a much lower one which was even below the Indian cost of production.

East-South agreements to develop economic relations have recently expanded to include an ever greater number of underdeveloped countries and a wider range of products, especially of manufactures. In 1973 alone, 130 new agreements were signed and in 1974–1975 the pace did not seem to slacken. The Soviet Union has doubled the number of underdeveloped countries with which it has agreements. By 1975 East-West economic agreements had been signed with nearly seventy underdeveloped countries of which thirty are in Africa, twenty in Asia, and thirteen in Latin America. There were 650 projects in the field of electric power generation alone. Economic agreements between the Soviet Union and Iran have reached $3 billion and include the steel, electricity, heavy machinery, and agricultural sectors in Iran. They also provide for the export of natural gas from Iran to the Soviet Union and the manufacture of paper and pulp in the Soviet Union for Iran (UNCTAD, 1975e: 10–11). By 1977 the Soviet Union had trade agreements with more than sixty, and the German Democratic Republic with more than forty Third World countries (UNCTAD 1979c).

UNCTAD suggests the following possibility:

[There may be] an emergence of a new pattern of specialization vis-a-vis the developing countries' needs. . . . In recent years, some socialist countries of Eastern Europe (in particular the USSR) have started to supply or have increased their supplies of industrial raw and semifinished materials to several, more industrially advanced, developing countries. . . . Some socialist countries of Eastern Europe have arranged long-term purchases of petrochemical products, mostly from factories they helped to establish (e.g. the USSR, Czechoslovakia, the

German Democratic Republic, Rumania and, among others, Afghanistan, Egypt, Lybian Arab Republic, Syrian Arab Republic. . . . The promising prospect of specializing in iron and steel products for the purposes of supplying the socialist countries have only been taken up in a modest scale as yet. It appears that only the USSR is importing on a more or less regular basis iron and steel products from India, Yugoslavia, Egypt (produced in plants it helped to establish). . . . The field of metal-transforming industries ... provides an especially suitable area. . . . The USSR and India have established such links in the trade of surgical instruments, lenses and other optical material, electric motors, simple gears and excavators. The USSR has agreed with Egypt that the latter will supply it regularly on a sub-contracting basis with specific components for motor cars. Also the shipyard in Alexandria, built with the assistance of the USSR, is exporting ships to the USSR. The partners have in several cases explored possibilities for specialization based on factories established in the developing countries by a socialist country (Czechoslovakia and India in engineering; Czechoslovakia, the USSR and Iran in machine tools; Rumania and Iran in railway carriages; the German Democratic Republic and India in electro-mechanical goods). The convergence of interests with respect to specialization and cooperation has been more visible in the textile industry, where the tendency of the socialist countries to shift towards higher-priced textile goods ... has been matched by the developing countries' ability to offer needed manufactured and semi-manufactured goods (UNCTAD 1976d: 7–9).

East-West and East-South as well as the traditional West-South collaboration in production, distribution, and finance do not take place and extend the international division of labor on an exclusively bilateral basis between each of these categories of countries. This collaboration also occurs on a multilateral or "tripartite" basis, involving enterprises from each of the three categories of countries in a single industrial or other type of project. UNCTAD sponsored a seminar in 1975 to examine and *promote* this significant new development in the international division of labor. In the documentation from this seminar we may read:

1. International cooperation between more than two enterprises from countries having different economic and social systems can materialize through various forms of multipartite deals. Tripartite cooperation, which is one of them, seems to be of particular interest in view of its intrinsic advantages especially in the framework of changing world economic conditions. In particular, it permits the extension of the developing countries of the profitable impact of growing East-West trade and economic cooperation. 2. International tripartite cooperation at the enterprise/organization level between countries having different economic and social systems is not confined to the industrial sector.

Successful tripartite projects have been undertaken or are being negotiated, or could be envisaged for future cooperation, *inter alia*, in the
fields of agricultural production and research and infrastructural development. . . . 11. Tripartite industrial cooperation has begun to develop significantly in recent years. It has developed from, and largely
relies on, the experience of bilaterial industrial cooperation. The survey
conducted by the secretariat found that many of the motives, sub-
stantive arrangements, problems and prospects of tripartite industrial
cooperation are quite similar in their nature to those which had already
been recognized in East-West industrial cooperation, largely through
the work carried out by the Economic Commission for Europe. According to existing evidence, Rumania was among the first countries
which promoted the tripartite form of industrial cooperation (UNCTAD
1975a: 4–7).

The cited document refers to 132 tripartite projects in thirty-three (plus
some unspecified) underdeveloped countried, 153 projects in seven (plus one
unspecified) East European socialist countries, and 168 projects in thirteen
(plus some unspecified) Western developed countries, for a total of 453 cases
of participation by individual countries in projects that are completed or
under implementation. At the time the report was written, 29 further such
tripartite contracts were under negotiation in thirty-three countries. The
surveyed tripartite projects that had been completed or were underway had
involved an estimated total cost of $21 billion at the time of implementation,
or $29 billion in current value.

Interest in tripartite agreements has continued to grow. UNCTAD reports that the total number of new agreements since 1975 is "not available,"
but that there is a "progressive trend." Thus, between 1975 and 1978 the
number of tripartite agreements has increased from twenty to fifty-eight for
Austria, and from twenty-one to sixty for the Soviet Union. While in 1975 a
total of thirty-three countries were involved in tripartite agreements, by 1978
the Soviet Union alone had such agreements with forty-six countries
(UNCTAD 1979c). The United States Department of Commerce reports:

> Polish trade officials have designated several industries in which
> Polish enterprises are interested in cooperative ventures with U.S.
> firms in third countries. This interest was indicated during the seventh
> session of the Joint American-Polish Trade Commission, held late last
> year in Warsaw. . . .
> Poland is offering to bid jointly with American firms in third coun-
> tries on projects relating to the following industries: electrical power
> installations, chemical plants and equipment, food processing installa-
> tions, chemical plants and equipment, food processing installations,
> wood processing equipment, and rolling stock. In all of these areas,
> Polish firms already are carrying out projects abroad.
> Polish experience in third country cooperation ventures with West

European countries dates back to the mid-1960s. Poland and a Swiss engineering company recently agreed to jointly develop coal resources in the Third World. . . . Other examples of Polish cooperative ventures in third countries with firms in Western Europe have involved the following industries: electric power stations, paper and pasteboard factories, machine tools, cement and sugar plants, and slaughter house equipment.

Polish officials believe that in many countries, Poland could supply labor intensive equipment, on-site project supervision and possibly even labor on advantageous terms. . . .

Commerce's Bureau of East-West Trade, established to bring business attention to commercial opportunities in the East European countries, stands ready to provide assistance or information (CA 27 February 1978: 9).

Eighty-three percent of the tripartite projects reviewed by UNCTAD were in manufacturing, including 43 percent in basic iron and steel industries together with basic chemicals, including fertilizers. UNCTAD adds, "this figure is far more negligible; it represents the equivalent of slightly more than one eighth of total imports of investment goods by developing countries during the last ten years 1964–1973" (UNCTAD 1975a: 10–16). The same document adds some further observations:

The survey found that intergovernmental action was one of the main factors influencing the development of tripartite industrial cooperation. . . . Out of the 23 tripartite industrial cooperation contracts for which a consortium leader was identified, Eastern European organizations appeared about twice as frequently as Western enterprises. However, when contributions were calculated as a percentage of the total cost of each project, the sample indicated that only 25% of Western contributions were one fifth of the total project cost or less, compared with 55% for Eastern European partners and 75% for the host developing country. . . . It was found that the enterprises in developing countries participating in tripartite industrial cooperation projects relied on their foreign partners principally for the supply of machinery and equipment and subsequently for project engineering, transfer of technology, assembly production and civil engineering. The sample clearly demonstrates the complementary nature of the specific contributions of the Eastern European and the Western partners in tripartite industrial cooperation project. . . . Such cooperation and in particular the joint delivery of investment goods to the industrial sector of developing countries is linked with the development of inter-enterprise cooperation between Eastern European and Western partners. . . . The availability of foreign credits was listed as one of the motivations in favour of tripartite industrial cooperation as well as a factor shaping into geographical structure. . . . An initial motive for a tripartite industrial cooperation project can be the availability of foreign credits earmarked for industrial cooperation (UNCTAD 1975a: 17, 49, 29).

Some further reasons, motivations, and "advantages" for the spread of such tripartite agreements are suggested by the same document elsewhere, albeit in more guarded language:

> It appears that an important incentive for participation in such co-operation by enterprises from both socislist and Western countries is to develop new markets or to consolidate export flows, either to the host developing country or region or to third countries. . . . Reportedly, an important motive for Western enterprises is a desire to develop opportunities for bilateral and multilateral industrial cooperation with Eastern partners, with a view to availing themselves of possible outlets in the growing CMEA market, since it is considered easier to work for that market if some experience has been acquired in previous fruitful co-operation, for example in joint plant construction. Tripartite cooperation has thus prompted Western firms to share part of their operational functions *inter alia,* as an indirect means of gaining, holding or extending medium and long-term market positions in the CMEA member countries (UNCTAD 1975a: 24–25).

Supplementary documents prepared by the UNCTAD Secretariat and by retained consultants for the seminar from East, West, and South permit a further appreciation of what is at stake in these tripartite arrangements:

> Experience has shown that actual cooperation between East and West is generally more extensive than the countries concerned will normally acknowledge publicly. . . . It should be noted that the third world does not generally feel that an *entente* between industrialized countries is necessarily in its interest. Rather, it would see an advantage in a competitive situation in which those countries try to outbid each other. . . . The systematic submission of joint tenders by enterprises belonging to the two systems may not, therefore, be equally appreciated by all developing countries. . . . For example, as far as the promotion of North-South cooperation is concerned, an industrialized country belonging to one system may find that its alliance with a country of the other system enables it to penetrate a third world market, access to which would previously have been politically difficult to achieve. . . . The industrialized partners may find that an East-West joint venture is less likely to have its interests harmed by the developing country in whose territory the operation takes place (after a coup d'etat or other political shift in one direction or the other for instance) than would be the case if the interests of a single industrialized country belonging to just one system were involved. The developing countries may consider that by entering into contracts with representatives of both systems they may benefit from the advantages of each and insure themselves against the inherent risk of establishing an exclusive association with one alone (de Lacharrierre 1975: 7, 4).

Tripartite arrangements do not, however, necessarily fulfill this function. In fact, they may reduce the options available to the buyer of technology if they provide a vehicle for reaching prior or separate agreements on the terms to be offered to the buyer by socialist enterprises and developed market economy firms that would otherwise compete with one another. When such agreements of a tacit or explicit nature exist, there is nothing to guarantee that any potential benefits that might arise from complementarities and division of labour between Eastern European and Western partners would necessarily be passed on to the developing country participant in the form of lower costs. Instead, the technology supplier may choose to exploit their dominant position within the tripartite arrangement to extract maximum returns. . . . The latter conclusion is supported by the experience of Sri Lanka with certain turnkey plants supplied for the public sector by enterprises of socialist countries of Eastern Europe, utilizing in part machinery obtained from firms of developed market economy countries. A recent study prepared for the first session of the Committee on Transfer of Technology indicates that the capital cost to Sri Lanka could have been lowered considerably had it been possible to order the equipment in question directly from several suppliers rather than through the socialist enterprises. In addition, the country would have avoided major difficulties in obtaining spare parts (UNCTAD 1975f: 2–3).

Nonetheless, Dr. Ivan Ivanov of the Institute of United States and Canadian Studies in Moscow, in a discussion paper prepared for the Tripartite Seminar at the request of the UNCTAD Secretariat and as its consultant, offers the following opinion:

It should be noted, in particular, that tripartite cooperation has been facilitated by the steady progress in East-West industrial cooperation. This appears to be the logical result of the open and complementary pattern of East-West commerce, which generates a multiplier effect in other world trade flows and therefore is trade-creative for developing areas too. East-West industrial cooperation (especially through subcontracting, co-production, licensing and joint marketing) is in fact very often primarily "triangular" in orientation, providing opportunities for the integration of exports of developing countries that call for more intensive utilization of their resources, including skilled labor and even technologically sophisticated inputs. . . . It is important, particularly in regard to the implementation of the New International Economic Order, that tripartite industrial cooperation should involve *all* groups of countries concerned, both producers and consumers, in mutually advantageous arrangements, thus providing an example for a general impprovement in multilateral understanding (Ivanov 1975: 5, 3).

Immediate Motives for East-West/South Economic Relations

Some of the motives, reasons, consequences, and implications of the important and rapid expansion of East-West, East-South, and tripartite trade and industrial cooperation are implicit—and sometimes explicit—in the discussion above. Nonetheless, further inquiry into these developments is necessary. We shall first examine the more immediate and perhaps cyclically variable motivations, and then proceed to the more fundamental, underlying, long-term reasons and implications after that.

For the capitalist West, the socialist East offers a life-buoy—as Joyce Kolko (1974: 150–161) suggests—in times of cyclical economic crisis and perhaps even more importantly, in the case of serious structural, economic, and political crisis. From the point of view of the Western governments with balance of payments problems, chronic and increasing balance of payments surpluses with the socialist East are evidently able to offer some relief. As United States Deputy Secretary of State Kenneth Rush noted in April 1973, "At a time when we have a trade deficit with most areas of the world, our balance of trade surplus with Eastern Europe is particularly welcome" (cited in Kolko 1974: 159). The national trade deficit is, of course, a reflection on the inability of private capital to sell enough abroad. Therefore, it should come as no surprise that the vice-president of the Chase Manhattan Bank declared: "Let's be quite honest. . . . We do have a balance of payments problem and we have to look for new markets" (cited in Kolko 1974: 160). He thus suggested that Nixon's and Kissinger's détente was born out of necessity.

Reflecting on Marxist theorizing about cycles and crises in capitalism and reviewing an earlier cycle, Wilczynski writes, "It is rather ironical that, during the 1958 recession, the Western countries' trade with other capitalist countries declined by 5 percent, whilst, with the Socialist Bloc, it rose by more than 6 percent" (Wilczynski 1969: 53). Ironical or not, this is the pattern in all capitalist recessions, most particularly including the one in 1973–1975, during which Western exports to the Soviet Union, Eastern Europe, and China rose while world trade as a world declined more than 10 percent in the one year of 1975 (as did Western imports from the East). Perhaps more significant still, the capitalist exports which rose most sharply to the socialist countries during a capitalist recession are those whose capitalist market demand is most affected in all recessions: capital goods and, particularly, machine tools. According to the *American Machinist* (cited in Mandel 1975b: 965), of the ten largest producers of machine tools in the world in 1974, three socialist countries of Eastern Europe accounted for 28 percent of total production and 15 percent of total exports; but four East European socialist countries accounted for 44 percent of the total imports of machine tools, worth over $1 billion, most of which the capitalist producers were unable to sell elsewhere in that recession year. Conversely, in capitalist boom times, capitalist interest in exporting to the socialist countries wanes somewhat, especially if payment is not made in convertible currency. This sudden loss of interest particularly affects capitalist exporters of raw materials from underdeveloped countries, who can then fetch high prices in hard currency for their raw materials in the Western industrial countries. In this case they become reluctant to sell them (or even to fulfill their delivery obligations) to the socialist countries. The circumstance may help account for the relatively low increase, considering the rise in the prices of raw materials, in imports by socialist countries from the underdeveloped countries during the 1972–1974 boom in raw materials prices.

Economic fluctuations and perhaps even cycles in the socialist economies themselves may also help account for variations in their foreign trade, or in its rate of growth. However, in the socialist economies, economic fluctuations would primarily influence their imports rather than exports, whereas the reverse holds in capitalist economies. Again contrary to the capitalist economies, in the socialist economies low growth rates of income or investment—or "hard times"—are likely to lead to an increase of imports from abroad, including the capitalist West. The pattern of "storming" (the rush to fulfill plan targets when behind schedule at the end of the plan period), which is familiar in domestic economic behavior in the East European socialist countries, seems to be reflected also in a temporal increase in imports to aid in the process of storming (UNCTAD 1975e: 14). Annual growth rates of national income, industrial production, and investment are known to fluctuate widely. Thus, between 1966 and 1974 the maximum annual growth rate of national income was 50 percent higher than the minimum annual rate in the German Democratic Republic (GDR), 100 percent greater in Bulgaria, 130 percent greater in the Soviet Union, and 288 percent (nearly four times) greater in Poland (UNECE 1975c: 7).

More significantly, but less demonstrably so, there appears to be a pattern of economic fluctuations in investment and income in the socialist economies of Eastern Europe. This pattern seems characterized by cycles of about eight years' duration, with four or five years of accelerated growth alternating with the remaining years of lower growth rates. (For a review of the evidence and of possible explanations, see Alexander Bajit, 1971, "Investment Cycles in European Socialist Economies: A Review Article.") The greatest amplitudes are in the rate of industrial investment and construction, implying the existence of investment cycles, and secondly, in industrial production. A temporal synchronization between the up and down phases seems to exist among the various countries, although in the 1960s the German Democratic Republic and Czechoslovakia appeared to lead the other countries by a year or two. The early 1950s seem to have been years of lower growth rates or downswing, while 1958 to 1960 witnessed accelerated growth or upswing, the 1961–1965 plan period downswing, and the 1966–1970 plan period upswing. Finally, there was another downswing during the five-year plan period from 1971 to 1975, during which the growth of industrial production, especially of consumer goods, was below plan and lower than in the previous plan period. The growth rates of foreign trade, and particularly of East-West trade, seem to have followed an inverse pattern: higher in the early 1950s and lower toward the end of the decade; 10 percent growth in the first half of the 1960s, 11 percent (unadjusted for inflation) in the second half; and a very much faster expansion of foreign trade in the 1970s.

Entirely satisfactory explanations for such apparent economic cycles in the socialist countries are not yet available. However, there is some suggestion that ambitious plans lead to upswings in investment. These lead to supply bottlenecks and restrictions, lags of wages behind productivity, shortages of consumer goods, and increased consumer dissatisfaction, expressing itself in political pressure and resulting in renewed lowering of the pace of investment (see Bajit 1971). Imports from abroad would seem to offer some possibility to supplement the supply of goods and especially to maintain the investment in machinery and equipment, particularly if these imports can be bought on credit. UNCTAD (1975e: 3 and 1976c: 3) notes that "the trend towards growing reliance by the socialist countries of Eastern Europe on the utilization of external economic factors in the course of the implementation of their current five-year plans was clearly reflected in the marked acceleration in the growth of the volume of their foreign trade, both in comparison with the levels achieved in the past and with the planned annual targets for 1971–75." Greater reliance than planned on foreign trade in Eastern Europe is, however, normal (UNCTAD 1972b: 3). The 1976–1980 plans envisage significantly lower rates of growth than those planned or achieved in the previous plan period (LM 16 December 1975). Other periods of reduced growth have witnessed a rise in Soviet demand for industrial imports to supplement inadequate domestic resources and production. The recent slowdown in Soviet and East European growth has again built up pressures leading to this kind of import demand. However, as imports have grown far more rapidly than exports (which have been restrained by depressed demand in the West), trade balance deficits have risen to over $10 billion a year, and import demand has had to be restrained again. UNCTAD (1975e) expected the "outward-looking policies" to be continued.

An UNCTAD report noted: "As a rule the current policy of the socialist countries appears to be progressively to replace, whenever possible, bilateral clearing arrangements by arrangements providing for payments in convertible currencies.... The multilaterialization of payments arrangements favours the establishment of rational price structures in inter-enterprise transactions" (UNCTAD 1975d: 6). The same document also anticipated complete transferability and possibly convertibility of the ruble, at least within CMEA. However, important economic and political impediments have emerged, imposed particularly by the Soviet Union for whom increased multilaterality implies threats to its economic and political control over her CMEA partners. Ausch argues:

The switch-over to multilateral trade and payments, to transferability and varying degrees of convertibility within CMEA, cannot thus be achieved by simple measures of monetary reform. All this can emerge only, on the other hand, as the concentrated expression of gradual changes within the individual countries and in the mechanism of co-operation, changes which must lead to *qualitative transformation* and to the abolition of the system of directive plan instructions; and, on the other hand, as a result of a general efficiency of the individual economies and of fundamental changes in the political pattern of the world. . . .

If the assumption is justified that the probability of doing away with the system based on directive plan instructions in the long run is greater in the other CMEA countries than in the USSR, the question may arise whether it should not be possible to create regional multilateralism and transferability in the trade between the other socialist countries and other parts of the world.

In order to examine the *realistic* possibilities of multilateralism and convertibility in the given economic and political situation of the CMEA countries, we must start from the expected possibilities and attitude of the USSR, the dominating economy within the CMEA and the main supplier and purchaser for the rest of the CMEA countries. Nobody who knows the situation is likely to dispute the fact that, for economic, ideological, traditional, and, last but not least, military reasons, the USSR is not likely to abandon in the foreseeable future her system of a planned economy based on directive plan instructions, although even there the mechanism tends toward flexibility. This fact itself sets certain objective limits to the progress towards a system of multilateralism. For political as well as economic reasons the USSR will also for a long time to come strive for bilateralism in her trade with capitalist countries. Profound changes would have to occur in the world's entire political pattern to induce the USSR to enter into multi-lateral trade with the latter and to introduce convertibility. . . .

There is, of course, steady pressure on the USSR from the developing countries to bring about the *external* convertibility of the ruble. It is possible that the USSR, after taking into account the position of the dollar, will meet these demands in some form with suitable restrictions (Ausch in Vajda, ed., 1971: 92–93, 90–91).

Advantages and Disadvantages of East-West/South Economic Relations

The international division of labor experiences its most rapid qualitative changes during periods of structural crisis in world capitalist accumulation. During these periods of erstwhile methods and relations of production, particularly those formerly leading industries in the most advanced sectors of the world capitalist system become relatively less profitable, even altogether unprofitable. Thus, the crisis of accumulation obliges capital to undertake important changes in the division of labor. This need, created by or at least magnified by the crisis, offers the opportunity to undertake changes for those sectors of capital that are able and willing to do so. The transformation of the division of labor—international, intranational, intersectoral, and intrasectoral—is also reflected in, and effected through, changes in the patterns of East-West, East-South, and West-South production and trade, as well as in the relations of these trade and production patterns among each region.

... for the West

Looking at the matter from the capitalist West, *Time* magazine (26 April 1976) refers to more than one thousand cooperation agreements between Hungary and the West, and offers the clue that "in their simplest form, such ventures involve little more than a thinly disguised exploitation of cheap Hungarian labor." Writing in the *American Economic Review*, Hewett adds further considerations:

> For the Western partner these "small deals" are quite profitable, since they shift the more labor-intensive, less profitable processes to an area where semi-skilled and skilled labor is relatively cheap and a good deal more *dependable* [no strikes] (Hewett 1975: 379–380; italics added).

Joyce Kolko (1974: 157) correctly points out that from the point of view of Western corporations, for the export of goods produced in East Europe, it is the stability (no strikes) and the low labor costs that are attractive to the industries from the strike-torn West. In Eastern Europe there is at least stability, and profit by any name can smell as sweet. These two economic *and political* reasons for expanding trade with and production in Eastern Europe appear repeatedly, often explicitly, in the United States business press, such as *Business International/Business Eastern Europe*. Moreover, investment in East Europe is not unlike the practice of "foreign investment" elsewhere. For example, International Harvester's manager of special operations notes that "the Poles have made a substantial capital investment in a facility to build an IH product. To the extent they have made the investment, IH doesn't have to make it" (BW 28 September 1974: 110). In the West, International Harvester will have extensive rights to market the Polish-built units, and in the underdeveloped countries the same bulldozers, loaders, and other equipment will be marketed partly by International Harvester under its own label and partly by the Poles without the IH label. "A number of Polish garment factories ... are producing entirely for the U.S. market" (BW 28 September 1974). Western sales of electronics were expected to more than triple between 1972 and 1978 (FT 25 February 1975). Xerox has already been using components manufactured in the Soviet Union for incorporation into equipment sold in the West (FT 25 June 1974). Exports of the Polski Fiat and Soviet Lada (Fiat) have been increasing:

> The Soviet Union plans to end production of its Moskvich, a medium sized car, by the early 1980s, and is looking to join with Western auto

company to produce a replacement that would be marketed internationally. . . . Parts would be made in both countries, and there might
be joint marketing, the trade group said. Some of the cars doubtless
would be intended for the home market, but officials clearly have their
eyes fixed abroad, where sales would fetch badly needed hard-currency
earnings (IHT 2 May 1978.)

These items illustrate significant trends in East-West economic relations
that in turn parallel the transfer of certain kinds of industrial production from
the West to some of the underdeveloped countries: labor-intensive industries,
such as textiles, clothing, and footwear, or manufacturing processes, such as
the fabrication of electronics components, are being transferred from economies where the cost of labor has become too high to keep them profitable to
areas with cheap labor; also of importance is the transfer of some heavy
industry, portions of automotive and related-equipment manufacturing, and
steel production to more advanced parts of the South—and of the East.
These industries include not only those in the West that are now becoming
"sick" because of problems in demand, cost of production, and relations of
production on the assembly line. They also include industries in which "labor
trouble" has been politically important in the larger context of the Western
world. Witness the strike initiatives in the Fiat, Renault, and Ford plants in
Italy, France, and Britain, or steel strikes in the United States and their
consequences for both the labor and political climates. What better strategy
than to shift some of the production in these industries to Brazil, the Soviet
Union, and Poland, where labor is not only cheaper but more disciplined?
Moreover, a politically effective domestic strategy does not necessitate the
transfer of all production. It is enough to transfer a little to make the threat of
another runaway factory credible when the next strike develops! Other
economic and political advantages of East-West trade and production relations for Western firms include the fact that, as *Business International*
(20 September 1974) entitled one of its reports, "Eastern European Partners Can Open Doors to Some LDCs." We have already observed how
East-West bilateral production for export to third markets (especially in the
Third World) and tripartite East-West-South production and distribution
arrangements are flourishing.

Another point of Western interest in the East is the role that the latter,
particularly the Soviet East, can play in providing fuels and raw materials in
the international division of labor. During the recent "energy crisis" and
renewed Western interest in the development of new sources of fuels and raw
materials, the regions of Siberia and the Soviet Far East have been under
continuous discussion by the Western press, with such headlines as "Mapping
out Siberia's Future," "Tapping Siberia's Riches," "Dusting off Siberian
Gas Plans," "Improved Prospects for Siberian Development," and "Billionaire Business in the East?" These regions have also been the object of
trade delegations and political negotiation at the highest level. At stake are

not only Soviet oil, gas, coal, timber, copper (negotiations with Anaconda were announced on the very day that Allende's Chile nationalized its copper mines!), and so forth, for consumption in the West, but also the sale of Western mining transport and pipeline equipment for multibillion dollar projects. Also at stake is the international political equilibrium in a multipolar world, in which joint United States-Japanese interest in the Soviet Tuymen gas project (Japan wants the gas but cannot finance it alone), and in the construction of another proposed Baikal-Amur railway line to transport petroleum—but also troops—just north of China's borders, threatens that country and its political and economic relations with Japan and the United States. Immediate economic and political obstacles have scuttled or delayed several such major East-West projects. Nevertheless, many individually less ambitious and noteworthy ones are proceeding and, as long as the détente permits, the prospects continue for developing more, bigger, and better enterprises. On the occasion of the West German chancellor's state visit to Moscow, the third gas-cum-pipeline deal, worth DM 1.7 billion ($.7 billion) was signed.

Advantages for Western capital in East-West relations are accompanied by some disadvantages, beyond the higher price of wheat resulting from Soviet purchases. Of course, in a competitive if highly monopolized world capitalist economy, East-West business signifies not only collaboration, but also competition for business—and very business-like waiving of ideological considerations. The Soviet Union is selling its Togliatti-built Fiats in West Germany under the trademark "Lada," and has undersold Fiat in Britain by one third. The *Financial Times* responded with alarmist headlines: "Comecon exports threaten Western motor producers" (FT, 18 February 1976). "Poland's drive into new car markets . . ."; "From the beginning, the Polski-Fiat 125 plant has been export-oriented, with about 70 percent of its production going overseas. . . . Having exported 70,000 cars last year the company is planning to tackle the U.S. market in 1977" (FT, 12 March 1976). The Soviet fishing fleet is ransacking the seven seas, to the increasing anger of its capitalist competitors. Not infrequently, socialist machine-building enterprises make—and occasionally win—competitive bids on turbines or other equipment for major capital projects. During the oil embargo against Holland, imposed by the Soviet-allied Arabs after October 1973, the Soviet Union delivered oil to Rotterdam. During a coal miners' strike in Franco's Spain, the Soviet Union delivered coal there. Part of the butter which the Soviet Union purchased from the Common Market "butter mountain" at half price was resold to Allende's Chile at the full world market price—in dollars. Perhaps the most widely remarked example of recent Soviet competition on world markets occurred when the Trans-Siberian Railroad, even with the decline in world shipping generated by the 1975 depression, carried one hundred thousand of the half-million containers, or 20 percent of the Japan/Korea-Western Europe ocean freight traffic. This was accomplished at 25, 50, and even 50 percent below ocean freight fares, and with faster delivery than the round-Africa route when the Suez Canal was closed (BW 12 January 1976, FER 21 November 1975). At the same time, growing at 6 percent a year, Soviet shipping itself has increased its world share by one third, to over two hundred million tons between 1970 and 1975, and charges 30 percent less than the Far Eastern Freight Conference rates (FER 13 February 1976). Experienced low-budget air travelers between the West and Asia or Africa are familiar with the cut-rate airfares offered by Aeroflot, below the lowest group/charter and similar fares of Western and other capitalist IATA and non-IATA airlines. Moreover, competition also works the other way around; so much so that Rockefeller has already proposed cooperation to West German capitalists such that the socialist countries will not be able to play one Western business partner off against another any more (FR 5 December 1975).

... for the South

The advantages of East-South economic relations from the point of view of the capitalist underdeveloped countries, or at least of their ruling classes, are fairly easy to see. To the extent that exports, and the imports from the East that can be consequently purchased, are supplementary to their trade with capitalist countries, and insofar as they need not "divert" exports away from convertible hard currency trade to inconvertible bilateral trade, this East-South trade represents largely a net gain to the underdeveloped countries, or rather, to their bourgeoisies. Most studies suggest that such exports to the East are in fact not "trade-diverting."

The construction of capital projects that, other things remaining the same (if that is imaginable), would not be undertaken without Eastern help are even more clearly a net gain—to those who benefit from them. Economic and military aid are available from the East on relatively favorable terms— generally lower interest rates, longer amortization on loans repayable bilaterally in merchandise rather than hard currency, and some grant aid or favorable renegotiation of accumulated debts. Such aid is of course welcome to those who benefit from it for their own economic, political, and military support, protection, or aggrandizement. Moreover, beyond the direct advantages, support from the socialist countries and the alternatives which it offers strengthen the recipient's hand in bargaining with capitalist—or other socialist—countries.

The terms of trade in East-South trade and the real cost of aid tied to a particular donor country for a given project have long been subjects of heated controversy. As early as 1964, when addressing the Afro-Asian Economic Seminar in Algiers, Che Guevara pointed out that, insofar as the socialist countries conduct trade with the underdeveloped ones at the "world market" prices set by the imperialist monopolies, the socialist countries exploit the underdeveloped ones through unequal exchange no less than do the developed capitalist ones. Prices in East-South (as well as in intrasocialist) trade—now notably in petroleum—have as a rule followed world market prices, albeit with a certain traditional lag that has been drastically reduced recently (from five years to one in intrasocialist trade since 1975). Indeed, a socialist cynic once remarked that after the whole world had become socialist, Switzerland might have to be retained as a capitalist country in order to provide "world market prices" for the socialist world to follow.

However, there have also been changes from some quarters in the West, in the underdeveloped countries themselves, very insistently by the Chinese, that the socialist countries of Eastern Europe charge even higher prices and pay lower ones than those going on the "world market." M. Sebastian, for instance, reviews:

> Authors like J. R. Carter, J. Berliner, M. Golman, Vassil Vassilev and Kurt Muller have charged that the Soviet Union sells it[s] commodities to the developing countries at 15 to 20 percent higher than the world prices and that it purchases mostly primary commodities from developing countries at a rate 15 to 20 percent lower than world prices. . . . Our analysis of the data forces us to conclude that India sold dear to and bought cheap from the Soviet Union. In the trade with the Soviet Union, India has been a net gainer: Similar conclusions have been reached by J. Bhagwati and Padma Desai, the NCAER and Dharm Narain (Sebastian 1973).

In view of this controversy, which also engages other authors whom we have consulted (Salvi 1971; Sankar De 1975; Nayyar 1975b and those in Nayyar, ed., 1975c), it is not possible to make a definite judgment here on this question nor to evaluate claims such as those of the Chinese in the *Peking Review* under the title, "Some Facts on Soviet Plunder of the Third World":

> It has been estimated that between 1955 and 1973, the Soviet Union through the exchange of unequal values plundered all kinds of third world resources to the tune of $11,300 million. . . . It has been estimated that the African countries in their trade with the Soviet Union had a loss of nearly $2,400 million between 1955 and 1974 due to unfavorable trade terms. More hair-raising is the degree of exploitation if viewed from the changes in the terms of bartering. While African countries in 1955 exported 1.8 tons of coffee in exchange for a Soviet metal cutting lathe, they had to export 4.2 tons for it in 1974 (PR 13 February 1976).

Sebastian found some individual cases of Soviet overcharging on some export items to India, and similar instances appeared in Allende's Chile and elsewhere, but whether these add up to a systematic pattern of exploitation—over and above the normal unequal exchange between more and less developed countries—is another question. What experience does show is that the socialist countries of Eastern Europe stick to business and drive as hard a bargain in international trade as anybody else.

Thus, after examining Soviet capital projects in India where, until 1970, 85 percent of Soviet aid was concentrated in steel (40 percent), oil, power, and heavy machine building, a study of "Soviet Social Imperialism in India" concludes:

> In the case of India too there is no basic difference between investments by the Soviet Union and by other imperialists. . . . (1) The Soviet social-imperialists have been able to force on the Government of India unequal contracts, without even the normal commercial safeguards [regarding, for instance, the almost "normal" delays in the delivery of contracted equipment and completion of projects]. (2) Machinery from the Soviet Union is sold at a very high price [at least in documented cases of the Bokara steel project and three petroleum refineries]. (3) Sales of components and raw materials, induced by the original investment, are very profitable. (4) The projects are designed not with a view to economy but to maximize sales. (5) Outmoded technology at transferred [and complete Soviet technological and management control is maintained until project completion]. (6) Indian technology is not encouraged and Indian conditions are not adequately taken into account [even when Indian technology and installed capacity are adequate to supply components of the project]. (7) The basic consideration of Soviet "aid" is to gain a foothold and break established Western cartels and earn super profits. . . . The pricing policy of the Soviet Union [is] to raise the price after a foothold has been established. . . . The commercial nature of the so-called aid is seen in that the repayment may begin even before the project goes into production, e.g., Bokara Steel plant credits were being repaid even before production began. . . . The Soviet Union then has up to now got the highest rate of repayment to "aid" given—almost 75% as against just 12% for U.S., 25% for UK and 50% for West Germany. . . . Up to 1969 grants were only 3.7% of total Soviet aid against 19% for US (CPI-ML 1976: 10–11, 4–5; material in brackets added by AGF from information supplied in pp. 3–10).

Similarly, an inquiry into "Special Gains from Trade with Socialist Countries: The Case of Tanzania" observed that, with regard to Eastern Europe, "It is essential to remember that the trade was carried out on convertible currency, and was not subject to effective bilateral balancing. . . . Tanzania has not derived any special benefits from its trade with socialist countries, other than gaining access to additional export markets" (Bienefeld in Nayyar, ed., 1975c: 262, 270).

The question of the advantages and disadvantages of East-South economic and other relations must be examined from some additional, broader perspectives as well. One of these perspectives is the socialist and capitalist underdeveloped countries' participation in the international division of labor. UNCTAD observes:

The development of East-West economic relations provides a number of opportunities for the expansion of East-South and West-South relations as well as tripartite links. . . . The expansion of East-West trade and economic cooperation is most likely to include trade-generating effects in the developing countries, as production expansion and modernization based on increased East-West trade and cooperation will raise the demand for industrial raw materials and semi-processed goods imported from the developing countries. The ability of the developing countries to respond to these opportunities could be enhanced by East-West partnerships. . . . Furthermore, the increased scope for an East-West-South specialization could contribute to the development of markets for exports of manufactures from the developing countries as well. Certain production operations which are no longer economically advantageous as a result of the opportunities opened up by expanded East-West production specialization could be shifted to the developing countries, under appropriate forms of cooperation agreements and contracts. . . . The institutional developments which have accompanied the growth of East-West trade and economic relations can help promote the expansion of global and integrated cooperation between the socialist, the Western and the developing countries (UNCTAD 1975e: 17–18).

For instance, in India:

A number of "conversion" deals have been entered into with the Soviet Union. In the cotton deal, the Soviets supplied Sudanese cotton (no doubt bought at "concessional rates") to Indian mills for turning these into textiles, and Indian compradores were paid a conversion charge of Rs. 16.5 crores. The entire output produced by Indian labour automatically accrued to the Soviet Union which had provided the capital (not all of it though) and thus got the surplus value produced (minus the conversion charge). . . .

In the cotton conversion deal the Soviets took advantage of the ailing state of Indian industry. Soon the Soviets proposed to extend the conversion deals to setting up "captive" units. This question was taken up during the Moscow visit (May 1972) of the Foreign Trade Minister, L. N. Mishra. He . . . [reported] that the Soviet Union had agreed to assist India in setting up certain labour-intensive industries. Later reports . . . revealed that the machinery for these units would be supplied by the Soviet Union and that the bulk of the products from these factories would be earmarked for export to the Soviet Union (CPI-ML, 1976: 16–17).

The collaborative insertion of the Soviet Union and India in the international capitalist division of labor, however, goes further. Another example is the Indo-Soviet protocol agreed upon in 1968 and signed on 20 February 1970:

The two sides agreed detailed examinations should be made at expert level, as early as possible for identification of the possibilities of exports, of products manufactured in Soviet assisted plants in India to Third World countries and for consideration of various aspects connected with the implementation of India's participation in Soviet assisted projects in such Third World countries. In particular, the Soviet side would examine the possibilities of assisting in exports of turbojets and components to be produced at Heavy Electrical Plant in Hardwar (CPI-ML 1976: 18–19, from official Indian documents).

The Declaration by the socialist countries . . . at the third session of the United Nations Conference on Trade and Development . . . circulated at the request of the representative of Bulgaria on behalf of the [9, including the Ukrainian and Beylorussian SSR] authors of the Declaration offers a similar prospect and perspective: One effective means for achieving a further development of economic relations between the socialist and developing countries might be a sectoral division of labour involving the use—on the basis of specifically and economically sound proposals—of the potential possibilities existing in various sectors of production, especially in the production of industrial products (UNCTAD 1972c).

Yet on the very same and the preceding page of this official declaration from the socialist to the underdeveloped capitalist countries, the socialist ones add:

At the same time the socialist countries reiterate their view that it is wrong to try to adopt an identical approach in any form to the socialist and to the developed capitalist countries, since such an approach is tantamount to bury in oblivion the entire historical phase of colonial rule and exploitation. . . . The socialist countries understand the specific problems of the least developed and the land-locked countries among the developing countries of Asia, Africa, and Latin America, and take these problems into account in their practical activities. The socialist countries will adhere to the forms and methods of international economic and technical cooperation which are in keeping with their social and economic system (UNCTAD, 1972c).

How is this declaration of principle compatible with the socialist countries' declaration on the same page offering a "sectoral division of labor . . . especially in the production of industrial products," which, as UNCTAD observed, "could be shifted to the developing countries" when and because these products "are no longer advantageous as a result of opportunities opened up by expanded East-West production specialization"? How should we understand Kosygin's declarations about the "division of labor between socialist and developing countries"? (*Times of India* 4 March 1976). We may well ask then why or how the underdeveloped countries' approach to the developed capitalist and socialist ones should not be identical. How do the socialist countries "understand the specific problems of the least developed" countries any differently from anybody else. How are the "forms and methods of international cooperation" that "are in keeping with the social and economic system" of the socialist countries of Eastern Europe any different from those of a still continuing "entire historical phase of colonial rule and exploitation" by the capitalist imperialist West?

Action speaks louder than words or official declarations. On the one hand, the socialist countries' offer their promise of understanding, and observe that "the causes of the continuing economic backwardness of developing countries are: the existing structure of international economic relations in the capitalist economic system, based on an obsolete and irrational division of labour . . . ," as stated in the above cited "Declaration" directed at the underdeveloped countries at the UNCTAD III conference in Santiago in 1972. On the other hand, the present author, like many others at the same conference, observed that on the most crucial issues the East European socialist countries, and particularly the Soviet Union, in fact lined up in debate *and* in vote—unless they abstained!—right behind the developed capitalist and imperialist countries led by the United States. At the various international conferences for the negotiation of international laws to govern the exploitation of the oceans and their seabeds, the coincidence of economic interests between the Soviet Union and the United States, West Germany, and others has also found them willing allies against the demands for protection pressed by the underdeveloped countries (FER 28 November 1975, and other sources).

At the Law of the Sea conference in Caracas, "on important particular issues the Soviet Union operated on the side of the Americans and against the developing countries, whose sympathy it otherwise woos" (FAZ 6 September 1974).

At the UNCTAD IV conference in Nairobi, "despite Indian Prime Minister Indira Gandhi's enthusiastic expression of appreciation for Soviet support for the Third World on her arrival last week in Moscow [Japan's Chief Delegate to UNCTAD IV, Toshio] Kimura was struck at Nairobi by the gap between Moscow's words and its actions. 'The Soviet Union and the East Europe bloc (the D Group) expressed great sympathy for the less developed countries, but their attitude did not differ from that of the B Group (the developed countries) on specific matters such as the common fund and accumulated debts.' " These last were the two principal points of contention between the capitalist developed and underdeveloped countries, in which the latter demanded a common fund to finance and stockpile raw materials and a moratorium on accumulated debt, both of which the United States, West Germany, *and* the USSR refused to accept. (Quotation and internal quotation of Kimura are from FER, 18 June 1976: 52).

Perhaps, if only because of its vast economic and political importance, the most critical case of East-South economic-political-military relations deserving further attention is that between the Soviet Union and India. Beyond the narrower question, "Does India buy dear from and sell cheap to the Soviet Union?" (Sebastian in EPW 1 December 1973), it is necessary to evaluate the development of Indian state monopoly capitalism, the Indian economic, political, and military subimperialism in South Asia, and the defacto triple American-Russian-Indian alliance supporting the Indian bourgeoisie's role in the area. We must consider the total Soviet support of Mrs. Gandhi's government while it was engaged in the "emergency" repression of the working class; the elimination of habeas corpus and the detention of reportedly over 180,000 political prisoners (NBI January–February 1976: 9); and a host of other measures, such as a ban on strikes and even on legal protection (forbidding petitions for injunctions) against employers who themselves broke the law (EPW 11 October 1975). These and other measures of emergency rule brought "an observable improvement in labor discipline," (NZZ 18 March 1976) and a decline by more than half of man-days lost thorugh strikes, with "the improvement . . . more impressive in the public sector enterprises" (FER 20 February 1976), which are precisely those most closely linked with Soviet aid. Aid to whom, we must ask. The only possible answer consistent with the facts is that this aid serves the big monopoly bourgeoisie in India, which has been the main economic beneficiary first of the Soviet-supported public sector in India, and ultimately of the emergency rule by its political representative, the Indira Gandhi regime. The fact that this regime enjoyed the political support of the Moscowline Communist Party of India (CPI-Dange), and that Mr. Brezhnev in his visit to India went so far as to call Mrs. Gandhi a great socialist whose government was leading India to socialism with broad support, does not change the real implications of Indo-Soviet relations (EPW 8 December 1973: 2161). On the other hand the economic and political independence of Mrs. Gandhi's government became apparent when, after Sadat's break with the Soviet Union, and on the grounds that "business is business" India wanted to sell its Soviet-licensed, Indian-built Mig jet fighter spare parts to Egypt, "the Indian government acknowledged . . . that the Soviet Union blocked India from supplying Egypt with spare parts for Mig-21 fighters" (IHT 18 March 1976).

Economic interests make strange political bedfellows, and so do political and strategic interests. Perhaps they should no longer occasion surprise after the multipolarization of ping-pong diplomacy. If we view this multipolarization from the perspective of the underdeveloped countries, their liberation movements, and their peoples, the question of the advantages and disadvantages of East-South no less than West-South relations presents itself with particular force. In reviewing and introducing the studies on economic relations between the socialist countries and the Third World collected under his editorship, Deepak Nayyar asserts:

Interestingly enough, economic ideology and political developments within the poor countries had little to do with the relationship. International political developments were far more important. To begin with, it was factors such a[s] cold war rivalries and the decolonization policies in Third World countries that sought to assert national economic independence. Later, it was a question of international balance of power in certain regions of the world, e.g., the Middle East and South Asia (Nayyar, ed., 1975c: 245).

Moreover, where "politics" was or is not immediately determinant, simple business is. For. "business is business," as the first secretary of a Soviet embassy in Latin America answered the present author, explaining why his government was not only maintaining but increased its trade *and* credits to Brazil after the reactionary military regime was installed there through the 1964 coup d'etat. The same answer probably applies to the fact that the Soviet Union increased its credits to Bolivia under Banzer's miltiary coup against the populist Torres (*El Mercurio* 19 April 1973). The same explanation, plus political competition with China and the United States, no doubt also applies to continued Soviet economic support for the Suharto government in Indonesia. Suharto's regime killed off five hundred thousand to one million people in its repression of capitalist Asia's largest Communist party and, a dozen years after its military coup, still keeps tens of thousands imprisoned without trial while the Soviet Union "will finance most of the expected $100 million cost of two dams and hydroelectric stations. . . . Moscow has been known to want expanded relations with Indonesia, the area's largest country (132 million people) in advance of Jakarta's expected full restoration of diplomatic relations with China" (FER 12 December 1975). Moscow also gave economic and military support to Egypt, whose government kept the Egyptian Communist party illegal and its members in jail for a decade, and finally broke off the "special relationship" at the behest of Kissinger and the right wing of the Sadat government. Similarly, Moscow has continued to support Syrian President Assad, even while Syrian troops suppress the Palestinians and the Muslims left in Lebanon, aided by the Americans and Israelis. Moscow's recognition of the American-imposed puppet Lon Nol regime in Cambodia, literally until the eleventh hour of its fall to the liberation troops, further illustrates the questionable nature of Soviet aid. On the other hand, the Chinese have continued to supply trade, aid, and even weapons, to the Pinochet junta in Chile, and to support the FNLA/UNITA opposition to the MPLA in Angola. All these and so many more cases call some of the advantages of socialist aid to the underdeveloped countries and their peoples seriously into question.

On balance, it appears that East-South economic relations tend to reinforce the existing role of the underdeveloped countries in the international capitalist division of labor, and/or to propel them further into the "new" directions now required by the process of world *capitalist* accumulation of capital. The economic and political advantages that East-South economic relations confer on the underdeveloped countries do not differ significantly from the "advantages" of imperialist and neocolonialist economic relations between the capitalist underdeveloped and the capitalist developed countries of the West. East-South economic relations thus do not seem particularly to promote the liberation of the underdeveloped countries from economic dependence. Nor do they necessarily further political liberation; East-South relations even hinder liberation struggles in all too many cases by lending support to the ruling classes and to even the most reactionary regimes among them. Within the capitalist underdeveloped countries, East-South economic relations do not significantly further the interests of the exploited producing classes—as distinct from the owning ones—any more than do capitalist West-South relations.

Those in the South who actually produce the exports to the East do not reap substantially more benefit from them than if they exported to the West (except to the extent that net employment opportunities are thereby increased). Imports from the socialist countries may sometimes be of greater "mass benefit" when they go to the public sector, but even this is not necessarily the case. The preferential East-South relations with the public sector in underdeveloped countries may often strengthen economically and politically the relatively more "progressive" sector of the local bourgeoisie, and thereby may offer the overall population various relatively greater benefits—directly through public sector projects and indirectly through this more "progressive" political influence. Moreover, insofar as socialist economic and other relations strengthen state capitalism and the state at the service of private capital in the underdeveloped countries, as on balance they undoubtedly do (all talk about "noncapitalist paths" notwithstanding), the socialist countries give further support and protection to capital and capitalism in the Third World and in the world as a whole.

... for the East

The growth of East-West/South economic relations derives also from the internal needs of socialist countries, and has far-reaching consequences for both their external policy and their internal structure. That is, it derives from their contradictions and contributes to their resolution. As long as the socialist countries have to take account of capitalist imperialism, if only to combat it—with over 8 percent of GNP and over 50 percent of research and development expenditures devoted to defense (Sivard 1976: 8)—political and economic developments in the capitalist world will necessarily affect the socialist countries. However, the effects of the capitalist world on the socialist countries go far beyond this, as the latter have not escaped the international capitalist division of labor.

Not only has socialism lacked an acceptable concept of its own to cover foreign trade and international economic relations, as Imre Vajda (1971: viii) points out, but it has not found any practice of its own that is acceptable to socialist. We observe in the epigraphs at the beginning of this chapter that, since the time of Lenin and Trotsky—and with the approval of both—the "socialist world" has continued to participate in the capitalist international division of labor, under the sway of imperialism.

When this international division of labor changes, the socialist countries find it convenient or necessary to change with it, lest—as in a game of musical chairs—they be left standing . . . and out! Thus, the director of Intercooperation, the official Hungarian agency concerned with relations between socialist and capitalist enterprises, observes: "We are aware that an epoch-making rearrangement in the international division of labor is taking place. We must find our place in this new international economic order" (*Time* 26 April 1976). Understandably, this imperative is greater for the smaller socialist countries of Eastern Europe, and particularly for Hungary, which depends so heavily on foreign trade, then it is for the relatively more self-sufficient Soviet Union. Nonetheless, the minister of foreign trade of the Soviet Union, N. Patolichev, believes that "in this age of scientific and technical revolution, no country, not even the most developed one, can advance its industry fast enough without using efficiently world achievements in science and technology" (quoted in UNCTAD 1972b: 39). The 1971–1975 five-year economic plans of the individual socialist countries of Eastern Europe (as well as Brezhnev's introduction of the Soviet plan at the meeting of the Central Committee of the Communist party in 1971, and the CMEA Comprehensive Programme for the Further Extension and Development of Cooperation adopted at its twenty-fifth session in 1971), laid particular emphasis on technological advances to improve labor productivity or to reduce costs, and on the expansion of and increased reliance on foreign trade. UNCTAD summarizes:

> The member countries of CMEA reiterated that the international division of labour between them would be developed with due regard to the world-wide division of labour. . . . The role of foreign trade as a specific factor of economic growth is becoming more prominent under the new plans. . . . The emphasis on imports of modern equipment, with growing demand for licenses and knowhow, is continuing. . . . Export-oriented industries are receiving priority in the allocation of investment resources and are encouraged to choose the best foreign-exchange-earning products. . . . The number of payments agreements negotiated in convertible currencies is increasing (UNCTAD 1972b: 3–6).

Moreover, an East European economist adds:

> However, it would be wrong to conceive of the advancement of trade with the Western countries as a factor which acts against systematic cooperation within the framework of CMEA. . . . Western comercial relations are apt to, and should, become complementary and supporting forces in the countries of CMEA, since division of labour among the socialist countries could be realized to the best advantage in a Euro-

pean [then why not world?], rather than an Eastern European, context (Berend in Vajda 1971: 27).

The increasing participation of the socialist countries in the capitalist international division of labor also has increasingly far-reaching and deep-going implications for the intrasocialist division of labor, for the structure of socialist society, and for domestic as well as foreign policy. As the former president of the Hungarian Economic Association, Imre Vajda, observed in the book under his editorship entitled *Foreign Trade in a Planned Economy:*

> Stalin's thesis of two parallel world markets has had to be rejected, and not only because the parallelism never materialized, although, despite the alienation of the two systems, they were never totally separated. The thesis also had to be abandoned because the socialist "world market' revealed itself to be a fiction, with in fact hardly any of the characteristics of a real market. . . . The marginal role which foreign trade came to play in the Soviet Union was to some extent due to the fact that the Soviet Union is a "big country." . . . Meanwhile it also became evident that the problems which arose in the field of foreign trade were not marginal in character and could not be neglected (Vajda 1971: viii–ix, 54).

Similarly, the UN Economic Commission for Europe observes that "the trade dependence of East European countries, and to an increasing extent, of the Soviet Union as well, has reached such a level of intensity that trade problems could not be treated independently from the objectives of internal economic and social development" (UNECE 1975b: 13).

Under the title "Prospects for Profits, Comecon," *Business International* advised its Western business clients:

> Symptoms of what Eastern Europe calls "the Western disease," i.e., recession, will be blocking the path to higher living standards in that area during the next five years. The Comecon countries, like their market-economy counterparts, know that only a full *international* recovery from recession can reignite industrial development. Until then, Comecon governments will walk the familiar tightrope between fear of social and political unrest and the economic need to enforce austerity. Specifically, sharp increases in the cost of energy and raw materials, the gradual disappearance of surplus labor, hefty rises in the East European external indebtedness and diminished export possibilities all spell a lower GNP—"social product" in Comecon terminology. In addition, prices are going up. (Hungary, and to some extent Poland, have already gone a long way toward allowing world market prices to determine domestic prices.) As a result of these factors, growth targets have been lowered in all the 1976–1980 five-year plans (BI 27 February 1976: 68).

Indeed, as cited in our epigraphs, Brezhnev himself, while addressing the

Congress of the Hungarian Communist Party on 17 March 1976, admitted that "because of the broad economic links between capitalist and socialist countries, the ill effects of the current economic crisis in the West have also had an impact on the socialist world." Even this is an understatement, for his colleague Comrade First Secretary of the Communist Party of Bulgaria Tudor Zhivkov explains one such impact: "It may be hoped that the crisis which is raging in the West may come to a rapid end, since it affects and creates uncertainties for the Bulgarian economy, which to a certain extent is dependent on trade with the countries of the West" (*Le Monde*, 17 April 1976).

One *might* have thought that crisis in the capitalist world might be welcomed by socialists and especially those in positions of leadership—the situation is "excellent," as the Chinese never tire of saying—because they sharpen the class struggle and might bring the advent of socialism nearer. On the contrary, Mr. Zhivkov hopes that the crisis will come to a rapid end. No doubt he and his fellow first secretaries of the Communist parties will do all in their power to help the crisis of capitalism come to a rapid end.

As for the immediate ill effects of the capitalist crisis, Mr. Zhivkov is of course right. As *Time* observed:

> The Eastern block has been caught in the same economic squeeze as Western Europe. Inflation sharply raised the prices of all the capital and consumer goods that had so confidently been ordered from the West. At the same time, recession in the West reduced the demand for Czechoslovak machine tools, Polish hams, East German radios, Hungarian textiles and other products. The result was a widening trade deficit . . . and the only way to bridge the gap was to secure more credits from the West (*Time*, 26 April 1976).

Moreover, the Soviet Union has reduced or eliminated the subsidy that it had in effect been according its CMEA trading partners through the delivery of raw materials and fuels at relatively low prices in exchange for importing manufactures from them (Hewett 1975). In part, the Soviets have been caught in the same capitalist world market squeeze (though simultaneously benefiting from the higher price of petroleum) and have been unwilling or, for internal reasons, unable to continue this subsidy at the expense of their own fuel and raw material-producing areas. Also in part taking advantage of the OPEC oil price increase, the Soviet Union increased the prices of its own raw materials and more than doubled that of petroleum sold to its CMEA partners, to reach two thirds of the world market price (FT 24 February 1975). Since 1975, however, the intra-CMEA prices, which previously were adjusted only every five years using a three- or five-year moving average of the previous period's world market prices, are adjusted yearly (on a still not clearly defined moving average). As a result, as a *Financial Times* (25 February 1975) headline put it, "Inflation goes East: Within five years there will be little difference between Comecon and world prices." Prices have certainly risen, although popular political opposition and the fear of uncontrollable social upheavals have restrained governments from raising prices as far as they have sought. However,

> whether to raise prices and risk popular unrest or allow subsidies to reach economically ruinous levels is the single most sensitive issue currently facing the governments of Eastern Europe. Bulgaria has already taken the plunge by raising prices of basic foodstuffs by some 30 percent with many more products and services to follow. Minimum wages were also raised, but the overall effect is a loss of purchasing power.... Hungary alone among Comecon countries is informing its population well ahead of its regular price rises.... Hungarian officials are also the only ones in Eastern Europe to admit inflation (FT 22 November 1979).

Higher prices are, however, not limited to foreign trade prices. Although the East has attempted a policy of absorption of price increases by the state through increasing subsidies on consumer items to keep the latter's prices stable, it has become impossible to continue this policy endlessly in the face of the inflation imported from the West and from the East itself. Accordingly, Rumania, Hungary, and Poland have been obliged to increase consumer prices as well (UNECE 1974c, 1975b). The consumer price index in Hungary rose 3.8 percent in 1975. Some prices, particularly for meat, rose much more, and as much as 30 percent on some items (NZZ 10 January 1975). In Poland, food prices were kept stable while the price index rose 2.9 percent in 1975; but in mid-1976, the state tried to raise prices in one fell swoop by up to 60 percent on some items. This attempt unleashed a popular reaction similar to that of 1970 that had brought down the Gomulka government, obliging the Gierek government to back down temporarily. Nonetheless, given the circumstances of the socialist economies, prices *must* be increased one way or another. During 1979 significant price increases in consumer goods have been announced and implemented in the Soviet Union, East Germany, Czechoslovakia, Hungary, Rumania, and Bulgaria (NYT 21 July 1979; GUA 2 July 1979). The absence of Poland from the list so far is explained by the political risk (or certain consequences) of raising prices to consumers, and the alternative recourse of reduced investment. "On January 1 [1980] ... in accordance with Hungarian Government policy, industry will be required to pay international prices for raw materials, with the Government gradually withdrawing its subsidies. ... From now on the salary bonuses for company directors are to be based largely on profits" (FT 17 December 1979).

The relations between socialist prices, pricing policy, and the capitalist price system, however, antedate and go deeper than those prevailing under the present inflation. The Hungarian economist, Bela Csikos-Nagy, writes:

> The price problem of the international market within CMEA cannot be solved without taking into account the connections with the world

market as a whole and the extent of separation between CMEA and the rest of the world market. The connection between the international market within CMEA and the world market outside it means that the market value judgments of the CMEA countries about the prices of individual products and about the relative prices of different products can be formed only by taking into consideration the price relations in the capitalist world market. Quite independent of the fact whether and to what extent a CMEA country has the opportunity of choosing between various main world markets, the concept of a "realistic" price necessarily involves the consideration of the price of the product outside the CMEA market. . . . In view of the actual mechanism of cooperation—it would be unrealistic to expect to be able to change over to a price basis reflecting the particular production conditions and exchange relations of the CMEA countries. In the given situation the real problem is not whether the principle of applying capitalist world market prices should be given up for the pricing principle based on our own inputs, but consists much more in doing away with the distortions which assert themselves—in contrast with the terms and the spirit of the Bucharest agreement—in the course of the practical application of the world market price principle. But neither should we be blind to the problems emerging from the adoption of capitalist world market prices, since they may sooner or later become serious hindrances to the progress of a purposeful division of labor (in Vajda 1971: 110, 106).

If this is true for intra-CMEA foreign trade prices, it soon becomes equally true for planning prices, which determine the decisions about investment and production; consequently, all possible subsidies notwithstanding, the same applies to consumer prices which determine consumption within any one of the socialist countries of Eastern Europe.

It was becoming evident that the problems of foreign trade were not marginal. According to Vajda, they also "played a substantial part in the process of reappraisal that could not be put off any longer . . . although it cannot be claimed that these problems were the only forces that brought about the pressure for economic reform" in Hungary. Moreover, as the Central Committee of the Hungarian Communist Party observed in 1966, "the new economic mechanism should establish a close relationship between internal and external markets. It should increase the impact of influences originating in foreign markets on domestic. . . ." (cited in Belassa n.d.: 64). This impact is not only necessary; it is desirable, if only its ill effects could be eliminated or if the problems causing these ill effects originating in the West could come to a rapid end. Unfortunately, however, the impact of foreign influences and resulting ill effects are not limited to price levels or price formation; since they affect—and are intended to transform—the decision-making process regarding investment, production, and distribution, these ill effects also extend to the structure and relations of production and consumption.

Two of the principal acknowledged problems of the socialist economies in

Eastern Europe are inadequate technological progress and low-quality production. The latter has been a constant complaint for decades, and has arisen more recently in regard to products made under Western license—for example, "Fiat" cars built at Togliattigrad, where the directors complain to the workers that "our factory receives too many protest letters because of the low quality of production" (cited by Carlo in Jahn, ed., 1975: 110). One of the less-acknowledged problems, emphasized by Ticktin (1973) among others, is the related inefficiency and wastefulness of the Soviet economy. For instance, the frequency of breakdown of engineering machinery, including the defense sector, is said to be three to four times that of the United States, and four times as many people are engaged in repairing machine tools as in producing new ones. The reasons for these deficiencies lie in the organization of the industrial process and the incentive system at the plant level. Organizationally, for example, whereas in the United States two thirds of research and development occurs within industrial firms, in the Soviet Union three quarters of R&D occurs in institutes that are independent of producing enterprises (Heymann 1973). Problems occur, however, beyond those on an organizational level, which the recent formation of vertically- and horizontally-integrated industrial conglomerates is designed to reduce; the planning and incentive system, which emphasizes the production of targeted quantities with existing technology and methods, does not provide adequate guidance and incentives—indeed often builds in disincentives—to innovate in the application of existing new technology, let alone to invent it within the enterprise, and to improve the quality of production. The importation of Western technology is meant to help overcome these problems, but it cannot in and of itself do so unless managers of socialist enterprises are given incentives, or are obliged to incorporate this technology and its derivatives into their own processes of production. The inevitable corollary of the entrance of Western technology, therefore, is the need to compete with it on the domestic market, and through exports on the world market as well. Yet this means further inroads of the capitalist market and its prices into the socialist economies. On the one hand, there is a natural resistance to this process from the adversely affected vested interests:

> The enterprises, the ministries, and the labor unions in Hungary comprise a formidable protectionist lobby which effectively opposes proposals for substantially opening the economy to foreign competition. . . .
> The organizational changes which would make Hungarian enterprises independently competitive on Western markets would be quite difficult and costly, requiring a substantial redistribution of power. . . . Probably the only true effective mechanism for compelling these changes is increased competition in Hungarian markets, primarily through lowered barriers to foreign trade, and a substantial curtailment of the extreme power of ministries over enterprises. . . . [I]t seems unlikely that such drastic changes will occur soon (Hewett 1975: 381, 380).

On the other hand, Ticktin (in Jahn, ed., 1975) argues that economic reforms and the introduction of foreign technology also have a mutually reinforcing spiral effect, in which the failure of the reforms to live up to expectations so far will lead to still closer ties with the West and to still greater concessions. The importation of technology whets the appetite for more of the same, and increases the attractiveness of the reforms. These require still further concessions to foreign firms and to the states of the imperialist West, on both of which the socialist countries will become increasingly dependent for credits to finance their imports of technology and capital. At the same time, domestic production will have to be increasingly diverted into exports to pay for the imports and to repay the credits. Thus, the beneficiaries of this process of East-West integration in the socialist countries, along with their ruling class, will become increasingly dependent on the West—and on economic and political stability in the West—to maintain their power in the East. Meanwhile, no less than in the underdeveloped capitalist countries, Eastern Europe and the Soviet Union will be importing not only Western factories, technology, and products, but the capitalist relations embedded in them, including speed of production, capitalist organization and criteria of decision making, capitalist wage structure and income differentials, capitalist consumption patterns and ideology, and capitalist class structures. In short, the socialist countries of Eastern Europe will be and are already importing capitalism:

> Poland's program for allowing foreigners to establish private businesses in the country—Eastern Europe's most forthright bid ever for capitalist investment—is even broader in its final form than was originally envisaged by planners. A key condition that investors be of Polish origin now living in the West has been dropped in the detailed regulations published in recent weeks. Instead, virtually anyone willing to put up the money evidently will be considered under terms that seem notably flexible. . . . The unique feature of Poland's new program is that business will be wholly owned and operated by foreign individuals or corporations. . . . The leadership's willingness to submerge ideological principles of state economic management to blatant expediency is a potentially important breakthrough in East-West ties. [At the same time] Poland has ceased building state apartments, ending a 30-year Communist program and opening the way for what is virtually private enterprise in provision of most private dwellings (IHT 22 June 1976).

Economic integration—now also on a regional basis and regardless of social systems—seems to be the watchword and order of the day throughout. Thus, the semiofficial Soviet news agency, Novosti, recently transmitted an article entitled "CMEA-EEC: Cooperation or Confrontation?" by the Soviet economist Nikolai Schmeljow:

> In this perspective the economy of Europe could achieve a significantly more complex character, which would rest on the mutually

complementary structure of the economies of the individual states. The question of the necessity and possibility of long-term programs of economic and scientific-technical development including the investment programs of the countries of the East as well as the West of Europe can already become real now. Through such programs, it would be possible to achieve a more rational system of inter-state specialization on the European continent, which rests on the natural and technical-economic advantages of the individual national economies. The economic preconditions for the concretization of a series of important all-European wide projects have in the meantime already matured in Europe: for the achievement of a unitary system of energy distribution, the construction of an all-European road network, a network of internal navigation and pipelines, the construction of common research installations, and the union of efforts for the protection of the environment. Not for nothing did European public opinion receive with the greatest attention the largest suggestion by the Soviet Union for the celebration of international conferences on a series of these problems (FR 11 August 1976).

Thus, no less than in the developed capitalist West or the underdeveloped capitalist South, the international economic relations of the socialist East and their sources in and effects on society are not class neutral but class based. The political pressure for internal economic reforms and related external economic "liberalization" comes from the ruling class, with both real and anticipated benefits for its members and some other privileged sectors. Liberalization benefits them economically through its resultant importation, production, and consumption, symbolized by the automobile. Perhaps more importantly, it also benefits them politically by buying the political support of the potentially disaffected bureaucratic, professional, and intellectual groups that neutralize or control the latent political pressure of the alienated working classes. These class imperatives and goals in the socialist societies of Eastern Europe and the Soviet Union are partly furthered and supported by accelerated participation in a world capitalist division of labor. This division permits the import of technology and its adjuncts from the capitalist West, and facilitates a convenient division of labor with the capitalist South, which additionally helps pay for imports from the West. From another point of view:

> These institutional developments are especially significant because they help integrate East-West (and South) trade into the system of world commerce, which detente has made politically feasible. . . . This institutional progress can be expected to promote both the continued growth and the greater stability of East-West economic relations (UNCTAD 1975e: 15).

After 2½ years as the U.S. ambassador to the Soviet Union, Walter

Stoessel, Jr., who left his post today, is temperately optimistic about the future of the Soviet-U.S. relations. . . . "It's hard to be certain," he remarked, "but I feel that the detente relationship or relaxation of tensions, whatever you call it, is rooted in sort of fundamental factors on both sides, for the Soviets and for ourselves, and that the factors will continue to operate." Most basic is "a concern on both sides about avoiding nuclear war, nuclear confrontation," Mr. Stoessel said. "I think there is a concern on both sides to try to put some kind of limitation on strategic arms. I think for the Soviets there are other interests also," the envoy said. "Their preoccupation with China leads them to want stability in some other areas. They are interested in trade, technology, and I think we are interested also in more trade as a way to get the Soviets more interested in a normal relationship, building a web of interests, which I still think is valid, although it's a very long-term business" (IHT 14 September 1976).

As Kissinger noted, "the key to U.S. strategy towards the USSR has been to create mutual vested interests in the preservation of the international order"; and as Brezhnev agreed, "we will be happy if our efforts to better Soviet-American relations help draw more and more nations into the process of detente—be it in Europe or Asia, in Africa or Latin America, in the Middle East or the Far East." Where does this leave the people's fight for national liberation and socialism?

Addenda, May 1978 and December 1979

Recent developments in the Soviet Union and Eastern Europe have extended and aggravated the economic and political tendencies examined above. *Business Week* reported under the title "Capitalistic Troubles of Eastern Europe":

> Eastern Europe . . . is suffering many of the same ills as the capitalist world: inflation, trade deficits resulting from higher energy costs, and slower economic growth. The average real national income (equivalent to GNP minus services) of the bloc rose at only 4.3% last year [1978], down from 7.8% annually between 1970 and 1975, and the combined trade deficit with Western industrialized countries soared. . . . Now the burden of servicing the accumulated debt threatens to put a damper on their ability to continue important vital equipment and knowhow from the West. As one solution, they are encouraging . . . agreements ranging from quasi-barter deals to direct equity investments (BW 13 August 1979).

The *Financial Times* of London reported that "none of the major Comecon economies is likely to achieve its five-year industrial growth target. . . . The worst results—all between 4.8 per cent and 5.8 per cent—were achieved by the largest economies, the Soviet Union, East Germany, Hungary, Poland, and Czechoslovakia" (FT, 1 March 1979). Industrial growth rates for all ten Comecon countries, including faster-growing Rumania, Bulgaria, Mongolia, Cuba, and Vietnam, declined from 6.4 percent in 1977 to 5.5 percent in 1978; growth targets have accordingly been revised downward for the most part for 1979 (FT 23 February 1979; 1 March 1979).

Poland experienced its lowest rate of economic growth since the Second World War in 1978 and again in 1979 (FT 3 December 1979). The planned rate of growth had already been reduced to 2.8 percent from an earlier target of between 3 percent and 4 percent, but the real rate of growth that was achieved was only 1 percent to 1.5 percent. Accordingly, the planned growth rate for 1980 has been revised downward to between 1.4 percent and 1.8 percent, which is the lowest growth target since 1945 when a socialist-planned economy was instituted in Poland (FT 11 December 1979). At the January 1980 Congress of the Polish Communist Party it was then announced that output had *declined* 2 percent in 1979, and the Prime Minister had to resign. In Hungary production increased only 1 percent to 1.5 percent in 1979 instead of the 3 percent to 3.5 percent that was planned for, and because of inflation real income declined by 1 percent to 1.5 percent. The outlook for 1980 is similarly bleak (FT 11 December 1979 and 3 January 1980).

In the Soviet Union:

> Industrial production was to increase between 1976–80 by 32%, which works out at an average annual increase of 6.5%. But in 1976, the increase was only 4.8%, in 1977 it was 5.7%, and the new plan for 1978 calls for no more than 4.5%. This leaves a target of nearly 8.5% to be reached in each of the remaining two years if the original 32% is to be attained during the whole five-year period—and this is outside the realm of economic possibility (IHT 1 February 1978).

Thus, it was only because the annual plan target for the growth of industrial production was lowered to 4.5 percent that a small overachievement was possible with 4.8 percent growth in 1978. Labor productivity grew by only 3.6 percent, representing half of earlier annual rates, and the second lowest since the Second World War (FT 20 January 1979). The year 1979 has been far worse. For the first nine months, instead of the planned rate of 5.7 percent annually, real growth was only 3.4 percent, the worst performance since the war. The growth of labor productivity at 2.4 percent was only half the target rate of 4.7 percent (FT 1 November 1979). Soviet grain production in 1979 reached 179 million tons instead of the planned 226 million tons, and 58 million tons below the 1978 record. Addressing the November 1979 meeting of the Supreme Soviet, President Brezhnev "delivered a sweeping attack on Soviet mismanagement and inefficiency," as well as on individual ministries and ministers, and called the unavailability of certain everyday consumer goods in stores "unforgivable" (FT 29 November 1979).

Also speaking at the 1979 Supreme Soviet, the chief of soviet planning, Mr. Baibakov, projected a growth of industrial production of 3.6 percent for all of 1979, and announced a target (lower than the 1979 plan rate) of 4.5 percent for 1980. The *Financial Times* comments: "If Soviet industry achieves its 1980 growth target of 4.5 percent, the total rise for the 1976–80 period would be 25.7 percent. This is far short of the Five-Year Plan of 36 percent and raises the possibility that the 1976–80 Plan may not be achieved until the end of 1982" (FT 29 November 1979).

The Five-Year Plan target for 1976–1980, whether at 36 percent or at 32 percent growth, was already well below earlier plan goals; and the severe shortfall, even if the Soviet Union achieves the now-projected 25 percent industrial growth by the end of 1980, gives ample cause for reflection. "Evidence that the Soviet economy is running out of steam is mounting [and] suggest[s] that the 1980s may be the first decade since World War II in which the Soviets will experience virtually no growth" (BW, 25 June 1979).

In an attempt to overcome some of their economic difficulties, the socialist countries of Eastern Europe continued to expand their imports from the West on a much greater scale than they were able to increase exports. As a result, their trade deficit and foreign debt rose rapidly. The debt rose by 35 percent in 1976, and reached $45 billion by the end of that year (this is considerably more than the projected $38 billion estimate cited on page 189 above). This increase caused so much alarm both in the West and in the East itself that the growth of the debt was reduced to 14 percent the next year, and reached $52 billion in 1977 and $56 billion at the end of 1978, of which nearly half is owed to Western banks. The trade deficit of the East European socialist countries was reduced from $11 billion in 1976 to an estimated $5 to $7 billion in 1977 and $6.5 billion in 1978. In the Soviet Union the trade deficit was reduced to $1.5 billion. The total debt is now projected to grow more slowly, to $66 to $80 billion by the end of 1980 (IHT 17 March, 11 April, 12 April, and 13–14 May 1978; FT 21 March 1979). Debt service has been eating up a quarter or more of foreign earnings and credits in most of Eastern Europe and over one half in Poland, and it has become necessary to make sharp cuts in imports to keep this burden from growing further. Poland, whose debt is estimated at $15 billion, has been obliged to reduce its investments and to announce increases in food prices again in order to answer its needs for increased imports of equipment and food (BW 20 March 1978; IHT 4 April 1978; FT 16 March 1979).

On the other hand:

> More than $18 billion in East bloc debt to the West was paid off last year in something other than money. The barter deal is fast becoming an important tool of trade as Communist debt balloons to as much as $50 billion. Says Gheorghe Mihaies of the Boston Consulting Group in Paris: "The East now sees barter deals as its only alternative to more debt in developing its industry and foreign markets." But from the Western viewpoint, this holds grave danger.

Primitive bartering, in which the Council for Mutual Economic Aid (Comecon) traded beef for locomotives, has become sophisticated. The Communists now want access to specific Western markets in return for big-ticket items such as chemical, steel, and auto plants. It is the buying back of surplus production from such plants that Western businessmen see as a threat to their markets. "It's becoming more and more difficult to prevent the import of sophisticated goods from the East," says Robert Ostier, trade specialist for Credit Lyonnais, one of France's largest state-owned banks. These market-share barter deals now account for about half of all barters with the East.

Compiling data. The disruptive potential in the buy-back barter has shocked apparently unprepared West European industries. Imperial Chemical Industries Ltd. has protested to the European Community in Brussels. The Germans are compiling data on the effect such deals could have on unemployment. Fiat wants to know why Russian-made Fiats sell better in France than its own products. French and German steelmakers complain that buy-backs could finish off weak companies; some in France are operating at only 30% to 40% of capacity (BW 23 January 1978).

Small and medium-sized Western companies suffer most as large concerns can market the goods accepted in payment for their exports through specialized trading subsidiaries. . . . However, the sources said they can see no alternative to more barter business in view of the East's desire to keep on importing from the West without increasing debts too much (IHT 6 April 1978).

The effects of the economic crisis and the recent Soviet and East European response are evident in numerous other press reports and headlines. "Russia Doubles Gas, Quadruples Coffee Prices" (IHT 2 March 1978). "Russian Prices Up" (GUA 2 July 1979). "Moscow Denies West's Credits Stretch Economy. Press Explanations Point Up Sensitivity" (IHT 1 August 1977). "Soviet Union Making Effort to Export Technology to West" (IHT 16 August 1977). "Soviets Seeking Partner in West For Car Venture . . . to produce a replacement [for its medium sized Moskvich] that would be marketed internationally. . . . Parts would be made in both countries" (IHT 2 May 1978). "E. Germans miss target . . . [for] the third successive year in the present five-year plan" (FT 20 January 1979). "East German Economy Starting to Sag under Weight of Energy Bill, Stagnant Exports" (IHT 17 April 1979). "E. German leaders worry about economy" (GUA 30 April 1979). "Prague Raises Cost of Fuel and Goods" (NYT 21 July 1979). "Prague Edging Cautiously Toward West Because of Economic, Political Difficulties. The most immediate cause of the opening to the West seems to be growing sense of desperation about the economy. . . . Seventy per cent of their plant and equipment now is obsolete or obsolescent" (IHT 11–12 February 1978). "The Polish economy is to grow by 1.4 to 1.8 percent next year ... the head of the Government Planning Commission told to Polish Parliament. ... The planned growth rate for this year was 2.8 percent but Mr. Wraszczyk said it would be 'markedly down on target. ...' The country will now have two consecutive years with a growth rate lower than in any year since World War II" (FT 3 December 1979). "Wage Cuts, Forced Overtime Spark Strikes in Poland" (ICP 2 April 1979). "Bulgaria Is Experimenting With Pay-Incentive Systems To Solve 'Efficiency' Problems. ... 'We know we cannot compete with the most highly developed countries until we solve the problems of quality and efficiency.'. ... Sofia is also improving its political and economic ties with the capitalist world to increase trade and investment that could help modernize its industry" (IHT 6 January 1978). "Sweeping Changes [in] Rumania Economy: 'New Mechanism' ... under which individual enterprises will be given a much greater degree of autonomy. ... Analysts in Washington said the growing importance of trade with the West may have been a factor in the decision to ease control. In recent years Rumania's trade with the non-Communist world has been greater than that with Communist states" (IHT 27 March 1978). "Rumania Bars Soviet-Block Cash for Gasoline, Stranding Tourists" (NYT, 2 August 1979). "Hungary Loosening Curbs on Alien Firms. Some Get A Majority Stake. Western Capital could encounter a more eager reception in East European countries soon. ... All the Eastern European countries are giving serious thought to improving their export performance over the next ten years. They'll need to complete in an increasingly competitive world market" (IHT 29 September 1977). " 'We know there is a risk in these steps, but we must expose our firms to the squeezes of the world economy and force them to make more efficient use of their resources, including labor,' Hungarian Deputy Prime Minister István Huszár told *Business Week*" (BW 13 August 1979).

HUNGAROCOOP Offers Itself as a Partner of Co-operation

What is co-operation?

A foreign company, normally producing any product, could call on the Hungarian industrial capacity to produce that same product to increase the company's commodity stocks.

In the course of the co-operation agreement, the Hungarian side, both the commercial and the industrial partners, will assure the plant, the convenable manpower, the plant manager, the necessary skilled-workers and the social provisions necessary for steady production. The technical conditions will be provided partly or entirely by the Hungarian side.

The special machines and tools necessary for production will be provided by the foreign side. These machines will be either bought or rented by the Hungarian co-operatives during the time of partnership. Similarly, the foreign party should give the knowhow and the raw materials and accessories, the latter will be given partly or entirely depending on the product. The Hungarian co-operatives will be interested in working with the consigner's experience in plant organization and training in order to assure a smooth and successful production run.

The produced article is at the foreign party's disposal on the spot of manufacturing. Generally, the foreign party's own staff if occupied with the sale of the product, but there could be cases when the Hungarian party either takes responsibility for a part of the goods, or could contract with the consigner for sales in a third market.

The basis of an active co-operation at HUNGAROCOOP is a 3–5 year contract to assure a mutually beneficial co-operation. (From an advertisement in *Business Week* 22 May 1978).

Beyond these immediate economic problems and the attempt to confront them through cooperation with the West and "new mechanisms" at home, even more serious economic and political problems loom on the horizon. The "civil rights" movement is perhaps only the tip of the iceberg of a political groundswell that could alter the balance of forces in the world as a whole. After suggesting that "the outlook is so bearish [pessimistic] for U.S.-Soviet trade . . . [because of] the Russian's lack of hard currency," *Fortune* examines another emerging problem:

The Arabs Won't Take Rubles

To avert an economic disaster, the Russians would have to begin importing large quantities of oil from the Mideast. And this would require much more hard currency than they can spare. If the CIA's projections of Soviet oil requirements for the 1980's prove accurate, the Russians in 1985 will have to spend about $10 billion a year for oil, *at current prices*. To pay such a staggering bill, Soviet non-oil exports would have to more than quadruple by then. The Russians are striving mightily to accomplish this (see "This Communist Internationale Has a Capitalist Accent," *Fortune*, February 1977), but an export increase of this magnitude within so few years seems impossible. The Russians would have no choice but to divert virtually all their hard currency from the West to the Mideast.

Satellites Need Oil Too

Whatever the dimensions of the Soviet Union's oil problem, it is bound to damage trade between the West and the East European satellite countries, whose huge debts are already worrying some Western creditors. These countries get most of their oil from the USSR, and the Russians will doubtless have to squeeze their satellites to relieve the pressure on themselves. Indeed, they have already begun to do just that. Since 1975 the Soviet Union has increased the price of the oil it sells to Eastern Europe by more than 150 per cent, to $9.10 per barrel. This is forcing the East European governments to divert more and more of their own money from the West to Moscow, and if the Soviet Union becomes unable to supply East Europe with the oil it needs, the satellites will have to divert their precious hard currency from the West to the Middle East (*Fortune,* 16 January 1978).

The CIA projections of Soviet oil imports have since been disputed by the Soviet Union (IHT 9 May 1978), and severely criticized as erroneous by a U.S. Senate study, which also draws on private expert opinion (IHT 23 May 1978). However, the CIA subsequently reconfirmed its earlier forecast of a Soviet oil shortage in the 1980s (IHT 22 March 1979). " 'We might be seeing the peak of Soviet oil production right now.' The C.I.A. estimated that Moscow would be importing 700,000 barrels a day by 1982. It now exports about one million barrels daily" (NYT 30 July 1979). Other indications also suggest that at least speculations about the East European oil-importing countries may not be very far off the mark.

If any of these projections and speculations are well founded, perhaps they offer part of the background for the foreign and military policy of the East European socialist states in the Middle East and neighboring Africa. At the same time, the Soviet Union "supports" self-determination for the people of the West Sahara, led by POLISARIO; and it makes the invading Morocco into its principal trading partner in Africa (LM 12–13 March 1978). Elsewhere, as the most important trading partner of Argentina, the Soviet Union defends that country in the United Nations against accusations of human rights violations. The Soviets want to install a nuclear power plant in the Philippines, which President Marcos governs under martial law (FR, 15 February 1978). The Soviet Union has broken the erstwhile United States monopoly on the sale of enriched uranium, of which it now supplies about half the consumption in Western Europe and more than that in West Germany and Spain.

China*

Still less of an attempt to analyze Chinese domestic society and the way it determines foreign policy can be made here than was possible in the discussion of other socialist countries. For present purposes, this major omission may perhaps be justified by the fact that, although China has 20 percent of the world's population, in 1970 it accounted for less than 0.7 percent of the world's foreign trade, less than Hong Kong, some of whose exports, however, are reexports from China. Our discussion will limit itself to the barest outlines of China's place in the international division of labor, as seen through its foreign trade and aid, with some added reflections about Chinese foreign policy.

*Written in July 1976 after the fall of Deng and revised in November 1976 after the ousting of the "Gang of Four," except for recent minor editorial modifications and addenda.

In apparent contrast to the socialist countries of Eastern Europe, China's foreign trade increases when its economic growth rate rises; and it falls when, as during the Great Leap and the Cultural Revolution, attempts are made to bring China's development onto a qualitatively different economic footing. During these two periods, 1959–1961 and again 1966–1968, China's foreign trade fell, albeit with a lag, but even more sharply than its agricultural and industrial output. In other years since the 1949 revolution, foreign trade has generally grown, though also at rather uneven rates. The following periods and fluctuations, or even cycles, can be roughly identified. From 1949-50 to 1958: rapid expansion of heavy industry on the Soviet model and with the latter's aid, which was also reflected in substantial growth of foreign trade. From 1959–1961: the withdrawal of Soviet aid, two consecutive years of disastrous harvests, and the Great Leap Forward, with absolute declines in both output and trade. In 1962–1966: renewed growth, now giving priority to agriculture rather than industry, again accompanied by growing foreign trade but at lower rates than in the 1950s. In the 1966–1968 period: the Cultural Revolution, involving a certain "involution" that was also reflected in absolute declines in foreign trade. From 1969 to the mid-seventies: generally renewed economic growth, "walking on two legs" of agriculture and industry combined, with moderate increases of foreign trade during the first years and substantial ones in more recent years. (For a review of this whole period see *Current Scene,* July and September 1974.)

Since the Sino-Soviet split in 1960, Chinese foreign trade with other socialist countries has declined from over 70 percent of its total trade to 17 percent in 1973, including only 1 percent with the Soviet Union. That is, over 80 percent of China's foreign trade is with the capitalist countries, of which over 50 percent is conducted with the developed ones; this includes about 20 percent with Japan alone, 20 percent with the underdeveloped countries, and nearly 10 percent with or through Hong Kong and Macao. Japan has consistently been China's most important single trade partner, followed by Hong Kong, replaced, however, in the number two spot by the United States in 1973 after Nixon's visit to Peking in 1972.

The commodity composition of China's imports has been about 50 percent manufactures, concentrated in iron and steel products and machinery and equipment, with a tendency to rise; chemicals 10 to 15 percent, with a tendency to fall; raw materials 20 percent; and foodstuffs, particularly wheat and soybeans, 20 percent. A portion of the wheat imports can be attributed to a sort of wheat/rice caloric arbitrage, in which China exports higher-priced rice to purchase cheaper wheat with an equal caloric content. The Chinese thus make a substantial "caloric profit" on the deal, which permits it to increase its total grain calorie consumption by about 1 percent (Griffin 1972: 133–134). The commodity composition of China's exports is roughly 30–33 percent foodstuffs; 20 percent raw materials and fuels, with a recent increase, among which oil has gained importance since the OPEC oil price increase; and 40–45 percent manufactures, with a tendency to rise (all data are from CS, December 1974). *Current Scene* summarizes: "Total PRC trade is a relatively low percentage of gross national product—about 5 per cent in 1973. . . . Although the PRC plays a minor role in international commerce, foreign trade plays a major role in stabilizing and developing China's domestic economy. China also depends on agricultural imports to help feed and clothe its huge population. It also relies on imports of machinery and equipment, metals, and advanced technology to support the growth and modernization of the industrial sector of its economy."

Since the advent of ping-pong diplomacy in 1971–1972, Chinese foreign trade policy has undergone significant developments and changes. Total foreign trade suddenly more than doubled between 1972 and 1974, and has grown at varying rates since then.

TABLE 4-8
China's Foreign Trade
(in U.S. $ millions)

	1971	1972	1973	1974	1975	1976	1977	1978	1979[a]
Turnover	4,720	5,920	9,870	13,765	14,714	14,000[b]	16,820	22,630	27,500
Imports	2,305	2,835	4,975	7,518	7,430	6–7,000	8,200	11,950	15,500
Exports	2,415	3,085	4,895	6,247	7,284	7,000	8,620	10,680	12,000
Balance	110	250	−80	−1,271	−146	0 to 1,000	+420	−1,270	−3,500

Sources: 1971–1973, CS December 1974; 1974, FER 20 June 1975; 1975, FER 26 March 1976; 1976 approximate figures from *China Quarterly,* June 1977; 1977–1979 from FT 2 July 1979, citing New China News Agency; 1979 figures are plan estimates.

[a]Estimated figures.

[b]Approximate figure.

In view of the steady zig-zags in China's policy, it is difficult and hazardous to say whether these imply a new trend, or to identify the nature of such a trend. Thus, the *Far Eastern Economic Review* wrote on 1 October 1976: "The issue is far from decided, however, and it would be premature to project any certain trends in China's foreign trade policy. The sudden fall of Teng Hsiao-Ping [Deng Xiaoping] is adequate proof of how quickly things can change." Nonetheless, the following observations may be made in this connection. The elimination in mid-1971 of Lin Biao, who stood for a strong self-reliant and antiimperialist line, and the ascension fo dominant influence of Zhou Enlai, was reflected in an expansive foreign trade policy. In early 1975, Zhou Enlai issued a document, "On Certain Problems in Speeding up Industrial Development," also known as the "Twenty Points," in which he argued that self-reliance should not mean isolationism. Therefore, he supported the importation of advanced—read capitalist—technology and the development, in part relying on the same, of petroleum production for export to pay for this technology import.

After Zhou's death in late 1975, not only this policy but the authorship of the Twenty Points document itself was attributed to Deng Xiaoping by the anti-"capitalist-roader" campaign against him, spearheaded by the "radicals" in early 1976. Deng was accused, among other things, of selling out China's patrimony. Imports and petroleum exports, which had leveled off already in 1975, declined in the first half of 1976, particularly in trade with Japan. However, the subsequent elimination of the radical Shanghai group of four in October 1976 and the consolidaiton (for the time being) of Hua Guofeng after the death of Mao would appear to have altered the general course of foreign trade policy again toward revindicating, developing, and expanding that charted by Zhou Enlai since 1971. The defeated radicals, who espoused a particularly self-reliant, anti-U.S.- and anti-Soviet-social-imperialist line, like Lin Biao, are now being characteristically accused of having been covert rightist capitalist roaders intent on the corruption of foreign influence. Beyond the general political significance of these events, several indications of probable resulting economic and foreign trade policy are noteworthy: the military and bureaucratic as well as urban support for "technocrat" Hua's "pragmatic" policies; the apparent ascendance of Economic Minister Li Xiannian and his possible appointment as Prime Minister; the apparent reinstatement of Railway Minister Wan Li, who had been dismissed with the fall of his mentor, Deng; and rumors of the possible revindication of Deng himself (the attack on whom has certainly been replaced by the much stronger attack on the "radicals").

At the time of this writing, several press reports are available that bear specifically on China's probable foreign trade policy for the near future:

> China's new authorities said in an editorial today [25 October 1976] that they would carry out the ambitious program of economic development originally put forward by the late Premier Chou En-lai [Zhou Enlai] early last year but criticized this year in the anti-rightist campaign. The pledge to return to Chou's plan, which called for the modernization of China by the end of the century, is the first official indication of the policies that Hua Kuo-Feng [Hua Guofeng], China's new leader, and his associates will pursue. It represents a major triumph for the veteran party bureaucrats, long championed by Chou [Zhou], who are often termed the "moderates" (IHT 26 October 1976).

The *International Herald Tribune* (12 November 1976) also reports with a Peking dateline:

> The Chinese officials who make their country's foreign trade policy seem like new men these days. In the wake of the purge of the radical "gang of four," they are talking frankly, realistically and optimistically about the future. What they have been saying to visiting businessmen and journalists during the past few weeks boils down to this: It's going

to be easier to do business with China, and there's going to be more business to do. . . . [Economics Minister Li Xiannian] said that the government wanted to import more capital equipment. He mentioned petrochemical technology, oil and mineral-exploration equipment, steel-making technology and power-generating systems—the sort of technology China has been importing in recent years. . . . But to go beyond that and predict a big boom in China trade is around the corner would be rash, given some realities.

Nonetheless, *Le Monde* (11 April 1976) reports under the headline, "The Sino-Japanese Economic Exchanges Are Taking Up Again with Startling Speed," that after the 12 percent decline in trade (6 percent according to IHT 6 October 1976) in the first semester of 1976, several important new contracts have already been signed.

Despite China's traditional policy of self-reliance—illustrated, and after the fall of Deng perhaps temporarily restrengthened, by the refusal of all offers of foreign assistance in the wake of its summer 1976 earthquake disasters—China has since 1972 embarked on a massive program of purchasing foreign technology and advanced high technology incorporating equipment, including the importation of various complete turnkey plants. The spectacular symbol of this policy, perhaps, is China's option offer to buy British/ French supersonic Concorde airliners after having already purchased ten American "ordinary" Boeing 707s; also reported is an agreement to import British Rolls-Royce engines for installation in China's military aircraft. More important in the long run, however, should prove China's new reliance on foreign technology, including the purchase of whole plants, particularly from Japan, to develop its industry. In 1973 alone, China contracted for the purchase of sixty-two whole plants for $1.2 billion, or six times more than in all of the 1960s combined (CS March 1974). Simultaneously, and through the implementation of this technological import policy, Chinese imports have risen much faster than her exports, despite net exports of petroleum since 1974. As a result, in 1973 China had a balance of trade deficit of a modest $80 million, after having had a surplus in almost every year since 1956, excepting 1956, 1960, and 1970, which were bad harvest years. Trade balances with the capitalist countries, however, had been in deficit in some other years as well, particularly every year between 1957 and 1964, and during the Cultural Revolution. With the socialist countries, on the other hand, China has had a consistent trade surplus in every year since 1956. In 1974, however, with exports increasing 28 percent and imports rising 51 percent, China's overall trade deficit rose to over $1.2 billion (FER, 20 June 1975). Some analysts, particularly Japan's foreign trade organization JETRO, have suggested that "China's deficit [is] here to stay," and would reach nearly $3 billion in 1978, falling to $1.5 billion in 1980, and then grow to a big surplus of nearly $12 billion by 1985 because of the projected major increase in the export of petroleum (FER 20 June 1975). In 1975, however, the Chinese trade deficit was already cut back to $150 million (FER 26 March 1976) through cutbacks on imports, including many already contracted for (FT 26 February 1975); and the surplus considered possible by the same Japanese foreign trade experts for 1976 and 1977 was borne out by events (Fer 20 June 1976; LM 17 April 1976, before the above-mentioned political events of October 1976). After the auspicious beginnings of Chinese oil exports, particularly to Japan but also to the Philippines, the thirty-million-ton target of oil exports to Japan was reduced again to ten million tons for 1977 and fifteen million tons in 1981–though in the meantime there is talk of Chinese export of oil to the United States (FER 23 January 1976). However, since October 1976 these targets have been raised, albeit constantly changed, again. (For later data see Table 4-7 and pages 246–247 below.) The political succession "time of troubles" put a break on the expansion of the economy and of imports to support that expansion. Indeed, Hua Guofeng later accused the Gang of Four: "As a result of their interference between 1974 and 1976 the nation lost about Rmb 100 billion (US $61.3 billion) in total value of industrial output, 28 million tons of steel and Rmb 40 billion in state revenues" (FER 6 October 1978).

Another apparent reversal of earlier Chinese policy has recently been to accept, indeed to seek, foreign credits and loans, which China previously rejected or did not need. So far, however, these have been on a 20 percent down payment and five-year repayment basis, rather than the long-term credits customary elsewhere. To pay for these increased imports and exports, China is, as already observed, banking particularly on the development of her on- and off-shore petroleum production and exports, and is currently promoting these with foreign technological help. Additionally, China is driving hard to increase her exports of manufactures, and no longer at bargain but at world market prices. Among these are machine tools, iron goods, instruments and medical equipment, bicycles, sewing machines, and chemicals. Increasingly, China is also stepping up exports of transistor radios, electric household and other goods, wristwatches, photographic equipment, tires, musical instruments, and of course clothing and footwear. For these consumer goods, China's preferred export market is in the developed capitalist countries, with which it has a balance of trade deficit. Not unlike the socialist countries of Eastern Europe, China already has a balance of trade surplus with the underdeveloped countries, despite the fact that it has recently increased its imports from some of these countries; the Chinese have been buying directly from them the raw materials that it had previously purchased on the London Metals Exchange and other developed capitalist markets (CS October 1972).

Socialist China's insertion in, acceptance of, *and use of* the capitalist international division of labor is also manifest in the utilization of overseas Chinese, and particularly the active capitalist businessmen among them, throughout Southeast Asia for China's *national* economic and political purposes and policy. These developments are most especially visible through

China's use of Hong Kong and Macao as *entrepots* in its economic relations with the capitalist West. Thus, these colonies, still maintained on Chinese soil with China's agreement—indeed at her insistence, as Portugal's recent attempts at decolonization show—play a unique role. A substantial portion of Hong Kong's exports constitute reexports from China, arising out of its *entrepot* function, which China maintains for various purposes of its own. Moreover, as the Hong Kong business magazine, *Far Eastern Economic Review,* points out:

> China's dogmatic resistance to the whole concept of foreign invest-
> ment—both in its own territory and in other underdeveloped coun-
> tries—is completely waived in the case of Hong Kong, where Peking
> indulges in investment with the greatest enthusiasm. . . . The People's
> Republic of China (PRC) publicly controls investments which annually
> bring it staggering sums in hard currency—much more than the $300
> million which is sometimes quoted as an estimate for these invisible
> earnings. This, of course, is separate from the $1,400 million or so
> which China is now earning yearly by supplying the colony with food,
> water, consumer goods and petroleum fuels, and the extra which it
> gains by employing Hong Kong as an entrepot . . . (nine banks in-
> corporated in the PRC control deposits of about $5 billion equivalent to
> 5/6 of all bank deposits and 1/3 of the assets of Hong Kong banks).
> Less easy to follow up . . . is China's involvement in banking, in-
> surance, transport, retailing, warehouse and cold storage facilities,
> property development and investment advertising, and the manufacture
> of cigarettes and monosodium glutamate. China also controls holding
> companies which could enable it to invest in virtually anything. Most
> recently, the Hong Kong Government has been asked to consider per-
> mitting the establishment of a PRC-controlled plant manufacturing
> machine tools and heavy machinery on Tsin Yi Island (FER 30 July
> 1976: 44).

The plant is to cost about $40 million initially and is intended to supplement China's already large *exports* of machine tools through and from Hong Kong (FER 30 July 1976: 80).

Socialist China's use of Hong Kong as a capitalist island colony must be related also to the economic, social, and political conditions that exist and are maintained through Chinese support in Hong Kong:

> Hong Kong probably has grosser inequalities of wealth than any
> society in the world. . . . In 1971 the Mongkok area of the Colony had a
> density of 400,612 people per square mile—more than ten times the
> population density of Tokyo. . . . [Hong Kong] has by far the highest
> level of utilization of plant in the textile industry in Asia: in 1965 looms
> were employed the equivalent of 24 hours a day for 360 days a year.
> No other country approached even 75% of this figure. . . . [I]n 1968

Hong Kong workers had the longest working day and the longest working week of city dwellers in Southeast Asia: 58% worked 7 days a week, 52% worked 10 hours or more a day. There is no legal limit. . . . [There] is widespread use of child labor. . . . Hong Kong *is* a rich territory which compiles a high budget surplus each year, and yet stolidly refuses to spend this surplus to help the local population. . . . In fiscal 1969–70, while the London-appointed colonial administration was spending HK $19,204,686 on its Social Welfare Department, the Colony's budget showed a surplus of HK $618,670,000. The bulk of this was sent to London to bolster the UK's reserves and support the pound. By 1972 one American source calculated that Hong Kong was providing as much as half all the backing of the pound (Hong Kong Research Project, 1974: 25–28).

Le Monde reports further that in 1971, 174,339 persons worked over 75 hours a week, including 13,700 over 105 hours, and that 36,000 children worked illegally. Hong Kong has the world's highest tuberculosis rate and the third highest suicide rate, as well as several hundred thousand drug addicts. Nonetheless, in this greatest and last of the world's island paradises of complete laissez-faire, even the most modest demands of labor for higher wages or better working and living conditions, let alone any possible movement for liberation or socialism, are condemned and combatted by the socialist revolutionary Peoples Republic of China as foreign "Trotskyist" agitation.

China has also been active in foreign aid. After beginning a moderate aid program in 1956, which dropped to near zero during the involution of the Cultural Revolution, China rapidly expanded foreign aid in the late 1960s, to reach levels of $500 million a year equivalents and more in the early 1970s (CS December 1973). Whereas during the whole 1956–1969 period the Chinese spent $1.1 billion on total aid, in the five years 1970–1974 alone the total reached $2.4 billion (FER 30 July 1976). The recipients of Chinese foreign aid have been more widely dispersed than those of other socialist countries, with about half concentrated in Africa, going up to two thirds in the 1970s, albeit distributed to twenty-three different countries in that continent (CS December 1973 and FER 30 July 1976). The most important project has been the construction of the TanZam railroad, designed to give Zambia an outlet for its copper through Tanzania so as to render it less dependent on South Africa, Rhodesia, and the then Portuguese-controlled Mozambique.

Other important recipients of Chinese foreign aid in Africa have been Somalia and Egypt, where China has competed with the Soviet Union, as well as Algeria and Ethiopia. In capitalist Asia, China has maintained the closest of relations with Pakistan and Sri Lanka. Some Chinese aid has also gone to a few countries in Latin America. Unlike Soviet aid, only 5 percent of China's aid has been allocated to heavy industry and the like in Pakistan (FER 30 July 1976). Moreover, the Chinese are known for extending aid on very much more favorable terms than do other socialist, let alone capitalist, countries, with interest-free loans for lengthy periods followed by periods of grace if necessary. Moreover, Chinese technical and other aid personnel in underdeveloped countries have the reputation of always adapting themselves to local standards of living, and doing their best to teach their local counterpart workers, even if the Chinese keep to themselves socially. Thus, with regard to the terms of Chinese aid and its execution at the grass roots level, the Chinese truly distinguish themselves most favorably from all other major providers of "aid," capitalist or socialist.

Nonetheless, when Chinese trade and aid relations with the underdeveloped capitalist countries are examined in the broader international and national political context of which they form an integral part, they appear no better—and often markedly worse—than those of many other countries. It is enough to list some of the countries and regimes to which Chinese aid has been extended—especially since the fall of Lin Biao—and the particular points in history when aid has been offered: Ayub Khan's Pakistan at the time of its genocide in East Pakistan/Bangladesh; the Nimeiry regime in the Sudan, after it brutally repressed the bid for power of progressive officers and the Moscow-allied Communists in 1971; Mrs. Bandaranaike's regime in Sri Lanka at the time of her brutal repression of the JVP uprising, also in 1971. (In this, notably, she had the support not only of China but of the Soviet Union, the United States, India, Pakistan, West and East Germany, Yugoslavia, and Egypt. While Soviet arms were shipped to the government, a Chinese freighter in Colombo harbor refused to supply its load of arms, supposedly destined for Africa, to the rebels in need, whom Zhou Enlai then condemned in his message of political support for Mrs. Bandaranaike.) Other recipients of Chinese economic and military aid have been Zaire's Mobutu, whose reactionary regime had been installed by the CIA; CIA agent Holden Roberto and his FNLA in Angola, long after it had become clear that only the MPLA remained a progressive force there; and General Pinochet in Chile, whom the Chinese supplied with credits and reportedly a shipment of small arms (the latter was denied to me by a Chinese spokesman). At the same time, at least in word if not in action, Chile was being condemned individually by virtually every other civilized country in the world, and by all of them collectively through the United Nations General Assembly. Additionally, China did not hesitate to normalize its relations with the Philippines after Marcos had established martial law there, and to make crystal clear to one and all its desire that the United States' military, economic, and political presence in Southeast Asia continue for a long time to come. This Chinese foreign policy does not seem to vary with the ups and downs of the political fortunes of its domestic leadership from one month or year to another. China's policy toward underdeveloped countries is only matched by its public political wooing and support of the most reactionary of all political forces and personages in the imperialist West, from Franz Joseph Strauss and Edward Heath or Margaret Thatcher in Europe to ex-Secretary of

Defense James Schlesinger in the United States and, last but not least, to the Shah of Iran and the ultrareactionary Prime Ministers Fraser of Australia and Muldoon of New Zealand. All this, of course, derives from only one major reason and explanation: Chinese opposition to the Soviet Union through all possible means, including the policy of "my enemy's enemy is my friend." (After having formulated this statement, a friend who recently returned from China told me that he heard this self-same formulation used by the Chinese themselves in the explanation of their foreign policy given in a Communist party cadre school in Tianjin.) Only this motivation can and does explain China's seemingly blind support of Pakistan against India and the Soviet Union, of Mobutu and Roberto in Africa, or of Pinochet in Chile and Strauss in Germany, not to mention the downright counterrevolutionary practice of the "Maoist" parties in Portugal and elsewhere when there appears to be a Soviet-aligned or Soviet-backed alternative liberation movement. The Soviet Union, in turn, pursues the same "my enemy's enemy is my friend" policy, supporting Lon Nol in Cambodia while Sihanouk is in Peking, and maintaining political contacts even with Chiang Kai-shek and his son's regime in Taiwan. The result, however, is that the economic and political liberation of the peoples of the world and their progressive organizations necessarily suffer; and this includes the Vietnamese, who did receive Soviet and Chinese aid in their war of liberation, but not as much as they should and could have received.

Addenda, May 1978 and December 1979

If the continuity of earlier economic and political tendencies in China seemed subject to any doubt in the discussion above, these trends in the the meantime been most spectacularly confirmed and if anything unexpectedly intensified. Since then all doubt has evaporated as to the nature of the "new," "pragmatic" course of Chinese political economy. The only doubt that remains, perhaps, is how new it really is. As anticipated earlier (p. 238), the strongest individual force behind this so-called pragmatic modernization policy, Deng Xiaoping, has returned to power for the second time. With his return has come a major campaign to implement the policy outlined in the "Twenty Points" and in two other important economic documents on scientific research and administration by Zhou Enlai. These echo Zhou's ideas already launched in 1964, which were subsequently scotched by the Cultural Revolution. The documents' inspiration and at least partial authorship, however, had come from Deng Xiaoping. The policy, in short, intends to convert China into a world power of the first order by the year 2000.

Indeed, it may be said that the de-Maoization of China has begun, which goes far beyond the derision of the Gang of Four, and since 1978 has included first veiled and then increasingly attacks on the Chairman himself (Victor Zorza in IHT 27 April 1978). Six months earlier David Bonavia still saw only "dismantling parts of Maoism—but not Mao." (FER 7 October

1977). Since then, this process of dismantling has gone much further, and aims to start again where China took an ideologically motivated left turn under the guidance of Mao over two decades ago. Hua Guofeng's ideological defense of the present course is based on a "pragmatic" speech that Mao gave in 1956 before China broke with the Soviet Union and when he let "a hundred flowers bloom." Hua's edition of the next volume of Mao's writings also conveniently takes the same date as the cutoff point. Not only the second-rank leadership, earlier purged during the Cultural Revolution of 1966–1969, was now being rehabilitated by or for the last National People's Congress in February 1978 (IHT 13 March 1978). Over one hundred thousand functionaries have been rehabilitated and reinstated (if young enough, pensioned if not) collectively in Decree Number 11 of 5 April 1978, which exonerates those who had been purged for right-wing deviation since 1957—that is, just after the period of the one hundred blooming flowers (IHT 19 May 1978). "A global measure of this amplitude is without precedent," and goes far beyond the reinstatement of individual party members to include many thousands outside the party as well (LM 12 May 1978). The minister of education who had been purged along with Deng has been rehabilitated posthumously; his educational policies, which sought to reverse the "low" quality of "antitheoretical" education of "open-door schooling" of the post-Cultural Revolution period, are now being applied full scale (CS December 1977). "Quality" again takes precedence over "quantity" in education: "In the sharpest departure yet from the egalitarian policies of Mao Tse-tung [Mao Zedong], China has begun to institute a new program of dividing schoolchildren into classes of fast, normal, and slow learners . . . [which according to some] will help bright students, producing 'men of talent' for China" (IHT 16 May 1978). Inequality of incomes is receiving new justification as a Marxist and higher form of equality. Income is to be distributed more in accordance with the quality than with the quantity of labor, and incentives to increase productivity are being reintroduced throughout the economy (FET 27 January and 17 February 1978). Former industrialists and businessmen are receiving restitution and are being encouraged to come "home" as Chinese capitalists. In the meantime, there are reports of substantial unemployment of 20 to 50 million in China and 50,000 in Shanghai alone; "a wave of dissidence sweeps China's youth" (BW 9 July 1979). These and many other changes, which the *Far Eastern Economic Review* (5 October 1979) calls "astonishing reversions to pre-1966 social policies," have been consecrated in the draft of a new constitution, which "stresses economic goals"; Western analysts believe "that [in it] is represented the most candid and complete statement of China's current leaders' preference for modernization and order instead of the late Mao Tse-tung's passion for ideological purity and class struggle" (IHT 2 March 1978). "All vestiges of Mao's utopian policy of technological self-reliance are being shed. China dispatched more technical and purchasing teams abroad in 1977 than in any previous year." "One China expert calls [it] 'possibly the largest transfer of technology in history'—as much as $20 billion for complete plants and processes by 1985. To pay for all that, China will not only have to draw on reserves (estimated at $4 billion) but enter the world export market in an aggressive and successful way. There are signs that it is already doing so" (BW 29 May 1978).

Chairman Hua Guofeng confirmed the tendencies of the Zhou/Deng twenty-point economic development program and of his own recent speeches. In his report to the National People's Congress in February 1978, he presented a ten-year economic program designed to make China an economic power by the year 2000. Chairman Hua said:

> By the end of the century the output per unit of major agricultural products is expected to reach or surpass advanced world levels and the output of major industrial products to approach, equal or outstrip that of the most developed capitalist countries (FER 17 March 1978).

For the *Far Eastern Economic Review* (17 March 1978), this is reminiscent of Soviet Premier Nikita Khrushchev's 1960 promise to bury the West. However that may be, China's growing competition with the West also involves increasing collaboration with the West.

China's foreign trade has more than tripled since 1970, with 85 percent of it currently with capitalist countries. Exports have risen from $2.1 billion in 1970 to $7.9 billion in 1977, and about $10 billion in 1978. Oil exports to finance imports increased from $5 million in 1971 to $815 million in 1975, and the exports of textiles tripled during the same period (IHT 17 November 1977; BW 29 May 1978; FER 5 October 1979). "China earmarks for export some of about everything it produces," according to a CIA report (IHT 17 November 1977). The trade deficits of the early 1970s gave way to a trade surplus of some $700 million in 1976 and $1.4 billion plus remittances of another $1.5 billion from Hong Kong in 1977, as imports were reduced during the time of troubles (IHT 13–14 August 1977; BW 3 April 1978). But then imports, particularly of factories, equipment, construction material, and after bad harvests also of wheat, increased again. In 1978 imports increased by 40 percent (to US $12 billion), twice as fast as exports, which rose to $10.7 billion, leaving a trade deficit of $1.3 billion. Accordingly, in 1979 imports were to grow by only 32 percent to $15.5 billion, and exports by only 15 percent to $12 billion, leaving a budgeted deficit of $3.5 billion (FT 29 June and 2 July 1979). Indeed, at the meeting of the National People's Congress in June–July 1979, Premier Hua Guofeng announced a three-year retrenchment program to "readjust, restructure, consolidate, and improve" the apparently over-ambitious modernization program inspired by Deng Xiaoping. It was agreed (against the desires of Deng?) again to reduce—albeit not to eliminate—the emphasis on heavy industry and especially on steel, in favor of more rapid growth in agriculture and light industry, and of increased incomes for peasants and workers (IHT 19 June 1978 and 23–24 June 1979; LM 24–25 June 1979; FER 5 October 1979).

The *Economist* asks whether this "marked retreat from the boldest visions" of Deng Xiaoping "also represents a personal and political setback for Mr. Deng," and answers with a qualified "no," surmising that he was himself a "prime mover behind the modificaitons" (ECO 9 June 1979). On the other hand, at the end of 1979, the *Financial Times* (19 December 1979) reports that "after a gap of nearly a year, China has again begun signing important contracts for technology. This is an unmistakable clue that its modernisation programme is cautiously under way again."

China's new eight-year trade agreement with Japan, its most important trading partner by far, is particularly important and symptomatic. This agreement provides for $20 billion of trade between the two countries. China's exports are to rise from seven million tons of oil and 300,000–500,000 tons of coal in 1978 to 15 million tons of oil and 3.5–3.7 million tons of coal in 1982. Prices will be bargained yearly in accordance with the movements of world market prices. Whatever these may be, during this first five-year period China is expected to have a trade deficit with Japan, as China will have imported $8 billion of plant and equipment, and $2 to $3 billion in construction materials, including steel, from Japan (FER 3 March 1978). The deficit appears to be covered by "deferred payments," which are equivalent to (but not called) credits for seven to twelve years, and which would mark a further departure from China's previous self-reliant policy of refusing loans and aid (BW 3 April, 29 May 1978). The financing of Chinese imports by West German banks (FER 28 October 1977) suggests a similar tendency. A less important trade pact was signed with the European Economic Community.

In 1979 China sought and accepted outright loans, often from commercial banks in many developed capitalist countries, and even in some underdeveloped ones, such as Argentina. With the entry of the Bank of China to borrow on world financial markets in 1979, loans and credits to China could reach US $40–50 billion in a year (FER 5 October 1979). The China International Trust and Investment Corporation has been established to "utilize foreign investment and introduce advanced technique, technology and equipment needed for the socialist modernization of China" (HOL 29 July 1979). The 1979 National People's Congress approved a foreign investment code contemplating exemption of foreign profits from Chinese taxes for the first three years and a further rebate on profits reinvested within China, as well as freedom to remit any profits abroad. The code established a minimum foreign investment of 25 percent in any joint venture in China, but no maximum (HOL 29 July 1979). Accordingly, "Peking is prepared to consider 100 percent foreign ownership of joint ventures in China, a U.S. legal expert says" (IHT 5 June 1979). The director of the foreign trade department of the Peking Foreign Trade Institute declared that China seeks foreign collaborations in the following fields: electric power industry, including hydrothermal and nuclear projects; energy resources, including coal and oil; transport and communications; raw or semiprocessed materials, such as plastics; precision machinery and electronics; iron, steel, and non-ferrous metals; and agricultural mechanization. Joint ventures would also "be encouraged primarily to produce commodities for export" (FER 5 October 1979).

China's pragmatic policy in foreign economy—and political—relations can be seen further in the assurances by the minister of foreign trade and by Chairman Hua himself that, despite the approaching expiry of the ninety-nine year lease of Hong Kong's New Territories, capitalists "should not worry" about that date or their investments in Hong Kong (FER 2 December 1977). After the Bank of China had begun to participate in syndicated loans for speculative land development in Hong Kong, by the end of 1979, according to a joke making the rounds in Hong Kong, the question is no longer "When will China take back Hong Kong?" but "By when will it have brought it back?" (FT 19 December 1979). China also began establishing special industrial export promotion zones in China itself (FER 5 October 1979).

Nonetheless, it would be saying too much to suggest that the pragmatic policy of modernization is fully established in China, or that disagreement and conflict about this policy are over. Thus, Victor Zorza suggested:

> The right-wing policy of modernization is urged by Teng [Deng]. The left-wing policy of sticking to socialist principles is favored by Hua. The extreme-left policy of reviving Mao's radical program is advocated by many followers of the "Gang of Four." . . . A strong Maoist faction in the army is making it difficult for Peking to disregard the views of the extreme left. The modernization urged by Teng requires the mobilization of the country's resources for the development of industry and agriculture, and this means that less would be available for the army. That is one reason why, apart from any ideological considerations, there is also strong army opposition to Teng. . . .
>
> Teng's modernization program—whether for the economy or for the army—needs a lot of time. It needs an assured peace with Russia, stability on the border, and a political atmosphere in which China could afford to concentrate on economic reconstruction. . . .
>
> What it needs, in short, is a settlement with the Soviet Union. This is the real foreign policy issue in the debate about modernization. . . . The major issue in the debate is whether China should re-establish a friendly relationship with the Soviet Union. This is linked directly with the struggle over domestic policy now in progress in Peking (IHT 18 May 1978).

Zorza also suggested that Brezhnev is anxious for a settlement as well, but is unable to offer sufficient concessions, while China is bargaining up the price of the same through its semi-alliance with the United States.

Important elements in the army still swore by Maoist self-reliance and the "Yenan Way," and were trying to reverse the policies pursued by Deng—so much so that there were complaints of an army plot against the political leadership (Zorza in IHT 23 November 1977). Chairman Hua Guofeng seemed to straddle the two positions, seeking to inherit the mantle of Mao while turning it partially inside out and supporting Deng's modernization campaign. However, Hua "would obviously prefer to make haste more slowly" than Deng, and even the respective public pronouncements of the two officials indicate serious disagreement on a number of issues (Zorza in IHT 27 February 1978). The press reported that "Peking Admits Leaders, People Split on Policy Shifts, Resistance to Change in Politics, Economy" (IHT 9–10 June 1979) and pointed to particular disagreements on the invasion of Vietnam. On the other hand, there are also those who dispute the split between Deng and Hua, arguing that "Hua is Chairman/Premier due to Teng's [Deng's] strength," which is so great that Deng can afford to let Hua keep these posts (FER 5 October 1978). With respect to China's foreign policy, the credibility grap—as David Bonavia (FER 15 July 1977) calls it—continues to widen to the point of becoming a gaping hole. For instance, after China sent a million men to defend Korea a generation ago and even while Chairman Hua made his first state visit abroad to North Korea in May 1978, the opinion is widespread that in fact China "is now one of the most concerned nations in Asia that the U.S. might withdraw its remaining troops from the peninsula" (USN 24 January 1977). The Washington-Peking-Tokyo axis has become a fact, and China invaded Vietnam "to teach it a lesson" as soon as Deng Xiaoping returned from his triumphant trip to the United States. Indeed, according to the *Washington Post,* Peking has even "proposed . . . to let the United States supply the technology and training with which they themselves could monitor certain Soviet missile activities and then report the findings back to Washington" (IHT 23 April 1979). Yet, no less than their predecessors, Hua and Deng take advantage of every official occasion to declare that "the situation in the world is excellent . . . and in China too."

Korea and Vietnam

It is perhaps appropriate to add a very brief note on Korea and Vietnam, without pretending to give them the careful examination that they no doubt deserve. The economic and political sacrifices and successes of the Democratic Peoples Republic of Korea and of Vietnam have won the just admiration of progressive and honest people around the world for many years, and they continue to do so today. Nonetheless, recent news has been disquieting, and bears consideration.

For many years, North Korea faithfully pursued its *juche* (self-reliance) policy, but in the early 1970s it started to look to the industrialized countries for imports—especially modern technology—so that the country could pull itself up to the technological level of its bitter rival,

South Korea. Trade with the West is now believed to account for half the North Korean total. No sooner were the trade doors opened, however, than the trade position deteriorated from a small surplus in 1970 to a burgeoning deficit from 1973, largely because of soaring import prices, including the cost of oil brought from the Soviet Union and China. . . . Pyongyang's difficulties are [also] due to falling prices received for exports. In addition, the North Koreans often invoiced in sterling, and the pound has been falling rapidly in value (FER 19 December 1975).

Nor is this all:

Two reasons are given for the North Korean economic misery. First: North Korea imported large quantities of Western products, in order to fulfill its six-year plan ahead of schedule. In doing so, it moved away from economic realities. Secondly: a significant fall in metals prices on the international metals exchanges hit the North Korean metals industry in its vital nerve. Thirdly: the increase of oil prices by the Soviet Union and China made the North Korean economic crisis worse (FR 22 October 1976).

As a result, North Korea's foreign debts rose rapidly; it became one of the few countries—and the only socialist one—to default on its loan repayments. Estimates of its foreign debt vary. One estimate for 1975 was $1,130 million, of which $700 million to socialist creditors (FER 19 December 1975). For 1976, external debt was valued at $1,800 million with socialist and $1,300 million with capitalist countries (FER 5 November 1976). South Korea offered what appear to be particularly hostile estimates of $2,144 million at the end of 1975, of which $902 million to socialist and $1,242 million to capitalist creditors (FER 9 April and 11 June 1976). For 1979, foreign debt outstanding is estimated between $1.8 and $2 billion (FER 17 August 1979). The most important debts to a capitalist creditor are owed to Japan; it is estimated that $270–$300 million of these were overdue in mid-1976, and North Korea had already defaulted on at least $120 million (FER 16 July and 5 November 1976). North Korea was accordingly obliged to restrict its imports, and its trade deficit with Japan declined from U.S. $143 million in 1974 to $59 million in 1977 (FER 17 August 1979). The Japanese are careful not to foreclose on any of these debts as long as possible—not only of humanitarian generosity, but in order to avoid a chain reaction of bad debts and export credit stoppage at home:

Tokyo: North Korea is again falling far behind its debt payment schedule, which has already been stretched beyond common practice by sympathetic creditor nations. . . . Even if a single creditor demands insurance payment and Tokyo complies, North Korea would automatically be blacklisted as a unreliable trade partner and Tokyo would have to stop underwriting exports to it. Until now, the Japanese have tried to live with North Korea's defaults, desperately hoping that the situation would improve without necessitating insurance claims (FER 9 April 1976).

On the other hand:

> Paris: North Korea's creditors have adopted a policy of "every man for himself" since Pyongyang has made it clear debt repayments will not begin for several years and it has become obvious neither the Chinese nor the Soviets will bail it out. When President Kim Il Sung was in Peking last year, it is believed to have agreed to cancel North Korea's $200 million debt. At the same time, Kim also intended to visit Moscow. . . . Although the Soviets contributed to Pyongyang's heavy debt burden by increasing the price of oil sold to North Korea in 1974, they have not offered to reduce the debt, estimated at $400 million (FER 11 June 1976).

By 1977, however, after three years of "Drought, Debt, No Market, North Korea [Is] Seen Recovering from Slump" (IHT 6 July 1977). Since then:

> North Korea starts to put its house in order. . . . But the North Korean domestic economy, while certainly austere, may not be in quite the state of disarray often supposed. . . . [Even so] Pyongyang now finds itself in a "Catch-22" situation. It needs to import more, so that in turn it can export more and thus has the wherewithal to pay its debts. But creditors are in no hurry to supply the Kim regime with more money—a hard fact of international trade and finance that North Korea is only now coming to grips with. The debt talks in Japan are seen as crucial, and Pyongyang floated what North Korea thought to be a reasonable plan for repayment. But Japanese traders are looking for more assurances (FER 17 August 1979).

Thus, the capitalist world crisis created, or at least seriously aggravated, an economic and political crisis of major proportions in North Korea, a country which had long distinguished itself in its self-reliant economic and technological development. This internal political turmoil generated countless and incessant rumors of a succession crisis, involing Kim Il Sung's son Kim Chong Il, his supporters, and his opponents. We have witnessed the expulsion of North Korean diplomats from Denmark for smuggling whiskey, cigarettes, and even drugs, and the subsequent revelation of similar systematic North Korean activity in Sweden, Finland, Malaysia, Argentina, and elsewhere. This spectacle could no longer be laid to aberrations of individual diplomats, but had to be accounted for through instructions that Korean diplomats do anything to earn additional foreign exchange for the state treasury (FER 5 November 1976, FR 22 October 1976). And why, we may ask, was the Democratic Peoples Republic of Korea still training Mobutu's military forces in Zaire—with public appearances at military parades—while the latter was helping the FNLA to combat the MPLA in Angola in 1975?

The Vietnamese achieved a historic military and political as well as moral victory over American imperialism on 30 April 1975. However, perhaps not surprisingly, they have found reconstruction difficult. Nayan Chanda reports:

> Vietnam has been forced into a major reappraisal of its economic strategy. The reasons are disappointment over the lack of aid from the socialist camp, and the growing urgency of providing food and other essentials to a country whose population now has peace-time expectations. . . . It is now clear Hanoi will trim some of its ambitious heavy industry projects and give top priority to agriculture and exports of farm products. And it is stepping up its search for capital and technology from the developed capitalist countries. This change of strategy is not only a fundamental departure from the economic philosophy embraced by the country since 1960—Soviet-style planning emphasizing heavy industry—but it is also noticeably different from the plan outlined in June by VWP Secretary Le Duan (FER 19 November 1976).

Earlier Chanda had reported that:

> Vietnam Workers' Party First Secretary Le Duan has made it clear in his latest speech that technology will be given priority over narrow ideological considerations in order to rebuild the country's battle-scarred industry. . . . Apparently, most investment will go towards building heavy industry in the north, while the south concentrates on light industry and agriculture. In a commentary on the speech, the Hanoi daily *Nhan Dan* went further and said that scientific and technical revolution "is the key to achieve the goal of socialism." If this is the official line, it is inevitable that massive foreign assistance will be required (FER 16 July 1976).

That this *is* the official line has been confirmed by other Vietnamese spokesmen, such as a Vietnamese ambassador who—to the express surprise of his listerners, including the present writer, at an Afro-Asian conference—used the self-same words in outlining the longstanding Vietnamese strategy of developing large-scale agriculture, with special emphasis on export. In his later report, Chanda informs that "the present Plan relegates heavy industry to third place—after agriculture and light industry. . . . 'We must admit,' [Foreign Minister] Trinh said, 'we have failed over the past several years to understand truly the extremely important position of agriculture' " (FER 19 November 1976).

However, agriculture, light industry, and the coal mines are to increase production not only for Vietnam consumption,

> but also to increase exports in order to obtain capital to finance heavy industry. As the [political] report [to the Fourth Party Congress in December] says: "Foreign trade must be·stepped up and become a

crucial part of the whole economic activity of our country. The aim of imports and exports is to acquire for ourselves modern techniques of the world and to bring higher economic results to production and labor." . . . Hanoi's urgency in boosting food and consumer good production have led to the adoption of an open-minded foreign policy and a realistic domestic policy. . . . While senior Hanoi officials have been visiting Western Europe and Japan seeking bilateral aid and trade, the country has joined the International Monetary Fund and Asian Development Bank and is prepared to accept joint ventures with foreign companies (FER 17 December 1976).

At the same time, Vietnam has joined the socialist countries' CMEA (Comecon). Active Vietnamese interest in foreign trade and the prospective passage of laws permitting private foreign investment—with minority shares and profit taking through commodity exports—have been reported by the Western press with increasing frequency (e.g., LM 27 April 1976; FR 13 December 1976). Particularly notable is the party's First Secretary Le Duan's statement—perhaps not yet superceded by the recent change in emphasis—that "special efforts must be made to build a petro-chemical industry" (FER 16 July 1976), and frequent reports that Vietnam has been inviting bids for offshore petroleum exploration by major capitalist, including American, oil companies (FER 28 May 1976).

Nayan Chanda reported:

> Vietnam is prepared to provide substantial incentives, including 100% foreign ownership, to investors in export industries in South Vietnam. And Western businessmen who have been informed of this policy by Hanoi think that as a result Vietnam before long could emerge as a competitor not only for foreign investment in Southeast Asia but as an exporter of light industrial products. Although Hanoi has yet to publish its investment code, senior Vietnamese officials have told businessmen that if they bring in machines and expertise to produce exportable commodities they can expect many advantageous conditions and a 10–15 year non-nationalization guarantee. It is not yet clear whether export promotion zones, as the old Saigon regime tried to establish . . . will be set up. But Hanoi appears ready to allow tax-free import of machinery and raw materials and duty-free export of the products from fully foreign-owned plants. This is a step forward from the original Hanoi plan for joint ventures with foreign companies, as first reported in the REVIEW (September 24). . . . The cost of the plentiful labour in Vietnam is expected by businessmen to be competitive with Southeast Asian countries, and skills are claimed to be as good as those in Hong Kong and Singapore (FER 31 December 1976).

On the other hand,

> In a major change from earlier denunciations of "neo-colonialist"

countries . . . [Vietnam] has quietly gone about mending diplomatic fences with Malaysia, Indonesia and the Philippines. . . . Hanoi's media has maintained a surprisingly low-key attitude to individual insurgency movements in South-east Asia. Indeed, there has been no evidence of material support from Hanoi for the insurgents, thus giving no substance to the specter that haunts the leaders of the region of 1 million M-16 automatic rifles captured in Saigon finding their way into insurgent hands (FER 16 July 1976).

Summarizing the political situation in Asia even after the 6 October 1976 reactionary military coup in Thailand, the regional editor of the *Far Eastern Economic Review* wrote:

Since the fall of Indochina, political obsessions in Asia have given way to economic anxieties. . . . To use a Chinese idiom, the pragmatists are taking over from the radicals—in China itself, in Vietnam, and in South Asia. . . . The communist countries are playing down proletarian internationalism with only very low-key backing for insurgencies. . . . The new pragmatism shows itself most conspicuously in Vietnam (FER 12 November 1976).

Addendum

Serious crop failures, caused largely by bad weather, have led the Vietnamese to reverse earlier plans for substantial investment in and expansion of industry, especially of heavy industry, and to shift to a massive new agricultural program instead. In addition to investment in agriculture, this program includes large-scale resettlement of people on the land and increased incentives for agricultural production (FER 4 February 1977 and 5 May 1978). At the same time, Vietnam has joined the IMF, the World Bank, and the Asian Development Bank; and it has established a foreign investment regulation in which "the incentives offered by Vietnam are very similar to . . . those of Taiwan, Malaysia, and South Korea, and are surprisingly liberal for a socialist country" (Tharakan n.d.: 11). Indeed, the New York Citibank's vice-president Edward G. Harshfield, who is based in Hong Kong, has visited Vietnam, and "has already made suggestions to the Vietnamese on ways of making investment in Vietnam attractive to foreigners" (FER 7 June 1977). Harshfield, who is also vice-chairman of the International Affairs Committee of the American Chamber of Commerce in Hong Kong, reports:

For institutions looking for new investment opportunities in Asia, the last April approval of the Foreign Investment Regulations, after 18 months of cogitation by the government of the Socialist Republic of Vietnam (SRVN) has undoubtedly created a new area of investment potential. It is unique that a socialist government should have taken the initiative in attracting private foreign investment. While this measure has displayed the pragmatic attitude of the Vietnamese in resolving their economic problems, it has also underscored the vast amount of capital and technology that are required for developing untapped economic resources of the country. The current investment strategy of Vietnam seems to be only a part of its external policy direction, and its attempts to move from heavy to lesser dependence on its neighbouring communist giants. . . . The SRVN's investment regulations are geared to attract foreign investment in three areas, namely petroleum, export-oriented industries and industries which cater to domestic demand. Equity ownership has been limited to three specific categories; investments in enterprises jointly owned by foreigners and Vietnamese state-owned organisation, where foreign equity could range between 30% and 49% of aggregate capital; production-sharing arrangements suited to energy based industries; the investment regulations do not specify equity ownership for export-oriented industries, and it is assumed that these could be fully owned by foreigners. A wide range of light industries could be developed in South Vietnam, which has the necessary skills and infrastructure, based on joint ownership or fully owned export-orientated operations. The most attractive element for investors in Vietnam is low wage costs. . . . Wage rates have also remained relatively stable in the past, and they can be expected to remain so in the future, as they are set by the Ministry of Labour. . . . Article 10 of the investment code . . . offers a non-nationalisation guarantee for 10 to 15 years. Although the Vietnamese officials have given assurances in private conversations that this period is negotiable . . . Article 26 states that: "In specific cases, if need be, the Government of Socialist Republic of Vietnam may approve more advantageous terms in favour of the foreign party" (FER 29 July 1977).

Before China's decision to set up its own export processing zones, Peking denounced such zones, which Vietnam has also offered to set up, as "nothing else but concessions where foreign capitalists make super profits on local cheap labour"; FER (8 July 1977) asked whether the message was intended for Vietnam.

To enforce its control over food prices, Vietnam suddenly outlawed and closed down private wholesalers of food. (Mostly of Chinese origin, many of these immediately started to leave as "boat people" who had the means to pay their way, and also to carry enough valuables with them to attract the Thai pirates.) At the same time, Vietnam signed its first full agreement for offshore oil exploration with a company from West Germany (FER 14 April and 21 April 1978). These and other apparent contradictions in Vietnam's policy are also expressed in the declarations of its highest leaders. Nguyen Duy Trinh, for instance, stated: "We must quickly and clearly realize the changes in international cooperation and, on this basis, more strongly emphasize our policy of being self-reliant . . . making every effort to produce a large volume of export goods" (FER 4 February 1977). In the first two years following its liberation, Vietnam is estimated to have received the equivalent of about $6 billion of foreign aid, of which about half has come from the Soviet Union. Aid from China has only been about $300 million a year, or about half of what the Vietnamese themselves had expected before it stopped altogether (IHT 24 January 1977; FER 9 December 1977). On the other hand:

> The Vietnamese government has turned down requests by several African and Asian nations to buy U.S. weapons that were left after the collapse of the South Vietnamese government, according to State Department and Pentagon sources. The Vietnamese also have declined to supply guerrilla movements in Thailand, Malaysia and the Philippines, the sources said.
>
> Vietnam's refusal to sell part of its huge stockpile of U.S. weapons—many of them no doubt in poor condition—is attributed, in part at least, to a desire to cement economic links with Western nations, including the United States, and the reluctance to be labeled an "exporter of revolution." Among the nations believed to have offered to buy weapons are Libya, Ethiopia, North Korea, Peru, Pakistan and Turkey. . . . On the surface it would seem like a great asset—a way of obtaining foreign exchange—but political considerations seem to have overruled any sales" (IHT 2 May 1979).

Instead some of these weapons have been used in the war between Vietnam and Kampuchea, which has caused so much consternation around the world.

Some Implications

In conclusion, some major claims of the socialist countries regarding the consequences of their very existence as well as their policy in the struggle for liberation and socialism elsewhere in the world appear to be half-truths; and half-truths are sometimes worse than outright falsehoods. This conclusion emerges from our examination of the participation of the socialist countries in the capitalist international division of labor, even without a detailed analysis of socialist societies themselves. The continued, indeed increasing and often enthusiastic, participation of the socialist economies in the capitalist international division of labor under the laws and rules of the latter is enough to cast the most serious doubt on the full veracity of the claims of the socialist countries regarding their socialism and its consequences.

Through countless official declarations by their authorized spokesmen, the socialist countries make two main set of claims: one, the mere existence and example of the socialist countries necessarily exercise a most beneficial influence on the capitalist world and its internal contradictions. These same contradictions are thereby ameliorated, reducing capitalism's otherwise natural bellicosity, exploitation of its working class, and oppression of its colonies and neocolonies. Secondly, the active *policy* of peaceful coexistence of the socialist countries, plus their selfless help to the peoples of the capitalist underdeveloped countries and their movements of national liberation, make a major positive contribution to the maintenance of peace, the furtherance of national liberation, and the promotion of or transition to socialism in the world. (For an example of such claims, see Dieter Klein's [1976] "Political Economic Aspects of the Fight Between Socialism and Capitalism," and his assertion that the "influence of socialism modifies the operation of the laws of capitalism. . . .") Although there is *some* truth to these claims, they cannot be accepted at face value. Upon further examination they have turned out to be half-truths, whose acceptance without serious qualification would be dangerous indeed for those who are committed to peace, liberation, and socialism.

The existence of the group of socialist countries, since World War II, has thus far contributed to the prevention of another major war through the balance of nuclear terror. However, it is less clear that this is a consequence of their *socialism.* It may be said to derive from the balance between two superpowers, regardless of how the Soviet Union may be defined. The multipolarity emerging from the Sino-Soviet split, as well as the increased power of Europe and Japan, may contribute to a mutual balance of power strategy similar to that known in the period preceding World War I, but certainly no thanks to the existence of *socialist* countries. The balance of power, however, is inherently unstable, and has not guaranteed peace in the past; there is no reason to believe that it will necessarily do so in the future.

With regard to capitalist and imperialist exploitation, Klein claims that because of the existence of socialism, and

> in view of the changed power relations, the influence of socialism in imperialism and the effects of the example of socialism . . . the monopoly bourgeoisie is, in the interest of assuring its dominance, obliged among other things to expand the sphere of social consumption, that is—with regard to the production of surplus value—of unproductive labor. . . . [Thereby socialism] also makes a significant contribution to the fight against reformist social democracy, and bourgeois conceptions of society generally. . . . The power of socialism imposes limits to the operation of imperialist aggressiveness and produces a limitation of the possibilities of imperialism to exploit other peoples. It even obliged imperialism to make certain concessions to these countries, which cannot be explained through private monopoly competition for maximum profits and which also enter into contradiction with the same (Klein 1976: 4).

It is undeniable that the existence of the socialist countries exerts an influence on the operation of national capitalism and imperialism, if only because it has *partially* (and temporarily?) withdrawn 30 percent of the world's people and their resources and markets from the sway of imperialism. However, it is less easy to demonstrate that the existence of socialism or its example has induced, or even helped to induce, capital to introduce the welfare state in some of its domains. These developments are to be explained primarily by the exigencies of capital accumulation along with certain demands of the working class in the West. However, the working class and its leadership in the West are far from having becoming more revolutionary, either by socialist example or through help or advice from the socialist countries; in fact the working class in the West has become more and more reformist and social democratic through the influence of the socialist countries of Eastern Europe and the Soviet Union. This was the case especially in the immediate postwar period, when Stalin helped sabotage the socialist revolutionary movement in Italy, France, and Greece, and would have done so in China if the Maoists had followed his advice or had submitted to his pressure. Nor has Chinese socialism, particularly in its most recent development, had such revolutionary effects on the working class in the West. Only Vietnam and Cuba can in any way be said to have had the kind of influence, particularly in sparking the 1968 movements, that Klein attributes to the socialist countries; and that influence was combatted tooth and nail by the very socialist countries to which he refers. It is equally or even more impossible to accept the claim that the existence of socialism has exercised a limiting influence on imperialist exploitation of the underdeveloped countries, nor obliged it to make concessions to the Third World in general.

If the socialist countries effect any counter influence at all, then it is through the provision of an alternative economic partner in Eastern Europe or the Soviet Union, as for India or Egypt. This has not been a *socialist* alternative, however, and could in principle have been offered by another capitalist imperialist rival, as is common throughout the world in the sale of arms (by the French), better petroleum deals (by the Italians), or in various other economic relations (with anybody and everybody). On the contrary, it can be argued with equal or greater force that the partial elimination of the imperialist domain in the socialist countries has obliged imperialism to increase its exploitation and oppression in other countries. Even with regard to Cuba and Vietnam, the reaction of imperialism and its local allies was to increase its repression of liberation movements in Latin America and Southeast Asia in the 1960s, even if the existence of the Soviet Union and Cuba went forward preventing the United States from crushing Cuba and Vietnam; the liberation of all of Indochina has thus far only intensified imperialist and local repression and reaction in other parts of Southeast Asia. This imperialist reaction, of course, is not to be blamed on the socialist countries; but it also does not afford them, especially the Soviet Union and China, much credit for limiting imperialism's possibilities of exploitation and repression, just because they exist. Where is the evidence that "the modification of the world power relations strengthens the liberation movements in the developing countries, helps nationalization measures against foreign monopolies and that the raw materials price dictates of the monopolies are broken?" (Klein 1976: 6). The mere *existence* of the socialist countries, particularly in view of their progressive reintegration in the capitalist international division of labor, has not furthered these movements and measures appreciably; the active policy of the socialist countries has only supported them in ways that require serious qualification.

Some socialist countries have certainly offered active support to Communist parties, liberation movements, and bourgeois nationalist governments intent on some measures to nationalize foreign property, or to get better prices for their raw materials. Nonetheless, this support has not gone toward particularly socialist revolutionary purposes, either on the part of the socialist countries or on that of the groups that have received their support in capitalist underdeveloped countries. More often than not—and particularly at the most critical moments, such as during the Spanish Civil War, the postwar period in Western Europe, and literally countless instances in the underdeveloped countries—economic, political, and military support from the socialist countries has been for downright counterrevolutionary purposes. (For postwar Western Europe, see for instance Claudin and Kolko.) Where this support has been used for socialist purposes, as in Indochina, the native revolutionary movement *itself* was revolutionary. Both the Soviet Union and China in fact repeatedly urged the Vietnamese to abandon their revolutionary pretensions as unsuitable or untimely, as Stalin had urged the Chinese similarly in 1947–1949. The Soviet Union in particular could and should have given the Vietnamese military aid, such as Mig-21s and Sam II missiles which could have afforded a defense against United States B-52 bombers and other weapons. However, the Soviet Union denied such aid to the Vietnamese, while Egypt was already supplied with these same Soviet weapons. Further, Peking and Moscow received Nixon while he was bombing Hanoi and mining its harbor and while the *Vietnamese themselves* were modifying the Soviet-supplied missiles in order to bring in the B-52s down with them—these events of course speak for themselves. Equally transparent are Vietnam's invasion of Kampuchea and China's invasion of Vietnam. As for "local" wars in the underdeveloped countries, neither the existence nor the policy of the socialist countries have presented or even impeded them in the past; neither do they give promise of doing so in the future.

Eastern Europe's support of the efforts of underdeveloped countries to raise the prices of raw materials has been limited indeed. The fact that the Soviet Union made common cause with the most diehard imperialist countries at the UNCTAD and Law of the Sea conferences against attempts of the underdeveloped countries to protect and raise raw materials prices through the Common Fund and other measures is an indication of how far this support went. If the Soviet Union supported the increase in the price of oil, was it not because coincidentally she is also an exporter of the same? Did the Soviet Union not equally welcome a high price for gold, of which she is the world's second most important producer/exporter—after South Africa? With respect to terms of trade and the international division of labor in general, we have seen that the socialist countries behave no differently from, and some-times worse than, the imperialist ones, except that for reasons of their own they prefer longer-term price and delivery arrangements, unless these be-come burdensome. Now, the imperialist countries also show increasing interest in stability of supply of raw materials but, like the Soviet Union, not through a multilateral common fund which would prevent them from exer-cising their own bargaining power bilaterally. Nationalizations have long since ceased to be an obstacle for imperialism. If the imperialist firm can invest its compensation in more profitable endeavors or transfer abroad to do the same elsewhere, and if nationalization promotes the formation of mixed com-panies between imperialist and underdeveloped state capital, then the im-perialist firms and their governments are more than satisfied and happy. Support for such nationalization measures from socialist countries is, of course, not so welcome to the imperialist ones if this support strengthens the bargaining hand of the underdeveloped state. Again, the objection is not that such support is *socialist*, but rather that it offers an alternative, which could be and often is similarly offered by another Western capitalist state. For the socialist countries, investment links with the state sector of the underde-veloped countries are, as we have seen, beneficial, particularly insofar as these relations provide a basis for exports of otherwise not highly com-petitive products of socialist heavy industry. For the underdeveloped coun-tries, however, these relations are not particularly more favorable than are those with a capitalist supplier. Everybody is made happy when, as is in-creasingly the case, there is tripartite East-West-South collaboration in major capital projects—everybody, that is, except the masses of people and their liberation movements in the underdeveloped countries, who are con-demned to suffer continued and increasing exploitation and repression from the bureaucratized and militarized state capitalism which West and East support in the name of the international division of labor.

We must attempt to examine, and demystify, the respective ideologies of each sector under a clear light: the Soviet theory of "non-capitalist develop-ment" under the leadership of the bureaucratic, and supposedly progressive, antifeudal and antiimperialist bourgeoisie in the Third World; the Chinese theory of "new democratic revolution" through the antiimperialist and anti-feudal alliance of four groups (workers, peasants, petty bourgeoisie, and national bourgeoisie) against feudalism and superpower imperialism; and the three-world theory, according to which the progressive and reactionary states of the second and third worlds should unite against the superpowers of the first world. We must unfortunately conclude that all these are little more than ideological figleaves for the economic interests and political policies of each sector. These ideologies have been invoked in support of their sponsors' respective foreign policies in Indonesia, India, Egypt, Ghana, Chile, Angola, and other countries in the Third World, as well as in international forums such as the United Nations, UNCTAD, the Nonaligned Nations Conference, and so forth. The socialist countries' indistinguishably reformist and some-times downright reactionary support for bourgeois regimes, and frequently equally indistinguishable ideological, political, and even material oppo-sition to popular revolutionary movements in the Third World, have led to political disaster in one country after the other. This "socialist" sponsored "Third Worldism" argues that the principal contradiction lies on the one side between the "national" bourgeoisies, allied among each other and with their workers and peasants, and on the other side their common imperialist enemy, rather than between the ruling but increasingly imperialist dependent bour-geoisies and their own proletariat and peasantry. We therefore conclude that socialist "Third Worldism" offers little hope and even a substantial threat to aspirations for national liberation and socialist revolution in a world inter-national division of labor based on superexploitation of the people by im-perialism in alliance with the local bourgeoisie.

One is left to wonder how and why the official pronouncements of self-styled communist and revolutionary socialist centers, parties, and move-ments continue to claim that "the situation is excellent" (Peking); "socialism is advancing stronger than ever" (Moscow); and "revolutionary possibilities are around the corner" at least in Southern Europe (Trotskyists). These claims conflict with the domestic and foreign policies—now including re-pression at home and wars abroad—that mark contemporary socialist coun-tries, communist parties, and revolutionary movements. Therefore, we face a grave crisis of Marxism that is costing the cause of socialism countless millions of supporters around the world.

The theoretical, ideological, and political dilemma of socialism today derives from and may be summarized by the complete abandonment, both in theory and in praxis, of the famous means and end of *The Communist Manifesto:* "Workers of the world unite." Both the theory and the praxis of proletarian internationalism toward the goal of communism have been re-placed by "socialism in [my] one country." Moreover, communism itself as the end goal of social development has in practice and apparently even in theory been replaced by "socialism." Although for Marx and Engels and still for Lenin socialism meant no more than an unstable transitional process or stage on the road to communism, "socialism" has been converted into an end station or steady state. Some "socialists" claim to have arrived already. Other more realistic ones (ironically called "idealists" by the former), such as Mao, only claim that their country is in the transition to socialism, which requires repeated and successful cultural revolutions (of which the first one in China failed). Of course, if "socialism" no longer means the transition to communism through proletarian internationalism, but becomes an estab-lished state in some countries and a distant goal for others, it becomes end-lessly debatable how one recognizes such a state if one sees it, and how one gets there if one does not recognize socialism today. Thus, the socialist has become like the person who looks for his lost watch alone under the nearest street light, claiming that there he can see better, even though the watch for socialism was lost somewhere else down another road, and has made the time of communism recede back into definite darkness.

The more we examine the "Marxist" theory that is supposed to guide and justify this "socialist" praxis under the plain light of day, the more indistinguishable does "Marxism" become from orthodox, everyday, bourgeois capitalist theory and praxis of "national development." Ever since the capitalist ascension of noncolonial Japan into the charmed circle of industrial powers, outside the West only the socialist countries have been able to achieve participation in the world capitalist economy (or even aspire to such participation, as in the case of China) on a remotely equal basis to that of the developed capitalist countries. These relations in the international division of labor seem ironic in view of the state goals of Marxism, but are perhaps not surprising on further analysis. *None* of the (under)developing capitalist Third World countries have escaped dependent capitalist underdevelopment, nor do any of them show prospects of doing so in the foreseeable future, despite Brazilian, Korean, Iranian, and Mexican miracles or oil booms. Only certain select "socialist" economies can now knock on the door of the capitalist inner sanctum. One reason is ironically that the Socialist East had been temporarily relatively isolated from the workings of the capitalist international division of labor; this isolation in turn—oh, double irony—was not voluntary, but was enforced by the capitalist powers during the Cold War in reaction to the socialist transformations of domestic property, and of productive and political relations. These transformations comprise the other grounds for the "success" of socialism (even the most nationalist dependent and state capitalist Third World countries like Nasser's Egypt never attempted such thoroughgoing changes). There is, however, a further and triple (and quadruple, quintuple) irony: Deng's China, Phan's Vietnam, Tito's Yugoslavia, Kadar's Hungary, Gierek's Poland, and perhaps last but not least Brezhnev's and/or his successor's Soviet Union, all have been pursuing the same course. Driven on by their own internal economic and political crises, these countries do not want to use "socialism" to challenge the West in its time of crisis by beating capitalism, but by joining in the capitalist world system as competitive partners on as nearly equal terms as possible. In the process, they lend the capitalists an economic, political, and thereby ideological hand in overcoming the world crisis of capitalism. Someone in the (East) German Democratic Republic suggests that socialists would win the race with the West as soon as they stopped running in the same direction. However, as long as they play catch-as-catch-can instead, the socialist countries, and with them the cause of socialism in much of the world, will remain caught in a "Catch 22" dilemma of being damned if they do and damned if they don't. Or is this Catch 22 simply the inevitable result of treading the path of "socialism in one country" while confronting the cruel ironies of an ancient triple Greek tragedy in the guise of the Modern World System?

Chapter 5
Rhetoric and Reality of the New International Economic Order

Driven by deteriorating economic conditions and encouraged by the apparent success of OPEC, Third World governments in the United Nations and elsewhere have demanded a new international economic order (NIEO). They seek more money through an improved international financial system; less restricted access to the markets of the developed countries, particularly for Third World manufactured exports; higher and more stable prices for their raw materials; controls against abuses in the transfer of technology, particularly by multinational companies; more sovereignty for and cooperation among Third World states, and other modifications in the international order. Despite a long succession of international conferences devoted to these issues, the progress achieved toward NIEO through negotiations between the South and the North (sometimes including the East as well as the West) has been virtually nil. Moreover, in the real world outside the conference rooms, the position of the Third World has deteriorated even further as an important part of the burden of the economic crisis in the North and of the oil price hike has been shifted onto the Third World through the operation of the existing international economic order. The prospects for reversing this deterioration of the Third World position, let alone for the establishment of a NIEO, are very dim for the foreseeable future. However, the deepening world economic crisis may lead to a new wave of protectionism in the West (and involution in the East), which would prevent the Third World from continuing in its present appointed role as exporter of cheap raw materials and low-wage producer of manufactures. As long as the Third World continues to play this role—and the demands for a NIEO seem designed only to enhance their ability to do so and thereby to increase the bourgeoisies' benefit—the masses of workers and peasants will continue to suffer from economic superexploitation and the concomitant political repression.

> Where the world goes, depends mostly on the United States.
> *U.S. Secretary of State, Henry Kissinger*

> In the sphere of international power politics, sincerity counts for nothing.
> *Michael Harrington*

The call for a new international economic order (NIEO) has become the theme of innumerable international conferences, forums, declarations, debates, and discussion in the press, as well as the subject of scientific research. Like all movements, that for NIEO seeks to add to its legitimacy by claiming a long pedigree and a venerable tradition. NIEO traces its roots back to the first Afro-Asian Meeting of the Nonaligned in Bandung, Indonesia, in 1955 on the one hand, and the first appearance of the Group of 77 countries (which now number more than 120 and then started with 75) at the first UNCTAD conference in Geneva in 1964. UNCTAD's Secretary General, Raúl Prebisch (the director of the United Nations Economic Commission for Latin America [ECLA]) already called for a new economic order in its opening session. A similar call in essence was heard at the Afro-Asian Economic Seminar, addressed by Che Guevara representing Cuba, also held in 1964 in Algiers. In the meantime, UNCTAD conferences and related Group of 77 caucus meetings have been held at New Delhi in 1968, Santiago in 1972, and Nairobi in 1976, all without producing any noticeable change in the old international economic order. The Nonaligned and Group of 77 countries for their part have met in Belgrade, Cairo, Algiers, Georgetown, Lima, Manila, Colombo, Dakar, and Havana, lately every year or two, in an attempt to define their positions and to shore up their bargaining power by presenting a militant united front in the sphere of international power politics.

The Background and Reasons for NIEO

At the initiative of the Third World's Nonaligned summit meeting in Algiers in 1973, under the leadership of Algerian President Boumedienne and while Foreign Minister Bouteflika was President of the United Nations General Assembly, the latter at its Sixth Special Session in May 1974 formally issued the Declaration and Programme of Action on the Establishment of a New International Economic Order in Resolutions 3201 (S-VI) and 3202 (S-VI). The General Assembly subsequently brought forth the Charter of Economic Rights and Duties of States in General Assembly Resolution 3281 (XXIX) in December 1974. The demands for NIEO were reiterated at the Seventh Special Session of the UN General Assembly in 1975, strengthened at the Nonaligned summit in Dakar in 1975, and again weakened at the Group of 77 meeting in Manila in 1976. NIEO has become a bargaining issue between the underdeveloped and the developed countries at every other international conference, particularly at UNCTAD IV in Nairobi in 1976 and at the North-South Dialog which lasted eighteen months from 1976 to 1977 in Paris. NIEO has also become the focus of attention at numerous nonofficial conferences, forums, and declarations, such as the Third World Forum (at meetings in Karachi, Santiago, Lima, and elsewhere); the Algiers Conference and the Association of Third World Economists; and the seminars and declarations at Cocoyoc (Mexico), the Hague, Stockholm, and elsewhere. The International Development Association, the European Institutes of Development Studies, the Bariloche (Argentina) Group, the Dag Hammarskjöld Foundation, the Overseas Development Council, the Club of Rome at its meetings in Berlin in 1974 and Algiers in 1977 and in its "RIO" report on *Reshaping the International Order* (prepared under the direction of Jan Tinbergen [1976–1977]), the United Nations Study on *The Future of the World Economy* (prepared under the direction of Nobel laureate, Wassily Leontief [1977], and countless research institutes, personalities, and individuals as well as very substantial press coverage have kept up the refrain about a NIEO. With all this smoke, where is the fire?

We may ask, first of all, *why* this crescendo about NIEO has built up *now*, particularly with a pedigree that goes back two decades and more. One reason, of course, is that the old economic order has disadvantaged the Vast Majority, as Michael Harrington (1977) calls it in his recent book, and some of the established elites as well (see chapter 1). The first United Nations Development Decade, launched in 1960, was a complete failure. That the second decade was off to a bad start became particularly clear with the onset of the 1973–1975 world economic recession and the realization that the world capitalist economy was entering (or had already entered) a new period of crisis.

> There is now widespread recognition that existing international development policies have largely failed to achieve their stated objectives. The hopes that were placed on the International Development Strategy for the Second United Nations Development Decade, when it was adopted by the General Assembly in 1970, have been essentially frustrated. . . . The Strategy had no significant positive impact on the pace of development of the Third World. Indeed, it now appears evident that the policy measures envisaged in the Strategy, even had they been fully implemented, would not have provided an adequate basis for the long-term development of the developing countries (UNCTAD 1977a: 1).

The reasons for this failure, according to the above-cited UNCTAD document, lay with the "central concept" of the strategy—that the expansion of the developed economies would be transmitted to the Third World. The "major assumption" asserted that trade barriers would be reduced. Both concept and assumption proved to be "defective" and "invalid" respectively. Additionally, the strategy "did not take adequately into account the fact" of the transnational corporations, and that "they tend to impose inappropriate patterns of development in the Third World." Moreover, a fourth major erroneous assumption was that "expansion in the gross product of developing countries would engender economic development in the broad sense." In stead, "income disparities appear to have widened, while poverty, unemployment, under-employment, malnutrition and hunger have become more widespread." In sum, "the weakness of the Strategy . . . can thus be attributed basically to the fact that its underlying concepts and assumptions were not in keeping with the realities of the world economic system," and to the "ill-founded assumption" that "governments would give high priority to implementing the Strategy." They have not done so, "though, as argued earlier, even full implementation would have been inadequate . . ." (UNCTAD 1977a: 1–3).

Recognition of these facts and of the inherent ill-foundation of previous strategy has become widespread indeed, so much so that even a longtime member of the very moderate social democratic Socialist Party of the United States was impelled to declare: "First of all, I was surprised to find out how much I agree with neo-Marxist theory that America is an imperialist power" with widespread responsibility for the underdevelopment and exploitation of the Third World, after he had spent many years combatting this "theory" (Harrington 1977: 252). This same recognition of "the realities of the world economic system" is also being expressed through the call for NIEO and the many scientific studies and political declarations related to it.

Two recent studies have received particularly widespread attention; they deserve such attention because they show—with the authority of their authors and backers—both how necessary and how hopeless the establishment of a *new* international economic order really is. The first is the three-year-long study under United Nations sponsorship by renowned world personalities and specialists, under the direction of Wassily Leontief (1977) and using his "input-output analysis," *The Future of the World Economy,* to the year 2000. The study begins with an income gap between developed and underdeveloped countries of 12 to 1 in 1970, and asks what would be necessary to reduce this gap to 7 to 1 by the year 2000. Previous and current development strategies, with targets of economic growth of 6 percent per annum and 3.5 percent per capita in the Third World, would not narrow this gap at all, according to the study. As may be seen in Table 5-1, real growth rates have *declined* in recent years and have been increasingly below these targets. Therefore, recent and foreseeable growth rates would widen the gap still further to 16 to 1 and more. During the first half of the 1970s, per capita output in the Third World, other than the fast-growing petroleum and manufacturing exporting countries grew at 2.2 percent; and twenty-nine countries with 40 percent of the Third World population saw their per capita income stagnate or even decline. Of ninety-eight Third World countries, sixty-three

TABLE 5-1
Economic Growth in Major Country Groups, 1960–1977

	Population 1977[a]	GDP per head 1977	Change in total GDP			Change in GDP per head		
	(Percent)	(Index)[b]	1960–1970	1970–1973	1973–1977	1960–1970	1970–1973	1973–1977
			(Percent per annum)			(Percent per annum)		
Developed market-economy countries	24	100	4.9	5.1	2.1	3.9	4.1	1.1
Socialist countries of Eastern Europe[c]	12	—	6.7	6.6	6.0	5.9	5.7	5.0
Developing countries:[d]								
Total	64	9	5.3	6.3	5.4	2.8	3.7	2.8
Medium- and high-income countries	23	12	6.0	7.8	5.9	3.2	5.0	3.1
Low-income countries[e]	41	3½	4.1	3.0	4.1	1.7	0.6	1.7
of which								
Least developed	8	3	3.1	3.2	3.3	0.8	0.8	0.9

From UNCTAD *Handbook of Trade and Development Statistics, 1979.*

[a]Shares in the total of the first three country groups shown.

[b]GDP per head in developed market-economy countries = 100.

[c]The figures for GDP relate to net material product.

[d]Excluding China and other socialist countries of Asia.

[e]*Per capita* income below $400 in 1976.

Source: UNCTAD 1979f.

countries with 65 percent of the population did not achieve the target of 6 percent annual growth, and sixty-eight countries with 75 percent of the Third World's population failed to achieve the target of 3.5 percent growth per capita (UNCTAD 1977c: 6). In order to narrow the gap to 8 to 1 in thirty years, growth rates would have to be 7 percent per annum and 5 percent per capita in the Third World, and 3.6 to 4 percent (instead of the previous 4.5 percent) in the developed countries (Leontief 1977: 3, 30–31) The world capitalist economic crisis—rather than any agreement on NIEO—is indeed reducing the developed countries' growth rates to these percentages and below. However, far from increasing the growth rates of most Third World countries, the same crisis has thus far brought their growth rates per capita ever closer to zero.

In analyzing how to achieve the projected necessary growth rates for the next thirty years, the same Leontief study calculated that in the Third World, agricultural land would have to increase by 229 million hectares or 30 percent; yields per hectare would have to be tripled; and agricultural output would have to rise by 5 percent per year (Leontief 1977:4). All of these increases far exceed any achieved so far. During the first half of the 1970s, Third World agricultural production increased at an annual average rate of 2 percent (UNCTAD 1977c: 8). Manufacturing production would have to reach 6 to 7 percent in African and 7.5 to 8 percent in Asian non-oil-producing countries, 8.5 to 9 percent in Latin America, and 14 percent per year in oil-producing Third World countries. Heavy industry would have to grow faster than light industry (Leontief 1977: 8). By the end of the century, the Third World would have to account for 14 percent of the world's exports (and remain net importers) of light industrial products, 7 percent of industrial materials, and 2.7 percent of machinery and equipment (Leontief 1977: 56–95). Real investment in the Third World would have to rise to 30 to 35 and in some countries to 40 percent of national product, the distribution of national income would have to become more equal, and balance of payments deficits would have to be substantially reduced (Leontief 1977: 11). Therefore, it would be necessary to establish a NIEO in which the terms of trade would favor producers of primary products; the Third World's dependence on imports of manufactures would be decreased and its exports of manufactures increased; official and other foreign aid would reach and even surpass the targets that are already further and further from realization; and the flow of capital investment would have to be substantially modified (Leontief 1977: 9). Moreover, "two general conditions are necessary: first, far-reaching international changes of a social, political, and institutional character in the developing countries, and second, significant changes in the world economic order" (Leontief 1977: 11). In brief, the obstacles are not technical but political.

Additionally, the other well-publicized recent study, entitled *Reshaping the International Order* (RIO), under the direction of Jan Tinbergen (1976–1977: 103), argues that not even a 5 percent growth rate per capita is enough to reduce income differentials,* and it is nonetheless doubtful whether all Third World countries could achieve and maintain such a growth rate. In his 1977 address to the Board of Governors of the World Bank President McNamara soberly observed:

> Development, despite all the efforts of the past 25 years, has failed to close the gap in per capita incomes between developed and developing countries. . . . The proposition is true. But the conclusion to be drawn from it is not that development efforts have failed, but rather that "closing the gap" was never a realistic objective in the first place. . . . It was simply not a feasible goal. Nor is it one today. . . . Even if developing countries manage to double their per capita growth rate, while the industrial world maintains its historical growth, it will take nearly a century to close the absolute income gap between them. Among the fastest growing developing countries, only 7 would be able to close the gap within 100 years, and only another 9 within 1,000 years [McNamara 1977: 7].

Thus, the most prestigious authorities have established that NIEO is needed for "the vast majority" of mankind—a need which has existed for a long time—and that the foreseeable prospects of achieving NIEO look very dim indeed.

If the need for NIEO has existed for so long and the prospects for it remain so dim, what then has moved so many Third World spokesmen to demand NIEO now? What has disposed representatives of the capitalist developed states to entertain, though not to accede to, these demands? A one-word, and therefore perhaps simplified, answer is likely to be OPEC. The nearly simultaneous and, in part, mutually related victory of Vietnam over American imperialism; its consequent monetary political weakness; the economic challenge of Europe and Japan to American power, and of the post-1973 economic crisis to the Western-led world capitalist system as a whole; and related to all of these, the challenge of OPEC—all have encouraged Third World spokesmen to air their demands and Western representatives at least to listen. In other words, the terms of Third World dependence are now subject to some negotiation. Thus, France's Foreign Minister Louis de Guiringaud said, "Just as there is no alternative to détente with the East, so there is none to the dialogue with the South. [There is] no political alternative . . ." (IHT 24 June 1977). Spokesmen for the socialist countries attribute these developments in turn to political changes in international relations in the wake of détente, and the growing economic power of

---

*The director of the RIO project, Jan van Ettinger, writes in a personal letter: "This statement is correct based on the German version you used. However, the original English version . . . reads on page 90: 'a 5 percent target . . . still fails *substantially* to reduce the income differential.' With apologies for the, on this point, incorrect German translation, I would highly appreciate if you could change your text. . . ."

the socialist world (IPW 1977). Realistically speaking, OPEC has not only given moral encouragement but also direct political and economic support to the spokesmen for NIEO. Moreover, as the Club of Rome soberly points out:

> There is still a lack of concrete indications that the rich nations are convinced of the need for structural change . . . it is surely correct that the majority of Western politicians are not driven to the conference tables by the misery of the poor nations, but by the poor economic situation in their own countries and through the strong shifts in the international system . . . which naturally explains their preoccupation with securing the supplies of raw materials and oil" (Tinbergen 1976–1977: 61, 57).

(Not to be outdone or left behind by Western politicians, the Club of Rome, which only as recently as 1972 had completely written off the Third World in its first report on *Limits to Growth* [Meadows 1972] with "zero growth," incorporated the Third World into a differentiated world economy in its second report [Mesarovic and Pestel 1974], and then placed the Third World at the center of its new concern for "reshaping the international order" under the guidance of Tinbergen [1976–1977].)

Numerous testimonials indicate that the West, led by the United States, was brought to the conference bargaining table, particularly at the North-South Dialog in Paris, by its concern to assure itself stable supplies of petroleum at acceptable prices, and secure conditions for foreign investment in the Third World. Henry Kissinger had failed in his initial attempt to break up OPEC (by dividing its members through stick and carrot threats and offers). The industrial oil-importing countries were obliged to parlay as long as the OPEC countries and the remainder of the Group of 77 maintained a common front, despite the West's hopes to divide them and the world into petroleum-producing and petroleum-consuming states at the Paris conference and elsewhere (Buira 1977; CE July 1977). In the diplomatic language of UNCTAD (1976a: iv):

> The question is no longer one of a moral imperative. There are solid reasons, both economic and political, which underlie the need for a positive response from the developed countries. . . . Today, the developed countries can be harmed by crisis conditions in the Third World. Disturbances which interrupt the flow of supplies, which lead to irregular movements in prices, and which prevent the orderly expansion of investment can have serious consequences on the economies of the developed countries. Nor is this all. The political aspects are no less significant. Instability, tension, and social unrest in the Third World must have their inevitable repercussions on the rest of the international community. The frustrations of the countries of the Third World could erupt in many ways and go well beyond the actions of their governments. The avoidance of tensions in the Third World will prove to be an increasingly important element in global peace.

Here, UNCTAD has laid out a perspective upon which the governments and bourgeoisies of the developed and underdeveloped capitalist countries can agree, even if portions of the rhetoric may sound unpleasant to some ears there. In many Third World countries has long been common practice to accompany or even to preface increasing domestic political repression by "compensating" progressive pronouncements on foreign affairs; these cost nothing internally, and even help to neutralize some of the real progressive political forces on the domestic scene. Why not generalize this ploy, and/or extend it to the "South" versus the "North" as a whole? "In certain cases, the agitation for a NIEO is used by some regimes for throwing all the blame of the worsening conditions of the masses on external forces alone, and for establishing an alibi for themselves" (Mansour 1977: 83)—and to provide a political publicity cover for intensifying the repression of the masses. Moreover, "since the propositions for a 'new international economic order' come from the representatives of the dominant classes [and] it is hardly to be supposed that the *pay offs* [if any] would in the first instance flow to the mass of the impoverished population, these additional resources could also flow into the weapons arsenals of the social war [against the masses]. For the moment, more speaks for this supposition than for the contrary one" (Senghaas 1977: 260). In a word, the progressive demand for any NIEO, let alone any measures toward its realization, may well be partially designed for increasing the political repression of the masses by local bourgeoisies in the Third World who find themselves hemmed in by the crisis of the old international economic order. An example par excellence is Mexico, whose President Echevarria was perhaps the loudest Third World spokesman for NIEO. President Marcos of the Philippines hosted the Group of 77 preparatory meeting for UNCTAD IV and the World Bank Group/IMF, and enforced martial law on the Filipino people along the way.

The Third World Demands for NIEO

In this international and domestic political context, the demands for and of NIEO need not surprise us. Gamani Corea, the secretary general of UNCTAD (one of the principal official institutional promoters of NIEO), speaking just before UNCTAD IV—scheduled to be one of the main instances of NIEO's negotiation—summarized:

> I am of the opinion that the underlying desire, indeed demand, of all is that the countries of the Third World be incorporated into the system of world wide trade. They do not any longer want to remain at the margin or outside of this system. They want to belong to it and to participate in the decisions and events that influence its development" (LM, 6 April 1976, cited in Senghaas 1977: 63–64).

Johan Galtung (1975:9) observes:

First, NIEO is essentially trade-oriented. There is even talk of expanding the world economy. . . . Second, as far as improving world trade is concerned NIEO only aims at terms of trade. There is very little mention of changing the division of labor. . . . Third, to the extent that there is talk of improved terms of trade it is the deterioration in terms of trade that is discussed . . . not the absolute level. . . . Fourth, to the extent that there is some talk of improved division of labor it centers on such tertiary sector institutions as transportation, insurance and finance institutions in general. . . . To summarize: what the New International Economic Order means, when translated into world reality, is some kind of "capitalism for everybody" charter (Galtung 1975: 8–9).

Manuel Pérez Guerrero, the head of the Venezuelan delegation to the North-South conference and serving as its president and as chief negotiator for the South, clarifies: "Those of us who promote a change in the system of international economic relations do not do so with the aim of eliminating the principles of economic freedom and private initiative" (Guerrero 1977: 23).

Michael Harrington (1977: 217, 232) is "struck by the utter moderation of what is proposed. . . . First the ideology of the demand for a New International Economic Order is impeccably capitalist. Second, the poor countries have been extraordinarily patient and long suffering. . . . Third, American capitalism could make money from a moderate increase in world social justice."

"The essentials of a new order" here summarized by UNCTAD for its IV Conference in Nairobi in 1976:

Emphasis [should be] on structural changes, rather than on aid. . . . First, a new structure is needed to govern the trade . . . in primary products. . . . Second, there is need for a reformed external framework to govern the industrialization of the developing countries. . . . Third, there is a basic need for a new international monetary system. . . . A fourth area . . . encompasses co-operation among the developing countries. . . . Fifth, a major expansion of trade and other exchanges between the developing countries and the socialist countries of Eastern Europe is required.

Additionally, and cutting across these, UNCTAD mentions the special needs of the least developed, landlocked, and island developing countries, and the need for a new institutional mechanism to negotiate the demands elaborated above (UNCTAD 1976a: 12–14).

These utterly modest proposals for greater integration of the Third World in capitalist world trade are reflected in the long list of concrete demands formulated in numerous international conferences. Of the many statements of such proposals, we may cite the convenient summary list put together by the United Nations Institute for Training and Research (UNITAR). Under the title "Progress in the Establishment of a New International Economic Order:

Obstacles and Strategies," UNITAR offers a catalog of specific research tasks:

UNITAR: Documentation on the NIEO 1974–77

Principal Issues Covered:

1. The attainment of U.N. global development assistance levels and other quantitative targets.
2. The linkage of development assistance with the creation of SDR's, and the utilization of SDR's as the central reserve asset of the international monetary system.
3. The negotiated redeployment of certain productive capacities from developed to developing countries and the creation of new industrial facilities in developing countries.
4. Lowering of tariffs and non-tariff barriers on the exports of manufactures from the Third World.
5. Development of an International Food Programme.
6. The establishment of mechanisms for the transfer of technology to the Third World separate from direct capital investment.
7. Regulation and supervision of the activities of transnational corporations in promoting economic development of the Third World.
8. Elimination of restrictive business practices adversely affecting international trade, especially the market share of developing countries.
9. Reform of the procedures and structures of the IMF, the World Bank and IDA to facilitate favorable conditions for the transfer of financial resources for development.
10. Improving the competitiveness of natural resources vis-à-vis synthetic substances.
11. Full reimbursement to developing countries of monies derived from customs duties and taxes applied to their exports.
12. Appropriate adjustments in international trade so as to facilitate the expansion and diversification of Third World exports.
13. Creation of buffer stocks through producers' associations and other means.
14. Renegotiation of Third World debts.
15. Promoting the participation of Third World countries in world invisible trade.
16. The establishment of a system of consultations at the global, regional, interregional and sectoral levels with the aim of promoting Third World industrial development.
17. Adoption of an integrated approach to price supports for an entire group of Third World commodity exports.

18. The indexation of Third World export prices to tie them to rising prices of the manufactured and capital exports of developed countries.

19. Free choice of States of their economic, social and political system and of their foreign economic relations.

20. The right of States to full permanent sovereignty over their natural resources.

21. The right of States to nationalize foreign property in accordance with their own laws.

22. Restitution and full compensation for the exploitation and depletion of, and damages to, the natural and all other resources of States, territories and peoples under foreign occupation, alien and colonial domination or *apartheid.*

23. The need of all states to put an end to the waste of natural resources.

24. The right of association of primary product producers, and the duty of other countries to refraim from interfering in such associations.

25. The use of funds released through disarmament for Third World development.

26. Exploitation of the sea-bed and ocean floor taking into account the particular interests and needs of developing countries.

27. Special measures to assist in meeting the developmental needs of land-locked, least developed and island countries.

28. Technical Co-operation among Developing Countries (TCDC) (indigenous technology).

29. Strengthening of Third World regional, sub-regional and inter-regional co-operation.

30. Technical and financial development aid and assistance to Third World countries.

31. Social questions (Employment and income distribution).

32. Restructuring of the Economic and Social Sectors of the United Nations.

Source: UNITAR n.d.: 4–5.

Note: *UN source materials:* General Assembly Resolutions and Decisions, ECOSOC, UNIDO, UNCTAD, UNEP, FAO, World Food Council, UNDP, ILO, UNESCO, UN Special Fund, World Bank, IMF, GATT, Center for Disarmament; UN Regional Commissions: ESCAP, ECWA, ECA, ECE, ECLA, additional UN sources, as appropriate; *Non-UN sources:* Conferences of Heads of State or Government of Nonaligned Countries, Conferences of Ministers of Foreign Affairs of Nonaligned Countries, Conference of Developing Countries on Raw Materials, OECD, European Security Act, Reports to the Commonwealth Secretariat.

André van Dam summarizes, "in essence NIEO may be considered as a new global model of industrialization, based on the worldwide distribution of labor, resources and capital, in that order of importance" (CE March 1976: 306). The sectors of capital which are domiciled in the Third World segment of this global model are bargaining for more profits from "their" labor and resources, in that order of importance.

NIEO Results So Far

They can pass resolutions at Colombo and in the United Nations until hell freezes over, but none of them will have any important impact until they negotiate with the industrial states.

USN 16 August 1976, quoting "a top American economic official"

What have been the results of the many-sided negotiations for NIEO so far? In the United Nations General Assembly sessions, where the Third World commands the votes but has no executive authority extending beyond rhetoric, a Third World united front has been able to pass NIEO resolutions with substantial majorities. These proposals have had the support of the socialist countries, and have attracted or neutralized some industrialized capitalist countries' votes as well. Thus, the original NIEO Programme of Action was adopted by consensus (without votes by the opposing minority), and the Charter of Rights and Duties was adopted with 120 votes for, 6 votes against, and 10 abstentions.

The Third World countries have met among themselves, excluded some of the more reactionary governments, and have sought to build a common front among the more progressive of them. At meetings such as the Nonaligned summits, they have taken more militant positions (than at the UN, for example) to further their collective self-reliance. At the meeting of the 77 in Dakar in 1975, with respect to negotiations on raw materials, a Third World "solidarity fund" was proposed to defend raw materials prices through producers associations; these would withhold some sales, and compensate potential sellers largely with OPEC, that is Arab, oil money from the fund. However, in preparation for negotiations with the industrial countries at UNCTAD IV in Nairobi, the UNCTAD Secretariat itself launched the proposal for an "integrated programme" and a "Common Fund" that would finance a stockpile of raw materials through contributions—and therefore votes and decisions—of all countries, including the industrial ones. In the meantime, in Manila at the Group of 77's preparatory meeting for UNCTAD IV, the 77 backtracked to a "stabilization fund" that would be jointly financed and managed by Third World and other countries (Amin 1976). The compromise agreement was on a fund with a "first window" of $400 million, largely to cover costs of administration, and a "second window" of $300 million, whose scope the West wants to keep as "limited as possible." The second window would assist poorer producers in increasing their commodity earnings. "In practice it will have only a marginal role in the world's commodity markets. Prices will still be determined by supply and demand. . . ."

Moreover, instead of treating eighteen commodities or even only twelve as a group, the "stabilization fund" provides for a commodity-by-commodity approach (FT 22 March 1979). "In the period since Nairobi, despite several preparatory meetings on as many as 12 commodities included in the Integrated Programme but not covered by international agreements, it has been possible to bring only one product—rubber—to the stage of a negotiating conference" (UNCTAD 1979e: 5). On other matters as well, the Manila meeting of the 77 represented a weak compromise on the lowest common denominator of the least offensive demands to be made at UNCTAD IV.

At the UNCTAD IV conference in Nairobi in May 1976, U.S. Secretary of State Henry Kissinger arrived with an alternative proposal, while the West Germans sought to obstruct any and all agreements until the last night's session. The integrated program proved unacceptable because it contemplated a wholesale approach to raw materials whereby the decline of some prices would be compensated by the rise of others through the Common Fund. Instead, the industrial countries, including the socialist ones, wanted a piecemeal approach that would guarantee their bargaining power at each turn. A stabilization scheme, financed by a solidarity fund against them, was of course anathema to the developed countries of East and West; but then the Third World had already dropped that proposal anyway. Mr. Kissinger proposed instead an International Resources Bank to be associated with the World Bank Group and controlled by the United States and the international financial institutions. This was unacceptable in turn to the Third World as well as many other countries. Three years later, the father of UN-ECLA and UNCTAD, Raúl Prebisch, wrote: "I was inclined to believe that the initiative had its merits and should be examined. Hence my discomfiture—which I freely admit—when, some time after leaving the State Department, Dr. Kissinger explained to an audience of businessmen that the purpose of his idea was to ensure a supply of low-price commodities for the industrial centres! That was the significance of one of the few initiatives made by the North in response to the appeals by the South" (Prebisch 1979: 1). Finally, West Germany retreated from its recalcitrant "minority of one" position—which had nonetheless served the purpose of softening everybody else's position. The only points agreed upon were to continue talking about the Common Fund and to adjourn the talks to the North-South Dialog in Paris, where the North would be in a relatively stronger and the South in a weaker position than in Nairobi. The results of UNCTAD IV with regard to other major issues proved similar: wholesale consideration, much less a moratorium or even cancellation, of Third World debt was also unacceptable to the industrialized creditor countries, again including those of the socialist East. Even Brazil and Mexico want debts to be considered case by case (that is, all creditors against one weak debtor each time); it was then agreed to continue discussion in Geneva. With regard to technology transfer, the West was more amenable to the establishment of a code of conduct, which in turn will be more effective as rhetoric than reality, if and when it is enacted. The

Conference on Technology, held in Vienna in 1979, was based on proposals for "a smorgasbord instead of a plan," prepared largely by government bureaucrats," considered "most definitely not a basis for action" (Lund Letter 1978 and 1979).

Evaluations of UNCTAD IV differ. By and large they have been negative, though perhaps less so than reactions to the previous three UNCTAD conferences which accomplished nothing at all. Because the developed countries are now themselves concerned about raw materials supplies and prices and about the mounting Third World debt problem, they have at least been willing to talk about them. Nonetheless, *Comercio Exterior* (June 1976: 661), for instance, summarizes: "On balance what happened at Nairobi leaves ... one unmistakable feature, failure." A relatively positive evaluation of UNCTAD IV is that of Miguel Wionczek (1976: 573) from Mexico. He argues that, if the conference was not a success, it was not truly a failure either for the following reasons: UNCTAD IV at least discussed real problems, which all countries will have to continue to discuss for another ten years; the Third World achieved considerable cohesion and successful political orchestration in its negotiation—after having already watered down its negotiating position at Manila—in part because the developed countries were unable to present a united front themselves (particularly since the Scandinavians supported Third World positions and West Germany retracted its precious lone opposition); and the documentation was prepared at a high technical level. However, UNCTAD IV failed to agree upon, much less enact, any significant concrete measure, and NIEO certainly moved no further along.

The next major conference, known as the North-South Dialog, was initially convened in Paris by French President Giscard d'Estaing especially to negotiate with the Third World, or rather, part of it. The Western countries wanted to talk about security for their petroleum supplies and investments in the Third World. The socialist countries were not invited, and only nineteen selected Third World countries were present to represent all the others. The latter, however, insisted that, as a condition for their participation, the questions of principal concern to them be considered as well. After long, drawn-out discussions about what subjects to consider, the North reluctantly agreed to the establishment of four commissions on energy, raw materials and trade, development, and money and finance. The North's efforts to split the South into oil and non-oil countries—and indeed to divide the OPEC countries themselves—failed at least partially, whch proved to be perhaps the most significant result of the conference. However, for this very reason, and notwithstanding some intra-Northern disunity, the relations of forces led to eighteen months of stalemate during 1976 and 1977. Since neither side wanted to close the door completely, the North-South Dialog in its last sessions finally came to a minimum agreement—mainly, to continue talking at later conferences. The dialog agreed on certain special measures to favor the least developed, landlocked, and island Third World countries, and to increase official development aid (ODA) to the Third World, although this promise has been made several times before. The target of 0.7 percent of the developed countries' GNP continues to recede, as "aid," however generously defined, has fallen to less than half of that. The other "agreement" was to accept the Common Fund in principle. Previously, it had been rejected outright. It was now agreed to consider the Fund in some form at least, and to discuss it again at the next conference in Geneva. Britain and several other industrial countries began to show a more accommodating attitude. On the other hand, these countries are trying to transform the proposed Common Fund from a stockpile into that of a bank. Not incidentally, this is what Mr. Kissinger had proposed in Nairobi (FER 28 April 1978). The Geneva conferences subsequently took place in November 1977 and March 1978. At the end of the last conference, the Group of 77 issued a statement saying, "we cannot fail to express in the most unequivocal terms that the conference is ending in complete failure" because of the "serious lack of political will by the industrialized and socialist states" (IHT 4 April 1978).

Besides sidestepping the Common Fund for raw materials, the Paris North-South conference only agreed to disagree about securing supplies and stabilizing prices of oil; debt relief for the Third World (a subsequent conference in Geneva made no progress on this issue either); and all other significant financial questions. Nobody wanted to call the conference itself a complete failure; but its results were "clearly miniscule . . . [and] the 'old' international economic order remains virtually as it was" (Amuzegar 1977: 141). For the head of the Mexican delegation, Jorge Eduardo Navarrete (1977a: 159), the conference was an experiment in the negotiated search for NIEO which is on the "border of failure." With respect to reaching any agreement on the principles of NIEO, "the effort has so far substantially failed" (Navarrete 1977b: 1059). Each side has overestimated its own and underestimated the other side's bargaining power, and neither had the "political will" to do better.

The "Report by the Secretary-General of UNCTAD to the Conference" of UNCTAD V, held in Manila in May 1979, observed:

> The issues incorporated in the agenda for the fifth session are relevant to many of the essential concerns of the international commodity in the current situation. They reflect the major problems presently facing the developing countries in the area of international economic relations. But they also reflect problems that must be of vital concern to the developed countries themselves. The problem of weak and fluctuating terms of trade continues to be one of the predominant concerns of the developing countries in the present context. The question of access to markets for the products of their emergent manufacturing sectors has acquired a new urgency against the background of a trend towards protectionism in the industrialized countries.

The severe inadequacy of the prevailing network of financial facilities, and indeed the limitations of the international monetary system as a whole, have been underlined by the vast shifts in payments positions of developed and developing countries in recent times. The need for much wider economic cooperation amongst the developing countries themselves has come to be highlighted by the persistence of their dependence on a few metropolitan powers for trade, technology and finance. All these issues figure prominently on the agenda for the fifth session. Taken together with issues in the field of technology, of trade between countries with different economic and social systems, of shipping, and with problems affecting specially disadvantaged categories of countries such as the least developed countries, they make up a wide and well-rounded agenda for UNCTAD V.

The issues by themselves are not new. Indeed it is important to recognize the continuity that exists between the fifth session and UNCTAD IV at Nairobi (UNCTAD 1979d).

The "success" of yet another major conference in making any "progress" toward NIEO, or indeed toward anything at all, was summarized by the press headlines and commentary after the conference: "UNCTAD main issue unresolved." "No consensus at Manila" (FT 28 May; 5 June 1979). "Little Else Accomplished" (IHT 5 June 1979). "UNCTAD V end in complete deadlock." "UNCTAD 5 a watershed—not a success" (GUA 4 and 6 June 1979). "UNCTAD dissatisfied with everybody" (ECO 2 June 1979). "Little accomplished beyond agreement to send major unresolved issues back to UNCTAD headquarters in Geneva for more efficient study and more conferences" (IHT 5 June 1979).

Progress toward NIEO through other international conferences has also failed to materialize so far. Of the various measures to deal with the Third World food problem discussed at the 1974 World Food Conference in Rome, none have been effectively implemented. Only the weather has since improved, so that there have been record crops in South Asia and surpluses in North America. However, good weather is normally followed by bad. The Law of the Sea conferences in Caracas, New York, and Geneva have gone from one stalemate to another. The Third World wants protection for its raw materials against the competition of seabed mining and deep-sea fishing by the developed capitalist and socialist countries. The underdeveloped countries demand a new institutional ocean authority and enterprise over which they would have substantial power. Meanwhile, the United States keeps threatening with the introduction of laws in Congress such that the American government itself may license the multinationals to exploit the sea and sea bottom if the Third World is not prepared to accept the regulation of the seas on American, West German and, last but not least, Soviet terms. At world monetary conferences in Jamaica and elsewhere, "the process of restructuring the international monetary system has come to a virtual halt. The various ad hoc

decisions . . . cannot be considered as constituting monetary reform"
(UNCTAD 1977b: 6). To the extent that there have been any such decisions
and reforms, they only favor capital in the industrialized countries and not
the Third World states. The few policy changes to date have further disadvantaged the bourgeoisies and have penalized the masses in the Third
World (as we will observe in greater detail below). The only areas in which
apparent reform has not come to a halt include: progress toward codes of
conduct by transnational corporations and for technology transfer (one may
wonder who, if anybody, would enforce such codes, and how); measures to
increase Third World participation in insurance, liner conference, and other
matters relating to shipping (though Liberia and Panama already lend or rent
their flags to foreign bottoms and banks); and the agreement and implementation of the "stabex" scheme to compensate some raw materials
producers for certain price declines within the Association of African,
Caribbean, and Pacific (ACP) countries through the European Common
Market. However, after a few years of operation, this "much vaunted special
relationship . . . is looking tarnished," as a "rift" and a "deadlock" have
developed between the EEC and the ACP countries over the financing of the
arrangement (GUA 18 June 1979). The final negotiating session, lasting
twenty-six hours, ended in "disappointment and bitterness," as the "EEC
was not prepared to negotiate further"; twelve ACP countries refused to sign
the new convention and a joint declaration (FT 28 June 1979).

In short, in the conference "ring around the rosy," "shrewd analysts
understood that the Seventh Special Session [of the UN General Assembly
in 1975] marked the 're-emergence of the moderates' in the Group of 77"
(Harrington 1977: 235). This trend was also reflected in the Third World's
backtracking at the Manila conference, its conciliations at Nairobi, and its
temporizing in Paris. In the meantime, the North did not make one single
significant concrete concession on NIEO or on anything else. Third World
spokesmen have become increasingly persuaded that asking for even the
most moderate "new" international economic order overnight is utopian, and
that the only realistic procedure is to follow the salami tactic, slicing off a
little bit at a time. But ultimately, won't this tactic be rather more like peeling
an onion, as NIEO is sought under each new layer, until there is nothing
left—except tearful eyes? To consider this question, we may look at what has
been happening in the real world outside the conference rooms.

We may divide the catalog of thirty-two NIEO demands (on pp. 273–
274) into major subject matter categories, and examine the evolution of
events with regard to these subjects, not so much at the conference tables, but
in the real world itself. The major subjects are: (a) money; (b) raw materials,
(c) manufacturing exports; (d) technology and transnational corporations;
(e) Third World state sovereignty; (f) Third World cooperation; and
(g) "social questions."

(a) Money and Finance: foreign aid and foreign debt; financial payments
to the Third World to return importers' tariffs and taxes, for restitution of

colonial damages, and in lieu of armaments expenditures; and special aid to less developed, landlocked, and island Third World countries (demands number 1, 2, 9, 11, 14, 22, 25, 27 and 30).

> No significant progress has been made so far in implementing the General Assembly's recommendations in the area of international monetary reform and development finance. . . . The effort to estblish a link between the creation of special drawing rights [SDRs] and the provision of additional development finance has so far been frustrated. . . . No agreement was reached . . . as regards development finance, compensatory financing, alleviation of the debt burden of developing countries or the reform of the international monetary system (UNCTAD 1977a: 12).

Arms expenditures, of course, have increased; and restitution of taxes or damages to the Third World is literally out of the question. On the contrary, as can be seen in TW, chapter 4, the Third World's prospects for debt or other financial relief have continued to recede inasmuch as its foreign debts have doubled or tripled during these past years with higher rates of interest, shorter terms of maturity, and more onerous conditions of debt management. Canada and some small European countries have unilaterally canceled the debts of a few poor Third World countries, and the late Senator Humphrey even introduced a bill in Congress to authorize the United States to do likewise. However, "Carter administration officials have no intention of a blanket or a significant write-off of loans to some poor nations, even if such a step is given legislative approval" (IHT 20 March 1978) and "in Bonn a government spokesman denied that West Germany has entertained any plans to take part in a write-off of Third World debts" (IHT 28 February 1978). The Third World countries with the largest debts, Brazil and Mexico, have themselves opposed all consideration of debt moratoria for fear of damaging their own credit rating, which they need to get new loans to pay off old ones.

The dollar has been devalued three times, reducing the real value of the dollar debt, but also of the Third World's dollar reserves; and the weakened dollar has caused an effective devaluation of those Third World currencies that are pegged to it in one way or another. These real monetary changes have, of course, occurred without the slightest consideration of the interests of the Third World. Moreover, the Third World countries and their populations have clearly suffered the most as a result of these changes, if only because they are the most defenseless against the worldwide inflation, particularly in prices of manufactures, that is fed by the reckless printing of devalued dollars by United States. The supposed measure to demonetize gold and to replace it by SDRs or some similar universal reserve currency have led on the one hand to the strengthening and price increase of gold, to the disadvantage of Third World countries which have little or no gold mines or stocks. On the other hand, of the SDRs and other funds created by the IMF and other financial institutions, only the equivalent of US $2.5 billion has been destined for non-oil-producing Third World countries. This amount is equivalent to about one percent of their current foreign debt and a very small share of total additional funds, almost all of which thus went to the rich countries. The "link" that the Third World demanded between additional money and development finance has been effectively denied. More important than its refusal in principle, an effective link has been denied in practice, except in the opposite direction.

(b) Raw Materials: terms of trade of raw materials prices; integrated program and/or producer associations for raw materials; food and agricultural programs; seabed and ocean management; and conservation of natural resources (demands 5, 10, 13, 17, 18, 23, 24, and 26). In this area there has been to date some successful maintenance of OPEC unity and prices, providing the impulse toward the remaining demands for NIEO. However, the effective price of oil was again eroded to an equivalent of $7 per barrel by world inflation and dollar devaluation before the price was again raised sharply in 1979. For a time the OPEC countries were not sufficiently united (in view of Saudi Arabia's effective veto power) to raise the oil price again, given their common fears of rocking the world economic boat on its current crisis journey. Although the oil-producing countries—inside and outside OPEC—increased the price of oil again in late 1978 and in 1979, they did so more out of disunity than unity, each charging the "spot price" that its market will bear. If market demand declines due to recession, so will the price of oil. Be that as it may and as we observe in chapter 2 and TW, chapters 3 and 4, most of the effective cost of the oil price hikes has also been passed on to the non-oil-producing countries of the Third World. Meanwhile, the industrial countries have increased exports to the OPEC countries, and have recycled the remaining OPEC surplus through their banks. Several other raw material-producer associations have been formed or strengthened; however, these associations and their price stabilization efforts have been unable to prosper much against the opposition of developed raw material-producing countries and low world market prices in years of recession and times of crisis (see TW, chapter 3). Other raw material producers do not have the relative monopoly power of OPEC, and prospects for their independent successful action through stabilization, let alone "solidarity" funds, are dim (TW, chapter 4).

Common action with the raw-material importing industrial countries is limited by the latters' own interests, which may admit some stabilization of supply and price, but more in favor of consuming than of producing countries. In any event, although the terms of trade for non-oil-producing Third World raw material-exporting countries improved briefly between 1972 and 1974, they on balance declined again with the 1973–1975 world recession and the post-1975 mild recovery. For non-oil-exporting countries in the Third World, the terms of trade have fallen by more than 10 percent since 1970, and suffered an "unprecedented deterioration in the balance of trade" of US $32 billion between 1970 and 1975. Of this sum $5 billion can be attributed to changes in volume, and $27 billion to changes in prices of the goods traded. In turn, of this $27 billion deficit caused by price changes, $8 billion can be attributed to international inflation and $19 billion to unfavorable changes in the terms of trade (UNCTAD 1977c: 15). The underdeveloped countries' terms of trade declined 4.7 percent in 1975, rose 3.7 percent in 1976, remained unchanged in 1977, and declined 11.2 percent in 1978 (UNCTAD 1979e). Terms of trade may have risen again in 1979, "but in 1980 a deterioration in the non-oil LDCs' terms of trade is expected, as European economies slow down in policy-induced response to rising domestic inflation and the U.S. recession" (FER 21 September 1979). From 1974 to 1978 alone, the terms of trade of all underdeveloped countries, including the oil-exporting ones, declined by 15 percent, representing a foreign exchange loss of $30 billion in 1978 (UNCTAD 1979e: 3).

The increased availability of food and even the higher price for coffee have been almost exclusively due to the weather, not to any negotiations for NIEO. Developments in seabed mining, monopolized by a few metropolitan and/or socialist multinational firms, threaten some of the Third World raw materials exporting countries with "unfair" competition. Natural resources in the West, East, and South, far from being conserved, are being ravaged more and more, if only because such exploitation is considered temporarily necessary during the "emergency" of the present economic crisis. There is no NIEO in this area either.

(c) Manufacturing Exports: tariff reduction and trade in invisibles (demands 3, 4, 8, 12, 15, and 16). We shall see in TW chapter 3, that the export of manufactures and their production especially for export have indeed been increasing in many Third World countries. We have also noted that the principal reasons for this trend have stemmed from the desire of international capital to produce at lower costs in the Third World; as a result, the Third World countries are competing with each other to attract such capital, each trying to offer the most favorable conditions of production, and especially the lowest wages, at the expense of the masses of their local populations. This modification in the international division of labor may constitute an aspect of a "new" international economic order, but it is not derived from any hard bargaining for access to the industrial countries' markets through the reduction of their tariffs, domestic excise taxes, or other restrictive measures as part of NIEO. On the contrary, this wave of cheap Third World manufacturing exports combined with the demands for protection raised by some sectors of local capital and labor—faced with competition and unemployment in the current economic crisis—have had the following result: the European Common Market, its member countries, and the United States have moved to increase tariffs and to impose quotas on the import of manufactures from the Third World. Examples include provisions for increased protection in the Multifibre Agreement negotiated at the end of 1977, and American restrictions on the import of shoes, textiles, as well as television sets, steel, and so forth. The outcome of this struggle between higher profits for some and protection for others remains uncertain, and will be further examined below.

(d) Technology and Transnationals (demands 6, 8, 28): the industrialized countries have agreed to talk about codes for transfer of technology and for the conduct of transnational enterprises. However, the real-life conduct of both continues to be just as determined by the global interests of transnational corporations as before. The developed sector contributes all too little toward the self-reliance of Third World countries through the selection of more appropriate technology, and still less through its development in the Third World itself. In fact, the latter's technological dependence on the transnationals in particular and on the industrial countries generally increases day by day. Moreover, while the Third World states talk about collective codes of conduct, most of these countries are individually reducing or even eliminating the few restrictive provisions on transnationals and technology transfer that they had imposed nationally or regionally in the late 1960s and early 1970s. Thus, Malaysia, India, Pakistan, Bangladesh, Egypt, Tunisia, Zaire, Mexico, Argentina, Chile, Peru, the Andean Pact as a whole, and other countries are all busily engaged in relaxing controls on foreign enterprise, and are competing with each other to grant more and greater concessions to international capital. It would be too long and tedious to document this trend in each individual case (some of this documentation is already provided in TW, chapter 6), but we may quote *Business Week*: "There is good news coming out of Latin America for U.S. and other foreign companies with a stake in this vast region. Major countries are opening their doors wider to private enterprise. Multinational executives consider the region to be one of the world's major investment opportunities" (cited in MR February 1977: 22). Major countries in Asia and Africa are also not far behind in opening their doors wide.

(e) Sovereignty and Equal Rights of Third World States: the Third World states are achieving formal equality among unequals where it counts least— for example, in the United Nations General Assembly. The Security Council, the Secretariat, and the UN specialized agencies remain under the near exclusive control of the larger developed states. International financial agencies, such as the World Bank and the IMF, remain under the control of United States (with the IMF partially controlled by West Europe); and if these institutions admit any Third World countries to their boards, they do so more to coopt them than to permit them to help steer world financial affairs in a different direction (of which more below). Collectively, the Third World states are admitted to the conference bargaining tables. However, as we have seen, the underdeveloped countries have no power there to impose even their rhetorical demands, while the metropolitan states and multinationals use their power to negate in practice even the little that they were moved to grant in principle. Individually, the Third World states use their sovereignty more often than not—as we have seen—to compete with each other in ever greater concessions to international capital and growing repression of their own populations without outside interference.

(f) Third World Cooperation (demands 28, 29): technical cooperation among Third World countries certainly does not mean the development or use of "indigenous" technology to promote economic and political self-reliance for the masses of their people. If such cooperation means anything, it partially protects capital in some Third World countries from competition by metropolitan capital, and/or opens some markets in certain parts of the Third World to capital from certain others. As an example, Brazil, Mexico, and India—often with transnational participation—have been selling advanced technology and/or sophisticated knowhow in petrochemical and machine-building industries to several Arab countries. In the meantime, although the Arab states have found it politically convenient to present a united political front with other Third World countries, Arab capital has flowed into the banks of New York, London, and Zürich. Seeking the economic and political guarantees of imperialism, Arab capital thus found protection for its profitable investments in Europe and North America and its loans to other Third World countries through the Eurocredit market (see TW, chapter 4). There has been hardly any Arab investment in, let alone solidarity with, the Third World directly, and what little there has been has come with very reactionary political strings and very attractive economic profits attached.

(g) Social Questions: employment and income distribution (demand 31). These "social questions" are examined in great detail in the chapters on growing unemployment and increasingly unequal distribution of income (chapter 1), sharpened superexploitation (TW, chapter 5), increasingly severe political repression (TW, chapter 6), and the militarization and other institutionalization of the state and society (TW, chapters 7 and 8) to serve the interests of international capital and its local junior partners. These Third World partners in turn demand a "new" international economic order to institutionalize their collaboration with foreign capital abroad and their exploitation of local labor at home. It is therefore not necessary here to elaborate what is "new" in the international economic scheme. It is enough to note that there will and can be no new international economic order between states without a new political order within these states.

Interpretation of and Prospects for NIEO

It becomes increasingly evident that the demand for NIEO signifies a political conflict between the governing classes in the Third World and the political representatives of international capital. The political conflict concerns the terms of the Third World bourgeoisie's economic integration in the world capitalist economy. How may we then interpret this conflict, and what is its likely outcome? "The most articulate and persuasive spokesman of the Third World, Mahbub ul Haq, provides here a graphic though disturbing picture . . ." according to the publisher of his book *The Poverty Curtain*. Haq has used his position as vice-president and director of Policy Planning and Program Review at the World Bank as a platform from which to launch his most active call for NIEO. Mr. Haq writes:

By 1972, I was becoming convinced, however, that the rich nations were mistaking the short-run weaknesses in the bargaining power of the Third World for permanent impotence. It was at that stage that I started arguing that the poor nations should "organize their poor power to wring major concessions from the rich nations and to arrange for a genuine transfer of resources." I advocated the use of collective bargaining techniques by the Third World for raising the prices of non-renewable resources, negotiating a settlement of past debts, staking out a claim for the exploitation of common-property resources like oceans and space, and levying international taxes on the consumption of the rich nations. While these views spread some shock waves in the Western world at that time, they were, on the whole, taken quite lightly. After all, where was the real collective bargaining power of the Third World that I was advocating so passionately? (Haq 1976: 143).

Where, indeed? Haq argues that the "poor" nations are often lightly dismissed by the "rich" ones for lack of economic bargaining power; he adds, "in the last analysis, however, the real bargaining power of the poor nations is political, not economic" (Haq 1976: 178; also see pp. 169–183). According to Haq the sources of this political power include the following: the poor nations will soon have the overwhelming majority of the population; some atomic bombs and delivery systems; a greater monopoly of natural resources; a wider market; some control over the "international commons," like the ocean—and OPEC. Haq thinks that the oil states are not likely to join the rich, but will stick with the poor, while the rich can be divided by driving a wedge between the United States and Western Europe and Japan. Bernard Lietaer (1978) argues that growing Third World debt will become so explosive that the North will have to defuse it through a sort of global Marshall Plan in its own interest; he proposes a world development stock exchange as a technically feasible way of financing this plan at least cost. Michael Harrington (1977: 242–245) thinks that "the United States is likely to be reasonable about Third World debt," not out of compassion but for money. Michael Hudson (1977) goes even further, and argues, under the title *Global Fracture: The New International Economic Order,* that the balance of payments deficit or debtor nations in the world—that is, the United States and most of the Third World countries—will line up together against the surplus or creditor countries in Europe, Japan, and the Arab world. On the other hand, the United States also has two other prongs in a "triple strategy": a consumer cartel to roll back commodity prices, and "confronting both Third World and industrial nations by U.S.-Soviet détente to keep the satellites of each system in their place" (Hudson 1977: 262).

Others are not so sanguine about the collective political bargaining power of the Third World. Guy Erb (1975: 138) reminds us that "for every instance of economic or political power exercised by the poor nations, examples can be cited of their persistent poverty and their political-economic weakness."

Michael Harrington dampens his own optimism in reviewing conversations with Third World ambassadors and high-level technicians at the United Nations: "It was an enlightening, depressing evening. I had asked, how, specifically, do you move toward a new international economic order. As far as I am concerned, no one among that shrewd, informed and Third World group had answered" (Harrington 1977: 218). *U.S. News* (9 August 1976: 27) reviews the relative strength and weakness of North and South, and suggests that the oil crisis gave the Third World "a false sense of power. . . . Rhetorically, they will make noises about forcing us to accept a new international order on their terms. But when it gets down to hard bargaining, they know that we have the power." The RIO report suggests that in the short run changes in the structure of power can only be produced through acts of violence, and that many such can in fact be expected in the coming years. To allow such violence to take its course on the international plane would lead to nuclear war, which is unacceptable; thus, the countries of the Third World will have to rely on other instruments, such as control over natural resources and of direct foreign investment and new coalitions, to improve its position of unequal power (Tinbergen 1976–1977: 119). However, we have already seen how weak these instruments are, especially against the economic, political, and military power of international capital and its metropolitan states. Third World coalitions are also fragile:

> The developing countries do not have enough power to impose demands that do not correspond to the interests of international capital. Their weakness is deepened by the tendency of many developing countries to seek individual economic advantages, which leads to a competitive struggle among them. It is true that, as is often emphasized, they all sit in the same boat; but the discussion is about who will be the first to be thrown to the sharks (Heyne 1976: 22).

Where Mahbub ul Haq sees the establishment of NIEO through a process of collective bargaining, Fawzy Mansour (1977) suggests that NIEO should be regarded as "an attempt to establish Global Social Democracy," which is "uncannily similar" to social democracy at the national level in the imperialist countries. Nonetheless, Mansour notes three crucial differences: (1) the global "dice are much more loaded in favor of the rich metropolis vis-à-vis the Third World periphery than they ever were in favor of capitalists vis-à-vis their own working populations." (2) "A similar alliance on a world scale—that is, between the center and the periphery of the world capitalist system—is almost a contradiction in terms, since there is no other planet from which to draw the enormous surplus necessary to finance it," as part of the development of the metropolitan countries was financed out of "the exploitation of Third World resources and populations; and (3) most important the Third World is much more heterogeneous than the nonbourgeois classes in the metropolitan countries, thus making coalitions much more difficult" (Mansour 1977: 11–12, 97).

This reasoning leads to two conclusions. One is the cooptation of the bourgeoisies, state machineries, and political leadership of the Third World; and the other is the use of such a political alliance to exploit and oppress the masses in the Third World still more effectively. In an interesting article in the most authoritative voice of the American establishment, *Foreign Affairs* (whose significance was not lost on Michael Harrington [1977: 231–232]), Tom J. Farer suggests:

> What in fact happened to mitigate class conflict . . . [in] the national societies of the West. . . . What, in essence, did accommodation involve? . . . There was the creaming off and co-optation of the natural elite of the working class. . . . There is no evidence that any existing wealth was redistributed; but there was some redistribution, albeit modest, of shares in the large increments. . . . Is the present struggle between the classes of nation-states not susceptible to mitigation by the employment of an analogous strategy of accommodation? . . . In many respects, indeed, the strategy of accommodation might in fact be easier to implement in the present case than in its predecessor. Our conflict is not with huge, anonymous masses whose demands have to be aggregated through fairly uncertain representational arrangements. For the most part, Third World elites are even less committed to human equality as a general condition of humanity than we are. They are talking about greater equality between states. And in their largely authoritarian systems, the state is they. . . . [They are] articulate, well organized representatives with whom to negotiate. . . . There is, moreover, no reason to doubt whether the negotiators can deliver their constituents. . . . A third factor facilitating accommodation is the very small number of representatives that have to be co-opted into senior decision-making roles in the management structure of the international economy. In Africa, only Nigeria. In Latin America, Brazil and Venezuela, perhaps Mexico. In the Middle East, Saudi Arabia and Iran. And in Asia, India and Indonesia (Farer 1975: 91–93).

Commenting on the North-South conference in Paris, Mexican Foreign Trade Bank's *Comercio Exterior* (July 1977: 835) suggests that "the capitalist system is in crisis and everybody is trying to save what he can"; CE goes on to observe that—beyond the limits of the North-South blocs—it is evident that the United States "has been successful in getting Saudi Arabia, and to a lesser extent Iran, to draw closer to its own positions and that the Third World has given evidence of its splits, although formally it voted in unison within the conference." It appears from our discussion of unequal accumulation (in TW, chapter 1) how this strategy of cooptation is being advocated also by the Trilateral Commission, whose members include President Carter and his National Security Advisor Brzezinski. Therefore, Mansour suggests that NIEO should more appropriately be called RIEO, a reformed international economic order.

It is on the basis of this RIEO that a new class alliance is merging at the level of the world capitalist system between the center of that system and the bourgeoisie of Third World countries. This class alliance is the manifestation, on the political level, of global social democracy . . . [which] is not *essentially* opposed by the center, or at least by the more forward-looking sections of it (Mansour 1977: 84).

Pedro Vuscovic (1978a: 265) already observes "the weakness of the governmental representations of the Third World in the forums of international negotiation as a result of the presence among them of regimes that are absolutely committed and subordinated to foreign interests."

There is another side of the coin of the cooptation of corrupted bourgeois and state interests in the Third World into a subordinate participatory role in the global social democracy of a new international economic order: the exploitation and repression of the "anonymous masses" by this same coalition of international and national capital. The current discussion concerns the distribution not of existing wealth, but only increments to it —as the Leontief and Tinbergen studies make quite clear. Yet, "as long as there is no other planet to draw the enormous surplus necessary to finance" whatever the accommodation between international and Third World capital may turn out to be, the anonymous masses of the Third World will have to agree to bear a substantial part of the cost of NIEO. If the masses cannot also be co-opted into the collective bargain of accommodation to this global social democracy—a prospect neither considered possible nor even contemplated by the bourgeois bargaining agents—then these masses will have to be forced to bear this burden. They will either do so, or revolt instead. The increasing exercise of force through economic exploitation and political repression is documented in TW, chapters 5 and 6.

Another approach and international campaign to face contemporary Third World problems is to meet the minimum basic needs for food, shelter, health, education (sometimes extended to clothing, employment, and political rights) of *all* people in the Third World. This approach gained international currency through the publication of the World Bank-sponsored study of *Redistribution with Growth* (Chenery et al. 1974) and the ILO conference and report on *Employment, Growth and Basic Needs* (ILO 1976). The question is whether the innocent- and attractive-sounding basic needs (BN) strategy and NIEO are complementary or competitive. Frances Stewart summarizes:

> At the level of popular international debate, a sharp dichotomy is developing between those who support Basic Needs as a development strategy and those who are advocates of the New International Economic Order (NIEO). Johan Galtung describes it as "Grand Designs on a Collision Course." Broadly, the main donor developed countries—notably the U.S. and the U.K.—and international agencies (the I.L.O. and the World Bank) are leading proponents of Basic Needs (BN) as a development strategy, while spokesmen of the Group of 77

are suspicious of BN, believing it to be a diversion, on the part of the developed countries, from their claims for a NIEO (Stewart 1979: 1).

Paul Streeten of the World Bank observes that "developing countries are apprehensive lest a basic needs approach adopted by donors implies sacrificing features of a New International Economic Order." Streeten goes on to argue that "the conflict can be avoided. . . . The way . . . is to strike a bargain: donors accept features of the NIEO if, and only if, developing country governments commit themselves to poverty eradication" (Streeten 1979: 43). Streeten seems to be giving the game away, albeit involuntarily. The developing countries' governments are being given another ultimatum by the developed "donor" countries and their institutions such as the World Bank: accept our terms, or else. Only if the Third World commits itself to the developed countries' BN strategy, will the latter accept some features of NIEO. If that is the "complementarity" of BN to NIEO, it should not be surprising that Third World governments are "apprehensive." No wonder that observers of this debate from the socialist countries could write in an UNCTAD Review:

> At a first glance, the conception of "basic needs" seems to aim at filling the apparent gap in the NIEO "philosophy" as regards the framing of appropriate internal strategies for developing countries. One may wonder, however, if, because of its genesis, application and potential ideological usefulness, it is not alien to the NIEO concept rather than being its complement. . . . BN is being suggested to the third world countries as a desirable course for their internal activities, to be supplemented and reinforced by industrialized countries. However, it can also be interpreted as a conceptual and ideological means for "controlling" the course of development of the developing countries since it is being linked with "resource transfer" and is also being suggested as a conceptual basis for the formulation of the International Development Strategy for the 1980s (Pajestka and Kulig 1979: 78).

Moreover, as Blaikie, Cameron, and Seddon (1979) suggest, we should distinguish between a liberal BN strategy that would be only a temporary palliative at best (and, as suggested above, blackmail at worst), which is proposed by the World Bank and ILO, and a radical BN strategy which would attack the root causes of the production and reproduction of mass poverty. The latter, of course, would be combatted rather than favored by the states and the institutions of both the developed capitalist and the vast majority of the underdeveloped countries, since it would require the complementary revolutionary institution of a real new international economic order (very different from the NIEO proposed so far) based on a new internal political order in the countries concerned. As we have argued above and will seek to demonstrate in the companion volume on the Third World, the real debate over NIEO so far concerns a Third World complement to the new international industrial order promoted by capital today, in which the number of people whose basic needs remain unmet can only grow.

However, if NIEO is essentially a "new global model of industrialization" (as the above-cited van Dam and our review of the demands suggest), and if the Third World bourgeoisies and their spokesmen are to have a secure and profitable place in it, the establishment of this global model must really proceed without too many obstacles. Nonetheless, numerous obstacles present themselves. The same world economic crisis which both promotes NIEO and generates the demand for it in some sectors of the Third World also places obstacles in the path of its realization. Some of these obstacles include inadequate investment and market demand, unemployment and, notably, protectionism and other restrictions and competitive modifications of international trade.

Protectionism and Other Obstacles to NIEO

"With continued high unemployment and business failures, official United States sources said: 'There is a rising tide of protectionism . . . which is rapidly becoming unmanageable and uncontrollable' " (FER 2 December 1977). Since mid-1977, the press has increasingly reflected concern about protectionism and moves toward its implementation all around the world.

> U.S. Tariffs, Global Risks . . . Protectionist forces are gathering strength in Europe and the less-developed countries (NYT editorial in IHT 19–20 March 1977).

> Don't rely on world-trade gains to speed weaker economies along the road to prosperity. New barriers could slow the flow of commerce in years ahead (USN 20 June 1977).

> Protectionist moves to cut the deficit would only make matters worse (BW 30 January 1978).

> A new protectionist offensive is beginning to roll in Washington . . . [which] could release all these forces in a protectionist landslide (BW 13 March 1978).

> The Gathering Forces of Protectionism . . . EEC shifts to Protectionism to Fight Unemployment Rise (IHT 6 October 1977).

> Bonn Warns Paris of Possible 'Super-Protectionism' (IHT 12 August 1977).

> Conversation with EEC Commissioner Wilhelm Haferkamp about the Dangers of Protectionism (Zeit 17 February 1978).

> Has Brussels [the site of the EEC Common Market Commission] begun the march back to the 1930's? (FR 23 July 1977).

The danger of a world depression . . . [is] very much on the minds of Japanese leaders today. Nobuhiko Ushiba, Minister of External Economic Affairs . . . is particularly worried about the threat of protectionism and the fragility of the world monetary system (IHT 10 May 1978).

GATT Warns on Protectionism Spread. Calls it Threat to World System (IHT 13 September 1977).

The *Far Eastern Economic Review* (FER 11 November 1977) devotes ten pages to "Protectionism. The game everyone wants to play."

Olivier Long, the director general of General Agreement on Tariffs and Trade (GATT, the intergovernmental organization for the regulation of world trade and the negotiation of tariff reductions), elaborates in greater detail "The Protectionist Threat to World Trade Relations":

> Protectionism is in the air for the first time in this generation. . . . There is evidence, convincing to most observers, that the will to resist protectionist pressures has weakened in some countries at the very moment when these pressures have become unusually insistent. Over the past two years, and most particularly in recent months, a significantly higher number than usual of protectionist moves have been initiated or tolerated by governments. Others have been seriously threatened. Competitive pressures are driving domestic industries in many countries to voice new demands for relief through restrictions on imports, or for government help for their own exports. The real possibility that these demands will be met—in encouraging protectionist influences everywhere, is threatening hopes of establishing more constructive relations between developed and developing countries and is clouding the prospects for rapid recovery from the present recession.
>
> The product sectors most affected by protectionist action are clear. Apart from special cases as restrictions on trade in beef introduced by the European Communities, Japan and others . . . they are textiles and clothing; shoes, steel; transport equipment (particularly ships); and certain sectors of light engineering, including especially electrical and electronic goods and ball-bearings. Significantly, these are all areas of trade in which there have recently been major shifts in comparative advantage towards producers who until the past decade or so were not significant exporters of the products concerned. . . .
>
> Our own best estimates in GATT, however, suggest that actions taken since 1974 have affected somewhere between 3 and 5 per cent of world trade. In other words, trade of some $30 to $50 bn. annually, previously unaffected by restrictions other than tariffs, has been subjected to restriction or disruption. . . .
>
> Of course, it is not only the industrialized countries which have in recent months intensified or introduced restrictions. Many developing countries have done so too, usually in response to balance-of-payments

difficulties or as an element in the development plans. But the actions by industrialized countries are in my view much more significant both in their present impact on world trade and in their implications for future world trade relations (Long 1977: 283–284).

To put it another way, there is a "worldwide tendency of cartel formation under the protection of state authority" (FR 27 June 1978). The GATT Tokyo round tariff reductions agreed upon in 1979 were limited almost entirely to trade among the developed countries, and have drawn widespread condemnation from spokesmen in and for the underdeveloped sector: "Tariff reductions [have been] made to measures for the rich. . . . It is, however, evident that the result of the Tokyo Round will be unfavorable for the majority of Third World countries" (CE editorial, March 1979: 81). "The outcome of the longest trade negotiations in history is likely to be less protectionism among industrialised countries, but at the expense of developing nations" (FER 9 February 1979). "UNCTAD says pact harms Third World" (FT 3 May 1979).

The president of the Central Association of German Chambers of Industry and Commerce, Otto Wolff von Amerongen, observes moreover that "only the strongest countries dare nowadays resort to patently and directly protectionist measures such as minimum prices for bulk steel or quantitative import restrictions on some textiles from developing countries." In other countries, "subtle forms of protectionism are the fashion today as never before. They include appeals to buy goods made at home . . . administrative regulations on foreign trade . . . insisting on certificates of origin for textiles" (von Amerongen 1977: 289–90). These nontariff barriers have increased enormously in recent years, and are "75% of what the Tokyo round [of tariff reductions] is all about" (BW 26 June 1978).

Japan has charged the United States with outright violation of the rules of the General Agreement on Tariffs and Trade (GATT), because of the unilateral way in which the United States imposed certain restrictions on imports of Japanese television sets and other electronic equipment (IHT 4–5 June 1977). However, the American stance in negotiations is even more serious. The editors of the influential Japanese newspaper *Yomiuri Shimbun* commented on the visit of the American trade delegation, headed by President Carter's chief tariff negotiator Robert Strauss, in November 1977:

> The behavior of the U.S. negotiators . . . was shocking because they tried to intimidate and almost dictate terms to this country. Many Japanese could hardly believe that this was the attitude of a supposedly friendly nation and ally. The negotiators attempted to bring Japan to its heels. (Quoted in WP, 24 November 1977, and cited in ICP 6 February 1978: 132).

They did. *The Wall Street Journal* (5 December 1977, cited in ICP 6 February 1978: 132) reported that the Japanese "conceded more than they may have wanted," and that a high Japanese official remarked, "we were pushed into a corner 40 years ago. It isn't good to see similar unfortunate and dangerous pressures being placed on us again." Forty years ago these pressures led to the Japanese attack on Pearl Harbor in World War II. Mr. Ushiba, the Japanese minister quoted earlier, further points out, "there is no question that the depression led to World War II" (IHT 10 May 1978). To reduce the American trade deficit and the Japanese trade surplus, Japan has been obliged to agree to increase its imports from the United States and to limit its exports, particularly of color television sets and steel. In addition, by devaluing the dollar, the United States has in effect obliged Japan to revalue the yen and to make its exports less competitive. In the United States, these measures were demanded not only by the government and by business—for example, the Committee to Preserve American Color Television (COM-PACT) includes eleven labor unions and five firms, led by the Zenith Radio Corporation and with the steel industry in the forefront—but also by labor. One fifth of American steel consumption is now being imported from abroad; major steel exporters now include Japan, Western Europe, Eastern Europe, Spain, South Africa, Brazil, Mexico, and South Korea. In response to these shifts, the United Steelworkers Union of America has been calling for import restrictions on steel, coupled with "an enforceable commitment by industry to modernize at their existing locations" in the United States (IHT 8–9 October 1977). The American union federation is also active: "AFL-CIO Economic Proposals Stress Import Quotas, Curbs to Protect U.S. Industry, Jobs" (IHT 12 December 1977) and AFL-CIO President "Meany Says Free Trade Is 'a Joke'; Urges U.S. Set up Strict Controls" (IHT 10–11 December 1977). American labor "plans a major push in Congress next year [1978] for an updated version of the Burke-Hartke bill of 1971–74, the most controversial of all protectionist trade initiatives. . . . The union-backed bill called for import quotas on a product-by-product basis rolled back to the 1965–69 average" (IHT 8 November 1977).

Europeans are just as actively promoting protectionism.

Europe Shifts to Protectionism to Fight Unemployment Rise

The European Economic Community, once a staunch crusader for free trade and competition, has quietly shifted in recent months to the camp of protectionism and cozy cartels to combat unemployment. . . . They advocate an urgent need for "organized" world trade—meaning import curbs dressed up as "voluntary" quotas. . . . EEC officials . . . claim that the community is doing no more than matching the efforts of Japan and the United States . . . to stave off a flood of cheap foreign imports. . . . Led by Britain and France, EEC countries have grown alarmed. . . . Even West Germany, an ardent backer of free market capitalism, now favors some trade controls (IHT 6 October 1977).

Quotas and voluntary restraints were once regarded as sores, now they are viewed as chic beauty-spots renamed "orderly marketing arrangements" and "ordered liberalism. . . ." At the Downing Street summit [on the world economy by Western heads of government in May 1977] French President Valéry Giscard d'Estaing introduced the concept of "organised liberalism" to justify his claim that "free" trade should be internationally organised. The concept was given a measure of substance by his Prime Minister, Raymond Barre, two months later. Barre, a former professor of economics, argued . . . that the free trade philosophy . . . has been rendered obsolete by recent developments. . . .

The fact remains that the developing countries are the principal targets of recent protectionist measures. . . . Whatever may—and must— be said about protectionism in Europe, it is now clear that developing countries must start looking elsewhere for their industrial market (FER 11 November 1977).

For dishonesty, cynicism and arrogance, the current attitude of the EEC to textile agreements with developing nations is hard to bear. It must be combated with all available weapons. Not merely because agreements have been broken. Not merely because textiles is the largest manufactured export of developing nations. But because this is the most conspicuous example of the drift towards a world not only of protectionism but of trade chaos.

When the world's largest trading bloc unilaterally tears up the single most important set of rules governing trading in a major community, it is clear that the jungle threatens. If the laws and conventions that govern it are undermined, trade itself will falter. The EEC is attempting to hold total 1978 textile imports to 1976 levels, at the same time as making payoffs elsewhere—including to Soviet bloc countries. The main immediate sufferers will be Hong Kong, South Korea and Taiwan, which are to make the major "sacrifices" to make room for these payoffs. . . . Meanwhile, as the EEC dangles wormridden carrots in front of some developing nations and makes political payoffs in the Mediterranean and Eastern Europe, the countries which will suffer are just those which over the years have proved most prepared to adjust themselves, through bilateral arrangements under the MFA and its predecessor, to European problems. Years of behaving with reason and understanding are rewarded with a kick in the teeth. It is primarily newcomers from the Mediterranean and Eastern Europe, many of which are signatories neither to GATT nor the MFA, whose imports to the EEC have grown most rapidly in recent years (FER 7 October 1977).

The Multifibre Agreement (MFA) was extended after long, drawn-out bargaining during 1977, but with escape clauses that may well be used to restrict textile imports further during the life of the agreement. Both industry and labor are showing signs of increasing concern. Representatives of employers and workers in the Western European textile and clothing industries have issued "solemn warnings . . . about the critical position with which these industries are faced." Spokesmen claim that in these industries, which now employ four million workers, more than one million jobs (750,000 textile and 300,000 clothing) were lost between 1965 and 1976; unemployment reached 30 percent in these industries in the latter year. For certain products, such as shirts and trousers, imports have recently accounted for up to 80 percent of consumption (COMITEXTIL n.d.). According to Folker Fröbel, employment in the textile and clothing industries of the original six European Common Market countries plus Great Britain declined by 762,000 jobs, or about 18 percent, between 1960 and 1975. Half of this decline can be attributed to improving productivity in these countries themselves, and about half to imports from Third World and socialist countries (Fröbel et al. 1977: 75). The International Textile, Garment and Leather Workers' Federation, which represents workers in both industrial and Third World countries, is under pressure from the industrial countries offer protection from imports produced by underdeveloped states, according to a personal communication from Federation General Secretary, Charles Ford, February 1978.

In the meantime, the United States has signed new "orderly marketing" agreements in textiles, clothing, and shoes with Brazil, Hong Kong, and South Korea; additional negotiations are underway with Taiwan and other countries. The previous agreement with the largest exporter, Hong Kong, allowed for a more than 6 percent annual growth rate of American imports, whereas the new one, after the "toughest bargaining," restricts the quota to 1.5 percent in the first year (FER 12 August 1977). The new five-year agreement with South Korea permits no growth in sensitive items for the first year, 2 percent growth in the second year, and 3.9 percent growth during the following years (FER 17 February 1978). As a result South Korea will not approve the expansion of textile production facilities for the time being (IHT 7 October 1977).

The growth of protectionism as a response to crisis conditions has repercussions on North-South relations in general.

U.S. Toughens Economic Policy Toward Developing Nations

With protectionism rising, the United States has been articulating a tougher economic policy toward developing countries, telling them, in effect, that some of their demands for a shift in the distribution of the world's wealth are simply out of touch with reality. The sharper tone in the North-South dialog between rich and poor countries is in marked contrast to the position of the Carter administration a year ago when it was emphasizing accommodation and conciliation. . . . Attitudes are hardening among European trading partners [with the Third World] as well. . . .

Positions of the United States and other industrialized countries have hardened against a background of stagnant economic conditions in the industrialized world and continued high unemployment. "The

North-South dialog is not exactly in the freezer, just in the fridge," said a Common Market Ambassador (IHT 6 February 1978).

It is difficult to ascertain the extent to which political demands for protectionism may place major obstacles in the way of NIEO and other changes in the international division of labor and profits. This political conflict is not yet decided one way or the other. Political demands for protection arise from all directions: from labor, ravaged and threatened by unemployment; business, concerned by low profits; industry, plagued by shutdown or runaways; and from governments, haunted by balance of payments deficits. Behind these political demands lurk two major and interrelated economic problems. The first stems from the general capitalist overaccumulation of the past, which now manifests itself in rates of profit, frequent cyclical recessions with poor recoveries, and the world economic crisis overall. The other economic problem arises out of the differential changes in productivity among particular economies and industries, and resulting changes in their competitiveness relative to each other. Both of these major problems lead to increasing competition for markets among businesses and states, reflected in competitive devaluation of currencies and outright protective measures. These tendencies manifest themselves, as we have observed, on both national and regional levels; they also create pressures toward the renewed formation of economic blocs: "a division of the developing world into spheres of influence, with Europe 'taking' Africa, leaving Southeast Asia to Japan and South America to the U.S." (FER 11 November 1977).

Demands for protectionism are the strongest in economies where investment and productivity have grown the least, and where the economic crisis is the most serious. Foremost among these is the United States, with not only the highest rate of unemployment among major economies, but also the most outdated equipment in many industries. In manufacturing, 21 percent of installed equiment was more than twenty years old in 1974, compared with 17 percent in 1970. Obsolescence has been particularly high in the transportation equipment, iron and steel, nonferrous metal, machinery, and rubber industries (USN 30 November 1974). Labor productivity in the major industrial economies increased at very different percentage rates over the past decade and a half, as shown in chapter 2, Table 2-1. In the United States and Britain productivity rose less than half as much as in France and Germany, where in turn it grew about half as fast in the 1960s and at about the same rate in the 1970s as in Japan. These differential changes in productivity, more than differences in wage rates, underlie the Japanese and to a lesser degree the West European competitiveness today (excluding Great Britain). For instance, between 1971 and 1976, yearly production of crude steel per worker was 480 tons in Japan, or double the 240 tons in the United States (ICP 6 February 1977: 132). Japanese steel, produced in efficient, new, oxygen-fed blast furnaces instead of the old open-hearth furnaces still widely used in the United States, forms the basis of the Japanese offensive in the export of steel and, in part, of steel-using products, such as ships and automobiles.

The devaluation of the American dollar and pressures for protectionism in the United States and Europe are the natural consequence of these changes. However, this response hits the still weaker exporting countries in the Third World with even greater force, as these countries are clearly less able to defend themselves than Europe and Japan. The devaluation of the dollar and the revaluation of the German mark and the Japanese yen in turn have generated very substantial increases in labor and other production costs in Germany and Japan, compared with American production costs when measured in dollars in the United States or third markets. On the other hand, with a cheaper dollar, foreign investment in the United States becomes much less costly and much more attractive. In consequence, the past few years have witnessed a vast new wave of European, Japanese and, of course, Arab foreign investment in the United States; foreign investors thus seek to produce for the large American market using American labor that, with today's exchange rates, has become cheaper than labor in Germany and several other countries. This foreign production—for instances, of Japanese television sets and German Volkswagens—within the United States is not subject to exclusion by American tariffs or quotas, and competes with electronic equipment and automotive parts and engines from Third World countries; exports from Mexico, Brazil, South Korea, and Taiwan, for example, are subject to import restrictions by the United States. At the same time certain technological advances, such as those in microcircuits on "chips" and lasers, have encouraged certain areas of production to "return" from the Third World to the industrial countries. These products are now to be produced through highly capital-intensive, labor-saving processes, such as cutting textiles and clothing with minicomputer-guided laser beams. Such protective obstacles attempt to block real and potential changes in the international division of labor in a "reverse" direction, through competitive devaluation, import restrictions, "reverse" foreign investment, and the use of new technology. This protectionism may pose significant problems in the way of the establishment of the NIEO sought by Third World leaders.

The overriding problem posing a threat to NIEO (as well as to other, larger, global questions) through protectionism and other brakes on world trade is, of course, the world economic crisis itself. On the one hand, as we have claimed throughout, the world crisis generates both the demand for NIEO and pressures to accelerate the modification of the international division of labor in assigning new and increasing tasks to various parts of the Third World. On the other hand, the crisis itself also places obstacles, such as protectionism, in the course of this process; it slows down that international trade, or its expansion, which serves as the vehicle of exchange required for this new international division of labor (NIDL). Thus, during the last recession in 1974 a modest expansion of world trade was maintained principally through exports from industrial capitalist countries to the Third

World and socialist countries—representing an extension of NIDL. In 1975 total world production declined by about 2 percent (5 percent in manufacturing and more than that in the capitalist industrial countries), and world trade declined by about 5 percent (GATT 1976: 1). Manufacturing exports from Third World countries, especially from Asia, encountered severe obstacles of market demand in the developed countries; and production and employment in South Korea, Hong Kong, Taiwan, and elsewhere suffered setbacks—signifying a contraction of NIDL (FER *Asia Yearbook* 1976). The cyclical recovery since 1975 was accompanied by renewed expansion of manufacturing exports, production, and employment in these and other Third World countries (GATT 1977).

GATT reviewed the essential elements of the cyclical recovery in its analysis of the "main features of 1976/77." These provide a basis for expectations in the recession in 1980 or thereafter.

> In the industrial countries the recovery of demand, was due essentially to a rise of roughly 4½ per cent in private consumption, substantial restocking, and a rise of about 11 per cent in the volume of exports. . . . Compared with the previous peak in 1973, the rise in world output stemmed entirely from the increase of industrial and agricultural output in developing countries, of industrial output in the Eastern trading area, and of agricultural output in the industrial countries; industrial output in industrial countries and agricultural production in the Eastern trading area stagnated (GATT 1977: 3,2).

The president of the European Economic Commission (EEC or Common Market), Roy Jenkins, observed, "we need the developing countries as much as they need us."

> It was their sustained buying power over the last six years that did so much to mitigate the effects of recession. In the European Community area alone, he will tell them, there would be 3 million more unemployed—9 million instead of 6 million—if the non-oil developing countries had cut their manufactured imports by the amount needed to pay the increased oil prices imposed in 1973 and 1974. Can the Third World go on bailing out our unemployment, particularly in the face of another price hike?
> Trade in manufactured goods with the newly industrialized countries . . . created a net gain of 900,000 jobs in the West in each of the years 1973–1977 (IHT 28 June 1979).

> Illustrative of this fact is that the developing countries accounted for 30 per cent of the *increase* in the value of developed market-economy countries' total exports of manufactures between 1973 and 1977, in contrast to 15 per cent of the *increase* in such exports from 1962 to 1973 (UNCTAD 1979e: 11–12).

Indeed, as the director-general of GATT, Olivier Long, has observed:

> To a large extent, it is to the developing countries that we owe the continued growth of world trade through the recent difficult period. Both in 1977 and 1978, the exports of industrialized countries grew faster to developing countries than to one another. For all the major industrialized countries, trade with the developing countries is of growing importance. . . .
>
> Let me quote some figures to show just how important trade with the developing countries has become for the industrialized countries. I take as my examples France, Germany, Japan, Switzerland, and the United States.
>
> The share of United States exports going to the developing countries rose from 29 per cent to 35 per cent between 1972 and 1977. For Japan, the increase was from 38 per cent to 46 per cent. . . . German exports to developing countries have risen from 11 per cent of total exports in 1972 to 17 per cent in 1977, French from 18 per cent to 24 per cent, and Swiss from 15 per cent to 22 per cent. In almost every broad product category—in the case of Germany, in *every* category without exception—the share of exports purchased by developing countries has risen over the same five years (GATT 1979a; emphasis in original).

> The increasing importance of developing countries as a market for the manufactures exported by industrial countries is particularly apparent from the following comparisons. In 1978, developing countries absorbed 20 per cent of Western Europe's exports of manufactures to all destinations, twice as much as the North American and Japanese markets taken together. In the category of engineering products, developing countries bought 25 per cent of Western Europe's exports while North America and Japan, taken together, accounted for only 9 per cent. Developing countries accounted for 46 per cent of Japan's total exports of manufactures, again more than North America and Western Europe taken together. . . . Finally, developing countries absorbed about 32 per cent of North America's exports of manufactures as compared with 26 per cent taken by Western Europe and Japan combined (GATT 1979b).

The rapid increase in these industrial exports to the Third World since 1973 has been concentrated in the OPEC countries and the Far Eastern exporters of manufactures. However, in order to be able to buy such industrial products, these Third World countries must be able to pay for them with foreign exchange earned through their own exports, and/or by running up debts, which they must pay off through further exports.

Nonetheless, "the North-South dialogue is alive with the sound of rising trade barriers . . . [and] failure by UNCTAD to reverse this may lead to beggar-my-neighbor warfare" (GUA 23 April 1979). Thus, World Bank

President Robert McNamara was prompted to devote a major part of his speech at UNCTAD V in Manila to "countering the new protectionism" (F & D, September 1979). Low profits and high unemployment obviously constitute the major cause in the increased pressures for such protectionism. For some sectors of business and industry, the high level of unemployment—as distinct from the low level of profits—may well not be of concern. On the contrary, a certain amount of unemployment is a desideratum for some sectors of business and for the state (as is documented in chapter 3 and Frank 1978d). For those who are already unemployed and those threatened by the prospect of becoming so, unemployment is a matter of concern. This concern can be translated politically into additional pressures for protectionism and support for political policies bearing on the establishment of NIEO and on "progress" toward a new international division of labor. Political pressure from labor will not likely be sufficient in any capitalist country to incur the enactment of such protectionist and related policies, but it can weigh in the balance along with perhaps more significant pressures from interested sectors of capital. Considering that unemployment has actually *risen during the recovery*, as GATT and the OECD observed, we may imagine what will happen to unemployment and business failures during the recession beginning in 1979–1980. We might speculate similarly on likely prospects for world trade, further protectionism, and "progress" toward NIEO.

In this context, we may also take seriously the speculations of *Business Week* and of chief U.S. tariff and trade negotiator Robert Strauss:

> The possibility remains that a discontented Congress could force outright protectionism on the [unwilling] Administration. The resulting retaliation by other nations very likely would leave the U.S. deficit about where it is, but at a vastly lower level of total trade (BW 30 January 1978).

> When Congressman Hawley and Senator Smoot took a small step toward protection in 1930, their bill became a vehicle on the Senate floor for the addition of 1,250 amendments providing protection for specific products. The Smoot-Hawley Act set off a wave of retaliation that locked us into this nation's greatest depression (Robert Strauss cited by BW 13 March 1978).

U.S. Congressman Abner J. Mikva reflects:

> I'm going to support the President [against protectionism]. But what do I go back home and tell the people who are unemployed? The Administration was against Smoot-Hawley, but the people were for it. I worry that Congress will reflect the mood of the country now as it did then (cited in BW 13 March 1978).

In 1979 again, the press states: "Protectionist Action by Congress Feared" (IHT 23 April 1979).

If Congress does what Strauss and Mikva fear, it can only aggravate recession in the world. The American administration may choose to emulate President Franklin D. Roosevelt, who torpedoed and sabotaged the very World Economic Conference which he had called in London in 1933, preventing the salvage of the then-existing world monetary system, and forcing Germany and Japan into bankruptcy; the current or future United States president might follow the example of Richard Nixon, when he suddenly scuttled the world monetary system and penalized Japan with a 10 percent surcharge tariff in his "New Economic Policy," initiated on 15 August 1971 (which the Japanese called the "Nixon shokku"); or the president might follow further in Carter's footsteps, recklessly permitting the dollar to be devalued without American intervention and breaking all domestic and most international economic promises. As the inevitable result of such policies, prospects for a world depression would grow still brighter, and those for NIEO ever dimmer.

Clearly, the new international economic order (NIEO) depends on—indeed, institutionalizes—the expansion of world trade as the vehicle for a new international division of labor. Here, the Third World bourgeoisies would negotiate the terms of their dependence to participate more actively and profit more handsomely alongside the increased exploitation and heightened superexploitation of their agricultural, industrial, and service (including government) workers. Indeed, this entire NIEO will likely be estblished and maintained only through the intensive political-economic repression of the masses around the Third World. If NIEO can only be realized at such great cost, then the significant aggravation of the world economic crisis, the substantial breakdown of world trade, and all other obstacles to NIEO can only signify the lesser evil for the mass populations of the Third World. As we argued over a decade ago in "The Development of Underdevelopment" (Frank 1966, 1969) such a crisis could offer some Third World countries greater opportunities for relatively more autonomous and "self-reliant" capitalist development, based on a more populist democratic alliance between sectors of the bourgeoisie and the working masses. Perhaps such an alliance and capitalist development during the world economic crisis and its aftermath would be temporary. A transitional period would then be replaced by the NIEO that Third World bourgeoisies now seek in their demands for integration in the imperialist capitalist system. Perhaps, however, this interregnum would be temporary in that it could give way to a really new international economic, social, and political order through the revolutionary destruction, here and there, of the old one. For the time being, the most realistic prospects would seem to promise the maintenance, and indeed the new extension and intensification, of the old international economic order under the guise of a "new" one.

UNCTAD observes in its usual diplomatic language:

> As far as the developing countries as a whole are concerned, it would appear that they have had to bear a disproportionate part of the

global burden of readjustment to the economic crisis. As a result of the deterioration in their terms of trade, already mentioned, and the slow-down in demand for their industrial raw material exports, many developing countries have had to meet unprecedentedly high external payments deficits, with consequent necessity for either cutting down their development programmes or raising additional foreign loans on the private capital markets. The total outstanding disbursed debt on the developing countries, which had amounted to about $114 billion in 1973, rose to $244 billion by 1977, and is estimated to have risen further in 1978, to almost $300 billion, with an increasing number of countries having to meet debt-service charges exceeding 25 per cent of their export earnings.

As a result of these and related adverse developments, real income per head in the low-income developing countries—where an accelera-tion of growth is most needed—has continued to stagnate in the period since 1973, while for the middle-income countries, the rise in real income per head has fallen far short of the target growth rate in the International Development Strategy of 3½ per cent per annum. More-over, the immediate prospects for economic recovery by this group of developing countries have suffered a further setback as a result of intensified protectionist measures adopted by a number of developed market-economy countries, which will seriously restrict the growth in their exports of manufactured goods.

It now seems evident that economic development in the third world cannot be accelerated, or even maintained at its current inadequate rate, without a fundamental restructuring of the existing international economic order designed to make it far more supportive of the de-veloping process. However, in the preoccupation of the developed market-economy countries with the continuing crisis in their own economies, there has been little evidence of their acceptance of the need for restructuring their economic relations with the developing countries. The strong emphasis being given by developed market-economy countries to measures of "economic recovery" has in fact certain negative implications for the ongoing negotiations on a new international economic order.

First, there is an implicit assumption in this emphasis that the key to the solution of current international economic problems lies in the economic recovery of the industrialized countries, and the consequent expansion of the world economy and of world trade. Such an approach essentially argues for a return to the processes which were at work in the world economy before 1974, i.e. for a continuation of the existing system, restored to its pre-recession trends, with some marginal ad-justments. In this concept, the third world's development would be dependent on the transmission—or "trickle down"—of growth from the developed countries via the expansion of developed country markets, and increased demand for raw materials and other products from the third world. Second, emphasis on economic recovery as the priority for action also implies that the current crisis is essentially cyclical in character and that economic recovery in the developed market-economy countries can be achieved independently of the structural reform of the international system. From this standpoint, therefore, the recovery of the industrialized countries becomes almost a prerequisite for any negotiation on the restructuring of the international system itself.

Such a diagnosis, however, fails to recognize the existence of any link between the current economic difficulties of the industrial countries and the underlying structural disequilibrium in the present international division of labour and in the international trading and financial system. In other words, it ignores the contribution that a restructuring of international economic relations which resulted in a substantial strengthening of the economies of the developing countries, and in a significant increase in their purchasing power, would make to the solution of the current economic problems of the developed countries, particularly by the impetus it would give to increasing world demand for the lagging output of the capital goods industries of the developed countries.

Recognition of such a link between the problems of the developed and the developing countries would imply that emphasis should shift to restructuring as the primary means to achieve stable and sustained economic recovery. In place of the indirect approach to third world development through measures designed to restore fast growth to the developed market economies, the emphasis would have to be on measures designed to create and promote the growth of effective demand in the backward and poor parts of the world which would, in turn, indirectly contribute to the recovery of the industrialized economies. A wider acceptance of this interrelationship by the developed countries would inject a new dynamism into the international negotiating process (UNCTAD 1979e: 4–5).

Nonetheless, in the eyes and interests of Henry Kissinger and those for whom he speaks, negotiates, and acts, "the present economic system has served the world well." Therefore, "the international negotiating process" at UNCTAD and elsewhere, aimed at "a restructuring of international economic relations," can lead to no more than the realistic and candid appraisal of Otto Graf (Count) Lamsdorff, Minister of Economic Affairs of the Federal Republic of Germany, on his departure from UNCTAD V in Manila: "We couldn't even find agreement on describing the state of the world economy today" (IHT 5 June 1979).

Chapter 6
Development of Crisis and Crisis of Development: A Summary Conclusion About Living in the Real World

This conclusion is deliberately not footnoted, since it represents a synthetic summary of the argument set out and documented in the preceding chapters of this book on the development of the present crisis in the industrial capitalist West, the socialist East, and the underdeveloped South. The last part of this conclusion goes on to offer a summary of the argument in the similarly documented companion volume, *Crisis: In the Third World*.

Many people throughout the world believe that we are living in a pre-revolutionary era analogous to the one at the end of World War I during which the world's first socialist revolution occurred in what is now the Soviet Union. This belief in the present progress of revolution and socialism has been promoted and sustained especially by the developments of the past decade and a half in Cuba and Vietnam, Angola and Mozambique, Ethiopia and Iran, and even Afghanistan, and by current or prospective developments in Zimbabwe and Namibia, Nicaragua and other parts of the Caribbean area, and other places in the Third World. The belief in prerevolutionary progress is also based on the widespread mass movements in Europe and North America during the late 1960s and early 1970s; the subsequent fall of the dictatorships in Greece, Portugal, and Spain; and the recent worker, women's and populist mobilizations, especially against economic and social policies, that seem to be sweeping through many industrial capitalist, underdeveloped and socialist countries (the last of which seems particularly significant to some observers) since 1976–1977. On the other hand, the industrial capitalist West, the socialist East, and the underdeveloped Third World South are also being swept by very strong conservative or reactionary, counterreformist or counterrevolutionary, and militantly nationalist winds.

To what extent is revolution or counterrevolution likely in the foreseeable future? As in any prerevolutionary or supposedly prerevolutionary situation, the answer depends on which way the class struggle and the imperialist struggle will go. The subjective political element or forces in this class struggle are in part limited and shaped by the objective economic factors. The subjective and ideological factors were elevated to particular prominence in Cuba, China, and Vietnam in the recent past, and there has been some considerable disappointment in the efficacy of these subjective factors in or starting from the countries named. This disappointment has marked their own leadership—suffice it to mention Mao Zedong, whose Cultural Revolution was obviously defeated—and many others both in these countries and in the world as a whole. Therefore, it may not be amiss to devote greater care to the objective economic factors in the fight for liberation and socialism. Recent events may raise some doubts about whether the objective truth is always revolutionary, as the old adage says, but surely it is still true that subjective illusion or falsehood can never be revolutionary.

According to the official pronouncements about the world and the above-mentioned apparent revolutionary advances, the Chinese say at every opportunity that the present situation is excellent. The Soviet Union says that socialism is advancing on the world at a giant's pace. The Eurocommunist and other Communist parties say that social mobilization and popular advances are accelerating and virtually carrying the world before them, although there have been temporary localized reverses in Latin America until recently. At the recent Conference of the Nonaligned in Havana and particularly since the recent events in Nicaragua and elsewhere, popular mobilization is said to be advancing by leaps and bounds around the Third World. Trotskyists say that at least in several countries of Southern Europe—in Portugal, Spain, France, Italy, and maybe Belgium—the revolution is practically around the corner or at least that the revolution could be around the corner if revolutionaries play their cards correctly. Even the United States is said to be marked by new large-scale popular movements. To what extent are these pronouncements objectively correct? To what extent is this optimism, which we should all support subjectively, really merited by objective political economic considerations? Indeed, calling them objective or subjective considerations, do existing revolutionary theory, organization, and leadership, which certainly all socialists and revolutionaries regard as essential to convert a prerevolutionary situation into a revolution, justify this revolutionary optimism? There are objective reasons to doubt it.

In fact, a good part of this contemporary revolutionary and national liberation mobilization is a defensive outgrowth of a growing world economic and political crisis and is so far objectively severely limited. The crisis is perhaps not entirely unlike previous crises, particularly the one that began in

1913 and lasted through World War II. This crisis included the two wars, the depression of the 1930s, the October Revolution, and the Chinese Revolution. The same crisis included the rise of facism as a counterrevolutionary movement, with some considerable success at least in certain times and places. An earlier analogous major crisis of capitalist development occurred between 1873 and 1895 and was associated with the rise of monopoly capitalism in the central economies and the rise of classical imperialism and colonialism from the central economies to the periphery—or more accurately within the world economy and political system that includes them both. My suggestion is that since the 1960s the world, or at least the capitalist world, has entered another analogous long crisis period of overaccumulation of capital and overproduction. This book has examined the development and manifestations of this crisis in the West, East, and South. The companion volume, *Crisis: In the Third World,* goes on to detail the manifestations of this world crisis in the underdeveloped countries.

Chapter 2 and 3 have analyzed the development of the crisis in the West, which may be summarized as follows. The postwar industrial expansion, like previous major expansions, produced more capital relative to the labor used (in Marxist terminology, an increase in the organic composition of capital), particularly in industry. Associated with relative overinvestment in capital equipment in industry there was relative underinvestment in productive capacity in the mining and agricultural sectors in most of the capitalist world. Not incidentally, this primary sector underinvestment is substantially responsible for the oil and agricultural crises of the 1970s and perhaps the 1980s. The increase in the organic composition of capital (an increase in the capital/labor ratio) and productivity, and the partly associated increase in worker bargaining power and militancy, have since the mid-sixties led to a decline in the industrial economies in the rate of profit and a reduction in the rate of growth, in some instances to an absolute reduction in the demand for industrial commodities and most particularly of capital or investment goods. The previous imbalance may now perhaps lead to a relative increase in the provision of raw materials from mineral (including seabed and perhaps Antarctic) and agricultural (especially agribusiness) sources. Additionally, productivity and production have grown at different rates in the major industrial capitalist economies. Productivity in Western Europe has grown at twice the American rate, and Japan's productivity, until recently, grew at twice the European and four times the American rate.

These developments have led to the following major consequences and manifestations. One has been the attempt to postpone or restrain, or indeed in some monopolized sectors to prevent, the decline in the rate of profit and restriction in the market through mass programs of printing money and credit creation. This effort took its most spectacular form in the United States through the deficit financing of the war against Vietnam, which flooded the world with dollars. Secondly, competition increased, particularly among national sectors of capital from one country to another, for the remaining market. This competition manifested itself most particularly in the repeated devaluations of the dollar, which were an attempt to maintain or increase the overseas market for American exports and to protect it and the American home market against the incursions particularly of Germany and Japan. Their currencies have been revalued and have risen very markedly against the dollar, without so far turning the balance in favor of the United States on the world market. The decline of the dollar has, however, cheapened American wage and property costs relative to those in Europe and Japan and has therefore reversed the flow of foreign investment, which is now going from these areas into the United States. Slack demand and increased competition have also accelerated bankruptcies and monopolization nationally and aggressive export drives and renewed protectionism internationally.

Another major manifestation of overproduction and inadequate demand has been an increase in unutilized excess productive capacity in industry. This industry-wide problem is particularly visible in the steel industry, which has been in a worldwide slump for some years and, after shutting down a number of steel mills, is still working at only 60 or 70 percent capacity in various parts of the industrialized world. In consequence there has also been a marked slump in investments. With excess but unused capacity and low profits, business sees no good reason to engage in mammoth new investment. The 1973 level of investment in the industrialized economies was not reattained until 1978, and in Britain has still not been reached. Thus, there is a gaping investment hole from 1973 to 1978. Now investment is threatening to decline again, because of a new recession. Moreover, the nature of investment has changed. Expansive investment to provide new productive capacity for more and new goods has increasingly been replaced by ratio-nalizing investment designed to produce at lower costs and most particularly with lower labor costs.

There has been much talk about new technology in the energy supply and in a number of other fields. Despite the fact that the price of energy has shot up rapidly since 1973 and did so again in recent months, there have not been any major new investments in the energy field except for prospecting and drilling for petroleum, which has increased markedly since 1973. There has been no major new investment in petroleum refining, which is one reason for the recent bottlenecks. There also has been no major new investment in alternative sources of energy from shale oil, coal, or nuclear fuel. The nuclear industry is economically in virtual shambles, which explains much of the adamant drive to sell nuclear reactors at home and abroad and has lead to the strong competitive reactions and squabbles internationally (e.g., between the United States and West Germany over Brazil and between the United States and France over Pakistan) and the strong "no nukes" reaction in many parts of the world. Alternative sources of energy, including solar energy and synthetic fuels, have been the subject of much talk, but so far it is all talk and no action. The main reason is that the general rate of profit and prospective markets do not yet justify major investment either in the energy field or in any other. The apparent exception of the computer industry and particularly the use of microchips is so far primarily a rationalizing investment designed to reduce labor costs of production and is not yet a major innovation that puts production on new footing. Before a major new investment program can be undertaken and such major new technology put into place, the profit rate has to be elevated again. In order to do that, vast economic, social, and political transformations on a world scale will be necessary. The beginnings of some of these transformations are reviewed in the preceding chapters and in the companion volume on the Third World, and they are summarized below.

Instrumental in both the decline in profits and their possible future recovery are another set of consequences and manifestations of the development of this crisis through recurrent and deepening recessions. Since the mid 1960s, recessions have become increasingly frequent, increasingly long, increasingly deep, and increasingly coordinated from one major industrial country to another. An index of the growth of these recessions is their impact on unemployment in the industrial countries of the OECD. In North America, Europe, Japan, Australia, and New Zealand registered unemployment rose to 5 million during the recession of 1967, in which the United States barely participated because, so to say, it kept the recession wolf from the door with the war against Vietnam. By the recession of 1969–1971, which did hit the United States, registered unemployment rose to 10 million in the industrialized countries. Unemployment then fell back to 8 million in the subsequent recovery from 1972 to 1973. In the next recession, which hit almost the whole capitalist world simultaneously from 1973 to 1975, and which was the deepest one so far since 1930s, registered unemployed rose to 15 million in the industrialized countries, of which roughly 9 million or 9 percent were in the United States. Since then, unemployment again declined to less than 6 million in the United States but continued to rise in the industrial capitalist countries of Europe and Japan, as well as Canada and Australia. Indeed, the number of unemployed in these countries rose so much during the so-called recovery after 1975 that total OECD registered unemployment increased from 15 million at the bottom of the last recession to 17 or 18 million in late 1979.

A new recession began in 1979–1980 in the United States and Britain and is visibly threatening elsewhere. No one knows for sure how long the recession will last. The Carter administration was talking about a so-called soft landing and hoped that the recession would be relatively mild and not very long, if only because of the 1980 presidential election. To the express dismay of President Carter, a confidential document leaked out of his administration, which objectively projected a much deeper recession, lasting into 1981, with unemployment rising again to at least 8 percent. Furthermore, there are very substantial reasons to anticipate the 1979–1980 (81?) recession may turn out to be even more severe than the one of 1973–1975. One reason is that this recession is more welcome and "needed" than the previous one, which did not drive enough capital into bankruptcy to clean up the capitalist house sufficiently and did not successfully break the back of labor organization and militancy. Therefore, the capitalist states will do even less to combat this recession domestically than they did in the last one. The Debt Economy, as *Business Week* aptly calls it, has grown so spectacularly in an atttempt to keep the wolf from the door, that further acceleration in the growth of debt threatens to aggravate a possibly impending crash of the already excessively unstable financial house of cards; this has made worried bankers even more prudent and has reinforced economic conservatism.

At the same time, the previously available financial and institutional resources against the spread of recession, such as the development of speculative Euro-and Asian-currency markets, and to counteract them the introduction of flexible exchange rates and international economic coordination through economic summit conferences and the like, have already been substantially exhausted or have failed outright. Internationally, moreover, the safety valve or net that the socialist and OPEC countries offered to capital through increased demand for Western exports is already significantly diminished and likely to be far less available during this new recession. After their last expansion, these economies have a limited capacity to pay or to absorb imports, and are not likely to come to the rescue of Western capital again as they did after 1973. Thus, there would seem to be significant limits to consumer, investment, and export demand during this new recession. The only obvious alternative and additional source of demand is increased military spending.

The new recession is beginning at a level of unemployment, particularly in Europe and Japan, that is vastly higher than the level prior to the 1973–1975 recession, and a level of investment that has only just reattained the 1973 level. Most serious "scientific" projections from official and institutional forecasters seem to be unable or unwilling to take due account of these factors in the preparation of their generally overoptimistic forecasts. The September 1979 Annual Report of the International Monetary Fund predicted a long and hard worldwide recession starting early next year as a consequence of the weakness of the American economy. At its annual meeting in Belgrade in September 1979, the IMF amended its forecast further downward for 1980 and said "world economic growth will be lower than the percentage shown in the annual report." We are facing the prospect of a recession that may be even more severe than the one of 1973–1975, at a time when the economic, social, and political manifestations and consequences of the last recession—including 17 million unemployed in the OECD countries—have not by any means been overcome. This sobering circumstance is itself a mark of the deepening crisis.

Another consequence—indeed an essential part—of this process of deepening crisis through successive recessions has been the attempt to reduce costs of production through austerity policies and cuts in welfare, which has resulted in increased unemployment. It can be demonstrated that in most industrial capitalist countries there has been a deliberate policy of unemployment. Past recessions or the present one are not due to government policy "made in Washington," as Paul Samuelson said about the 1979–1980 recession. The recessions are an essential part of the crisis of accumulation, which is an integral aspect of uneven capitalist development. But these recessions are demonstrably further promoted by the policies made not only in Washington, but also in London and Bonn, in Paris and Tokyo and elsewhere. For instance, when the new head of the Federal Reserve Board—the central bank of the United States—Mr. Volcker, was interviewed in the Senate for the approval of his nomination, he said that he didn't know if there was a recession yet, but recession or no recession, the principal task was not combatting any possible or existing recession, but combatting inflation. What he meant, in plain English, was that he proposes to pursue monetary policies, and that he would ask government to pursue fiscal policies, designed to restrain wages and to decrease purchasing power to combat inflation rather than to increase purchasing power in order to combat unemployment. It is neither incidental nor accidental that Mr. Volcker's appointment was greeted with great jubilation in Bonn, Paris, Tokyo, and all other major financial and political capitals of the Western world.

World capitalist political leaders, such as President Carter (who was elected on a "fight unemployment" platform but predictably soon switched to making "inflation the public enemy number one" instead), French Prime Minister Raymond Barre (France's best-known economist), Labour Ministers Callaghan and Healey followed by their conservative successors Thatcher, Howe, and Joseph in Britain, and many others, have repeatedly declared that they would prefer to pursue conservative deflationary monetary, fiscal, and other economic policies to combat inflation even at the cost of growing industrial shutdowns (as in the French steel mills, whose workers have reacted vociferously) and rising unemployment.

The same argument is advanced everywhere: We need to combat and hold down inflation because it hurts all of us equally at home (although inflation characteristically reduces real income from work and raises the real values of property) and particularly because inflation at home would price us out of the world market, cut out export capacity, and therefore create unemployment. The principal cause of inflation supposedly is high public spending and high wage demands (although wage costs are a small and declining component of selling prices, and the evidence shows that prices are pushed up by the attempt to protect profits in monopolized industry). These same arguments are used everywhere to defend the imposition of austerity policies and to demand political restraint in public spending (except for defense and other business expenditures) and in "responsible" union wage demands, which are to be kept below the rate of inflation (both of which result in a decline of real wages and income, especially at the lowest end of the income scale). In addition to resting on very doubtful scientific grounds domestically, however (as suggested in the parentheses above), these arguments suffer from the logical fallacy of composition: When everybody pursues the same policy (as when everybody gets up on their toes to improve or maintain their view of a passing parade), nobody finds their relative cost and export position (or vantage point) improved by their efforts; everybody ends up with lower wages (or comfort). The analogy, however, only goes so far: Diminished comfort may be an entirely unintended consequence of crowd behavior, but lower wages definitely are not an unintended consequence of herding people against "the public enemy number one: inflation." Indeed, there is reason to believe that the lower wage objective is the principal economic purpose of the political slogan to fight inflation (which is felt by everybody) at the cost of unemployment (which hits only some people directly but immediately weakens labor's power everywhere to defend its wage level and working conditions). In view of these official pronouncements, theories, and policies, it should come as no surprise that the world capitalist press has blithely summarized them by saying "the world needs a recession."

Austerity policies have been imposed in every one of the major and minor capitalist economies in an attempt to get workers to tighten their belts. This attempt has been more successful in some places, less successful in others. Certainly in the United States and in Britain real wages have gone down. In other industrial economies there is some evidence that wage rates have gone down and some evidence that they have not gone down. But if we refer not to wage rates, but to the mass of real wages paid out after we consider the increase in unemployment of those who receive no wages at all, then real wage receipts have fallen since 1973. Another major attempt to cut costs of production is to change the way people work by reorganizing the work processes on the shop floor and in the office. In general, the new work processes involve the speed-up of work and fewer skills on the part of the worker. At the same time, there has been a worldwide capitalist cut in welfare. The motto in the capitalist world today is to shift from "unproductive" to "productive" expenditures, beginning with armaments, and "welfare: farewell." Although President Carter was elected on promises to cut defense spending and to promote peace, he increased budgeted military expenditures (in real terms that discount inflation) first by 3 percent and then by 5 percent a year and then launched a new cold war offensive, which received a major expression in his State of the Union message in January 1980.

All of these domestic policies have also been implemented wherever possible, and certainly in most parts of the Western world, through social democratic governments and often with the support of Labour and Communist parties. Communist support of all kinds of capitalist austerity measures has been very visible in Italy and Spain. In Spain the Secretary General of the Communist Party, Santiago Carrillo, took the initiative in proposing the Spanish austerity policy in the so-called Pact of Moncloa after the election of Prime Minister Adolfo Suarez. Austerity and income policies are also implemented in many places through the direct collaboration of labor unions, including even Communist unions as in Italy, who call on their members to tighten their belts. The argument is to pursue a sort of lesser evil policy, according to which it is better to tighten belts voluntarily than to be obliged to do so by some alternative right wing, or as the Communists in Italy would say, fascist government. In some, indeed many, places this union and Communist policy has led to considerable militancy on the shop floor and revolt of the mass base. This revolt has been visible most particularly in Italy and in Britain, where workers have rejected the social contract and collaboration with the government austerity policy that the union leadership had so far implemented. (The Spanish Communist Party and its unions have suddenly decided to oppose the austerity policy there, but to what extent is yet to be seen.) In Britain this militancy on and off the shop floor has led the newly elected Conservative government to an explicit determination to try to put a tight rein on labor mobilization, the unions, and their power through legal action against picketing and other union organization and through explicit policies to increase and use unemployment to discipline labor. In the past, and the right hopes also in the future, a significant increase in unemployment makes militant union aciton for higher wages, or even to maintain their real wages, increasingly difficult. Indeed, before—and if— capital is to recover "adequate" levels of profit and to launch a renewed investment drive that could bring capitalism out of its present crisis of accumulation and into a new period of expansion, not only will capitalism have to have a new technological base, but both the profitable introduction of new technology and such investment will have to be based on another major political defeat of labor as happened between the 1920s and 1940s.

These circumstances have led to very marked shifts to the right of political center in most industrialized countries. Britain and West Germany are obvious cases in point and so is the United States. The extremely right wing Joseph Strauss as the next Prime Minister of Germany is now a realistic prospect. Marked shifts to the right are not only manifest on these domestic political levels, but in more aggressive if not bellicose international policies, as manifested by the installation of mobile intercontinental MX missiles in the western United States, the NATO decision to station a new generation of American nuclear missiles in Western Europe, the U.S. Senate's apparent refusal to accept SALT II, and the Pentagon's plans for a new mobile intervention force, all of which were decided *before* the new Soviet push into Afghanistan (and which certainly entered into Soviet calculations of whether an invasion would lead the West to pose any *additional* threats and costs to the Soviet Union beyond the aforementioned and the Sino-American alliance). The Western shifts to the right also manifest themselves in a whole variety of other fields, such as in education (as a counteroffensive against the progressive measures of the 1960s), health, immigration, and race and sexual relations (against the women's movement), and on the ideological level in general, where the "new right" is advancing by leaps and bounds in most industrial capitalist countries.

The social democrats and liberals find themselves relatively unarmed against these shifts to the right. Keynesian and neo-Keynesian economic and social policies demonstrably do not work any longer, particularly in an economy with so-called stagflation (or slumpflation in the 1973 to 1975 recession), that is simultaneous unemployment and inflation. Keynesianism will work even less in the 1979–80 (81?) recession. The apparent reason is that Keynesian medicine is either to increase purchasing power if there is unemployment, thereby supposedly strengthening inflation, or to reduce purchasing power if there is inflation, thereby certainly increasing unemployment. Therefore, when government and economists face simultaneous unemployment and inflation they are left without a Keynesian policy to pursue. Not long ago the *New York Times* counseled that we should have a prudent economic policy: Neither to increase purchasing power to fight unemployment nor to restrain purchasing power to fight inflation. That is, prudent economic policy today is to do nothing at all because economists and governments really don't know what to do. No wonder that *Business Week* says that the American Economic Association is only concerned with trivialities and does not know how to tackle any of the major economic problems that face us and that economics is intellectually and politically bankrupt. This is a very realistic appraisal by the business community, but it holds not just for post-Keynesian economic "science" but for postwar social democratic ideology in general. The American dream of bigger and better and continuous prosperity is finished in the United States and elsewhere in the West. In his famous July 15, 1979, Sunday night speech on the crisis of confidence, President Carter said that the vast majority of Americans think that the next five years will be worse than the last five years. Carter's appraisal is quite realistic, but he might have added that the last five years have already been worse than the twenty-five years before that. This crisis of confidence confronts the political right, left, and center with a growing ideological problem of what to offer. The same Carter speech is itself a manifestation of complete ideological bankruptcy. The only universal agreement in the commentary on Carter's speech was that he offered absolutely no domestic solution to the crisis of confidence (which reflects the decline of American economic and political—in a word, imperialist—power) or even to the energy crisis which he defined as a subproduct of this crisis of confidence. Carter himself sought and found an apparent "solution" in Iran and Afghanistan.

It is open to question whether the left has escaped this crisis of confidence and of ideology. The previously quoted official and officious statements to the effect that everything is going fine may be no more than not very substantial fig leaves covering a serious ideological crisis on the left as well. This ideological crisis of the socialist left and Marxism is a reflection or counterpart of a real economic and political crisis and also manifests itself importantly in the so-called socialist countries from the Soviet Union to China and the smaller socialist countries of Eastern Europe and Southeast

Asia and perhaps also Cuba. These countries are caught up in the political economic crisis of the West as well as in one of their own, which may both be part of a single crisis in a single world system. Although it is not good to appeal to authority, it is perhaps convenient to cite Comrade Brezhnev from the Soviet Union, who says, "Because of the broad economic links between capitalist and socialist countries the ill effects of the current crisis in the West have also had an impact on the socialist world." The Prime Minister of Bulgaria, Comrade Zhikov, goes one step further and says: "It may be hoped that the crisis which is raging in the West may come to a rapid end; since it affects and creates uncertainties for the Bulgarian economy, which to a certain extent is dependent on trade with the countries of the West." Not only do these leaders of "socialist" countries recognize that the world capitalist crisis affects them, and does so negatively in their estimation, they also hope and ask that this crisis go away so that they can continue with business as usual. That in itself is both an element of and a manifestation of very serious crisis in socialism and Marxism, because in the past and still during the last serious crisis of capitalism between the two world wars, Marxist socialists welcomed such a crisis on the theory that it would lay the basis for the possible revolutionary destruction of capitalism and its replacement with socialism. The fact that the "socialist" Soviet Union, Bulgaria, and other countries in Eastern Europe, not to mention China, which has entered into a political and economic alliance with the United States and Japan against the Soviet Union, now all hope that the crisis will go away and that they are actively collaborating with the capitalists to overcome the crisis (and even compete with each other in helping capitalism to do so) means that socialism and Marxism itself are in very serious ideological trouble. The "socialist" countries are very clearly committed in words and even more so through their actions to the maintenance—and even prosperity—of capitalism in the West and these "Marxist socialists" seem to all intents and purposes literally to have abandoned any hopes and any policies to contribute in one way or another to the demise of capitalism in the West. This socialist integration in and apparent commitment to the world capitalist system is documented in chapter 4 and summarized below.

That "socialism" is banking on the capitalist West is visible in the economic arena through the accelerated integration or reintegration of the socialist economies in the capitalist international division of labor through trade and production. During the last decade the "socialist" countries have vastly increased their trade with the West in order to import Western technology. As a result they have run a balance of payments deficit with the West, which they have covered in part by running up vast debts that have risen from about $7 billion in 1971 to approximately $60 billion today. In part—and this is particularly significant politically—the socialist countries cover their deficit with the West through their balance of payments surplus with the underdeveloped countries of the Third World with which they are also increasing trade ties. Thus, the socialist countries import technology from the West and to pay for it export two thirds fuels and raw materials and one third manufactures. But in turn their exports to the Third World consist of two thirds manufactured commodities of a lower order of technological development, and their imports from the Third World consist of two thirds raw materials. The socialist economies occupy an intermediate place in the international division of labor in which the pattern of the Socialist East-Third World South relations are similar to the Capitalist West–Socialist East relations.

This policy of economic integration and cooperation between the socialist countries and the capitalist ones in the West and South goes beyond simple trade and increasingly includes the most complex network of productive arrangements. Western firms increasingly produce in the socialist countries through complex arrangements ranging from licensing to foreign investment, in which the Western firms provide the technology, know-how, and often the management and marketing, and the socialist economies provide cheap skilled labor and labor discipline, that is, no strikes. Even China, which was famous for its policy of self-reliance, and Vietnam, which won the war against American imperialism in large part because of its policy of political and military self-reliance (despite military aid from the Soviet Union and China), have now permitted and indeed encouraged foreign investment in their countries—in Vietnam's case with 100 percent foreign ownership to produce manufactured commodities for the world market. Thus, the capitalist West increasingly produces in the socialist countries at low cost through a variety of complex production agreements for export to the West and to the Third World.

From the point of view of capital in the West, this increasing production and trade with the socialist economies represents one of the important means of trying to stem and reverse the tide of the growing economic crisis. This "socialist" safety valve for capitalist crisis manifested itself in particular ways in the 1973 to 1975 recession, when the capital equipment which then found no market in the West was bought by the East and OPEC countries, and thus helped to keep Western business afloat during that recession. The same socialist helping hand to capitalism manifests itself economically through the reduction in production costs which are lower in the East, and subsidized by "socialist" society, and politically through the already several times exercised capitalist threat to move production facilities to a socialist country if union militancy does not exercise "self-discipline" at home.

I have questioned whether the "socialist" countries form a "socialist world" outside and apart from the world capitalist system and have argued that these countries are increasingly an integral part of the world capitalist division of labor, production, and trade—and concomitantly of the world capitalist social and political system. Stalin claimed a year before he died that there were two world markets, and though history has shown him to have been wrong, many people still claim that there are two social systems (though hardly anyone would claim only two political systems). Indeed, many

Marxists and others argue that, though there may be only one (capitalist) world market, the capitalist law of value and market forces does not operate within the socialist economies. These capitalist foreces clearly do operate, however, in Yugoslavia, complete with competition, monopoly, and unemployment; and the evidence is increasing that they also operate in "socialist" Eastern Europe. Rumania's violation of Comecon agreements by suddenly charging East European tourists high prices in hard (capitalist) currencies for gasoline at the roadside pump is only a spectacular manifestation of the eastward spread of the capitalist world inflation and the economic reorganization. This economic "reform" has been most deliberate in Hungary to adapt the organization, financing, prices, varieties, quality, work processes, and marketing of domestic production to the exigencies of competition on the capitalist world market. Moreover, although the socialist countries can plan their economies, the underfulfillment by nearly half of the growth targets in the current five-year plans in the Soviet Union and similarly in most of Eastern Europe suggests that whatever their considerable domestic difficulties are, they are not unrelated to the development of the crisis in the West, which particularly in Eastern Europe has increased import costs while restricting export possibilities to pay for them. Therefore, the capitalist law of value (and not just a separate socialist one as Stalin argued) does seem to operate within the socialist economies, although perhaps less so in the relatively more autonomous Soviet and Chinese economies (though they also have followed the OPEC oil price upward in their external sales including those to other socialist countries). If some of these socialist economies are successful in solving these problems during the current crisis (as Deng Xiaoping promises for China by the year 2000 through the four modernizations), the further question arises whether ironically only some countries that have passed through a socialist revolution will therefore be able to join the inner circle of metropolitan economies in the world capitalist system—while intermediate capitalist economies, like Brazil or Iran when ruled by the Shah, fail to do so. However, the intensive rivalry to the point of war between "socialist" states poses a serious obstacle to their success, as each—so far the Soviet Union, China, and Vietnam—is intent on preventing the success of another rival. (This most intense rivalry among socialist states contending for world and regional leadership positions and the resulting otherwise surprising alliances with capitalist nations are reminiscent of the similarly intense competition and alliances for the mantle of declining British world and regional leadership positions among the United States, Germany, France, Russia, and Japan during the periods of world crisis and wars over the past century.)

The socialist integration in the capitalist world has been all the more visible in the détente between the Soviet Union and the United States, which has been due not simply and perhaps not even primarily to peaceful coexistence under the nuclear sword of Damocles, but also to the political counterpart of growing economic integration. Perhaps it is appropriate to quote Mr. Kissinger in this regard: "The key to U.S. strategy towards the U.S.S.R. has been to create mutual vested interests in the preservation of the international order. Relations between the U.S. and the U.S.S.R. have become so stable that dramatic new departures could no longer be expected." For his part Mr. Brezhnev added, "We will be happy if our efforts to better Soviet American relations help draw more and more nations into the process of détente, be it in Europe or Asia and Africa or Latin America, in the Middle East or in the Far East." On the other hand the emerging Washington-Peking-Tokyo axis requires little comment, and the Chinese foreign policy of visible and invisible alliance with anyone they hope will aid and abet their anti-Soviet policy speaks for itself. The Chinese policy seems to be simply that "the enemy of my enemy is my friend," no matter whether that be the Shah of Iran, the CIA puppets in Africa, Senator Henry Jackson in the United States or Joseph Strauss in West Germany, all of whom have been Chinese favorites because they represent the most avid anti-Soviet forces in the West. This is not to suggest that the Soviet policy is vastly better in that respect, because the record of recent years shows that although the Soviet Union has supported some progressive causes, it has also supported some very reactionary ones—Lon Nol in Cambodia, the Videla regime in Argentina, and Morocco, with which the Soviet Union have vastly increased trade ties. Despite certain support for national liberation movements here and there, and notwithstanding some claims among the Nonaligned, it seems objectively less than realistic, indeed unjustifiably optimistic, to hope that Soviet, let alone Chinese or Vietnamese foreign economic, political, or military policy will in the foreseeable future support the transformation of any movement of national liberation into a socialist revolution in Africa or elsewhere, especially if their own interests counsel that others' national or socialist interests be abandoned to their fate or even opposed, as in Somalia, Eritrea, and Southeast Asia. The motto of "proletarian internationalism" rings increasingly hollow.

The Third World was and is an integral and important part of the world capitalist economy. (This integration is documented in chapter 1 and further examined in chapter 5.) Unless the working class in the West and the working class in the South can prevent it, the Third World is destined to play a major role in the attempt of capital in the world capitalist eocnomy to stem and reverse the tide of the growing economic crisis (see the companion volume TW for a detailed analysis). In the first place, since the Third World is an integral part of the capitalist world, the crisis is immediately transmitted from the center to the Third World through growing balance of payment deficits. As demand in the industrialized countries declines or grows more slowly, prices for exported raw materials other than petroleum decline or grow more slowly. At the same time, the vast world inflation in the industrialized economies increases prices of manufactured commodities imported by the Third World. Therefore, the terms of trade have been shifting again against the underdeveloped countries during this crisis (despite a temporary raw materials price boom in

1973–1974 which was completely reversed again after 1974), and the nonpetroleum-exporting underdeveloped Third World countries have faced increasingly serious balance of payments problems and a mushrooming foreign debt. Moreover, it is not accidental or incidental that the OPEC surplus is more or less equivalent to the increase in the balance of payments deficit of the Third World, suggesting that most of the increases in the prices of petroleum since 1973 have ultimately been borne by the Third World.

A significant portion of the OPEC surplus has been recycled through the banks in the imperialist countries to the Third World to cover their balance of payments deficits through private loans at increasingly onerous conditions and costs. Their growing debt, in turn, is then used increasingly as a political instrument to impose austerity and superausterity policies in the Third World. This blackmail through the renegotiation and extension of debts has received many newspaper headlines in the cases of Peru and Zaire, but it has also become standard International Monetary Fund (IMF) and private banking operating procedure elsewhere throughout the Third World. As these countries' foreign debt increases, they have to get the debt refinanced both through private banks and through official loans. The IMF then declares that if the government does not devalue the currency to make exports and foreign investment cheaper, lower wages, cut the government budget especially for welfare expenditures and take other antipopular measures, and if it does not throw out Minister A and replace him with Minister B who is more likely to institute the IMF-supported policies, then the country will not get the IMF certificate of good behavior and without it neither official loans nor loans from private banks will be forthcoming. This political-economic club has been used to beat governments into shape to adopt policies of superausterity throughout the Third World. However, the same thing has also happened to Portugal and it has happened to Great Britain. When the IMF led by the United States offered Britain a $3.9 billion loan in 1976, it gave Britain virtually the same treatment it had previously reserved for banana republics and the like—perhaps an indication that Britain is underdeveloping into a kind of Third World country. However, just as unemployment and recession are not simply or even primarily due to government policy decisions, so are superausterity measures in the Third World not simply the result of pressure from the industrialized capitalist countries through the IMF. These external political pressures are simply reinforcing tendencies that have another much broader economic base in the capitalist attempt to maintain or revive the rate of profit by producing at lower costs in the Third World (and also in the socialist countries) with national political support for these repressive measures.

Costs of production are reduced by moving industry to the Third World, particularly labor-intensive industries, such as textiles and certain kinds of electronic equipment, but also some very capital-intensive industries, such as steel and automobiles. It is perhaps symbolic that the Volkswagen beetle is no longer produced in Germany but is now made in Mexico for export to the other parts of the world. From the point of view of the world capitalist economy this is a transfer of part of industrial production from high- to low-cost areas. From the point of view of the Third World, this move represents a policy of export promotion, particularly of so-called nontraditional industrial exports. Third World manufacturing export promotion has two seemingly different origins. In the first case, the economies that had advanced most in the process of import substitution, like India, Brazil, and Mexico, have turned to export some of their manufactures that began as import substitutes, from textiles to automobiles, some produced by multinational firms. In the second case, from the very beginning foreign capital went to other Third World countries to set up manufacturing facilities to produce for the export rather than for the domestic market. This movement started in the 1960s with Mexico (which combined both kinds of industry but in different regions) on the border with the United States and in South Korea, Taiwan, Hong Kong, and Singapore. In the 1970s it spread to Malaysia, the Philippines, and increasingly through India, Pakistan, Sri Lanka, Egypt, Tunisia, Morocco, the Ivory Coast, and to virtually every country on the Caribbean. These economies offer cheap labor, and they compete among each other with state subsidies to provide plant facilities, electricity, transportation, tax relief, and every other kind of incentive for foreign capital to come to their countries to produce for the world market. In the case of Chile the military junta went so far as to offer to pay part of the otherwise starvation wages so that foreign capital could keep its costs down.

To provide these low wages and indeed to reduce wages from one country to another competitively, as each tries to offer more favorable conditions to international capital, requires political repression, the destruction of labor unions and/or the prohibition of strikes and other union activity, the systematic imprisonment, torture, or assassination of labor and other political leaders and in general the imposition of emergency rule, martial law, and of military government. In fact, the whole state apparatus has to be adapted to the Third World role in the new international division of labor.

This repressive movement has swept systematically through Asia, Africa, and Latin America in the course of the 1970s and is demonstrably not simply due to some kind of autonomous political force to combat communism (which has become a rather doubtful policy at a time when even the United States has socialist allies and some socialist countries collaborate with the repressive regimes). Demonstrably, this repressive political policy has very clear economic purposes and functions to make these economies more competitive on the world market by lowering wages and to suppressing those elements of the local bourgeoisie who are tied to the internal market. This sector of the bourgeoisie pressured for certain kinds of mild restrictions on the operations of multinational corporations in a number of Third World countries during the late 1960s and early 1970s. Since then, these restrictions have increasingly been removed, and one government after another is falling over itself to offer favorable conditions to international capital.

The motto now is to work for the world market rather than for the internal market. Effective demand on the national market is not and is not intended to be the source of demand for national production—demand on the world market is. There is no reason to raise the wages of the direct producers, because they are not destined to purchase the goods that they produce. Instead, the goods are meant to be purchased far away on the world market. An important exception is the small local market of high income receivers, which is supposed to expand. Thus, there is a polarization of income not only between developed and underdeveloped countries on the global level, but also on the national level. Within the underdeveloped countries the poor are getting poorer, both relatively and often absolutely, and the rich are getting richer. In some cases, such as in Brazil until 1974 but less so since then, the attempt to develop a high income market for part of local industry has been very successful. However, in Brazil as elsewhere in the Third World, this "development model" is based on the depression of the wage rate (which as a consequence has been cut by about half in Brazil, Uruguay, Argentina, and Chile and is increasingly being forced down in Peru and elsewhere) and the forced marginalization and unemployment of labor (which has already increased vastly in the Third World and continues to do so). Both of these processes are rapidly increasing the misery of the masses and the polarization of society in the Third World. Moreover, since in general the internal market is being restrained and restricted, the sector of the bourgeoisie that depends on the internal market, as in Chile and Argentina, also has to be repressed. Therefore, big capital must institute a military government that will repress not only labor but even a sector of the bourgeoisie and the petit bourgeoisie. The governing alliance is between the sector of local capital allied with international capital and their military and other political executors. This arrangement involves a very substantial reorganization of the state in the Third World and often is militarization so that the Third World can more effectively participate in the international division of labor in the interests of capital facing an economic crisis in the imperialist countries and its state monopoly capital allies in the Third World itself.

In some places since late 1976, in others since 1977 and 1978, there appears to have been a reversal of this tendency toward military coups, emergency rule, and martial law. There have been elections in India and Sri Lanka, pseudo elections in Bangladesh and the Philippines, elections in Ghana and Nigeria with promise of their military regimes to step down and hand over power to civilian rule, announced elections in various parts of Latin America, and some perhaps significant liberalization in the military regime in Brazil. Some people attribute these developments to President Carter's human rights policy, though it is a bit difficult to sustain the efficacy of this policy when in quite a few crucial cases it either was absent or was restrained in the higher "national interest" of the United States. Other people attribute the liberalization to increasing mass mobilization in many parts of the Third World, or to a supposed failure of the new policy of export promotion and—certainly according to many Brazilians—to the renewed and prospective importance of a policy of import subsitution and the widening of the internal market. However, at this time any such redirection of the Third World economies generally is hardly observable. Such a renewed import substitution in the Third World would be objectively aided and abetted by a far-reaching protectionist drive or the substantial breakdown of the system of international trade and finance elsewhere in the world. As the world economic crisis deepens, this eventuality is admittedly a distinct possibility; but so far it has not come to pass. In the Third World progressive import substitution of consumer goods—though less so of capital goods producing for the export market—would require a relatively more equal distribution of income and a politically more benign regime to permit or reflect a broader coalition or alliance of classes and sectors. In other words, these people argue that the dark days of the mid-seventies are over and that we are again facing the prospect of a redemocratization or at least of limited democracy in many parts of the Third World. Even a measure of democracy would offer better conditions for popular mobilization and for the continuation or acceleration of national liberation movements and of socialist revolutions in the Third World.

On the other hand, it may also be argued with considerable evidence that these recent developments do not represent the reversal of the emerging new model of economic integration of the Third World in the international division of labor in response to the development of the world crisis, but rather that this apparent redemocratization is simply the institutionalization of the new model of economic growth based on export promotion. It was necessary to have very severe political repression as a midwife to institute this new model; but once the model is in place and more or less working, it is possible to ease off a bit on the political repression. Then, indeed, it is not only possible, but it becomes politically necessary and desirable to get a wider social base for the political regime and to institute a kind of limited political democracy by handing over the government from military to civilian rule. But these political modifications would not be made in order to overturn the present economic order and again to promote import substitution, let alone so-called noncapitalist growth or some variety of "socialism." Instead, this supposed redemocratization would be to maintain and to institutionalize the new insertion of the Third World in the international division of labor as low-wage producers during the present world economic crisis. If we look realistically at what is happening in Asia, Africa, and Latin America, there is very considerable economic and political evidence for this latter explanation of what is politically going on today in the Third World. This evidence is presented and analyzed in detail in the companion volume, TW.

A political counterpart of this economic alternative is a renewed populist alliance of labor and other popular forces and parties with some bourgeois ones. This alliance would press for the amelioration of politically repressive regimes and their gradual replacement by formally or superficially more democratic but essentially technocratic ones to implement the same fundamentally exclusivist and antipopular economic policy. In the pursuit of such unholy alliances around the Third World, it has become opportune(ist) to resurrect all kinds of bygone politicians or even their ghosts. These politicians did not have left wing support in their heyday when they did not pursue very progressive policies, but they now receive support from the left to implement policies that are far more rightist than their previous ones. However, these rightist policies now appear as the lesser evil compared to more recent, often military, governments and policies. For lack of better alternatives the opposition, including the left, is now rallying behind bygone civilian political figures like Frei in Chile, Siles Suarez in Bolivia, Magalhaes Pinto in Brazil, Awolowo and Azikwe in Nigeria, Aquino in the Philippines, Pramaj in Thailand, Indira Gandhi in India, and even the ghost of Bhutto in Pakistan, as well as accepting new old men like the Ayatollah Khomeini in Iran to lead "progressive" movements, which are likely to maintain the essentials of the status quo and certainly will not offer any real development alternatives.

To the extent that these policies and politicians are a realistic political alternative in the Third World, orthodox development theory and ideology, as well as progressive dependence or even (not as revolutionary as hoped) new dependence theory—not to mention the Chinese "three worlds" theory and the Soviet supposedly "noncapitalist" third way to national liberation, democracy, and varieties of socialism—are all completely bankrupt. Today none of these theories and ideologies can offer any realistic policy alternatives and practical political economic guidelines for the pursuit of economic development or national liberation, let alone of socialist construction. Independent national development in the Third World has proved to be a snare and a delusion; and self-reliance, collective or otherwise, is a myth that is supposed to hide this sad fact of life in the world capitalist system. Political compromises with the capitalist status quo by the avowedly revolutionary socialist parties and particularly the Communist parties around the Third World are another part of the ideological crisis of the left in the face of the present world crisis.

Abbreviations

Organizations

AEI	American Enterprise Institute, Washington
AI	Amnesty International, London
APHA	American Public Health Association, Washington
BIS	Bank for International Settlements, Basel
CIAL	Centro de Información de America Latina, Paris
CMEA	Council for Mutual Economic Assistance, "Comecon," Moscow
ECE	UN Economic Commission for Europe, Geneva
ECLA	UN Economic Commission for Latin America, Santiago
EEC	European Economic Community (Common Market), Brussels
FAO	UN Food and Agricultural Organization, Rome
GATT	General Agreement on Tariffs and Trade, Geneva
GEREI	Groupe d'Etude des Relations Economiques Internationales, Paris
IBRD	International Bank for Reconstruction and Development (World Bank), Washington
IDEP	UN African Institute for Economic Development Planning, Dakar
ILO	UN International Labor Office, Geneva
IMF	International Monetary Fund, Washington
INRA	Institut de Recherche Agronomique, Paris
NACLA	North American Congress for Latin America, New York
OECD	Organization for Economic Cooperation and Development, Paris
OPEC	Organization of Petroleum Exporting Countries, Vienna
PCI	Partido Communista Italiano, Rome
PRIO	Peace Research Institute, Oslo
RBI	Reserve Bank of India, New Delhi
SIPRI	Stockholm International Peace Research Institute
UNCTAD	United Nations Conference on Trade and Development, Geneva
UNDESA	United Nations Department of Economic and Social Affairs, New York
UNECAP	United Nations Economic Commission for Asia and the Pacific, Bangkok
UNECE	United Nations Economic Commission for Europe, Geneva

UN ECOSOC	United Nations Economic and Social Council, New York
UNIDO	United Nations Industrial Development Organization, Vienna
UNITAR	United Nation Institute for Training and Research, New York
URPE	Union for Radical Political Economics, New York
USBLS	U.S. Bureau of Labor Statistics, Washington
USDA	U.S. Department of Agriculture, Washington
WBG	World Bank Group, Washington

Periodical Publications

AEI	*AEI Economist,* Washington
AER	*American Economic Review,* Menasha, Wis.
ALT	*Alternativa,* Bogotá
AMPO	*Japan Asia Quarterly,* Tokyo
AP	Associated Press, USA
APR	*America Presse,* Paris
BA	*Business Asia,* Hong Kong
BCS	*Bulletin of Concerned Asian Scholars,* San Francisco
BDS	*Bulletin of the Department of State,* Washington
BE	*Business Europe,* Geneva
BI	*Business International,* New York
B3W	*Blätter des Informationszentrum Dritte Welt,* Freiburg
BLA	*Business Latin America,* New York
BS	*Business Standard*, India
BSR	*Business and Society Review,* New York
BW	*Business Week,* New York
CA	*Commerce America,* Washington
CC	*Capitalism and Class,* London
CE	*Comercio Exterior,* México
CEE	*Commercio Exterior,* English-language abridged edition, Mexico
CHA	*Chile-America,* Rome
CJB	*Columbia Journal of World Business,* New York
CON	*Contemporary Crises,* Amsterdam
CP	*Cuadernos Politicos,* México
CRI	*Critique,* Glasgow
CS	*Current Scene,* Hong Kong
DA	*Dialectical Anthropology,* Amsterdam
DB	*Debate Proletario,* México
DC	*Development and Change,* The Hague
EBE	*Economic Bulletin for Europe,* UNECE, Geneva
ECO	*Economist,* London
EDC	*Economic Development and Cultural Change,* Chicago

EIU	*Economist Intelligence Unit, Quarterly Economic Review,* London
EJ	*Economic Journal,* Cambridge, England
EO	*Economic Outlook,* OECD, Paris
EPA	*El Pais,* Madrid
EPW	*Economic and Political Weekly,* Bombay
ES	*Economy and Society,* London
ESE	*Economic Survey of Europe,* UNECE, Geneva
ESP	*O'Estado de São Paulo*
FA	*Foreign Affairs,* Lancaster, Penn.
F&D	*Finance & Development,* IMF and World Bank, Washington
FAZ	*Frankfurter Allgemeine Zeitung*
FER	*Far Eastern Economic Review,* Hong Kong
FEX	*Financial Express,* New Delhi
FMT	*Financial Market Trends,* OECD, Paris
FOR	*Fortune* magazine, New York
FP	*Foreign Policy,* Washington
FR	*Frankfurter Rundschau*
FT	*Financial Times,* London
GM	*Gazeta Mercantil,* São Paulo
GUA	*The Guardian,* London
GUW	*The Guardian Weekly,* London
HB	*Handelsblatt,* Hamburg
HBR	*Harvard Business Review,* Cambridge, Mass.
HOL	*Holiday,* Dacca
HS	*Historia y Sociedad,* México
ICP	Intercontinental Press, New York (incorporating Inprecor, Brussels)
IDS	Institute of Development Studies, Sussex
IHT	*International Herald Tribune,* Paris
INF	*Informativo,* Paris
IPC	*Inprecor,* Brussels, Paris
IPW	*IPW Berichte,* Berlin, DDR
IRP	*Instant Research on Peace and Violence,* Tampere
JCA	*Journal of Contemporary Asia,* Stockholm
JEL	*Journal of Economic Literature,* Menasha, Wis.
LAER	*Latin American Economic Report,* London
LAPR	*Latin American Political Report,* London
LEV	*Leviathan,* Frankfurt
LM	*Le Monde,* Paris
LMD	*Le Monde Diplomatique,* Paris
LT	*The Times,* London
LTM	*Les Temps Modernes,* Paris
MAR	*Mining Annual Review,* Mining Journal, London
MBS	*Monthly Bulletin of Statistics,* United Nations, New York

MD	*Marxismus Digest,* Frankfurt
MEI	*Main Economic Indicators,* OECD, Paris
MEN	*Mensaje,* Santiago
MR	*Monthly Review,* New York
MRC	*El Mercurio,* Santiago
MRP	MERIP (Middle East Research and Information Project) Reports, Washington
NIB	*New India Bulletin,* Montreal
NJ	*National Journal,* AEI, Washington
NLA	*NACLA Latin America and Empire Report,* New York
NLR	*New Left Review,* London
NT	*New Times,* Moscow
NW	*Newsweek,* New York
NYT	*New York Times*
NZZ	*Neue Zürcher Zeitung,* Zürich
OBS	*Observer,* London
OO	*OECD Observer,* Paris
PD	*Problemas del Desarrollo,* México
PF	*Punto Final,* Santiago
PN	*Pugwash Newsletter,* London
PR	*Peking Review*
RAPE	*Review of African Political Economy,* London
RBI	Reserve Bank of India, *Reports on Currency and Finance,* New Delhi
SA	*Scientific American,* New York
SCB	*Survey of Current Business,* Washington
ST	*Sunday Times,* London
SZ	*Süddeutsche Zeitung,* München
TE	*El Trimestre Económico,* México
TI	*Times of India,* New Delhi
TIM	*Time,* New York
TRA	*Transaction,* New York
UBS	*Union de Banques Suisses Report,* Zürich
USN	*U.S. News and World Report,* Washington
WD	*World Development,* Oxford
WER	*World Employment Report,* ILO, Geneva
WK	*Wirtschaftskonjuntur,* Berlin
WP	*Washington Post*
WSJ	*Wall Street Journal,* New York
WW	*Wirtschaftswoche,* Frankfurt
WWA	*Weltwirtschaftliches Archiv,* Kiel
YLS	*Yearbook of Labour Statistics,* ILO, Geneva
ZA	*Zona Abierta,* Madrid
ZT	*Die Zeit,* Hamburg
ZW	*Zerowork,* New York

Bibliography

Abercrombie, K. C. (1975) The International Division of Labour and of Benefits in Food and Agriculture. Paper presented at Society for International Development Conference on World Structures and Development-Strategies for Change. Linz, Austria, September 15–17, 1975.

Adler-Karlsson, Gunnar (1971) *Der Fehlschlag. Zwanzig Jahre Wirtschaftskrieg zwieschen Ost und West.* Wien: Europa Verlag.

Ake, Claude (1976) "The Congruence of Political Economies and Ideologies in Africa" *The Political Economy of Contemporary Africa.* Peter C. W. Gutkind and Immanuel Wallerstein, eds. Beverly Hills, London: Sage.

Alavi, Hamza (1972) "The State in Postcolonial Societies: Pakistan and Bangladesh" *New Left Review,* London, No. 74, July–August reprinted in Kathleen Gough and Hari P. Sharma, eds. *Imperialism and Revoluion in South Asia.* New York: Monthly Review Press, 1973.

Albrecht, Ulrich; Ernst, Dieter; Lock, Peter und Wulf, Herbert, (1976) *Rüstung und Unterentwicklung. Iran, Indien, Grichenland, Turkei. Die verschärfte Militarisierung.* Hamburg: Rowohlt.

Altavater, Elmar et al. (1974) "On the Analysis of Imperialism in the Metropolitan Countries. The West German Example" *Bulletin of the Conference of Socialist Economists,* London: Spring.

Amerongen, Otto Wolff von (1977) "Protectionism—a Danger to Our Prosperity" *Intereconomics,* Hamburg, No. 11–12.

Amin, Samir (1970) *L'accumulation à l'échele mondiale. Critique de la théorie du sous-développement.* Paris: Editions Anthropos.

—— (1973) *Le développement inégal. Essai sur les formations sociales du capitalisme périphérique.* Paris: Les Editions de Minuit.

—— (1976) After Nairobi—Preparing the Non-Aligned Summit in Colombo. An Appraisal of UNCTAD IV. Dakar, United Nations African Institute for Economic Development and Planning, DIR/2747, June.

—— (1977) *The Future of Southern Africa.* Introduction. Dakar, IDEP reproduction 402; Dar es Salaam: Tanzanian Publishing House.

——, Frank, Andre Gunder and Jaffe, Hosea (1975) *Quale 1984.* Milano, Jaca Book. Also in Spanish *Como será 1984.* Madrid: Zero, 1976.

—— et al. (1975) *La crise de l'impérialisme.* Paris: Les Editions Minuit.

Amnesty International Report 1976. London: Amnesty International Publications.

Amnesty International Report 1977. London: Amnesty International Publications.

This listing includes works cited in *Crisis: In the World Economy* and in *Crisis: In the Third World.*

AMPO (1977) "Free Trade Zones and Industrialization of Asia" *AMPO, Japan-Asia Quarterly Review,* Tokyo, Pacific Resources Center, Special Issue.

Ampuero, Raúl (1977) "El nuevo poder militar" *Nueva Politica,* México, v. II, Nos. 5–6, Abril–Septiembre.

Amuzegar, Jahangir (1977) "A Requiem for the North-South Conference" *Foreign Affairs,* Lancaster, Penn., October.

—— and Fekkrat, M. Ali (1971) *Iran: Economic Development under Dualistic Conditions.* Chicago, The University of Chicago Press.

Annual Register of Political Economy (1978) *La Crise Contemporanea.* Milano: Jaca Book.

APHA (1975) *Health and Work in America: A Chart Book.* Washington, American Public Health Association, U.S. Government Printing Office.

Armstrong, P. J., Glyn, A. J., Harrison, J. M. and Sutcliffe, R. B. (1976) Reconstruction: Metropolitan Capitalism from the Second World War to Korea. Oxford, University of Oxford Institute of Economics and Statistics, January Mimeo.

Arrighi, Giovanni and Saul, John (1973) *Essays on the Political Economy of Africa.* New York: Monthly Review Press.

Arroio Junior, Raimundo (1976) "La miseria del milagro brasileño" *Cuadernos Politicos,* México, D. F., No. 9, July–September.

Arroyo, Gonzalo (1976) "Capitalisme transnational et agriculture traditionelle: Formes d'integration" *Political Economy of Food* Proceedings of an International Seminar. Tampere Peace Research Institute. Research Reports No. 12.

Aziz, Sartaj (1977) "The World Food Situation and Collective Self-Reliance. *World Development,* Oxford, v. 5, Nos. 5–7, May–July.

Baade, Fritz (1960) *Der Wettlauf zum Jahre 2000.* Oldenburg.

Bairoch, Paul (1973) *Urban Unemployment in Developing Countries.* Geneva: International Labour Office.

Bajit, Alexander (1971) "Investment Cycles in European Socialist Economies: A Review Article: *Journal of Economic Literature,* Menesha, USA, 9. No. 1.

Balakrishnan, K. (1976) "Indian Joint Ventures Abroad—Geographic and Industry Patterns" *Economic and Political Weekly,* Bombay, May.

Ball, George W. (1971) "Suez Is the Front to Watch" in *After Vietnam. The Future of American Foreign Policy,* Robert W. Gregg and Charles W. Jr. Kegley, eds. Garden City, New York: Anchor Books.

—— (1976) *Diplomacy for a Crowded World. An American Foreign Policy.* Boston: An Atlantic Monthly Press Book.

Bank for International Settlements (1978) Forty-eighth Annual Report, 1 April 1977–31 March 1978. Basel, 12 June.

—— (1979) Forty-ninth Annual Report, 1 April 1978–31 March 1979. Basel, 11 June.

Bartra, Roger, (1974a) *Estructura agraria y clases sociales en México.* México: Ediciones Era.

—— (1974b) "Modos de producción y estructura agraria en México" *Historia y Sociedad,* México, D. F., 2. época, No. 1.

BCC (1975) Can Business Help Solve the World Food Problems. Exploring the Alternatives. Business Communications Co. First Annual Food Conference Held March 19.

Bein, David O. (1977) "Rescuing the LDCs." *Foreign Affairs,* Lancaster, Penn., v. 55, No. 4, July.

Belassa, Bela (n.d.) "The Firm in the New Economic Mechanism," *The New Hungarian Quarterly.*

Benaim, Raymond (1976) Une firme multinationale d'elevage au Maroc: Le King Ranch. Paris, Institut National de la Recherche Agronomique. Mimeo.

Benoit, Emile (1973) *Defense and Economic Growth in Developing Countries.* Lexington Mass.: Heath

—— (n.d.) Growth Effects of Defense in Developing Countries. Mimeo.

Bergmann, Denis (1977) "Agricultural Policies in the EEC and their External Implications" *World Development,* Oxford, v. 5, Nos. 5–7, May–July.

Berlinguer, Enrico (1977) *La cuestión comunista.* Barcelona: Editorial Fontanara.

Bhagat, S. (1977) "India: Gandhi Aims at 'Normalisation'" *Inprecor,* Bruxelles, No. 65, January 13.

Bitran, Daniel y König, Wolfgang (1977) "Las empresas transnacionales y las exportaciones de manufacturas de América Latina. Algunas consideraciones." *Comercio Exterior*, México, D. F., v. 27, No. 7, Julio.

Blaikie, Piers, Cameron, John and Seddon, David (1979) The Logic of a Basic Needs Strategy: With or Against the Tide? Norwich: University of East Anglia, School of Development Studies, June (mimeo).

Blair, John M. (1974) "Market Power and Inflation: A Short-Run Target T Return Model" *Journal of Economic Issues,* v. VIII, No. 2, June.

Block, Fred (1975) "Contradictions of Capitalism as a World System" *Insurgent Sociologist*, Eugene, Oregon USA, v. 1, No. 2, winter.

Boddy, Raford and Crotty, James (1976a) "Wages, Prices and the Profit Squeeze" *The Review of Radical Political Economics,* New York, URPE, v. 8, No. 2, Summer.

—— (1976b) "Wage-Push and Working Class Power" *Monthly Review,* New York, v. 27, No. 10, March.

Bondestam, Lars (1976) "The Politics of Food in the Periphery with Special Reference to Africa" *Political Economy of Food.* Proceedings of an International Seminar. Tampere, Peace Research Institute. Research Reports, No. 12.

Bratenstein, Roger (1974) "First Steps Towards a Cyclical Theory for LDC" *Intereconomics* No. 10, October.

Braun, Oscar (1976) The New International Economic Order from the Point of View of Dependence Theory. Paper presented at First Congress of Third World Economics. Algiers, January.

Braverman, Harry (1974) *Labor and Monopoly Capital. The Degradation of Work in the Twentieth Century.* New York: Monthly Review Press.

Briones, Alvaro (1975a) "El neofascismo en América Latina" *Problemas del Desarrollo,* México, D. F., No. 23.

——— (1975b) "Neofascismo y nacionalismo en América Latina" *Comercio Exterior,* México, D. F., Julio.

——— (1976) "América Latina: crisis enconómica y fascismo dependiente" *Comercio Exterior,* México, D. F., Agosto.

Buira, Ariel (1977) "Diálogo Norte-Sur: final del juego" *Comercio Exterior,* México, D. F. v. 27, No. 9, September.

Buring, P. (1977) "Food Production Potential of the World" *World Development,* Oxford, v. 5, Nos. 5–7, May–July.

Burns, Arthur F. (1977) "The Need for Order in International Finance" *Columbia Journal of World Business,* New York, v. XII, No. 1, Spring.

Busch (Klaus), Schöller und Seelov (1971) *Weltmarkt und Weltwährungskrise.* Bremen: Margret Kuhlman für Gruppe Arbeiterpolitik.

Buxedas, Martin (1977) "El comercio internacional de carne vacuna y las exportaciones de los países atrasados" *Comercio Exterior,* México, D. F., v. 27, No. 12, Diciembre.

Campbell, H. (1977) The Commandist State in Uganda. University of Sussex, England. Political Studies Research in Progress Seminar Paper, April.

Cardoso, Fernando Henrique (n.d.) O"modelo brasileiro" de desenvolvimento: dados e perspectivas. (Uma interpretaçao socioeconómica.) Mimeo.

Carlo, Antonio (1975) "Die strukturellen Ursachen der Sowietischen Koexistenzpolitik" in *Sozioökonomische Bedingungen der Sowietischen Aussenpolitik,* Jahn, Egbert, ed. Frankfurt: Campus Verlag.

Carrillo, Santiago (1977) *"Eurocomunismo" y estado.* Barcelona: Editorial Crítica.

Castells, Manuel (1976) *La crise économique et la société américaine.* Paris: Presses Universitaires de France.

Chenery, Hollis et al. (1974) *Redistribution with Growth.* London.

Chile-America (1977) "Améica Latina bajo la hegemonia militar" Seminario de Bolonia. *Chile-América,* Nos. 33–34, Julio-Agosto.

Chomsky, Noam (1974) *Peace in the Middle East? Reflections on Justice and Nationhood.* New York: Vintage Books.

Chossudowsky, Michael (1975) "The Neo-Liberal Model and the Mechanisms of Economic Repression. The Chilean Case." London: Coexistence.

——— (1976) La recesión económica argentina. Julio. Mimeo.

——— (1977) "Legitimised Violence and Economic Policy in Argentina"

Cahier de Recherche, Ottawa, Dept. of Economics, University of Otawa, No. 7613. Mimeo. Published in *Economic and Political Weekly,* Bombay, April 16, 1977.

Chubin, Shahram (1976) Implications of the Military Build-Up in Non-Industrial States: The Case of Iran. May. Mimeo.

CIAL (1976) La militarización del estado en América Latina. Paris, Centro de Información América Latina, No. 1. Mimeo.

Clairmont, Edmond de (1975) "Dialogue ou Confrontation Nord-Sud? *Le Monde Diplomatique,* Paris, December.

Clairmonte, Frederick F. (1975) "Dynamics of International Exploitation" *Economic and Political Weekly,* Bombay, August 29.

Claudin, Fernando (1970) *La crisis del movimiento communista. v. 1 De la Komintern al Kominform.* Paris: Ediciones Ruedo Ibérico.

——— (1977) *Eurocomunismo y socialismo.* Madrid: Siglo XXI.

Cleaver, Harry (1976) "The Political Economy of Malaria de-Control" *Economic and Political Weekly,* Bombay, September 4.

——— (1977) "Malaria and the Political Economy of Public Health" *International Journal of Health Services,* Farmingdale, New York, v. 7, No. 4.

Cleveland, Harold van B. and Brittain, W. H. Bruce (1977) "Are the LDCs in over their Heads?" *Foreign Affairs,* Lancaster, Penn., v. 55, No. 4, July.

Collins, Joseph D. (1971) "The World Bank and the 'Small Farmer' in Guatemala" *Notes du G.E.R.E.I.,* Paris, Institut National de Recherches Agronomiques, No. 3.

Comblin, Joseph (1976) "La doctrina de la seguridad nacional" *Informativo,* Paris, Centre Ecumenique de Liasons Internationales, No. 23, Julio.

Comité Brésil pour l'Amnistie (n.d.) Bresil Dossiers, Paris, v. 1.

COMITEXTIL (n.d.) The European Textile and Clothing Industries and the International Division of Labour. Bruxelles, Comité de Coordination des Industries Textiles (1977). Mimeo.

Committee for Freedom in India (n.d.) *Democracy or Dictatorship in India?* A Handbook of Facts Documents Analysis. Chicago.

Córdova, Arnaldo (1977) "Los orígenes del Estado en América Latina" *Cuadernos Políticos,* México, D. F., No. 14, October–December.

CPI-ML (n.d.) Soviet Social Imperialism in India. A CPI-ML Publication. Reproduced by IPANA, Wesmount, Quebec, Indian People's Association in North America (1976).

CSE (1976) The Labour Process and Class Strategies, Pamphlet No. 1. London, Conference of Socialist Economist.

Dandekar, V. M. and Rath, Nilakantha (1971) "Poverty in India" *Economic and Political Weekly,* Bombay, January 2 and 9.

De, Sankar (1975) "Foreign Aid and the Communist Bloc" *Economic and Political Weekly,* Bombay, December 13.

Declaration by the Socialist Countries . . . at the Third Session of the United

Nations Conference on Trade and Development (1972) UNCTAD, TD/154, 25 April.

Del Monte, Matías (1977) El caso venezolano: reflexiones sobre una nueva variante de militarización en un país latinoamericano. Mimeo.

Demac, Donna and Mattera, Philp (1977) "Developing and Underdeveloping New York: the 'Fiscal Crisis' and the Imposition of Austerity" *Zerowork*, Political Materials, New York, No. 2.

Denison, Edward F. (1979) "Explanations of Declining Productivity Growth," *Survey of Current Business,* vol. 59, no. 8, part II.

Devron, Jean-Jacques (1976) Dévéloppement rural et technologies alternatives dans la strategie de la Banque Mondiale. Paris, Institut National de la Recherche Agronomique. Mimeo.

Diwan, Romesh (1977) "Projections of World Food Demand for and Supply of Foodgrains: An Attempt at Methodological Evaluation" *World Development,* Oxford, v. 5, Nos. 5–7, May–July.

Domhoff, G. William (1967) *Who Rules America?* Englewood Cliffs, N.J.: Prentice-Hall.

Dos Santos, Theotonio (1975) Imperialismo y dependencia. Ensayos sobre la crisis actual del capitalismo. México, Ms. 3vs. Published as Dos Santos 1978.

—— (1977a) "Socialism and Fascism in Latin America Today" *The Insurgent Sociologist,* Eugene, Ore. USA, v. VII, no. 4, Fall.

—— (1977b) "La crisis del milagro brasileño" *Comercio Exterior,* México, D. F., v. 27, No. 1.

—— (1978) *Imperialismo y dependencia.* México, D. F.,Ediciones Era.

Du Boff, Richard (1977) "Unemployment in the United States" *Monthly Review,* New York, v. 29, No. 6, November.

Echeverría, José (1977) "Fascismo y colonialismo en el caso chileno" *Chile-América,* Roma, Nos. 33–34, Julio–Agosto.

Edwards, Richard C. (1975) "The Impact of Industrial Concentration on Inflation and the Economic Crisis" in *Radical Perspectives on Economic Crisis of Monopoly Capitalism,* by URPE/PEA. New York: Union for Radical Political Economics.

Ehrensaft, Philip (1976) "Polarized Accumulation and the Theory of Economic Dependence: The Implications of South African Semi-Industrial Capitalism" in Peter C. W. Gukind and Immanuel Wallerstein, eds., *The Political Economy of Contemporary Africa,* Beverly Hills, London: Sage Publications.

Ellman, Michael (1975) "Did the Agricultural Surplus Provide the Resources for the Increase in Investment in the USSR during the First Five Year Plan? *The Economic Journal,* Cambridge, Eng., December.

Epstein, Edward C. (1975) "Politicization and Income Redistribution in Argentina: The Case of the Peronist Worker" *Economic Development and Cultural Change,* Chicago, v. 23, No. 4, July.

Erb, Guy F. (1975) "The Developing World's 'Challenge' in Perspective" in Guy F. Erb and Valerina Kalbab, eds., *Beyond Dependency. The Developing World Speaks Out.* New York: Overseas Development Council.

Erdman, Paul E. *(1977) The Crash of '79.* New York: Pocket Books.

Evers, Tilman (1975) Subdesarrollo y estado. Elementos de una teoría del estado en el capitalismo periférico. Berlin, Instituto Latinoamericano de la Universidad Libre de Berlin. (Ponencia para el coloquio sobre "Procesos de Urbanización en el capitalismo desarrollado y subdesarrollado" 29 September, 2 October 1975. Giessen, Alemania Federal) Mimeo.

Eyer, Joseph and Sterling, Peter (1977) "Stress-Related Mortality and Social Organization" *The Review of Radical Political Economics,* New York, URPE, v. 9, No. 1, Spring.

Faire, Alexandre et Sebord, Jean-Paul (1973) *Le nouveau déséquilibre mondial. Une prospective des rapports internationaux.* Paris, Bernard Grasset.

FAO (1974) "Population, Food Supply and Agricultural Development" Chapter 3 in *The State of Food and Agriculture 1974.* Rome, Food and Agricultural Organisation, also prepared for and incorporated in United Nations World Food Conference. Assessment of the World Food Situation. Present and Future. E/Conf. 65/3.

Farer, Tom J. (1975) "The United States and the Third World: A Basis for Accommodation" *Foreign Affairs,* Lancaster, Penn., October.

Feder, Ernest (1973–74) "Six Plausible Theses about the Peasants' Perspectives in the Developing World" *Development and Change,* The Hague, v. V, No. 2.

―――― (1974) "Notes on the New Penetration of the Agricultures of Developing Countries by Industrial Nations" *Boletin de Estudios Latinoamericanos y del Caribe,* Amsterdam, No. 16.

―――― (1976a) "Agribusiness in Underdeveloped Agricultures. Harvard Business School Myths and Reality" *Economic and Political Weekly,* Bombay, July.

―――― (1976b) "McNamaras's Little Green Revolution. World Bank Scheme for Self-Liquidation of Third World Peasantry" *Economic and Political Weekly,* Bombay, v. XI, No. 14.

―――― (1977a) Capitalism's Last-Ditch Effort to Save Underdeveloped Agricultures: International Agribusiness, The World Bank and the Rural Poor. The Hague, Institute of Social Studies. also published in *Journal of Contemporary Asia,* Stockholm, v. 7, No. 1.

―――― (1977b) "Agribusiness and the Elimination of Latin America's Rural Proletariat" *World Development,* Oxford, v. 5, Nos. 5–7, May–July.

―――― (1977c) "Regeneration and Degeneration of the Peasants. Three Divergent but not Incompatible Views about the Destruction of the Countryside." Published in Spanish as "Campesinistas y descampesinistas" *Comercio Exterior,* México, Diciembre.

—— (n.d.a) The New Penetration of the Agricultures of the Underdeveloped Countries by the Industrial Nations and their Multinational Concerns. Den Haag, Institute of Social Studies and Institute of Latin Ameican Studies, Glasgow, Occasional Paper No. 19, 1975.

—— (n.d.b) Strawberry Imperialism. An Enquiry into the Mechanisms of Dependency in Mexican Agriculture. Den Haag, Institute of Social Studies also published in México, Editorial Campesina, 1977 (distributed in England by America Latina) in Spanish: *El imperialismo fresa. Una investigacion sobre los mecanismos de dependencia de la agricultura mexicana.* México, Editorial Campesina, 1977.

Fellner, William ed. (1979) with contributions by Denison, Kendrick, Perlaman, and others on productivity. *Contemporary Economic Problems 1979.* Washington: American Enterprise Institute for Policy Research.

Foxley, Alejandro y Arrellano, José Pablo (1977a) "El Estado y las desigualdades sociales" *Mensaje,* Santiago, Chile, No. 261, agosto.

—— (1977b) "El tamaño y el papel del Estado" *Mensaje,* Santiago, Chile, No. 262, Septiembre.

Frank, Andre Gunder (1966) "The Development of Underdevelopment" *Monthly Review,* New York, September (reprinted in Frank 1969, chapter 1 and elsewhere).

—— (1967) *Capitalism and Underdevelopment in Latin America.* New York: Monthly Review Press, 1967, 1969. London: Penguin, 1971.

—— (1969) *Latin America: Underdevelopment or Revolution.* New York: Monthly Review Press.

—— (1972a) *Lumpenbourgeoisie and Lumpendevelopment. Dependency, Class and Politics in Latin America.* New York: Monthly Review Press.

—— (1972b) "La política ecónomica en Chile: del Frente Popular a la Unidad Popular. *Punto Final,* Santiago, sup. del No. 153, 14 Marzo.

—— (1973) "Reflections on Green, Red and White Revolution in India" *Economic and Political Weekly,* Bombay, January 20.

—— (1974) *Carta abierta en el aniversario del Golpe Chileno.* Madrid, Alberto Corazon Editor, Serie Communicación B No. 40 (incorporating Frank 1972b).

—— (1976a) *Economic Genocide in Chile. Monetarist Theory versus Humanity.* Nottingham, Spokesman Books, Spanish edition, Madrid: Ediciones Zero, 1976.

—— (1976b) "Economic Crisis, Third World and 1984" *World Development,* Oxford, v. 4, Nos. 10–11.

—— (1977a) "On So-called Primitive Accumulation" *Dialectical Anthropology,* Amsterdam, No. 2.

—— (1977b) "Emergence of Permanent Emergency in India" *Economic and Political Weekly,* Bombay, v. XII, No. 11, March 12.

—— (1977c) *Reflexiones sobre la crisis económica.* Barcelona, Anagrama, also published as *Reflexions sur la nouvelle crise economique mondiale*. Paris: Maspero, 1978 (incorporating Frank 1976b and 1977d). English ed.: *Reflections on the New World Economic Crisis*. New York: Monthly Review Press, 1980.

—— (1977d) "World Crisis and Underdevelopment" *Contemporary Crisis*, Amsterdam, No. 1.

——(1978a) *World Accumulation 1492–1789*. London: Macmillan and New York: Monthly Review Press.

—— (1978b) *Dependent Accumulation and Underdevelopment*. New York: Monthly Review Press and London: Macmillan.

—— (1978c) "Mainstream Economists as Astrologers: Gazing through the Clouded Crystal Ball" *U.S. Capitalism in Crisis*, New York: Union for Radical Political Economics.

—— (1978d) "The Economics of Crisis and the Crisis of Economics." *Critique*, Glasgow, No. 9 (incorporating Frank 1978c) in Spanish *Cuadernos Políticos*, México, No. 12, April–June 1977, and *Zona Abierta*, Madrid, No. 13, 1977.

—— (1978e) "Equating Economic Forecasting with Astrology is an Insult to Astrologers." *Der Gewerkschafter*, Frankfurt, v. 26, No. 1976, *Transicion*, Barcelona, vol. 1, no. 1, October. University of East Anglia School of Development Studies, Discussion Paper no. 52, mimeo. *Contemporary Crises*, vol. 4, no. 1, Jan. 1980.

—— (1978f) "Is a Left Eurocommuism Possible?—A Review of Claudin" *New Left Review*, London (original published as "Es posible un Eurocomunismo de izquierdas?" *Cuadernos para el Diálogo*, Madrid, 21 Enero 1978). Also in *Kritik*, Berlin, v. 6, no. 17.

Frei Montalva, Eduardo (1976) "El mandato de la historia y las exigencias del porvenir" *Chile-America*, Roma, Nos. 14–15, Enero–Febrero.

Freyhold, Michaela von (1977) "The Post-Colonial State and its Tanzanian Version" *Review of African Political Economy*, London, No. 8, January–April.

Fröbel, Folker; Heinrichs, Jurgen and Kreye, Otto (1976) "Tendency towards a New International Division of Labour. Worldwide Utilisation of Labour Force for World Market Oriented Manufacturing" *Economic and Political Weekly*, Bombay, Annual Number, February.

—— (1977) *Die neue internationale Arbeitsteilung. Strukturelle Arbeitslosigkeit in den Industrieländern und die Industriealisierung der Entwicklungsländer*. Hamburg, Rowohlt. A few citations of quotations, whose pagination here is preceded by roman numerals, were taken over from these authors' original manuscript and were not included by them in the final published book. Wherever possible, their quotations from English language sources were used in the English original generously supplied by the authors. English ed.: *The New International Division of Labour*, Cambridge University Press, 1980.

Galtung, Johan (1975) Self-Reliance and Global Interdependence. Some

Reflections on the 'New International Economic Order.' Society for International Development, European Regional Conference, Linz, Austria, Conf. Doc. No. 12-e.

Gandhi, Ved P. (1974) "India's Self-inflicted Defence Burden" *Economic and Political Weekly*. Bombay, August 31.

GATT (1972) *El comercio internacional en 1971.* Geneva, General Agreement on Tariffs and Trade.

—— (1976) *International Trade 1975/76.* Geneva, General Agreement on Tariffs and Trade.

—— (1977) Prospects for International Trade. Main Conclusions of GATT Study for 1976–77 Published. Geneva, General Agreement on Tariffs and Trade. Press Release GATT 1196, 7 September.

—— (1979a) "The Outlook for International Trade and the Management of Interdependence." Speech by Olivier Long, GATT director general. GATT Press release 21 June.

—— (1979b) Prospects for International Trade. Main Conclusions of GATT Study for 1978–79 Published. Geneva, General Agreement on Tariffs and Trade. GATT Press Release 4 September.

George, Susan (1976) *How the Other Half Dies. The Real Reasons for World Hunger.* Harmondsworth, England: Penguin Books.

Ghai, Dharam (1975) The Unemployment Crisis in the Third World. Society for International Development European Regional Conference, Linz, Austria, Conference Doc. 14-e.

Glyn, Andrew (n.d) "Capitalist Crisis: Alternative Strategy: Socialist Plan," Oxford, mimeo (1977), published in revised form as *Capitalist Crisis: Tribune's "Alternative Strategy" or Socialist Plan,* London: Militant, 1979.

—— and Sutcliffe, Bob (1972) *British Capitalism, Workers and the Profits Squeeze.* Harmondsworth, England: Penguin Books.

Gordon, David M. (1975) "Capital v. Labor: The Current Crisis in the Sphere of Production" in *Radical Perspectives on the Economic Crisis of Monopoly Capitalism,* by URPE/PEA. New York: The Union for Radical Political Economics.

—— (1978) "Up and Down the Long Roller Coaster" in *U.S. Capitalism in Crisis,* by URPE. New York: The Union for Radical Political Economics.

—— (1980) "Stages of Accumulation and Long Economic Cycles" in T. K. Hopkins and I. Wallerstein, eds., *Processes in the World-System,* Beverly Hills, Calif.: Sage Publications.

Griffin, Keith (1972) The Green Revolution: An Economic Analysis. Geneva, United Nations Research Institute for Social Development.

—— and Azizur Rahman Khan, eds. (1976) Poverty in Asia. Geneva, ILO, Mimeo.

Guerrero, Hernán y Varela, Andrés (1977) "Y después de Pinochet, que?" *Comercio Exterior*, México, D. F., v. 27, No. 10, October.

Guevara, Roberto (1977a) Nuevas formas de militarismo en América Latina. Belgrado, Semana Latinoamericana, 7–14 de Noviembre. Mimeo.

—— (1977b) "El partido militar en América Latina" *Chile-América,* Roma, Nos. 33–34, Julio–Agosto.

Gustafsson, Mervi (1977) Food Aid in International Relations: The Case of the United States. Tampere, Finland, Peace Research Institute, Research Report No. 14.

Halperin Donghi, Tulio (1969) *Historia Contemporánea de América Latina.* Madrid: Alianza Editorial.

—— (1972) *Hispanoamérica después de la Independencia. Consecuencias sociales y económicas de la emancipación.* Buenos Aires: Ed. Paidós.

Haq, Mahbub ul (1976) *The Poverty Curtain: Choices for the Third World.* New York: Columbia University Press.

Harrington, Michael (1977) *The Vast Majority: A Journey to the World's Poor.* New York: Simon and Schuster.

Harrison, John (1974) "British Capitalism in 1973 and 1974: The Deepening Crisis," *CSE Bulletin,* Spring.

Hayes, Carlton J. H. (1941) *A Generation of Materialism 1871–1900.* New York: Harper & Brothers.

Helleiner, G. K. (1976) "Transnational Enterprises, Manufactured Exports and Employment in Less Developed Countries" *Economic and Political Weekly,* Bombay, Annual Number, February.

Heller, Walter W. (1975) "What's Right with Economics?" Presidential Address delivered to the American Economic Association, December 29, 1974. *American Economic Review,* Menasha, Wis., March.

Hewett, Edward A. (1975) "The Economics of East European Technology Imports from the West" *American Economic Review,* Menasha, Wis., May.

Hewitt de Alcatara, Cynthia (1976) Modernizing Mexican Agriculture: Socioeconomic Implications of Technological Change 1940–1970. Geneva, United Nations Research Institute for Social Development.

Heyman, Hans (1973) "La economía soviética. Problemas de la productividad de la economía soviética" (Translation from the English original in) *El Mercurio,* Santiago, 24 Abril.

Heyne, H. (1976) "Neue Weltwirtschaftordunung—Veränderung für die Dritte Welt?" *Blätter des Iz3w,* Freiburg, Germany, No. 54, June.

Hinkelammert, Franz (1970) "Teoría de la dialéctica del desarrollo desigual" *Cuadernos de la Realidad Nacional,* Santiago, CEREN, No. 6 especial, Diciembre.

Holloway, John and Picciotto, Sol (1977) "Capital, Crisis and the State" *Capital and Class,* London, No. 2, Summer.

Hong Kong Research Project (1974) *Hong Kong: A Case to Answer.* Nottingham: Spokesman Books.

Hopper, David (1976) "The Development of Agriculture in Developing Countries. It Needs Additional Technology and Capital from the Development Countries" *Scientific American,* New York, v. 235, No. 3, September.

Hudson, Michael (1972) *Super Imperialism. The Economic Strategy of American Empire.* New York: Holt, Reinhart and Winston.

—— (1977) *Global Fracture. The New International Economic Order.* New York: Harper and Row.

Hveem, Helge (1975) The Political Economy of Raw Materials and the Conditions for their OPECization. Oslo, International Peace Research Institute, March. Mimeo.

—— (1976) The Political Economy of Producer Associations. Oslo: International Peace Research Institute. Mimeo.

IBGE *Annuario Estadistico.* Rio de Janeiro, Instituto de Geografía e Estadistica.

IHT (1977) "The Euromarket" *International Herald Tribune,* Zurich, December Part I.

ILO (1975) *1975 Year Book of Labour Statistics.* Geneva: International Labour Office.

—— (1976) *Employment, Growth and Basic Needs: A One World Problem.* Report of the Director General of the International Labour Office to the Tripartite World Conference on Employment, Income Distribution and Social Progress and the International Division of Labour. Geneva: International Labour Office.

IMF (1977) "La deuda externa de 75 países en desarrollo no petroleros aumentó notablemente en 1976" *Boletin del FMI—Bulletin IMF,* v. 6, No. 17, Washington, September in *Comercio Exterior,* México, D. F. December.

"Les intellectuels communistes dans la tormente" (1978) *Les Nouvelles Littéraires,* Paris, No. 2639, 15 Juin.

Ivanov, Ivan (1975) Tripartite Industrial Co-operation: Recent Situation, Problems and Prospects. Discussion Paper. Geneva, UNCTAD, TAD/SEM.1/7, 12 November.

Jacoby, Erich H. (1975) "Transnational Corporations and Third World Agriculture" *Development and Change,* The Hague, v. 6, No. 3, July.

—— (n.d.) Agri-Business and the United Nations System. Stockholm: University of Stockholm.

Jahn, Egbert (1975) *Sozioökonomische Bedingungen der sowjetischen Aussenpolitik.* Frankfurt: Campus Verlag.

Jolly, Richard; Kadt, Emmanuel de; Singer, Hans and Wilson, Fiona, eds. (1973) *Third World Employment. Problems and Strategy.* Harmondsworth: Penguin Books.

Kaiserlich Iranischer Botschafter (1976) *Iran Wirtschaftsdaten und Investitionsmöglichkeiten.* Bonn.

Kaldor, Mary (1976) "The Arms Trade and Society" *Economic and Political Weekly,* Bombay, Annual Number, February.

Kaplan, Marcos (1969) *Formación del estado nacional en América Latina.* Santiago: Editorial Universitaria.

Kende, István (1973) *Guerres Locales en Asie, en Afrique et en Amerique Latine (1945–1969).* Budapest, Centre pour la Recherche de l'Afro-Asie de l'Academie des Sciences de Hongrie.

Kennedy, Paul (1977) "Indigenous Capitalism in Ghana" *Review of African Political Economy,* London, No. 8, January–April.

Kim, Chang Soo (1977) "Marginalization, Development and the Korean Workers' Movement", *AMPO,* Tokyo, vol. 9, no. 3.

Kindleberger, Charles P. (n.d.) *Manias, Bubbles, Panics and Crashes and the Lenders of Last Resort.* Cambridge, Mass.: M.I.T. Mimeo.

Kissinger, Henry A. (1975) *The Kissinger Study of Southern Africa.* Nottingham, U.K.: Spokesman Books.

—— (1976) "UNCTAD IV: Expanding Cooperation for Global Economic Development" Address by Secretary Kissinger. *Department of State Bulletin,* Washington, No. 1927, May 31.

Klein, Dieter (1976) "Politökonomische Aspekte des Kampfes zwischen Sozialismus und Kapitalismus" *IPW Berichte,* Berlin, DDR, No. 3.

Kolko, Gabriel (1968) *The Politics of War. The World and United States Foreign Policy, 1943–1945.* New York: Random House Vintage Books.

Kolko, Joyce (1974) *America and the Crisis of World Capitalism.* Boston: Beacon Press.

Kondratieff, Nikolai D. (1935) "The Long Waves in Economic Life" *The Review of Economic Statistics,* Cambridge, USA. Reprinted in The American Economic Association, *Readings in Business Cycle Theory.* Philadelphia, 1944.

Kowarick, Lucio (n.d.) The Logic of Disorder in Capitalist Expansion in the Metropolitan Area of Greater São Paulo: São Paulo, CEBRAP, University of São Paulo. Mimeo.

Krishnappa, S. (1973) "Politics of Defence" *Economic and Political Weekly,* Bombay, March 10.

Labrousse, C. E. (1932) *Esquisse du mouvement des prix et des revenues en France au XVIIIe siècle,* Paris Lib. Dalloz, 2 vols.

Lacharriere, Guy de (1975) The Role of East-West Co-operation in the Development of Tripartite Co-operation. Paper prepared by Mr. Guy de Lacharriere, Consultant. Geneva, UNCTAD TAD/SEM.1/16, 18 November.

Laclau, Ernesto (1977) *Politics and Ideology in Marxist Theory. Capitalism, Fascism, Populism.* London: New Left Books.

Ladejinsky, Wolf (1973) "How Green Is the Indian Green Revolution?" *Economic and Political Weekly,* Bombay, December.

Langdon, Steve (1977) "Debate: The State and Capitalism in Kenya" *Review of African Political Economy,* London, No. 8, January–April.

Lavigne, Marie (1973) *Le programme du Comecon et l'intégration socialiste.* Paris: Editions Cujas.

Legassick, M. (1974) "South Africa: Capital Accumulation and Violence" *Economy and Society,* London, v. 3, No. 3.

Leitenberg, Milton (1977) A Survey of Studies of Post W.W. II Wars, Conflicts and Military Coups. Ithaca, Cornell University Center for International Studies. Peace Studies Program. Mimeo.

Leontief, Wassily et al. (1977) *The Future of the World Economy. A United Nations Study.* New York: Oxford University Press.

Leys, Colin (1976) "The 'Overdeveloped' Post Colonial State: A Re-evaluation" *Review of African Political Economy,* London, No. 5, January–April.

Lietaer, Bernard A. (1978) "El próximo conflicto Norte-Sur" *Comercio Exterior,* México, D. F., v. 28, No. 3, Marzo.

Lock, Peter and Wulf, Herbert (1977) Register of Arms Production in Developing Countries. Hamburg, Arbeitsgruppe Rüstung und Unterentwicklung. Mimeo.

Lockwood, Lawrence (1973) "Israeli Subimperialism?" *Monthly Review,* New York, v. 24, No. 8, January.

Long, Olivier (1977) "The Protectionist Threat to World Trade Relations" *Intereconomics,* Hamburg, No. 11–12.

Lowy, Michael and Sader, Eder (1977) "La militarización del Estado en América Latina" *Cuadernos Políticos,* México, No. 13, Julio–Septiembre.

Luckham, Robin (1977) "Militarism: Arms and the Internationalisation of Capital" *IDS Bulletin,* Sussex, England, v. 8, No. 2, March.

Lund (1978) Letter on Science, Technology and Basic Human Needs, December.

——— (1979) Letter on Science, Technology and Basic Human Needs, March.

McCracken, Paul (1977) *Towards Full Employment and Price Stability.* Summary of a report to the OECD by a group of independent experts. Paris: OECD.

——— et al. (1977) *Towards Full Employment and Price Stability.* Summary to the OECD by a group of independent experts. Paris: OECD.

MacEwan, Arthur (1975) "Changes in World Capitalism and the Current Crisis of the U.S. Economy" in *Radical Perspectives on the Economic Crisis of Monopoly Capitalism.* New York: Union of Radical Political Economics.

MacKay, Donald, ed. (1977) *Scotland 1980 the Economics of Self-Government.* Edinburgh: Q Press.

McNamara, Robert S. (1973) Address to the Board of Governors World Bank Group. Nairobi, September.

——— (1974) Address to the Board of Governors World Bank Group. Washington, D.C., September 30.

——— (1977) Address to the Board of Governors, World Bank Group. Washington, D.C., September 28.

Magdoff, Harry (1969) *The Age of Imperialism. The Economics of U.S. Foreign Policy.* New York: Monthly Review Press.

Mamdani, Mahmood (1976) *Politics and Class Formation in Uganda.* New York: Monthly Review Press.

Mandel, Ernest (1975a) *Late Capitalism.* London: New Left Books.

―――― (1975b) "Prospects for the International Capitalist Economy" *Intercontinental Press,* New York, July 7.

―――― (1975c) "Folgen der Weltwirtschaftkrise auf die Entwicklung der Arbeiterkämpfe im EG-Bereich" Ein Interview mit Ernst Mandel von Adelbert Reif. *Monthly Review,* Deutsche Ausgabe, Frankfurt, v. 1, No. 5, Oktober.

―――― (1978) *Crítica del eurocomunismo.* Barcelona, Editorial Fontanara. *Critique of Eurocommunism.* London: New Left Books.

Mansour, Fawzy (1977) Third World Revolt and Self-Reliant Auto-Centered Strategy of Development (A Draft). Dakar, United Nations African Institute for Economic Development and Planning, Reproduction 406.

Marchais, Georges (1973) *Le défi démocratique.* Paris: Bernard Grasset.

Marini, Ruy Mauro (1973) *Dialéctica de la dependencia.* México: Ediciones Era.

―――― (1974) *Subdesarrollo y revolución.* Ed. Rev. México: D. F. Siglo XXI.

―――― (1977a) "La acumulación capitalista mundial y el subimperialismo" *Cuadernos Políticos,* México, D. F., No. 12, Abril–Junio.

―――― (1977b) "Estado y crisis en Brasil" *Cuadernos Políticos,* México, No. 13, Julio–Septiembre.

―――― y Pellicer de Brody, Olga (1967–1968) "Militarismo y desnuclearización en América Latina" *Foro Internacional,* México, El Colegio de México, v. VIII, No. 1.

Marx, Karl (n.d.) *Capital.* Moscow: Foreign Languages Publishing House. 3 v.

Mato, Daniel (1977) "La deuda externa de América Latina" *Comercio Exterior,* México, v. 27, No. 11, November.

Meadows, Donelle and Dennis (1972) *The Limits to Growth.* New York: Universe Books

Meillassoux, Claude (1975) *Femmes, greniers et capitaux.* Paris: François Maspero.

Melman, Seymour (1974) *The Permanent War Economy: American Capitalism in Decline.* New York: Simon and Schuster.

MERIP (1977) "Labor Migration in the Middle East" *MERIP Reports,* Washington, No. 59, August.

Mesarovic, M. and Pestel, E. (1974) *Mankind at the Turning Point.* New York: Dutton.

Metra Consulting Group (n.d.) *Iran: A Business Opportunity.* London: Financial Times Limited.

—— (1977b) "La Conferencia de Paris: un final esperado" *Comercio Exterior,* México, Septiembre.

Meyer, Herbert E. (1974) "A Plant that Could Change the Shape of Soviet Industry" *Fortune,* Chicago, November.

Michalet, Charles-Albert (1976) The Multinational Companies and the New International Division of Labour. Geneva, ILO World Employment Programme Research Working Papers, WEP 2–28, WP 5, November.

Miliband, Ralph (1969, 1973) *The State in Capitalist Society. The Analysis of the Western System of Power.* London: Quarter Books.

Mills, C. Wright (1956) *The Power Elite.* New York: Oxford University Press.

Mishra, H. K. N. (1974) "Progress of Industrial Sector in the Fourth Plan 1969–74" *Economic and Political Weekly,* Bombay, June 8.

Moran, Theodore H. (1971–72) "New Deal or Raw Deal in Raw Materials" *Foreign Policy,* Winter.

—— (1973) Transnational Strategies of Protection and Defense by Multinational Corporations: Spreading the Risk and Raising the Cost for Nationalization in Natural Resources. *International Organization,* Madison. v. 27, no. 2, Spring.

Morris, Jacob (1975) "The Weird World of International Money" *Monthly Review,* New York, v. 27, No. 6, November.

Münster, Anne Marie (1977) Der Ubergang von der Elektromechanik zur Elektronik und die damit verbundenen Verwertungsmöglichkeiten im Rahmen transnationaler Produktion. Starnberg. Mimeo.

Murray, Robert (1975) *Multinational Companies and Nation States. Two Essays.* Nottingham: Spokesman Books.

NACLA (1975a) "The Food Weapon-Mightier than Missiles" *Latin America and Empire Report,* New York, v. IX, No. 7, October.

—— (1975b) "US Grain Arsenal" *Latin American and Empire Report,* New York, v. IX, No. 7, October.

—— (1976) "Merchants of Repression: U.S. Police Exports to the Third World," *NACLA Latin America and Empire Report,* vol. X, no. 6, July–August.

—— (1977) "Electronics: The Global Industry" *Latin America and Empire Report,* v. XI, No. 4, April.

—— (1978a) "Agribusiness Targets in Latin America" *NACLA Report on the Americas,* New York, v. XII, No. 1, January–February.

—— (1978b) *Report on the Americas* (1978b) v. XII, No. 2, March–April.

Nairn, Tom (1977) *The Break-Up of Britain. Crisis and Neo-Nationalism.* London: New Left Books.

Navarrete, Jorge Eduardo (1977a) El diálogo Norte-Sur. Una búsqueda negociada del nuevo orden económico internacional" *Nueva Política,* México, v. 1, No. 4, Octubre–Marzo.

—— (1978) *Iran: A Business Opportunity for the 1980s.* London: Metra Consulting Group Limited.

Nayyar, Deepak (1975a) The Impact of Transnatinal Operations on Exports of Manufactures from Developing Countries. A study prepared for the UNCTAD Secretariat, August.

—— (1975b) Socialist Countries and the Third World. Towards a Political Economy of the Relationship. Paper presented at a conference on New Approaches to Trade. Sussex, England, Institute of Development Studies, September. Mimeo.

—— Ed. (1975c) "Special Issue on Economic Relations between the Socialist Countries and the Third World" *World Development*, Oxford, v. 3, No. 5, May.

—— (1976a) Transnational Corporations and Manufactured Exports from Poor Countries. Sussex, England, University of Sussex, Economics Seminar, Paper Series 76/17.

—— (1976b) "India's Export Performance in the 1970s" *Economic and Political Weekly*, Bombay, May 15.

Nehru, Jawaharlal (1960) *The Discovery of India*. New York: Doubleday Anchor.

Nordhaus, William (1974) "The Falling Share of Profits" in A. Okun and L. Perry, eds., *Brookings Papers on Economic Activity* no.1.

Oberg, Jan (1976) "Towards a New Military World Order. A Sceptic Contribution to the Discussion of a New Economic World Order." Lund, Department of Peace and Conflict.

—— (1977) "The New International Economic and Military Orders as Problems of Peace Research", *Bulletin of Peace Research Proposals*, vol. 8, no. 2.

O'Connor, James (1972a) *The Fiscal Crisis of the State*. New York: St. Martin's Press.

—— (1972b) "Inflation, Fiscal Crisis, and the American Working Class" *Socialist Revolution*, San Francisco, No. 8, March–April.

OECD (1976a) *Collective Bargaining and Inflation: New Relations Between Government, Labour and Management*. Final Report on an Internatinal Management Seminar Convened by the OECD. Paris: Organisation for Economic Co-Operation and Development.

—— (1976b) *Study of Trends in World Supply and Demand in Major Agricultural Commodities*. Paris: Organisation of Economic Co-Operation and Development.

—— (1979) *Economic Surveys, United States*. Paris: Organisation of Economic Co-operation and Development, November.

Oliveira, Francisco (1973) "La economía brasileña: crítica a la razón dualista" *El Trimestre Económico*, México, D. F., v. XL (2), No. 158.

Osorio Urbina, Jaime (1975) "Superexplotación y clase obrera: el caso mexicano" *Cuadernos Políticos*, México, D. F. No. 6, Octubre.

Owen, Henry and Schultze, Charles L. eds. (1976) *Setting National Priorities: The Next Ten Years*. Washington: The Brookings Institution.

Pajestka, Josef and Kulig, Jan (1979) The socialist countries of Eastern

Europe and the New International Economic Order. Trade and Development, An UNCTAD Review. Geneva, no. 1, Spring.

Parvus et al. (1972) *Die langen Wellen der Konjunktur Beitrage zur Marxistischen Konjunktur- und Krisentheorie,* von Parvus, Karl Kautsky, Leo Trotzki, N. D. Kondratieff und Ernst Mandel. Berlin: Prinkipo.

Paul, Samuel (1974) "Growth and Utilisation of Industrial Capacity" *Economic and Political Weekly,* Bombay, December 7.

Payer, Cheryl (1976a) "Third World Debt Problems: The New Wave of Defaults" *Monthly Review,* New York, v. 28, No. 4, September.

—— (1976b) "Third World Loans Might Make our Banks Beggars" *Business and Society Review,* New York, No. 20, Winter.

Pérez Guerrero, Manuel (1977) "Un nuevo orden económico internacional" *Nueva Política,* México, v. 1, No. 4, Octubre–Marzo.

Petzoldt, Volker, (1976) "Consideraciones sobre el estado militar en América Latina" *Actualidades,* Caracas, v. 1, No. 1.

Piñera, Sebastian y Meller, Patricio (1977) "Pobreza, distribución del ingreso y rol del estado" *Mensaje,* Santiago, No. 263, October.

Pinochet Ugarte, Augusto (1975) Objetivo Nacional del Gobierno de Chile. Santiago, 23 de diciembre.

Pinto, Aníbal y Knakal, Jan (1973) El sistema centro-peripheria 20 años después. Santiago, Instituto Latinoamericano de Planificación Económica y Social. Mimeo.

Plaschke, Henrik (1975) "International Subcontracting: on the Migration of Labour-Intensive Processing from the Center to the Periphery of Capitalism" in *Instant Research on Peace and Violence,* v. V.

Poulantzas, Nicos (1968) *Pouvoir politique et classes sociales.* Paris, Maspero. 2 vs., in English *Political Power and Social Classes.* London, New Left Books, 1973.

PREALC (1976) (Regional Employment Program for Latin America and the Caribbean) The Employment Problem in Latin America: Facts, Outlooks and Policies. Santiago, ILO, April.

Prebisch, Raúl (1979) "Aspects of international economic co-operation: Some reflections on the vicissitudes of development." *Trade and Development, An UNCTAD Review.* Geneva, no. 1, Spring.

Radice, Hugo (1975) East West Industrial Cooperation and the Transition to Socialism. Paper prepared for a conference on New Approaches to Trade. Sussex, England, Institute of Development Studies, September. Mimeo.

Raj, K. N. (1976) "The Economic Situation" *Economic and Political Weekly,* Bombay, July 3.

Resnick, Idrian (1975) "L'état dans l'Afrique Contemporaine" in *Les inégalités entre états dans le système international: origines et perspectives,* Ed., par Immanuel Wallerstein. Quebec: Choix.

Revelle, Roger (1976) "The Resources Available for Agriculture" *Scientific American,* New York, v. 235, No. 3, September.

Review (1979) Special Issue on Cycles and Trends. *Review* vol. II, no. 4, Spring.

Rey, Pierre-Philippe (1971) *Colonialisme, néo-colonialisme et transition au capitalisme. Exemple de la "Comilog" au Congo-Brazzaville.* Paris: François Maspero.

Roberts, Dick (1977) "Imperialism and Raw Materials," *International,* London, vol. 4, no. 1, Autumn.

Rockefeller, Nelson A. (1969) *The Rockefeller Report on the Americas. The Official Report of a United States Presidential Mission for the Western Hemisphere.* Chicago: Quadrangle Books.

Rodríguez, Mario V., (1976) "Fundamento de la nueva institucionalidad (El concepto de Seguridad Nacional)" *Mensaje,* Santiago, No. 253, October.

Rosefielde, Steven (1974) "Factor Proportions and Economic Rationality in Soviet International Trade 1955–1968" *American Economic Review,* Menasha, Wis., v. LXIV, No. 4, September.

Rostow, Eugene V. (1972) *Peace in the Balance. The Future of American Foreign Policy.* New York: Simon and Schuster.

Rostow, W. W. (1978) *The World Economy: History and Prospect.* Austin, University of Texas Press.

Rudra, Ashok (1977) "The Left Front Government" *Economic and Political Weekly,* Bombay, September 3.

Ruz, Mauricio F. (1977) "Doctrina de seguridad nacional en América Latina. Contribución a un debate" *Mensaje,* Santiago, No. 261, Agosto.

Sabolo, Yves and Trajtenberg, Raúl (1976) The Impact of Transnational Enterprises on Employment in the Developing Countries. Preliminary Results. Geneva, ILO, WEP 2-28/WP 6.

Sachverständigenrat (1974) Jahresguatchten 1974, Bonn.

Sader, Emir (1977) "Fascismo y dictadura militar" *Chile-América,* Roma, No. 33–34, Julio–Agosto.

Salvi, P. G. (1971) *Comecon and the Emerging Nations.* New Delhi: Writers and Publishers Corporation.

Sarkar, N. K. (1974) Industrial Structure of Greater Bangkok. Bangkok, United Nations Asian Institute for Economic Development and Planning.

Sau, Ranjit (1973) "Growth and Fluctuation in Indian Economy" *Economic and Political Weekly,* Bombay, Special Number August.

—— (1977) "Indian Political Economy, 1967–77. Marriage of Wheat and Whisky" *Economic and Political Weekly,* Bombay, April 9.

Saul, John S. (1976) "The Unsteady State: Uganda, Obote and General Amin" *Review of African Political Economy,* London, No. 5 January–April.

Saul, S. B. (1969) *The Myth of the Great Depression, 1873–1896.* London: Macmillan.

Schertz, Lyle P. (1974) "World Food: Prices and the Poor" *Foreign Affairs,* Lancaster, Penn., April.

Schui, Herbert (1976) "Die Unternehmer haben die Krise selbst verschuldet" *Frankfurter Rundschau,* March 6.

Schumpeter, Joseph A. (1939) *Business Cycles.* New York: McGraw Hill.

Sebastian, M. (1973) "Does India Buy Dear from and Sell Cheap to the Soviet Union?" *Economic and Political Weekly,* Bombay, December 1.

Sebord, Jean-Paul (1977) *D'un deuxième monde à l'autre. Essai prospectif sur l'Europa du sud et le Monde Arabe.* Paris: Editions Anthropos.

Senghaas, Dieter (1977) *Weltwirtschaftsordunung und Entwicklungspolitik. Plädoyer für Dissoziation.* Frankfurt: Edition Suhrkamp.

Senghaas-Knobloch, Eva (1976a) "The Impact of Periphery Capitalism on Constitution and Composition of the Labour Force. Some Reflections on the New ILO Strategy for Employment and Development." Västerhaninge, Summer. Mimeo.

—— (1976b) "Weibliche Arbeitskraft und Gesellschaftliche Reproduktion" *Leviathan,* No. 4.

Sherman, Howard (1976a) "Class Conflict and Macro-Policy" *The Review of Radical Political Economics,* New York, URPE, v. 8, No. 2.

—— (1976b) "Inflation, Unemployment and Monopoly Capital" *Monthly Review,* New York, v. 27, No. 10, March.

—— (1979) "A Marxist Theory of the Business Cycle." *Review of Radical Political Economics,* vol. 11, no. 1, Spring.

Shetty, S. L. (1973) "Trends in Wages and Salaries and Profits of the Private Corporate Sector" *Economic and Political Weekly,* Bombay, October.

Shivji, Issa G. (1970) *Tanzania: The Silent Class Struggle.* Lund, Zenit Reprint.

—— (1976) *Class Struggles in Tanzania.* New York, Monthly Review Press (incorporating Shivji 1970).

Shourie, Arun (1974) "India—An Arrangement at Stake" *Economic and Political Weekly,* Bombay, June 22.

Shuman, James B. and Rosenau, David (1972) *The Kondratieff Wave.* New York: World Publishing.

Sideri, Sandro (1972) "International Trade and Economic Power" in *Toward a New World Economy.* Rotterdam: Rotterdam University Press.

—— (1973) Manuscript prepared at UN ECLA in Santiago, and no longer available for complete citation.

Simiand, F. (1932) *Les fluctuations économiques à longue période et la crise mondiale,* Paris: Alcan.

Sinha, N. P. (1976) "Malaria Eradication: What went Wrong?" *Economic and Political Weekly*, Bombay, June 26.

Sivard, Ruth Leger (1976) *World Military and Social Expenditures.* Leesburg, Virginia USA, WMSE Publications.

Smith, Adam (1973) *An Inquiry into the Nature and Causes of the Wealth of Nations,* New York: Random House (original ed., 1776).

Souza, Herbert (1975) "Las multinacionales y la superexplotación de la clase obrera en Brasil" *Problemas del Desarrollo,* México, D. F., Año IV, No. 23, Agosto–Octubre.

Stalin, Joseph (1953) *Economic Problems of Socialism in the U.S.S.R.* Moscow: Foreign Languages Publishing House.

Stewart, Frances (1979) The New International Economic Order and Basic Needs: Conflicts and Complementarities. Unpublished paper presented at the Nordic Symposium on Development Strategies in Latin America and the New International Economic Order, University of Lund Research Policy Institute, September.

Streeten, Paul P. (1979) "Basic Needs: Premises and Promises." Washington: World Bank Reprint Series Number 62. Reprinted from *Journal of Policy Modeling* 1 (1979).

Subrahamanyan, K. (1973) "Indian Defence Expenditure in Global Perspective" *Economic and Political Weekly,* Bombay, June 30.

Swainson, Nicola (1977) "The Rise of a National Bourgeoisie in Kenya" *Review of African Political Economy,* London, No. 8, January–April.

Swamy, Subramanian (n.d.) "What Is Happening in India? Democracy or Dictatorship in India" *Committee for Freedom in India* Chicago.

Sweezy, Paul M. (1953) *The Present as History.* New York: Monthly Review Press.

Terzian, Pierre (1977) "OPEC Surpluses: Myth and Reality" MERIP *Reports,* Washington, No. 57, reprinted from *Arab Oil and Gas,* Paris, March 16.

Testa, Victor (n.d.) "Aspectos Economicos de la Coyuntura Actual 1973–1975." Mimeo.

Tharakan, P. K. M. (n.d.) Multinatinal Companies and a New International Division of Labor. Brussels, European Centre for Study and Information on Multinational Corporations. Mimeo.

Ticktin, H. H. (1973) "Towards a Political Economy of the USSR" *Critique,* Glasgow, No. 1, Spring.

—— (1975) "Das Verhältnis zwischen Wirtschaftreformen und Entspannungspolitik der Sowietunion" in *Sozioökonomische Bedingungen der sowietischen Aussenpolitik,* Egbert Jahn ed. Frankfurt: Campus Verlag.

Tinbergen, Jan (1976–1977) *Reshaping the International Order* (RIO). Amsterdam: Elsevier. Citations here from the German translation: *Wir haben nur eine Zukunft. Reform der Internationalen Ordnung.* Opladen: Westdeutscher Verlag, 1977.

TNI (1974–1975) World Hunger: Causes and Remedies. Report presented to the World Food Conference, Rome. Amsterdam. Mimeo. Published in revised form in *International Journal of Health Services,* Farmingdale, New York, v. 5, No. 1, 1975.

Trajtenberg, Raúl with Jean-Paul Sajhau (1976) Transnational Enterprises and the Cheap Labour Force in Less Developed Countries. Geneva, ILO. World Employment Programme Research, Working Paper WEP 2-28/WP 15, December.

Treverton, Gregory F. (1977) "Latin America in World Politics: The Next Decade" *Adelphi Papers*, London, International Institute for Strategic Studies, No. 137.

Trilateral Commission (1975) *The Crisis of Democracy,* by Michael Crozier, Samuel P. Huntington and Joji Watanuki. Report on the Governability of Democracies to the Trilateral Commission. New York: New York University Press. Copyright © 1975 by the Trilateral Commission.

Triplett, Jr., Glover, B. and Van Doren, David M. Jr. (1977) "Agriculture without Tillage" *Scientific American,* New York, v. 236, No. 1, January.

Turnham, David (1971) *The Employment Problem in Less Developed Countries. A Review of Evidence.* Paris, Development Centre of the Organisation for Ecnomic Co-Operation and Development.

Turok, Ben and Maxey, Kees (1976) "Southern Africa: White Power in Crisis" in *The Political Economy of Contemporary Africa,* Peter C. W. Gutkind and Immanuel Wallerstein, eds. Beverly Hills, London: Sage Publications.

Udry, C. A. (1976) "A New World Order?" *Inprecor,* Bruxelles, No. 61–62, 11 November.

UNCTAD (1972a) Handbook of International Trade and Development Statistics. New York, UNCTAD TD/STAT.4. UN Sales Number E/F.72.II.D.3.

—— (1972b) Trade Relations among Countries Having Different Economic and Social Systems. Review and Analysis of Trends and Policies in Trade Between Countries having Different Economic and Social Systems. Geneva, UNCTAD TD/112, 20 January.

—— (1972c) Declaration by the socialist countries at the third session of the United Nations Conference on Trade and Development, Santiago, UNCTAD TD/154, 25 April.

—— (1974) Problems of Raw Materials and Development. Note by the Secretary-General of UNCTAD. Geneva, UNCTAD/OSG/52, 4 April.

—— (1975a) Tripartite Industrial Co-Operation. Geneva, UNCTAD TAD/SEM.1/2, 25 November.

—— (1975b) Tripartite Co-Operation Arrangements for the Transfer of Technology to Developing Countries. Geneva, UNCTAD TAD/ SEM. 1/13, 12 November.

—— (1975c) Financial Flows to and from Developing Countries. Geneva, UNCTAD TD/B/XV/Misc. 3, 3 June.

—— (1975d) The Scope of Trade-Creating Industrial Co-Operation at Enterprise Level between Countries having Different Economic and Social System. New York, UNCTAD TD/B/490/Rev. 1.

—— (1975e) Trade Relations among Countries having Different Economic and Social Systems. Review of Trends and Policies in Trade between Countries having Different Economic and Social Systems. Geneva, UNCTAD TD/B/560. 30 June.

—— (1975f) Review of the World Commodity Situation and Report of International Action on Individual Commodities. Commodity Trade: Review and Outlook. Report by the UNCTAD Secretariat. Geneva, UNCTAD TD/B/C.1/174. January.

—— (1975g) An Integrated Programme for Commodities. A Common Fund for the Financing of Commodity Stocks: Amounts, Terms and Prospective Sources of Finance. Report by the Secretary-General of UNCTAD. Geneva, UNCTAD TD/B/C.1/184. 24 June.

—— (1975h) An Integrated Programme for Commodities: The Impact on Imports, Particularly of Developing Countries. Report by the UNCTAD Secretariat. Geneva, UNCTAD TC/B/C.1/189. 13 June.

—— (1975i) Report of the Committee on Manufactures on Its Seventh Session. Geneva, UNCTAD TD/B/C.2(VII)/Misc. 3.

—— (1976a) New Directions and New Structures for Trade and Development. Report by the Secretary-General of UNCTAD to the Conference, Nairobi, TD/183.

—— (1976b) Preservation of the Purchasing Power of Developing Countries' Exports (Item 8-Supporting Paper) Geneva and Nairobi, UNCTAD TD/184/Supp. 2, May.

—— (1976c) Trade Relations among Countries having Different Economic and Social Systems. Nairobi, UNCTAD TD/193 May.

—— (1976d) International Specialization in Industrial Production and its Impact on the Expansion of Trade and Economic Relations between the Socialist Countries of Eastern Europe and the Developing Countries. Geneva, UNCTAD/TSC/24. 21 January.

—— (1977a) The Evolution of a Viable International Development Strategy. Report by the Secretary-General of UNCTAD. Geneva, TD/B/642, 30 March.

—— (1977b) Implementation of International Development Policies in the Various Areas of Competence of UNCTAD. Report by the Secretary-General of UNCTAD. Geneva, TD/B/642/Add.1. 31 March.

—— (1977c) The Recent Economic Experience of Developing Countries in Relation to United Nations Development Objectives. Report by the UNCTAD Secretariat. Geneva, TD/B/642/Add.2. 13 April.

—— (1979a) Trade relations among countries having different economic and social systems. Geneva, UNCTAD TD/243.

—— (1979b) Statistical review of trade among countries having different economic and social systems. Geneva, UNCTAD TD/243/Suppl. 1.

—— (1979c) Tripartite industrial co-operation in third countries. Geneva, UNCTAD TD/243/Suppl. 5.

—— (1979d) Restructuring the international economic framework. Report by the Secretary-General of UNCTAD to the fifth session of the Conference. Geneva, UNCTAD TD/221.

—— (1979e) Evaluation of the world trade and economic situation and consideration of issues, policies and appropriate measures to facilitate structural changes in the international economy. Geneva, UNCTAD TD/224.

—— (1979f) Evaluation of the world trade and economic situation and consideration of issues, policies and appropriate measures to facilitate structural changes in the international economy. Geneva, UNCTAD TD/224/ADD. 1.

UNDESA (1974) *1974 Report on the World Social Situation.* New York, United Nations, Department of Economic and Social Affairs. E/CN.5/521/Rev.1.ST/ESA/24.

UNECE (1974a) A Review of Commercial Policy Developments Affecting East-West Trade, 1968 to 1973. Part B of pre-publication text of the *Economic Bulletin for Europe,* Geneva, v. 25, UNECE, TRADE (XXII)/1 Add.1, n.d.

—— (1974b) *Bulletin Economique pour l'Europe,* Geneva, UNECE, v. 25.

—— (1974c) "Recent Economic Developments in Eastern Europe and the Soviet Union" Chapter 2 in *The European Economy in 1974.* Pre-publication text of the *Economic Survey of Europe 1974.* Geneva, UNECE (XXX)/1 Add.1.

—— (1975a) Recent Changes in Europe's Trade. Pre-publication text of the *Economic Bulletin for Europe,* v. 27. Geneva, UNECE (XXIV)/1, 17 November.

—— (1975b) "Recent Economic Development in Eastern Europe and the Soviet Union" Chapter 2 in *The European Economy in 1975.* (Pre-publication text of the *Economic Survey of Europe 1975*) Geneva, UNECE (XXXI)/1 Add.1.

—— (1975c) Long-Term Economic Growth of East European Countries: Objectives, Major Factors and Patterns between 1960 and 1990. Geneva, UNECE, EC.AD. (II)/AC.1/R.1/Add.3, 14 July.

—— (1976) "Recent Economic Development in Eastern Europe and the Soviet Union" Chapter 2 in *The European Economy in 1975.* Geneva, UNECE (XXXI)/1 Add.1.

UNECOSOC (1975) The Role of the Public Sector in Promoting the Economic Development of Developing Countries. Report of the Secretary-General. New York, E/5690 and E/4690/Add.1. Mimeo.

UNIDO (1974) Industrial Development Survey. Special Issue for the Second General Conference of UNIDO. New York, ID/CONF.3/2 (ID/134).

—— (n.d.) Industrial Free Zones as Incentives to Promote Export Oriented Industries. Vienna. Mimeo.

Union Bank of Switzerland (1976) Prices and Earnings around the Globe. A Comparison of Purchasing Power in 41 Cities. Zurich.

—— (1978a) Prices and Earnings around the Globe. A comparison of Purchasing Power in 41 Cities. Zurich.

—— (1978b) Business and Technology Today and Tomorrow. Zurich: UBS Publications in Business, Banking and Monetary Problems, No. 52.

UNITAR (n.d.) Progress in the Establishment of a New International Economic Order: Obstacles and Strategies. New York: United Nations Institute for Training and Research.

URPE (1975) *Radical Perspectives on the Economic Crisis of Monopoly Capitalism* with Suggestions for Organizing Teach-Ins and Teach-Outs. New York. URPE/PEA.

—— (1977) Special Issue on the Political Economy of Health, *Review of Radical Political Economics*, v. 9, No. 1, Spring.

—— (1978) *U.S. Capitalism in Crisis*. New York: Union for Radical Political Economics.

U.S. Senate (1969) Hearing before the Subcommittee on Western Hemisphere Affairs on the Committee on Foreign Relations. United States Senate, Ninety-first Congress, First Session, November 20.

—— Foreign Relations Committee (1977) Foreign Debts, the Banks and U.S. Foreign Policy. Washington, Aug. from spanish translation *Comercio Exterior*, México, November 1977.

U.S. Tariff Commission (1970) Economic Factors Affecting the Use of Items 807.00 and 806.30 of the Tariff Schedules of the United States, Report to the President. Washington, TC publications 339.

Utrecht, Ernst (1976a) Industrial Estates and Australian Companies in Singapore. Sydney, Transnational Corporations Research Project. Research Monograph No. 2.

—— (1976b) Transnational Corporations in the Developing World. Transnational Corporations Research Project, University of Sydney. Research Monograph. No. 1.

Vaitsos, Constantino V. (1976) Employment Problems and Transnational Enterprises in Developing Countries: Distortions and Inequality. Geneva, ILO. WEP 2-28/WP 11. October.

Vajda, Imre and Simai, Mihály eds. (1971) *Foreign Trade in a Planned Economy*. Cambridge: At the University Press.

Valenzuela, Carlo J. (1976) "El nuevo patrón de acumulación y sus precondiciones. El caso chileno: 1973–1976" *Comercio Exterior*, México, Septiembre.

Vasconi, Tomás Amadeo (1976) El estado militar en América Latina. El caso chileno. Enero. Mimeo.

Vernon, Raymond (1971) *Sovereignty at Bay. The Multinational Spread of U.S. Enterprises*. New York: Basic Books.

Vuscovic, Pedro (1975) "América Latina: la crisis de un patrón de desarrollo y sus consecuencias políticas" *Comercio Exterior* México, v. 25,
No. 12, Número aniversario 25 años.

—— (1978a) "La restructuración del capitalismo mundial y el nuevo orden
económico internacional" *Comercio Exterior,* México, v. 28, No. 3,
Marzo.

—— (1978b) "El neofascismo en América Latina" *Zona Abierta,* Madrid,
No. 14/15.

—— y Martínez, Javier (1977) Once proposiciones sobre la situación
actual de América Latina. Mimeo.

Waksman Schinca, Daniel (1977) "El proyecto de la OTAS" *Nueva
Politica,* México, v. II, Nos. 5–6, Abril–Septiembre.

Wallenstein, Peter (1976) "Scarce Goods as Political Weapons: the Case of
Food" *Journal of Peace Research,* Tampere, XIII, No. 4.

Wallerstein, Imanuel (1974) *The Modern World. Capitalist Agriculture
and the Origins of the European World-Economy in the Sixteenth
Century.* New York: Academic Press.

—— (n.d.) Semi-peripheral Countries and the Contemporary World Crisis.
Mimeo. Published in *The World Capitalist System.* Cambridge University Press, 1980.

Watanabe, Susumu (1976) "Minimum Wages in Developing Countries:
Myth and Reality" in *International Labour Review,* Geneva, V. 113,
No. 3, May–June.

Weisskoff, Richard y Figueroa, Adolfo (1977) "Examen de las pirámides
sociales: Un estudio comparativo de la distribución del ingreso en
América Latina" *El Trimestre Económico,* México, v. XLIV(4), No.
176, Octubre–Diciembre.

Weisskopf, Thomas E. (1978) "Marxist Perspectives on Cyclical Crisis" in
U.S. Capitalism in Crisis, by URPE. New York: Union for Radical
Political Economics.

—— (1979) "Marxian Crisis Theory and the Rate of Profit in the Postwar
U.S. Economy." *Cambridge Journal of Economics,* vol. 3, no. 4,
December.

Wilczynski, J. (1969) *The Economics and Politics of East-West Trade. A
Study of Trade between Developed Market Economies and Centrally
Planned Economies in a Changing World.* London: Macmillan.

Wionczek, Miguel S. (1976) "La IV UNCTAD: exámen de problemas
reales" *Comercio Exterior,* México, Mayo.

—— (1977) "La deuda externa de los países de menor desarrollo y los
euromercados: un pasado impresionante y un futuro incierto" *Comercio Exterior,* México, v. 27, No. 11, Noviembre.

Woddis, Jack (1960) Africa. *The Roots of Revolt.* New York: The Citadel
Press.

Wolpe, Harold (1972) "Capitalism and Cheap Labour-Power in South

Africa: from Segregation to Apartheid" *Economy and Society,* London, November.

Wolpin, Miles D. (n.d.) Military Dependency vs Development in the Third World. New York, Department of Political Science, State University of New York. Mimeo.

World Bank (1975) *Undernutrition and Poverty.* Washington, International Bank for Reconstruction and Development. Bank Staff Working Paper, No. 202, April.

Yago, Glenn (1976–1977) "Whatever Happened to the Promised Land? Capital Flows and the Israeli State" *Berkeley Journal of Sociology,* Berkeley, California, XXI.

Zarnowitz, Victor ed. (1972) *The Business Cycle Today.* New York, National Bureau of Economic Research, Distributed by Columbia University Press.

Index